The

Amorous Busboy

of

Decatur Avenue

A Child of the Fifties Looks Back

ROBERT KLEIN

A TOUCHSTONE BOOK
Published by Simon & Schuster
New York   London   Toronto   Sydney

The names and other identifying characteristics
of some people have been changed.

TOUCHSTONE
Rockefeller Center
1230 Avenue of the Americas
New York, NY 10020

This Touchstone Edition 2006

TOUCHSTONE and colophon are registered
trademarks of Simon & Schuster, Inc.

For information about special discounts for bulk purchases,
please contact Simon & Schuster Special Sales:
1-800-456-6798 or business@simonandschuster.com

Designed by Jan Pisciotta

Lyrics from *Let the Ball Roll* by Irving Caesar and Gerald Marks
reprinted by permission of Marlong Music Corp.

Manufactured in the United States of America
10 9 8 7 6 5 4 3 2 1

The Library of Congress has catalogued the hardcover edition as follows:
Klein, Robert.
The amorous busboy of Decatur Avenue: a child of the fifties looks back /
Robert Klein.
p. cm.
1. Klein, Robert, 1942–. 2. Comedians—United States—Biography.
3. Actors—United States—Biography. I. Title.
PN2287.K673A3   2005
792.702'8'092—dc22   2004063691
[B

ISBN-13: 978-0-684-85488-5
ISBN-10:   0-684-85488-0
ISBN-13: 978-0-684-85489-2 (Pbk)
ISBN-10:   0-684-85489-9 (Pbk)

For Mom and Pop,

my sister Rhoda,

and my son, Allie, light of my life

Acknowledgments

Thanks to Mark Gompertz of Simon & Schuster, who originally proposed that I write this book. His warm encouragement and guidance were invaluable. Gratitude to Allie Klein, my number one son, for his patience and comments regarding my manuscript. Beth Thomas, copyeditor, did a fine job making things clearer and more to the point. Thanks to Mel Berger, my literate literary agent, who appreciated my work and gave me more than ten percent of his support. Thanks also to Rory Rosegarten, my manager.

Contents

Pre-Preface

One of the most important elements of a book is its subject matter. One cannot overestimate how significant the content of a book is with respect to its overall quality. This is a generally conceded notion among literary people, though there are several revisionist contrarians in the intellectual strata of Canada who feel that the cover of a book is far more crucial to its value than what's inside. This matter has been argued many times by greater minds than mine, and certainly more eloquently. Nevertheless, I remain convinced that while the cover is of no small importance, the essential element—the factor that determines whether a book is good or bad, the thing that no book should do without—is the assemblage of words on its pages. It was with this in mind that I set out to write a book.

The important question was what the book would be about. This presented a perplexing dilemma on which I spent many long hours thinking of ideas, some of which excited me, most of which I dismissed. After thoughtful consideration, I decided to write a book about sixth-century Chinese pottery. I typed one word—"The"—and immediately hit a creative brick wall, which found me sitting in front of the computer, alternately motionless and banging my head against the wall in frustration. I felt hard lucky to be cursed so early in the project with that most dreaded affliction of the author: writer's block. I got up from the keyboard and cleaned the cat box after which I washed the windows after which I vacuumed the house after which

I made a five-pound pot roast and watched it cook for three hours. I went back to the computer, and there was still no result. I could not understand why I, a creative person, was making no progress in writing this book, as I got up from my chair for another round of distractions.

It was while cleaning the porcelain bidet in the master bedroom that the answer dawned on me: I don't know a fucking thing about sixth-century Chinese pottery. Why this had not occurred to me before, I cannot say; maybe I *thought* I knew something about sixth-century Chinese pottery. I happen to believe that an author should know what he's writing about, though those same Canadian intellectuals feel that ignorance of the subject of one's book is a blissful approach to writing. I respectfully disagree. Wasn't it William Faulkner who said "Write about what you know"? Maybe not, but it still strikes me as highly pragmatic advice, given my multiple failures in trying to write books about: sea turtles, circumnavigating the world, building jet engines at home, the social structure of chickens, and fungi of the skin. All of these subjects interest me, especially the pathology of dermal mitosis–athlete's foot—which aroused my curiosity after I saw a nifty Learning Channel documentary. Interest is one thing, knowledge is another. My knowledge of all of these subjects could fill, to the brim, a paragraph.

What *do* I know about? The subject that I have spent the most time learning about and know quite well is: me. I have spent numerous decades hanging around with myself, observing me, experiencing what I experience from the intimate to the mundane. Nobody knows me like *I* knows me, and I knows me well. What do I writes about me? I writes what I feels; and why am I suddenly talking in slave dialect? In a young lifetime of memories and their concomitant stories, a few rushed to the front of the line, begging to be told. The book is about the adventures of a child who becomes a young man: how he thinks and dreams and lusts and fears and laughs and handles adversity.

Sound interesting? You bet. So if you're reading this in the bookstore and have come this far, don't dare put it back on the shelf and fail to buy it. Mrs. Linda Bradstreet of Cummings, Minnesota, did just that and died of a virulent fever two days afterward. Harold Dugan of Sinclair, Maine, perused this book and read this very piece before he placed it back on the shelf and left the store. He was run down by a car, suffering brain damage that destroyed his already impaired sense of taste. Take no chances, buy this book. Or borrow it from the public library, which apparently also mitigates the unpleasantness that results from not buying it. This book is, in places, emotional dynamite, so please don't sue me if you go out and do something radical under its influence. It is also comedic nitroglycerin, causing many laughs from the reader: large, physical, bellyaching laughs. Though they make the spirit soar, these laughs can cause injury to the cheeks, abdomen, and lips, as well as raise the blood pressure. Despite those side effects—which, as with a pharmaceutical company, it is my ethical obligation to reveal to you—my book is well worth the read. And believe me, I am completely objective.

Preface

I think it was in the seventies that I first met my editor. I seem to remember bell-bottom jeans and sideburns, both huge. In any event, it was in the last century, in my dressing room after a performance. He was working for a publishing house. "You should write a book," said the guy who would become my editor. He had a huge head of curly hair growing out in all directions like a sunflower; it was the first time I had ever seen a Jewfro. "Really, I think you should write a book," he repeated. Write a book. I liked the sound of it, to be able to say: "I wrote a book." It appealed to me greatly to share something in common with Doctorow, Dostoyevsky, Fitzgerald, and Melville, minus a minor aspect or two—like the content.

His suggestion aroused in me that lifelong respect for the written word and the individual who writes it, passed on to me by my father and several of my teachers. To be a writer, automatically conveyed the notion of intelligence and erudition, never mind that the opus might be kindred to *Curious George Vomits at the Circus*, a book with more pictures than words. I had seen Dale Evans, Roy Rogers's partner in the saddle, on *The Mike Douglas Show*, promoting her latest book about her favorite subject, Christian faith. I believe Mike said it was her fourteenth book, which sent the audience into applause and awe. Ms. Evans acknowledged it by smiling proudly. Then Mr. Douglas asked her the most relevant, highly literary question: "Let me ask you this about your book, Dale: How long does it take you to turn out one of those babies?" This was hardly a question in the mode of a *New York Times* book critic. I do not mean to be patronizing, but Dale Evans, no doubt a good-hearted person, was hardly a woman of letters, though she could say she'd written fourteen books. I put the idea of writing a book on hold.

"I still say you should write a book," said this editor when I bumped into him twenty years after he first said it.

"So you still think I should write a book?"

"Yes, absolutely."

"Well, the idea is intriguing, I must say. I've performed on television, Broadway, in movies, on records, and of course the comedy material I write and perform. I've written articles for magazines and a screenplay for Warner Brothers. I *should* write a book."

"Oh, you should," he said.

"You know something? I absolutely agree, it's a great idea, writing a book. I'll write a book."

"I think you definitely should," he said.

"You're right, it's time I wrote a book."

"There's no doubt in *my* mind," he said. "*You,* my friend, should . . . write . . . a book."

"A book about what?" I said. There was a twenty-minute silence. "Well, that's not important, we can always think of something later," I said.

That's the reason I wrote this book. Because I should write a book.

Post-Preface

Writing can have its ups and downs, its roller-coaster swings; it can run that sort of bipolar, high-tide-low-tide gamut, from the stuff that's exceptional to the stuff that stinks to no stuff at all. There are the good days when I can't wait to get to the keyboard to pour into it a fusillade of imaginative ideas. And there are the difficult days of staring at a blank screen without a cogent thought to my name, listening to the whooshing sound of the idle computer mocking me. There is a creative progression and retrogression to most artistic pursuits, but when there is more ebbing than flowing, the going gets rough. Writers can be left wondering if they will ever write a decent word again: self-pitying, baffled as to how the muse who was so ubiquitous yesterday could abscond so rapidly today.

Even given all the pinnacles and low points in creating a book, no aspect has been more difficult for me than choosing a title. I think it can be generally agreed that a title's main purpose should be to attract the potential reader's eye, regardless of its pertinence. Relevance, as a criterion for choosing the name of the book, can weigh the process down with dull titles that won't sell, such as: "Some Stories About When I Was Younger" or "Boy I Had Fun and Was Terrified and Had Sex in the '50s and '60s" or "Robert Klein: My Early Life, Vol. I." I want a title that will grab book lovers and suck them in like a magnet, making the purchase of this book inescapable. I have a meeting with my editor from Simon & Schuster about the matter. "Have you come up with a title yet?" he asks.

"Yes, I believe I've come up with a real winner, can't miss."

"Splendid, what is it?"

"Well, I've given it a lot of thought, and all things considered, I'd like to call the book *Harry Potter and the Order of the Phoenix*."

"How can you use that title? It's already the title of another book."

"You can't copyright a title; there's no legal reason why we can't use it," I say.

"It's not a question of legalities, it's the title of one of the best-selling books of all time, for God's sake."

"Precisely," I say. "Can you think of a better reason to use it? It worked very well for them. It's tried and tested."

"But the reader would be expecting an entirely different kind of book," he says.

"That may be true, but by the time they realize it, they will have already paid for the book and read some of it, and we will have made the sale."

"Don't you think that's rather unscrupulous, to deceive a person buying the book like that?" he says.

"Don't you read the trades?" I say. "Haven't you noticed how difficult it is to sell books? We need all the help we can get. Besides, you're not supposed to tell a book by its cover."

My editor is getting frustrated. "You simply cannot use the title of a book like that, only recently a best-seller."

"I'm beginning to see your point. Too recent. How about *The Old Man and the Sea*? That title sold millions."

"No, that won't do, either," he says.

"The Bible?"

"No, no, no."

"*Portrait of the Artist As—*"

"No. You know something? You're crazy," he says. "A better title for you would be 'A Young Man Who Became an Annoying Lunatic in His Old Age.' Now get out of my office."

"Wait just a minute, no, no, just a minute. Say that again."

"Get out of my office."

"No, not that, the other thing."

"What other thing?"

"The title, I think you got it."

"'A Young Man Who Became an Annoying Lunatic in His Old Age'? I was just being sarcastic."

"I don't care what you were being, it's perfect: 'A Young Man Who Became an Annoying Lunatic in His Old Age.' A little long for the talk shows, but right on the money. It covers every aspect of what a good title should. It's bizarre and eye-catching, plus it's perfectly apt. It also assuages that ethical hang-up of yours, since nobody has used it before."

My editor is at his computer furiously searching for something. I assume it's a fine-print escape clause in my contract. "I'll be damned. You can't use that title," he says. Then he reads aloud from the computer: "*A Young Man Who Became an Annoying Lunatic in His Old Age,* translated from the Farsi by Mohammed El Farouq, published 1938, Sunlabi Publishers, Tehran. How do you like that?"

"Bad luck," I say. "Well, at least the book is written, that's twenty-five percent of the whole deal right there. Can you give me another six months on the title, or think of one yourself?"

"Get out of my office."

" 'Get Out of My Office'? No, that one doesn't do it for me. It's not catchy enough, and they'll think it's about someone who works in an office."

"Get out of my office," he says.

"You really like that one, don't you. I'll give it some thought. But I'd like *you* to keep an open mind, too, so don't give me an answer now, but just think about *Gone With the Wind,* would you?"

Chapter One

Careful Parents

My grandparents came from the two largest cities in Hungary—Budapest and Debrecen—in 1903. My mother and father were born and raised in Manhattan, and my childhood and that of my sister, Rhoda, were spent in the Bronx, so the great outdoors was not exactly in the lexicon of my urban parents, being a concept as alien to them as reading the catechism. The only hunting my father ever did was for bargains at Macy's, though he did bring home a copy of *Field & Stream* once that he found on the subway, and read it on the toilet. When he moved his bowels he liked to price kayaks. My mother hated eating at outdoor barbecues and was particularly disgusted by insects, so when a picnic was unavoidable, she never packed rye bread with seeds, because the seeds looked like ants. She made a big deal about mosquito bites and the danger of infection, and I got the impression early on that the world outside our home was a dangerous place. Any contemplation of an activity that involved risk was discarded as foolhardy. As a result, I was not destined to be an explorer or a test pilot or an airborne ranger or a motorcycle daredevil.

My mother and father were careful, cautious people; wary people. This ensured the certainty of careful, cautious children; wary children. In my sixteen years living in our apartment building, there was never a crime committed on the block. Nevertheless, when our doorbell rang, my sister and I were instructed to always ask: "Who is it?" and never open the door unless there was a response and the respondent was someone known to us. Anyone else had to be viewed through the peephole in the double-locked steel door. We lived on the sixth floor and viewed the world through well-placed window guards and stern warnings about leaning out too far. Parental invocations repeated over and over again like mantras became well absorbed and governed a good deal of how I dealt with my childhood world. This was, of course, their purpose. "Be careful, be careful, watch out, watch out, don't take any chances, it's not safe, it's not safe, that can take your eye out, stop that, you'll get hurt, you can lose a leg doing that, don't take candy from strangers." These were just a few.

Not unexpectedly, caution became my modus operandi. My entire childhood was pervaded by endless warnings and pleadings and reminders of dire consequences: "Watch out for that lamp cord! If you're going out at night, wear white so the cars can see you! Never touch a light switch with wet hands! My God, don't cut that bagel toward your neck!" Statistically speaking, the possibility of severing one's head while slicing a bagel seemed remote indeed, yet Ben and Frieda Klein took no chances. Danger lurked everywhere. Even the garbage incinerator had a poster full of warnings promising five years in prison for throwing carpets or naphtha down the chute. I didn't even know what naphtha was, but I pitied those naughty souls in Sing Sing who were doing hard time for throwing it out with the garbage. I felt equally bad for those criminals who, in a fit of pique or defiance, had torn the tags off their mattresses. Yet it was their own fault, as they should have been forewarned by the clearly visible printed admonition.

This atmosphere of constant vigilance and circumspection put a definite crimp in my activities. For example, it was the passion of the little boys on the block to act out the movies we saw every Saturday at the David Marcus Theatre on Jerome Avenue. Period pictures like *Robin Hood* and movies about pirates, the ones with dueling scenes, were special favorites. We would fashion swords out of appropriate pieces of wood or branches that we found where we played, in the vacant lots that would not be built on for another five years. One day my father, in his bellowing voice, called me to supper from the sixth-floor window while I was in the middle of a furious duel with Michael Newman from Apartment 2F. Then my father screamed at the top of his lungs a bone-chilling addendum to the dinner call, that embarrassed me in front of all the other pirates: "Stop it now! You're gonna take your eye out! Oh, you're gonna get it when you come up here! Are you gonna get it!" I reluctantly cast away my sword, which everyone leaped for because it was a beauty. I had spent much time shaving the bark and shaping a large twig from the sumac trees that abounded in the area and had survived the ecological insult of castaway junk and discarded tires. Alas, I was not as hardy as they were, and it was I who had to face my furious father.

It was an anxious and unhappy trip up the elevator home. Though my father was frequently more bark than bite, that bark could be terrifying, along with the anticipation of an occasional smack. I did receive a hard one across the face this time, signifying the seriousness he attached to the issue. In short, my dueling days were over, at least during the hours that my father might be home, though I had to be careful lest some adult neighbor tell on me.

I was forbidden a cap gun for playing cowboys and Indians because my father considered caps to be explosives, and besides, he said, "It gives me a headache." My mother said she'd heard of a boy who went deaf from a cap gun. Certain bad boys would light fires among the rubbish in the lots, sometimes bringing a fire truck to the scene—an event that caused much excitement and heads popping out of windows. In order to make sure I never lit fires, my father issued a two-pronged warning. First he reminded me of the pain associated with fire, and second that if I were caught, I would have a criminal record. Could reform school be far behind? The possibility of a life behind bars, like the animals in the Bronx Zoo, was quite an unappealing prospect.

No lesson was more repeated than the absolute command to look both ways before stepping into the street, which was referred to as the gutter. This was boilerplate stuff for all neighborhood children, as we lived in an urban environment with a fair amount of vehicular traffic, and the street was our playground. We were taught a song in school called "Let the Ball Roll," though we all forgot at times. These were the words of the song: "Let the ball roll, let the ball roll. / No matter where it may go. Let the ball roll, / Let the ball roll. It has to stop somewhere, you know. / Often a truck will flatten the ball. / And make it look like an egg. / Though you can get many a ball, / you never can get a new leg." The song notwithstanding, there wasn't one of us who had not had a frightening close call while chasing a ball into the street, with a car screeching noisily to a stop and a cursing driver relieved to know that he had not killed someone's child.

As usual, my father took the radical scary approach and made use of object lessons, frequently showing me newspaper accounts and pictures of boys hit by cars, maimed by firecrackers, burned by starting fires, killed by falling out of buildings, disabled by baseball bats, and paralyzed by horseplay they saw in the movies. On-site object lessons, when available, were also part of his repertoire. On one occasion he pulled me out of a curb-ball game hard by the arm and began walking me down the Decatur Avenue hill toward Gun Hill Road. "Where're we going, Dad? I was in the middle of a game."

"Never mind your game. This is more important. This is life and death." I could see a crowd and a police car in front of Frank's fruit store. My father, never letting go of my arm, forced his way through the crowd toward the object of everybody's curiosity. It was a horrifying sight. A woman was lying barely conscious in the gutter. She had been hit by a car, her grocery bag spilled over, with potatoes and apples rolling down the steep hill toward Webster Avenue. Her right leg was terribly mangled and bloodied so I could see the bone. The blood flowed down the hill as well, forming tiny eddies in the grooves and bulges of the cobblestones. I was stunned and felt sick. My father grabbed me aside. "See that? That's what happens when you don't look both ways."

"How do you know she didn't look both ways, Dad? Maybe she did and the driver didn't see her."

"Don't be a wise guy," he replied.

My mother had her own crusade for safety and longevity. When I requested her written permission to play hardball in the Police Athletic League, she looked at me incredulously, like I was a lunatic asking to eat a bicycle, and said, "Hardball? Hardball?" She hardly contained her emotion as she launched into a quick and illustrative horror story (she always had one on hand) of a boy mutilated by a hardball. Her voice would always drop to a somber sotto voce whisper when she got to the description of the affliction: "Hardball? Sure, like that boy on Hull Avenue who got a hardball right in the head. [whispers] *He walks backward now.*"

"How about football?" I suggested.

"Football? Football? Like that boy on Perry Avenue who got hit by all those boys and now [whispers] *he can't spell his name and thinks he's Abraham Lincoln.* He was an excellent student, and now *he sells* The Bronx Home News *and plays potsy with the girls.*"

Even playing checkers had its risks and parental provisos, though it was not forbidden. "A boy on Webster Avenue [whispers] *died from a checker.*" Yes, the idiot had tried to swallow one and choked in full view of three friends, or so the story went. Anyway, what could you expect thirty years before the Heimlich maneuver? I never had even the slightest desire to swallow a checker.

My father played baseball as a kid on East Seventy-seventh Street, and he regaled me with stories of his adventures as a catcher in hostile neighborhoods. He referred to the oft-quoted definition of catchers' equipment as "the tools of ignorance," because it was, he emphasized, the most dangerous position on the field and was to be avoided. Never mind that *he* played catcher; the point was that *his* experience should be enough to keep me from a similar fate. There was an implication that he had suffered so I wouldn't have to, though I suspect he had a lot of fun playing catcher despite the lumps and bumps. Like many American fathers, he taught his son to catch and throw. When I was very little, he naturally threw softly to me. The trouble was that in the name of safety, he continued to throw like that to me when I was twelve and older. At a time when my friends and I threw fast and hard in pepper games, my father was lobbing baby throws and yelling, "Careful! Watch out!"

Softball was acceptable as long as I didn't play catcher or slide, and watched out for swinging bats. There came a time, I believe it was the age of nine, when my father decided I was old enough to get a proper glove, bat, and hard ball—with conditions. "Listen to me," he said. "Never, never throw a hard ball at someone's head." This admonition seemed self-evident, but I solemnly promised. "Keep your eye on your mitt, and don't let anybody steal it. Most of all, watch out that you don't get hit in the head with a bat and never never swing your bat around anyone else."

"Okay, Daddy, I promise."

The Hijinks sporting-goods store, located under the noisy elevated Woodlawn train across from the movie theater, was the sports-equipment mecca for the neighborhood boys. Anytime we passed the store, we would press our noses to the window to admire the merchandise. But today I was not just looking. Today was to be that most joyous and rare occasion when an actual purchase would be made. Jinks himself, the proprietor, showed us an assortment of left-handed mitts and beautiful bats. The smell of new leather permeated the place, with row upon row of boxes holding treasures that every boy wants, school jackets and authentic uniforms. I chose a first-baseman's glove, a Ferris Fain model, and a smallish brown bat, a Frankie Frisch model. Actually, my father chose the bat. Frisch had been an excellent bunter for the New York Giants of the thirties, and I think my safety-conscious father reckoned that I would emulate the bat's bunting namesake and rarely swing it. On the walk home, my father extolled the virtues of bunting and how important it was to the game. He strangely omitted the fact that bunting involves facing the pitcher with your legs spread and your fingers exposed, so if no contact was made, a boy could take a ball in the balls.

I carried the bat, rubbing my hand along its smooth surface, feeling its heft and the perfectly formed knob on the end. I shadow-bunted as we walked, in homage to my father. His warnings in mind, I nevertheless wanted to try a swing, so I ran thirty feet ahead of him to a place on the sidewalk without people. I swung and announced in radio fashion that I'd just hit a home run to win the World Series. "Watch out there," my father said. Then he caught up to me, and I ran ahead again and swung again and homered again. On the next at-bat, I took an imaginary pitch for a ball. On the next pitch, I swung and hit something. It was my father's head. He let out a "Yow!" and grabbed his head, and I was afraid that I'd killed him like that boy in the *New York Post* who had whacked his brother. "I'm sorry, Daddy, oh God, I'm sorry! Are you okay?" He just rubbed his jaw and said, "See? I told you not to swing it around people! I told you!"

I went from horrified to ashamed as he took the bat from my hands. The amazing thing was that despite his pain, he actually seemed pleased that the incident had happened, that it had vindicated his lectures on caution. "I told you. Now you'll learn." He preferred being someone who was hit by a bat and could say "I told you so" to prove his point. After all, what would I have learned if I hadn't hit anybody? He made sure I knew he was feeling pain. As a lesson, in addition to fear, there was guilt, which could also make a strong impression on me.

One of the most interesting of the ironclad safety measures was that my father insisted I wait one hour after eating before going in swimming; something about dangerous cramping. This was probably derived from some myth about a kid who drowned in the East River in 1924 after eating an entire pot roast. Waiting a bit after a meal before swimming is not a bad idea. But with true Ben Klein hyperbole, I was warned that if I didn't wait one full hour and not a second less, I would instantly sink like a rock and die a choking, gurgling death. "You'll go right to Davy Jones's locker," my father would say ominously. I had a rough idea of what Davy Jones's locker was: a place of ruin and dead bodies and sharks eating them. The specter of death by drowning is a potent one to a ten-year-old. I recalled a scene from a movie in which a man was tortured by having his head held underwater until he was begging for mercy and nearly dead. I remembered being held underwater myself by bigger boys during horseplay, and I had never forgotten being knocked over by an ocean wave, most of which I inhaled, and the desperate fight for breath, which I thought would never come again.

I was therefore scrupulous about waiting the full amount of time, regardless of the hot sun and the sight of other kids swimming happily ten minutes after eating. Their parents were evidently irresponsible. The idea of waiting *exactly* one hour was etched into my brain like a mental tattoo, as if the food would know precisely what period of time had passed since I ate it. One hour—okay; fifty-nine minutes—dead. When I got a little older, my father explained that I really didn't need to wait a full hour. The actual amount of time a child would have to wait before swimming depended on what the child ate, and my father was the arbiter at the pool or beach who would decide such things. "What did you have, a tuna-salad sandwich? With a pickle?"

"Yes."

"Thirty-three minutes. Peanut butter and jelly? Twenty-seven minutes. Bologna and cheese? Forty-two minutes. Frankfurters and beans? Too heavy. You can't go in swimming this year."

Protecting the children from harm is admirable, but there are limits, and I sometimes got the sense that my mother and father would have preferred to keep me wrapped up in a padded room at home for safety's sake: hardly a prescription for an intrepid child. In retrospect, I would say my parents had a different approach to child rearing than, say, Evel Knievel's parents, or the Flying Wallendas of circus aerial fame. With all due respect, the family Wallenda has exhibited certain lemming-like tendencies and has diminished considerably in size over the years. This is a result of their specialty, the most dangerous aerial stunt ever performed. It is called the Seven and consists of a pyramid of seven Wallendas with a young lady on a chair at the top. It is performed about sixty feet above the arena with, quite literally, no net. The unfortunate dearth of Wallendas can be traced to this questionable no-net policy stubbornly adhered to by the family and its patriarch, Karl Wallenda. My mother would not have approved of my participation in such an enterprise, and never would have signed the permission form. My father would have shown me newspaper photos of a splattered aerialist on the circus floor to discourage me from such pursuits. It was a sad fact but true, something I had to live with every day of my childhood: I would never climb Mount Everest.

Chapter Two

Challenging Mrs. Graux

My academic education from kindergarten through high school was acquired entirely in the public schools of New York City. It was, for the most part, a good fundamental education that used orthodox, one may say, old-fashioned methods. We memorized our multiplication tables, and we memorized the important dates of American history. My sixth-grade teacher, Miss Links, took great pride in her ability to recite the names of the presidents . . . backward.

We were imbued with the proper patriotism associated with the Revolutionary War and the founding of the United States of America, though it was taught through the distant prism of myth and legend. We learned that George Washington and company were infallible, godlike men, the kind of men whose names Bronx schoolchildren would memorize almost two centuries later. I am referring to those indelible yet fallacious images from textbooks and old calendars of George Washington chopping down the cherry tree, or throwing a dollar across the Potomac. None of the complex nuances of risk, intelligence, luck, British blunders, or European politics were presented to us as necessary components of the Revolutionary War. It was simple: The British wore bright red uniforms that were easy to see, and they marched in a line to be slaughtered by the clever American colonists who hid behind trees in the manner of the Indians from the French and Indian War. (The French and Indian War. Even as a subsequent history major, this is a war I still can't quite figure out. It seems to have been at least partially fomented by the French, as usual, and they *lost*, as usual.)

In any case, with respect to the American Revolution, I have since learned how compromise, particularly the putting off of the slavery question to another time—was so crucial to the forming of the United States and the creation of the Constitution. To be sure, many of the true facts of the founding of the union have come out at the millennium, when historians and DNA experts were given the latitude to declare that the great author of the Declaration of Independence, Thomas Jefferson, actually did have sex with his slave and sire at least one child. As for George Washington, I have done a good deal of reading about him and have concluded that he was an even more extraordinary man than we were taught. The nonsense we were fed about his father's cherry tree and other myths was straight out of Mason Locke Weems's inaccurate, glorifying biography *Life of Washington,* published after the president's death.

The truth is that Washington's life had all the elements of greatness. He risked hanging by the British; with little previous experience, he became a worthy general; he willed that his slaves be freed and compensated after his death; he was the one man, admired by all, who could unite disparate factions to form the union; and, most spectacularly, he gave up power at its pinnacle, a course of action unprecedented in the world up to that time. Through a convergence of fate and luck, he was the right man at the right time, the Father of Our Country in every way, to whom we owe so much. We purport to be a patriotic people. I know George Washington would be proud to know that we celebrate his birthday every year with a mattress sale. And tawdry used car dealers hawking on TV, wearing wigs and three-corner hats and holding hatchets.

Though the teaching of history was clouded with inaccuracy and anecdote, the basics of the other subjects we learned in school were sound. We were taught early to read and write, and each child had his or her own pace. We were divided into three groups according to our reading skills, each with a different text according to difficulty. The less sensitive teachers would simply call them Groups One, Two, and Three. The more tactful teachers would give them names like Bluebirds, Robins, and Eagles, but everyone knew that the Eagles were the best readers and the Bluebirds were the dummies.

"Dummy" was a common noun in the early fifties, and a favorite of certain teachers, political correctness being an unknown concept at the time. Unlike anyplace I knew this side of the Iron Curtain, New York City had the depersonalizing practice of using numbers instead of names for schools: Think Steel Factory #8 in Minsk. Still, we were encouraged to take pride in our school, often exemplified by singing the school song at the weekly assembly in the auditorium. Instead of singing a sentimental anthem to the likes of the Abraham Lincoln School or the Mark Twain School, we were content to sing about the glory of Public School 94 or Junior High School 80. These were true school songs sung by enthusiastic children, full of emotion and spirit, and all paying homage to the glorious name of two- and three-digit numbers. Here are some of the lyrics as I remember them. An up-tempo march: "I wanna be the kind of boy that 94 can boast about. / I wanna be the kind of boy that it can never live without." The female pupils sang the word "girl," which came out in the aggregate "I wanna be the kind of birl that 94 can boast about." I remember another marching song in tribute to my junior high school: "80 . . . dear 80 . . . , your name will rise above." I can't remember what 80 was supposed to rise above, but I assume 79. There were even spiritual, slow hymns designed to draw tears: "We revere the halls of 113. We praise thee, oh glorious 113."

The school buildings themselves, P.S. 94 and J.H.S. 80, were more interesting by far than their names. These particular architectural types of New York City public schools were designed and built in multiples for economy. They still dot the city and serve their intended purpose. They were handsome, sturdy structures of mortar and stone, unlike the flimsy stucco temporary-looking schools one sees in the Sun Belt and California and much of the rest of America. The city schools were built extremely well during the Depression thirties, when men were hungry for work: skilled stonecutters, metalworkers, and carpenters. The buildings displayed architectural details purely for aesthetics, the kind that would rarely, for economic reasons, be placed on a public building today. There were massive white pillars at the entrance to 80, which reminded one of the Parthenon and the antebellum South, with a touch of Thomas Jefferson's Monticello: all right in the middle of the Bronx, mind you. The rapidly growing Bronx, haven of the overcrowded Manhattanites, with its optimistic art deco pretensions.

Our student body was as sturdy as the buildings we learned in: highly motivated, well-behaved first- and second-generation Ameri-can kids that we were. There were dress codes that seem quaint now. The boys were required to wear neckties, and the girls wore dresses or skirts. Once a week there was an assembly in the auditorium for which the boys wore white shirts and blue ties, while the girls wore white middie blouses complemented by a blue scarf.

The teachers at the elementary level were all women: As I recall, I did not have a male teacher until the seventh grade. Many of these women were unmarried and childless, and while having children is not necessarily a prerequisite for being a good teacher, in their case it would have helped. They seemed to have no clue about the dynamics of childhood, with its exuberance and curiosity, which were easily mistaken for misbehavior in their minds. There was none of the infor-mality seen in today's schools. In those days elderly people looked older than they do today, from their clothes to their state of mind, not to mention today's increased life span and youth-driven culture. In any event, my memory is of strict old ladies, with old-fashioned long dresses, black lace-up shoes, and hair back in a bun, like Miss Grundy from the *Archie* comic books. Margaret Hamilton on a broomstick also comes to mind. They disdained humor, all the worse for a class clown like me, so I had to be extremely careful about how and when to be funny. They tolerated no talking, fidgeting, or other crimes of the classroom. They were teaching in one of the best schools in the vast city, with energized, nonviolent children and a corps of parents encouraging their kids to achieve. Yet they continued to keep order as if they were at San Quentin, and violators were subjected to humiliat-ing punishments such as confinement in a corner or the clothes closet, along with vicious verbal assaults.

One teacher, Miss McIntosh, wore a black dress every day, in mourning for her long-dead brother, along with a three-by-two-inch iron crucifix that looked like it weighed five pounds and could incin-erate Dracula in four seconds. Whether it was the dearth of dry cleaning or the infrequency of her baths is unclear, but an odor emanated from the woman like the bottom of a bird cage. I used to say that she wore a perfume called Keep Your Distance, one of the first jokes I ever made up. The perverse thing is, she knew she stank; she made excellent use of this fact in exacting her many punishments in the enforcement of discipline. If a student talked too much, she would order him under her desk for the full array of olfactory torment. If he fidgeted excessively, he was required to sit in her stench for the allotted time.

Corporal punishment—that is, striking a student—was no longer allowed at that time, it being the progressive postwar era in New York City. The teacher could not technically hit the child, but the old crones found ways of skirting the rules. The push-probe-pull method was popular, in which the teacher would not hit you but would poke you with her gnarled, witchlike fingers and grab your face like a taffy pull until you screamed, though technically she did not *hit* you. The pull-and-choke was also a favorite. It was executed by pulling the compulsory necktie up like a hangman's noose until the errant boy's face turned the school colors. Many on the faculty of my elementary school, P.S. 94, had not graduated from colleges and universities, as is required today, but had attended two-year so-called normal schools, which were an early source of teacher training. They learned the best methods that the nineteenth century had to offer, including strict discipline, rote memory, and no nurturing whatsoever. Despite the rules, there were indeed rare incidents of tiny smacks to the arms and minor cracks to the head, and rulers as weapons. But we were cowed children, respectful of authority, who were used to an occasional bop on the head from our parents. In addition, the incidents were neither bloody nor brutal, the teacher knowing in an instant that the point was made. But one day Mrs. Graux went over the line. Way over the line.

Mrs. Graux (pronounced "Grow") was a sixty-four-year-old widow teaching the fourth grade. She was not the youthful sixty-four one would assume today. She was an old sixty-four, the strictest teacher in the school, and every pupil's nightmare. At the end of third grade, one opened the envelope containing fourth-grade information gingerly, like the bailiff reading the jury's decision. "Who you got? Graux?" It was a one-year sentence. She looked the jailer's part. There was a strange lack of mobility in her neck that placed her head in a permanent tilt to the left, giving one the impression that she was looking at you askance, which she probably was. She wore tiny spectacles low on her nose, with a deadly stare and scowl that could be truly frightening. A master of surprise, Mrs. Graux would sometimes smile before ripping into her prey like a *Tyrannosaurus rex*, whether the attack was verbal or otherwise. One did not talk back to Mrs. Graux. One did not talk fresh to Mrs. Graux. I had managed to get through the school year with a combination of occasionally charming the old lady and staying out of her way.

In truth, I was too much of an extrovert to stay permanently submerged, completely out of her sights. I had always been able to favorably impress adults in general and teachers in particular. I knew what they liked in a child. This may be a cynical view, but being able to please my elders was a primary force in my early life, and it worked to my advantage. This turned out to have benign consequences, perhaps due to the high quality of grown-up I depended on and trusted. It was a good thing I didn't experience an eccentric uncle who liked to bounce me on his lap—when I was fourteen. Though it was difficult, I did a decent job of picking and choosing my moments to score a point or two with Mrs. Graux, a hard-core case, which I hoped would be added to the bank of good points in the event of subsequent misbehavior.

My big opportunity to clinch a spot on her good side occurred just before the Christmas break. On the last day before vacation, we had a class party at which we were permitted to sing songs of the season and eat nuts and raisins. The impending holiday put an extra measure of goodwill and jollity into the school atmosphere, as I have found to be the case everywhere during that season. Given that the students were almost all Jewish, a number of them got up and sang Chanukah songs. I observed that Mrs. Graux was bored but, to her credit, tolerant. She endured a barrage of musical homage to menorahs, dreidels, and potato latkes, none of which she knew or cared the least bit about. No one—vegetarian, omnivore, or carnivore—can resist the flavor of a

well-seasoned, crispy potato pancake: in Jewish parlance, a latke. I
assume that Mrs. Graux unfortunately lived and died without experiencing this pleasure. In any event, in the middle of all these
Chanukah songs, I could see in her gentile eyes, on this cold December day, the genuine longing for a good old Christmas carol. I could
hardly blame her. "Menorah, Menorah Burning Bright" and "Let's
Spin the Dreidel" have less musical resonance than "The First Noel"
or "Silent Night" or Handel's *Messiah*. Having a nice choirboy voice
worthy of an eighteenth-century castrato, and being fond of Christmas carols, I seized the moment, stood up in front of the classroom,
and proceeded to perform a lovely rendition of "Silent Night." I could
see the teacher melt as I sang in my boyish soprano. My classmates
appreciated the performance as well. Despite the Jewish upbringing
of most of them, they were Americans, assimilated enough to have
heard Perry Como sing this beautiful tune dozens of times. I reached
the finale: "Sleep in heavenly peace, sleep in heavenly peace."
Incredibly, I saw a teardrop roll down the teacher's cheek. It was the
first, and certainly the only, occasion on which Mrs. Graux showed
any tenderness whatever, and *I* was the cause. It was sheer theatrical
guile and cynical calculation that I used to soften her: my first lesson
in the power of . . . well . . . show business. I had in effect manipulated
Mrs. Graux, but she was oblivious to that, having been thoroughly
cheered by my song. She and the class gave me a hearty round of
applause, because I sang damned well. This was good but did not
compare to the self-interested satisfaction I got from Mrs. Graux's
reaction. As she wiped away a tear, she said sincerely, "That was for
me. Thank you, Bobby, that was beautiful."

Bobby was not a name Mrs. Graux used in addressing me as a general rule. It was more likely to be Klein or dummy. From that point
on, I felt like I had a little credit in the bank with Mrs. Graux.

Most of our parents were first-generation middle-class Jews involved
in white-collar work. They sent their children to school every day,
neatly and properly dressed, clean handkerchief, homework completed. They had a strong sense of getting their fair share of opportunities in the hopeful postwar liberalism. Yet they were compliant

people who believed in and communicated to their children respect for authority. I was taught to ask a policeman for a dime if I got lost, in order to call home. If a neighbor woman complained to my father that I had misbehaved, her word as an adult authority was not questioned. If a teacher wrote a note to my parents about an offense in class, it was automatically assumed that she was right, and I was warned, "You better not be a troublemaker, or it will go on your permanent record and you won't be able to get into college and get a job." After one of these behavior letters, my father said the least prophetic thing he ever said to me: "Robert, don't be the class clown; being a comedian doesn't pay." But that's another story.

One of the girls in my class, Lauren Kay, was an anomaly among us. Lauren came from an atypical home for our neighborhood. She had an older brother named Sam, who was in the sixth grade and considered the toughest boy in the school. In addition, there were several other older brothers who were said to have had trouble with the law, and around whom much legend formed. The fact that few of us had ever met them added allure to the rumors. It was said that Lauren's parents were "a little slow," and they were the only family in the neighborhood receiving public assistance. Lauren's mother was a peculiar-looking woman, rarely seen, whose clothes and sloppy makeup gave her a clownish appearance. Lauren's father was the superintendent of the building they lived in, and given to singing on the street as he put out the garbage cans for collection. He wore a sleeveless undershirt in the appropriate weather and sported a tattoo of a naked lady on his forearm that he got in the navy. He enjoyed making the children laugh by removing his dentures and collapsing his cheeks. At these times he was well lit but always harmless. Lauren was embarrassed by him, and as a result, she never invited her fellow students to her house. She had a tough exterior and a panoply of profane language that only the boys could match. She could be intimidating in an argument and sometimes got into fights after school.

Lauren was by no means a homely child, though she had an inch-square red blotch, a rare birthmark on her right cheek which is called "port-wine stain." (Gorbachev, the pivotal Soviet premier, had one on his bald head that looked like a country on a map.) Some of the chil-

dren called Lauren Ink Face behind her back, though few would dare
say it directly to her and risk a fight. She was not well dressed or particularly popular, and some of the children treated her warily, but she
and I got along well. I could make her laugh, and she was not a child
who laughed often. I think she admired my pluckiness in making the
class crack up on occasion and risking the wrath of the teacher. One
of my most popular shticks was placing my right palm under my left
armpit and flapping my arm like a country water pump. It made an
authentic fart sound that couldn't be distinguished from the real
thing. Farts have always been, and always will be, funny to human
beings, for reasons unknown.

Poor Lauren. I felt a little sorry for her, since she apparently came
from a troubled home and was poor to boot. She did not come to
school in the well-pressed, well-starched blouses, like the other girls;
she had fewer outfits than they. Mrs. Graux displayed an obvious disdain for her as one of the slower learners. One day as our class was
settling down after lunch for the afternoon session, Mrs. Graux was in
a particularly foul temper. Lauren was having a conversation with
Susan Gilbert, and Mrs. Graux gruffly told her to take her seat. The
child began to comply, but not quickly enough for the teacher, who
forcefully grabbed Lauren's sweater and hurled her with an emphatic
"I TOLD YOU TO SIT DOWN AND SHUT UP!"

"Don't you push me!" Lauren shot back.

There was a stunned silence. "WHAT DID YOU SAY?" Mrs.
Graux said slowly, with all the venom she could muster. Then she
leaped, like the predator she was: "HOW DARE YOU SPEAK TO
ME LIKE THAT, YOU BRAT!"

In an instant, she had hit the girl square across the face and
knocked her down. There was a good deal of gasping, none of us
ever having seen such an assault by a teacher or such a surly retort
by a pupil to a teacher's command. It did not happen at P.S. 94. Mrs.
Graux quickly calmed down and assumed an almost casual air. She
attempted to play down the incident by beginning a history lesson,
but we were all in a kind of shock, and, like the teacher, merely went
through the motions. Lauren silently sobbed in her seat, her head
buried in the dreary oak desk with its three generations of carved

graffiti. Steeped in humiliation, she never looked up the rest of the day. No one could concentrate with the specter of a little girl sobbing into her desk for three hours. Mrs. Graux completely ignored her, which made the whole scene all the more cruel. None of the children dared leave their seats to comfort her. The three o'clock bell mercifully sounded, and we all grabbed our books and coats and poured out the door to line up for dismissal in the hall. Lauren did not speak to anyone while walking home from school. Eric, a good-natured fat boy; Harold, the class Episcopalian; and I were the only children who approached to console her. But she could not be consoled. I touched her shoulder, and she looked at me, not so much with anger but rather with a look of pure misery that said, "Leave me alone."

Though stickball season was just beginning, the weather giving late-March hints of the spring to come, I had no desire to play that afternoon. I couldn't get the incident out of my mind. I didn't say anything to my parents that evening for some reason I cannot explain. But after school and the next morning, the class talked of nothing else. There was some minor bravado from a handful about teachers not being allowed to hit students, but no one suggested a remedy. Many blamed Lauren for not having taken her seat immediately and for talking back. After all, they reasoned, a teacher has to keep order and can only take so much. It was pitifully evident that Mrs. Graux's long-term intimidation of us had had a deep effect.

The next day the teacher came to class with the sunniest disposition we had ever seen in her. She complimented one of the girls on her pretty dress and the bright green bow in her hair, and she kidded me about needing a haircut. It was not in Mrs. Graux's nature to kid. She sat down at her compulsively neat desk, but instead of immediately beginning our lesson, as she normally did, she told us a story that she characterized as "amusing"—about how her neighbor's cat had eaten the family goldfish. It was a clumsy attempt to reestablish some sense of normalcy in the volatile atmosphere. Everyone kept sneaking peeks at Lauren, who mostly stared at her desk and traced the graffiti on its surface with her index finger. Her face was a blank. She appeared to have a small pink mark on her cheek, the one opposite the port-wine stain. After several unsuccessful attempts at humor and casualness, Mrs. Graux told us to take out our textbooks, and we resumed our lessons. At recess, the boys played their usual punchball, and the girls jumped rope, but the tempo of the games was a snail's pace involving more speculation about the day before than enthusiasm for playing. We somnambulated into the afternoon session like little zombies. Nothing was the same; the mood was somber and fearful. Perhaps there was some collective guilt. We were sheep, and helpless.

About one-thirty, Mrs. Graux was teaching arithmetic at the blackboard when a man entered the door at the front of the room. "You Mrs. Growx?" he asked, pronouncing her name as it was spelled, without the silent French X. The class broke out laughing at the maladroit pronunciation. "You Mrs. Growx?" he repeated.

"I am Mrs. GRAUX," she snapped. "Who are you and what on earth are you doing here?"

He stepped closer to her and said, "You hit my daughter. You ain't got no right to do that."

"What are you talking about? I hit your daughter!" Mrs. Graux turned paler than usual as it dawned on her whom she was talking to.

"I am Lauren's father, and you hit her," he continued relentlessly.

The teacher assumed her most terrifying scowl and began the verbal assault that worked so well on the kids: "HOW DARE YOU COME IN HERE. WHO DO YOU THINK YOU ARE?"

The simple fellow, thinking he'd been asked a question, replied, "I told you, I'm Lauren's father, and you hit her, and that ain't right." He was almost nose-to-nose with her now, and the class froze with fear. The laughter that had accompanied the man's abrupt entrance had turned into the scary silence of twenty-eight children who had no control over the unfolding events.

"You're drunk! I can smell it on your breath!" she shouted.

"I ain't drunk," the man replied. Lauren, already a diminutive child, was nonetheless attempting to make herself even smaller. She was trembling and angry, though she did not cry. Mr. Kay began pointing in the old lady's face. "You hit my daughter," he repeated again and again. Many of the children were stealing quick glances at

Lauren, and she knew it. Some of them looked down at their desks in order to block out what was happening.

"You ain't got no right to hit my daughter."

"I DID NOT HIT YOUR DAUGHTER!" Mrs. Graux blurted out. At that, the class looked at one another knowingly but silently.

"Don't gimme that, you did, too," said Lauren's father. "Look at that mark on her face."

"What are you talking about? She's always had that mark on her face." Lauren began to cry. The teacher's scowl turned into a calm smile, and she addressed the class: "Boys and girls," she said. She always used "boys and girls" on those rare occasions when she was in a kindly mood. "Boys and girls, I didn't hit anyone, did I?" There was total silence as she panned the room. "Did any of you see me hit Lauren?" As the nonresponse continued, Lauren looked up from her desk and swept the class with her eyes. As she looked at each student, he or she looked away, embarrassed and frightened. One could see the hurt and fury in her face as she realized how alone she was. The father looked at the children, too, confused to be contemptuous of us.

"Once again, I say, did I hit Lauren?" No one stirred. A broad, misanthropic smile crossed Mrs. Graux's slanted face. She was in complete control, as usual.

I had assumed that since everyone in the class had witnessed the assault, someone would speak up and tell the truth. I was fervently hoping, however, that it wouldn't have to be me. It is difficult for me to recall what I was thinking in the crucial moments before I spoke. In my memory, it was as if I had decided to give up my own life for a principle, like diving on a grenade to save others; essentially, a heroic suicide. But this was not a movie. I raised my hand as if in a dream and said very quietly in a monotone: "Mrs. Graux, I saw you hit Lauren."

There was an audible gasp from the company assembled. Mrs. Graux's face contorted in a way I had never seen, and her stare could have melted the glass in her old-lady spectacles. She walked ominously toward me, and I began to shake, thinking she would surely strike me. Her voice was hushed, with a venomous quality that more than compensated for its lack of volume. "What . . . did . . . you . . . say?" she growled, almost sotto voce.

My reply seemed to take forever in coming, and I couldn't look at her. "I . . . saw Lauren hit you . . . I mean . . . I saw you hit Lauren, Mrs. Graux."

She was bending over me as I sat. My lips were trembling, and tears began streaming down my cheeks. Her voice ascended gradually in volume to a piercing scream, like a Greek chorus. "Robert Klein. How dare you ACCUSE ME! YOU ARE A LIAR!"

"No, Mrs. Graux, I'm not lying. Maybe you didn't mean to—"

"GET OUT OF THIS ROOM, YOU LIAR! GET OUT INTO THE HALL UNTIL I TELL YOU TO COME BACK, YOU LIAR!"

The last thing in the world I wanted to do was bawl in front of the class, but despite my best effort to hold it in, the dam broke, and I began to cry. As I walked, head bowed, toward the door, my eyes confirmed what I feared most of all: I had wet my pants. Lauren's father took her hand and led her, sobbing, out of the room just behind me. The teacher slammed the door, the sound echoing in the cavernous hall like thunder and retribution.

Out in the hall, Lauren's father offered me a filthy handkerchief to wipe away the torrents of tears. His breath reeked of the liquid courage he had consumed before coming to the school, and his speech at this point was slurring badly. "Youse . . . youse all righ— okay, kid?" he said. I could not speak, stuttering between intakes of breath, the way children do when they are crying hysterically. "You're a brave boy, kid," he said, and I could see that he was shaken and trembling, like we were. Mrs. Graux could scare grown-ups, too. Lauren looked at me, standing humiliated in the hall. She put her arms around me and, to my surprise, hugged me without saying a word. I had never seen her show such affection before. She was not the tough kid I had known but a little girl in terrible distress who had received the support of two ineffectual people—her tipsy father and a nine-year-old boy—and she was grateful. Perhaps it was a small respite from her pain. She touched my cheek with her hand and said almost imperceptibly, "Thank you."

As I stood against the wall wilting, I watched Lauren and her father, his arm around her shoulder as he gently wiped away her tears with his handkerchief. Then they walked down the hall. He may have been drunk, and he may not have been an award-winning father, but he loved his child just as my daddy did. This day he had been as good and protective a parent as any parent ever was. What a woeful silhouette they made against the bright sunlight coming through the window at the end of the hall. It was as if they were walking into a better tomorrow, but I knew that Lauren was going home to the same troubled environment. Yet wasn't it all a matter of perspective? Her parents couldn't afford summer camp or a new car, but did they love their children any less? Were they any less deserving of compassion and fair play?

The three remaining months of the term were almost unbearable. Mrs. Graux never spoke to me again or called on me in class. To her, I was a nonperson, which was almost worse than the occasional lethal stare. Her anger, though, wasn't reflected in my grades, which were all excellent. I even got an S (satisfactory) in conduct on my final report card. The only blot on my official record was an N.I. (needs improvement) in the category called "works and plays well with others," which was untrue but tolerable. It was Mrs. Graux who had not worked and played well with others. It was Mrs. Graux who had lied. Thankfully, my schoolmates did not share her disdain, and after a few days, our relationship was normal again.

Most of the children were a little nicer to Lauren. At first she shunned their modest advances, but after a while, she was participating in the school-yard games and the general give-and-take with the others, the need to be liked and to belong being what it is. Mrs. Graux, though she seldom spoke to Lauren, treated her as if nothing had happened. The incident was never mentioned again. I felt no sense of having been heroic; I received no congratulations, even from Lauren, though I knew she was grateful. I guess in the end, everyone had eyes and ears and a conscience and knew what I had done and they had not.

I never told my parents or anyone else about the affair for over twenty years. The story came out of me casually when I was thirty, on a shrink's couch one day when I was particularly down on myself, and it startled me with its clarity. It was incomprehensible to my shrink that I had forgotten the story and did not see its importance. "Don't you understand?" she said in her slightly Viennese accent. "You did the right thing and the noble thing. You risked much as a nine-year-old, for principles like truth and justice." I conceded that maybe I had, but what of it? So many years later, that explanation of the events seemed pompous to me. Leave it to me to have repressed the memory of an altruistic deed, guilty, neurotic bastard that I am.

Chapter Three

The TeenTones

The Bronx block I grew up on, Decatur Avenue between 211th Street and Gun Hill Road, was a steep hill worthy of San Francisco, so the ten or so snowfalls each winter were fervently anticipated, the hill being a wonderful sled run. I learned to play softball, curb ball, two-hand touch football, and stickball on an uphill incline, in the street and the vacant lots on what I reckon to be a five-degree angle.

On the northern, 211th Street side lay the southern boundary of Woodlawn Cemetery, the eternal home of many of the famous and accomplished, like Fiorello La Guardia and Bat Masterson, and later, Duke Ellington and Miles Davis. The surface of the cemetery was fifteen feet above the street, separated from it by a concrete wall adorned with stickball boxes.

A stickball box was a rectangle approximately twenty inches across and thirty inches high, drawn with chalk or tar on the wall. The pitcher aimed the Spaulding rubber ball, called a Spaldeen, at the box, and this determined balls and strikes. The batter tried to hit the ball as far and hard as he could, its distance determining whether it was a single, double, triple, or home run. There were many such homemade boxes on the walls of the handball courts of public schools and parks. Our home field, however, was the cemetery wall. There was some graffiti on the beige concrete, most of it of an ethnic character, as in "Scotch," "Irish," and a delicately written "Yea Jews." There were some messages of a profane nature, but they were lame and stupid, like "Mary blows" or "Fuck you," and were quickly painted over by diligent citizens.

Political graffiti was rare, given the fifties-bred monolithic attitudes about world affairs. No one was against the Korean War, and of
course Communists were our enemy, though a few brave left-wingers
managed to write a fair amount of "Free the Rosenbergs" here and
there around the neighborhood during the saga of the trial and subsequent execution. People put up hundreds of posters on the lampposts
and in storefronts around Election Day, but these could hardly be
called graffiti. They touted the candidates, most of whom were
Democrats, while the pictures of the hopeless Republican candidates
suffered the humiliation of penciled-in mustaches and blackened
teeth.

The southern, Gun Hill Road border of my block was a busy east-
west thoroughfare of traffic and stores, and also a pronounced hill,
appropriate to its name. I have seen places in Michigan and Iowa that
call themselves "hill," but they are optimistically or ludicrously
named. Mine were real hills, up and down which children ran and
played, and old people huffed and puffed.

The area is purportedly steeped in Revolutionary War history,
George Washington allegedly having visited the nearby Van Cortlandt
Mansion several times: a questionable assumption. It is true that the
New York City records were hidden in that house after the British
captured the town, and that colonial troops evacuated as far north as
Morrisania and Kingsbridge in the Bronx, with Washington using the
Morrisania Mansion as a temporary headquarters. The major battle
closest to my neighborhood was fought about six miles to the southwest of Decatur Avenue and Gun Hill Road, at a place called Washington Heights, in the northern part of Manhattan Island. It was one
of the biggest disasters of the Revolutionary War, and it caused Washington to retreat across the river to New Jersey. First in war, first in
peace, and first to flee to the suburbs (though he returned to the city
later). After the war, President George Washington, his wife, and the
Custis step-grandchildren liked to take daylong carriage rides from
lower Manhattan, across the Harlem River, all the way north to
Kingsbridge and back again. Kingsbridge is about two miles from my
home, so that's about as close as the Father of Our Country came to
Gun Hill Road.

Some of our streets were named after heroes of the War of 1812, which was fought on the high seas and hundreds of miles to the south, from Washington, D.C., to New Orleans. Other streets were named after Civil War generals. Perpendicular to streets named Hull, Decatur, Perry, and Bainbridge, the small shops on Gun Hill Road reflected the needs of the residents on the smallest of scales, in an era that could not have imagined the Home Depot. Within a four-block perimeter, there were groceries and butcher shops, dry cleaners, hardware stores, and appetizing stores, which was the name given to smoked-fish-and-pickle emporiums whose tangy smell caused us to salivate like the proverbial Pavlovian dog. The pickles and sauerkraut were stored in huge barrels, much the way they had been delivered for two hundred years. The countermen could carve smoked salmon and marinated herring with the skill of surgeons, a skill that was passed on by the generations. We would buy a nickel's worth of sauer-kraut in a paper bag for a snack, as naturally as a kid would get a ham-burger at McDonald's today. There were shoemakers, pharmacies, barbershops, delicatessens, small dress shops, and candy stores. The candy stores had five-stool soda fountains where one could leisurely sip an egg cream, as well as purchase newspapers, magazines, and school supplies. They were also favored hangouts and places to exchange gossip. All of these stores were within walking distance of one's home, generating a steady stream of pedestrians with reusable cloth shopping bags or carts, gathering the necessities of life.

There was a most personal aspect to this. When you've known all of the merchants for twenty years, when the same Italian immigrant has resoled your shoes all your life, and the barber has cut your hair since you had to sit on two phone books, there is a comfortable, famil-iar sense of order and loyalty. The ownership of these businesses hardly ever changed.

Most central of all the shops was the bakery, since fresh-baked bread purchased daily was the order of the day, the staff of life being far from a cliché to us. The Jews preferred the coarser rye breads, while the gentiles liked the white, though everybody loved the pas-tries and ordered birthday cakes, all of which were baked on the premises. There was a palpable European-village feel to the neighborhood that wasn't happenstance, the majority of the residents being first-generation Americans and European immigrants. It was largely a Jewish population, particularly to the north of Gun Hill Road, with a sizable minority of Irish and Italians, especially to the south. Two parishes, Saint Ann's and Saint Brendan's, had parochial schools whose students wore uniforms. Many of the parochial school boys still wore knickers, a remnant of early-twentieth-century America, while the girls wore modest blue dresses called gamps.

Gun Hill Road was a noisy street of cobblestones, built as in a previous century, a technique no doubt borrowed from Europe. Where horses once clopped and gripped, automobiles now rattled and rumbled with the sound of tires on bumpy cobble, and the Third Avenue El train screeched as it cautiously made its way around the sharp Webster Avenue turn. The Number 15 Gun Hill bus had a nice diesel roar as it tugged up the hill westward, and when a large truck made its way up Decatur in low gear, the windows shook and the vibrations bounced off the four buildings, creating a canyon of booming noise. Then, of course, there were the horn blowers whose cars were blocked in by a double-parker. These were the most conspicuous sounds from outside, but there was always the background din: of human voices and children playing and the half-mile-distant White Plains Road train going fast into the Gun Hill station and the frequent zoom and percussive clatter and occasional whistle of the New York Central trains speeding through the tiny Williamsbridge station, north to Chatham and south to Grand Central, the tracks not two hundred yards from my sixth-floor window on the world.

I describe some of these sounds, the trains, for instance, as a blind man might, because I couldn't see them from my window, and yet they were an important part of the pastiche of my childhood. Somehow the screech of the El on the turn stands out: For some reason, I associate it with feeling depressed. Late at night, the cacophony would tone down to an occasional barking dog, but it never disappeared completely, the busy Bronx being what it was.

Decatur Avenue was my world until kindergarten, at which time I walked the three blocks west to Kings College Place and Public School 94. Parents had not the slightest compunction about sending their young children off to school without supervision; the big kids presumably kept an eye on the little kids. The terms "little kids" and "big kids" were important designations in the neighborhood, which defined who you and your friends were. Exactly at what age a little kid became a big kid was unclear, but you could tell one from the other— perhaps junior high school was a dividing line. The standard safety instructions for children were about looking both ways before crossing the street, being wary of strangers and not taking candy from them, and something about watching out for perverts. Some kid from the neighborhood had seen a man on Hull Avenue who opened his raincoat, flashed his genitals, and ran. This was the only crime I remember hearing about in our safe, cozy neighborhood.

The route to and from P.S. 94 was parallel to Woodlawn Cemetery, which seemed to elicit some curiosity among the children. It was not unusual for us to stop and watch a funeral near the black steel picket fence where it became level with the street. The parklike setting and the mountains of flowers were beautiful and fascinating. Strangely, the mourning of the participants seemed to escape our notice. Whether this was the blithe denial of children is not clear to me; but it was so. It was not until the fifth grade, at the age of nine, that I began connecting the concept of death with the ubiquitous cemetery looming a few feet from my home, school, and play area.

It was a vertical existence, living in 3525 Decatur Avenue, our art deco apartment building that housed eighty-six families. I lived on the top floor, Apartment 6F, with a front view looking down on the street: definitely a preferred location, since the rear apartments faced the building twenty feet to the west. There was a good deal of looking out the window for us front dwellers, to see what was happening on the block and to keep an eye on the children playing in the street below. When the ice-cream man came jingling on Decatur Avenue, all the kids looked up toward their apartment windows and hollered, *"Ma!"* at the top of their lungs. Each mother knew her own child's cry, like the millions of birds on the Galapagos Islands know the cry of their chicks. The mothers would throw down ten cents from heights of seventy feet, which in retrospect was dangerous. My safety-conscious mother would wrap the coin in a paper bag and toss it aerodynamically, gracefully, but most important, harmlessly, into my arms. What a sweet and thoughtful mama. The parents who were mad at their kids would toss the dime right into the kid's head with a force of four G's on it, as when David hit Goliath between the eyes.

For us apartment dwellers, life was an up-and-down affair. When I went out to play, I did not tell my mother that I was going out, but rather that I was going down. It was routine discourse on the street: "Are you going up now?" "No, I just came down." "Oh. I came down a long time ago. I'm going up now. Call me when you go up." I would take the elevator up, but I preferred the wide staircases for my trips down, as most of the kids did—descending in rapid, noisy, rhythmic clumps, jumping from the last four steps, consummately childlike. Each landing was well lit by the sunlight through the ample windows, and the big stucco walls of the hall were perfect for a few tosses with the ever present rubber ball carried in the pocket of my dungarees— my play pants, changed into from my school pants.

The halls smelled of pies baking in the afternoon and boiled chicken and broiling lamb chops in the evening, all of it mixed with the scents of hundreds of people. I could always smell women's perfumes, which lingered particularly in the elevator. The grown-ups were pure elevator types, going down in them as well as up, never taking the stairs. It became my dream to live in a place someday where I could say I was going out instead of going down, complete with a backyard and trees and no dog shit on the ground.

Until they were built on later, for most of my childhood there were three hilly vacant lots on the block. The two at the north end of the block, closest to the cemetery, were our unofficial playgrounds. On the west, relatively level side, we played softball, while the east lot was used for cowboys and Indians and soldier games. We were brought up in the glory of World War II and the concomitant Hollywood movies about it, so that all of us liked to play soldier. I saw *Halls of Montezuma* and *Sands of Iwo Jima* three times and could not hold back tears at the end. A particular favorite was called Who Dies Best? In this war game, the contest was about who could die the most authentic death after being shot. The shooter would announce the caliber and type of weapon, and the victim would charge the foxhole, get shot, grab his stomach, and fall as spectacularly as possible. We made not the slightest connection between our game and the reality of war and combat, not seeing the irony of being exuberant in a sensational death—albeit a painless one—as the movies and newsreels had always sanitized the carnage.

The steep bumpy terrain of the northeast lot provided a thrilling, if brief, sled run in the winter and was hyperbolically called Dead Man's Hill. In season, there were major weekend softball games among the biggest kids on the block, some of whom were sixteen and seventeen, and it was a great rite of passage for a thirteen-year-old to finally be allowed to play. Nobody paid attention to the boulder behind first base in fair territory, called the Big Fat Rock, which was the size of a Volkswagen Beetle, and upon which we played King of the Mountain.

All of the lots were repositories of castaway junk, broken glass, the occasional dead rat, and the fecal matter of dozens of local dogs in a time long before scooper laws. It was standard procedure to check one's shoes constantly, especially before entering the house, as we were forever stepping in it. My mother would have me bend my leg back at the knee so she could inspect the soles of my shoes, like a blacksmith examining a hoof. Removing the foul stuff in the street could be difficult. It required ingenuity and improvisation, using whatever tools we could find in the lots, like newspaper and small pieces of wood. If all else failed, the metal edge of the curb was the last resort.

The street itself—called the gutter as opposed to the sidewalk— was a major playground, and there were games for all seasons. Fungo stickball, in which the batter threw the Spaldeen up and hit it without a pitcher, was a staple. So were curb ball and association football, which could be played with as few as two boys on a side. Parked cars were reference points for someone going out for a pass, as in: "Go to the Buick, fake, and then I'll hit you at the Plymouth." Cars coming up and down the street were a bother, but someone would yell "Car!" and play would suspend until it safely passed. It was strictly against the unwritten rules to yell "Car!" if none was there, and no one ever did.

We also played with the Spaldeen on the sidewalk. Box baseball was popular, which used the lines between the four-foot squares of concrete as boundaries, placing the players about sixteen feet apart, and the boy who was pitching would put a spin on the ball so that it bounced off the sidewalk oddly, making it more difficult to hit with the opponent's open palm. We also flipped baseball cards from the curb to the wall of the building; the nearest card to the wall won, and the winner took the loser's cards. Blackjack and poker became popular, with baseball cards as the street currency that was valuable indeed, especially the rare ones, though none of us ever thought of the cards as a future investment. When they outgrew them, the big kids would have a "hot scramble," in which they would throw hundreds of cards out the window like a ticker-tape parade, and forty little kids would scramble to collect them in the street below, like they were nuggets of gold.

We played skully, in which we struck bottle caps weighted with wax, by releasing the middle finger from under the thumb, which made them slide across the sidewalk. Marbles were strangely out of vogue on Decatur Avenue at that time. The girls jumped rope and played jacks on the sidewalk. They played with the Spaldeen as well, but instead of stickball and curb ball, they would bounce the thing while reciting old rhymes: "A, my name is Alice, and my sister's name is Alicia, and we come from Albany." On every word with the letter A, they would cross a leg over the ball and then go to the next letter of the alphabet, and so on: a more literate approach to game playing. Potsy was another favorite of the girls, and the only game that girls and boys sometimes played together, though as a boy got older, he did not especially want to be seen playing potsy. I don't remember the rules of potsy, but it involved throwing your keys and hopping.

One September day, we were playing stickball in the asphalt gutter, and a small black truck arrived at the building across the street from mine. It said MORTUARY DIVISION on the two doors in the back, and a police car accompanied it. Word quickly spread that they were there to remove a dead body from the building, and the curious, including us, formed a crowd around the vehicle. Dozens of heads popped out of windows to see what was going on, as they always did when an ambulance, fire truck, or police car made an appearance on the street, or a loud verbal ruckus ensued between two people after the same parking space. The attendants came out of the building carrying the body in a leathery black bag, placed it in the truck, and drove off to the morgue.

My friends and I did not resume our game. Instead, we sat down on the curb and began discussing what we had just seen; about what happens to a dead body; about heaven and hell; and the most difficult concept of all—finality. That night was the first of many that I thought and dreamed, indeed obsessed, about death. There were two aspects to my obsession: One was the fear that my mother or father would die; and the second was my contemplation of the state of death itself, what it would be like to die and be buried. The burial part was particularly distressing to my claustrophobic nature, fueled no doubt by my reading *Tales from the Crypt* comic books at my aunt Laura's candy store on Tremont Avenue. While my father chatted with my aunt at the counter, I would sit in a musty booth at the back and absorb tales of people buried alive who came out of the grave dead, dripping rotting flesh, and exacted revenge. There was a horrible odor in the back of the candy store of must and decay, caused by decomposing sugar syrup and the leftover soda in the returnable bottles. I associated the foul smell with graves and the stench of decaying bodies that I could almost sense leaping off the page of the brilliant but ghastly comic-book illustrations.

I worried constantly about my father's health, which as a matter of fact was excellent. When he took a nap, I would make it a point to see that he wasn't dead, checking his chest for motion to prove he was alive. If the breathing seemed imperceptible, I would intentionally make a loud noise to evoke from him a groan or a movement of his body to indicate that my greatest fear had not been realized. For some reason, though I loved her as much, I did not have the same concern about the sudden death of my mother. I would hear in school that someone's father had died—usually of a heart attack—much more often than I would hear the news of a mother's death. The mothers seemed more frequently to die a lingering death from cancer.

These questions of life vis-à-vis death vexed me as a child. I did not want to be buried in some lonely, distantly located cemetery that no one would visit, especially since my ashes could be conveniently located in the living room. And how could I know or care if anybody was visiting? I'd be dead, right? As a small child, I had visited my grandparents' graves once in the old Mount Hebron Cemetery, near the World's Fair grounds. Unlike Woodlawn, there was row upon row of graves crowded together with tall headstones, which gave the site a close, claustrophobic feel in addition to its significance as a place of death. I was especially haunted by the graves of children who had died forty years earlier: Were they still children? Many of these headstones contained metallic photographs of the children, which was a custom of the day. Some were about my age and buried six feet beneath the cold ground. I had several bad dreams after the cemetery visit, so my parents avoided taking me again, which was fine with me. In contemplating cremation, however, *Tales from the Crypt* once again crept into my thought process, and burning alive is only slightly less appalling than buried alive—well, not *alive*, exactly, because you're dead, and you're not supposed to feel anything. Maybe I could hedge my bet and get cremated in a fireproof suit.

After seven years at P.S. 94, it was time to move on to junior high school, which stretched my parameters—in truth, my world—eight blocks south and west to Mosholu Parkway. Once again I walked to school. I never took a school bus in my life. There I encountered the social culture of my fellow teenagers. In the evenings (excluding the dead of winter), a hundred kids or more would gather on the Mosholu Parkway fence, across the street from the school.

It was in junior high school that I first encountered male teachers and different teachers in different classrooms for various subjects, which was called "departmental" and seemed so grown up. The change of periods was a refreshing departure from the humdrum of one classroom and one teacher from nine to three.

It was also at this time that I made some friendships that have lasted a lifetime. Hanging out frequently on the parkway fence had to wait until high school, however, as my parents kept a tight rein on my

weekday evenings. DeWitt Clinton High School was an all-boys insti-
tution that 90 percent of the neighborhood boys attended. It had a
sort of macho tradition and a long and venerable list of distinguished
graduates, such as Burt Lancaster, James Baldwin, Paddy Chayevsky,
and Neil Simon. It also had a police car permanently parked near the
front entrance, for those students who were less distinguished. When
I was a little boy, I could not help but notice the distinctive red-and-
black Clinton jackets worn by the big kids, as if they belonged to
some mystical fraternity. The walk to DeWitt Clinton was twelve
blocks or approximately one half mile, but the center of my social life
became Mosholu Parkway, specifically, the three-foot-high steel pip-
ing that constituted the fence where the guys and chicks would
gather. Decatur Avenue became just a place to sleep.

The parkway was an exciting experience, given the energy and
vitality of its inhabitants, synergized by their sheer numbers. Most
were good kids and attentive students, with a sprinkling of "rocks,"
who in a later era were referred to as "greasers." That type was portrayed in a cartoon way on television as Fonzie from *Happy Days*,
which was created by Garry Marshall, who hung out on the parkway
several years before I did. His sister Penny was more my contemporary, and I held hands with her cute gum-cracking redheaded friend
Margie Pace. A stylish young fellow named Ralph Lifschitz would
park his little British automobile, a Morgan, amid the admiring kids.
In a few years, he would metamorphose, like a caterpillar into a but-
terfly, as Ralph Lauren. Interestingly, Calvin Klein lived a few buildings away, but I cannot recall him hanging out on the parkway.

I had, for the first time, achieved a kind of social status. I was
funny; clowning was my old standby, my longtime ticket out of
anonymity—and fights. I had a new passion: singing in a rock-and-roll
vocal quartet called the TeenTones. Doo-wop vocals were all the
rage, and our harmony was good for amateurs, bearing in mind that
amateurs could quickly become recording artists in the fledgling
rock-and-roll business of the mid-fifties, or so we hoped. Our group
began attracting the attention of the kids on the parkway; people listened, clapped, and showed appreciation. When the weather was
inclement, we would sing inside and vibrate the concrete halls of the

junior high school, which became a recreation center in the evening. At DeWitt Clinton, the rehearsal room of choice was the men's room, with its marvelous echoes and unfortunate bouquet. When we harmonized in the men's room, it sounded like we were singing in a recording studio, albeit an unsavory one. It was definitely our best sound. Oddly, whenever we harmonized anywhere else, it sounded like we were singing in a men's room.

I was a TeenTone to the core. From the moment my gaze fell in the morning on the beige ceiling of the family living room where I slept on a convertible bed, to the nighttime parallel-line shadows of the streetlights coming through the venetian blinds upon which I plotted my future before sleep, I thought and breathed TeenTones. You could say the group was my obsession, my hope, my ambition. School was just a six-hour interruption of the life of a TeenTone. Bellowing three- and four-part harmonies freed me. They call it doo-wop now, but I don't recall that expression used in the fifties, when groups like Frankie Lymon and the Teenagers, the Heartbeats, and the Cadillacs were hitting the charts. We idolized Frankie Lymon and his group particularly, because they were young high school kids like us.

In any event, the TeenTones were not in that elite group just yet, our performances largely confined to park fences and school toilets, yet people told us we were good, and we believed them, and it fueled us to rehearse the hit tunes and make up new ones. We were a neighborhood hit, and I began to notice the rapt and admiring attention of postpubescent girls who had paid little attention to me before. Life was looking up for the TeenTones, and now there was talk of auditioning for an appearance on the *Original Amateur Hour,* a creaking but nonetheless network television program on ABC. *Ted Mack's Original Amateur Hour* was outdated even by nineteen-fifties standards, but TeenTones couldn't be choosers, and the prospect thrilled us and gave us ever more incentive to improve.

All of this heady stuff was swirling in my mind one chilly November evening as I walked the eight blocks or so to rehearsal. I was wearing my Clinton jacket, which, though very much in vogue, was not warm enough to match the cold and brisk wind of a Bronx winter. Local mothers and fathers had always dressed their little boys up for the season—"You don't want to catch cold"—with mittens, sweaters, scarves and bulky, unstylish coats. The worst of it was that we were forced to wear hats with ear laps—there was nothing shmuckier or less cool than ear laps. For a big kid, it was a macho sign to one's peers to brave the cold with less, not more: no jackets below the waist, no hat.

I was headed for the parkway. The TeenTones would be practicing at the junior high school, which was open three nights a week for basketball, Ping-Pong, and knock hockey. Our favorite rehearsal venue was the first-floor boys' toilet; but if the odor and traffic became unmanageable and interfered with our artistry, the echo of the concrete stairwells would do nicely. Anyway, we had discovered that the girls couldn't watch us if we sang in the boys' room. We made a perfect acoustical accompaniment to the bouncing of basketballs and the cracking of knock-hockey pucks, and small groups of kids gathered to listen.

I walked up the hill with an icy wind in my face and my hands in my jacket pockets, toward Reservoir Oval, which was a park and athletic field converted from the old Williamsbridge Reservoir in one of those wonderful Depression-era construction projects designed to create work. And beautiful work it was, the kind of workmanship one would seldom see today, featuring a carved stone main building and walkways of octagonal tiles. The Oval was about a mile in circumference, and though it had a decorative five-foot-high fence (pickets of black painted steel with a horizontal beam at the top and bottom), one could enter at several ornate stone entrances placed around it. In a time-saving pinch, the fence could be climbed, as its function was more aesthetic than utilitarian. My route would take me about one quarter of the way around the Oval before I had to proceed west several more blocks to Mosholu Parkway and the school. The Oval had an upper level inside the fence, which ran next to the circular street (called Reservoir Oval Avenue), forming two large concentric circles or, more properly, ovals. I had the option of walking around the top level or on the sidewalk across the street: I had gone both ways many times on the way to school, but I usually preferred the outside-street route in the evening.

Inside the park, one could descend the thirty steps to the lower level, where there was a football field, a running track, tennis courts, and several playground areas containing swings, seesaws, and monkey bars. This was not considered a wise thing to do after dark, as the lower level was said to be the gathering place for youths bent on lower pursuits. These guys were from east of the Oval and beyond, a different neighborhood altogether, and strangers to us. We had heard stories of kids who'd ventured down at the wrong time and had been harassed and beaten, and some had had money stolen. It was referred to as getting jumped. In the daytime, evidence of these strangers' pleasure and malfeasance could be seen in the bushes: beer bottles, cigarette butts, and discarded condoms.

When I got to the top of the hill near the entrance to the Oval, I saw two old men in the dim light of the lampposts. They had just entered and were strolling around the upper level of the park, conversing with their hands behind their backs. There was no one else in sight. I could see the slight shine from their satin yarmulkes, which told me that they were fresh from evening services at the Gun Hill Jewish Center, one hundred yards to the left. As this was a Wednesday night, the turnout would be sparse, indicating that these old gentlemen were pious indeed. Perhaps the sight of them provided a sort of comfort, as the presence of grown-ups usually did in dark and deserted places. So that night I chose the inside-park route. I undertook a brisk pace along the upper walk of the Oval. In short order, I was overtaking the two men, whose tempo was more leisurely, and as they heard my footsteps, each turned a little anxiously to see who was behind him. I suppose it amused me that they might consider me a threat, followed immediately by the empathetic desire to reassure them and let them know that I was just a good boy who meant no harm, on his way to a TeenTones rehearsal. I wanted to shout out, "Just passing! Not going to jump you!," but I didn't. I created a Boy Scout voice for a most cheery and innocent "Good evening," and passed by them innocently, like a figure from a Norman Rockwell painting, humming the various harmony parts we would be rehearsing shortly. I had another few minutes of walking to do before I would exit, and the coast was clear.

It was then that I heard voices about two hundred feet behind me and to the right. It was certainly not the old men. These were the more vigorous, assertive voices of youth. As I turned, I could see, in the sparse light, three figures climbing the fence, and nimbly at that, into the park. There was a gleam off their bodies that became, on clearer view, the shining leather and silver accessories of motorcycle jackets, which were not usually the favored attire of honor students. After they had traversed the narrow grass section and hit the stone of the park walk, I could hear distinctly the definitive clack of motorcycle boots, which in the Bronx of that time (like the jackets) were a social statement, none of it having anything to do with motorcycles. They began walking in my direction purposefully. I could have bolted and outrun them to the park exit, given my lead; or jumped the fence and run down the hill. Shame overcame fear, and boyish pride took hold. I did not run, though I instantly changed my walking style to a more arrogant, tough gait, like someone not to be messed with. There was always hope—the hope that they had another engagement down in the belly of the Oval to drink beer, smoke, and get laid.

But their steady encroachment and the awful sound of six heavy boots on stone belied any innocent stroll in the park, and I began to feel like a dead duck whose continued humming was so much delusional bravado. I felt like a boy who had made a bad decision. I dared not look back, not wanting them to see me sneaking peeks, though a proverbial chill ran up my spine, and my pulse was revved to frightening heights; I was trembling. Clack, clump, clack, clump. They were close now, and I could hear their voices like hissing snakes, but I could not distinguish what they were saying. Then they were surrounding me, two in front and one behind, and would not let me pass. It was a surreal instant when the numb distance of a dream—seeing the scene from the outside, as if I weren't in it—momentarily overcame fear. I tried to keep walking, but the two in front gave me a vicious push so that I almost fell. They were big, maybe sixteen-year-olds, and they stood with their feet planted a wise-guy length apart. In the paltry park light, I could not clearly see their facial features, but something in their hands was shiny. "What do you want?" I said.

There was silence for a few moments, as much silence as you could hear in the Bronx if you excluded traffic and fire engines and the screech of the elevated train and a million people. Where the fuck were the people now? To think that those distant sounds represented human beings, grown-ups with whom I could find sanctuary. But they were in the wrong place. Or, more accurately, I was. I thought of my mother: She could be looking out the window right now, five blocks away. Then the extraneous sounds faded out, and all I could hear was the quiet whoosh of the wind blowing through the barren branches, sweeping along a few leaves and twigs. It was as if there was no one else in the world but we four. Oh, for a beautiful green-and-white police car!

"Whaddaya want? I got a rehearsal," I repeated, in my best Bronx street dialect. Who knows, maybe they were TeenTone fans, but they had to notice my shaking knees. "I gotta go, I'll be late," I said.

The tall one came right up to me, holding something in his hand, and pushed it against my stomach. "Shut up or you get *this*," he said, like a cliché from an early James Cagney movie. I instinctively placed my hand on the object and explored it gently with my fingers like a sightless person. It was cylindrical and cold to the touch. *This* was no cliché. *This* was a homemade twenty-two-caliber firearm commonly called a zip gun: a device of wood and pipe, with rubber bands providing the tension for the hammer. It was pointed two inches from my gut, and the fucking moron holding it had his finger on the trigger. The newspapers were full of stories of boys killed by zip guns. The other two flashed switchblade knives that had sprung open with consecutive loud clicks. The light reflected not only off their leather apparel and weapons but off their shiny greaser hairdos as well, with the little spill hanging down over the forehead like Sal Mineo had.

These observations were made by me in the span of a second, a very long and anxious second. My body was in full flight-or-fight mode, though running was out of the question, the gun having skewed that equation. Fighting was a poor option as well, given the weapons and my appalling dearth of fighting prowess and, I guess, courage. I knew instinctively that I could not joke my way out of this, as I had with previous minor scrapes. The situation did not look good, and there was nothing for a boy to do, so without thinking (or rather, thinking a mile a minute), I pretended to faint.

I slid gently to the stone walk in a kind of pseudo swoon, being careful to avoid hitting my head. I couldn't believe I'd done it. Was it believable? "He fainted," the tall one said. He sounded worried. "Holy shit," said another one. "Let's get the fuck out of here," said the third, and he clicked his knife closed. After a few seconds of possum-like stillness, I opened my eyes and looked up and got a good view of the tall one. "McVay!" I blurted out. "Klein!" he said, just as surprised. It was a guy from my biology class: Ace McVay, six foot four, skinny as a rail, with a hideous complexion that looked like a relief map of the Himalayas. His real name was Percival, though it was generally considered that one called him that at significant risk. He had begun his high school career as an honor student but was now on the verge of flunking out, if he attended class at all. He was known as a tough guy at school, though I can't remember much evidence to verify that fact. It was just the way he carried himself, the "I don't give a shit" attitude, the boots and jacket, and a hell of a name—Ace McVay.

"Oh, fuck, he knows you. What the fuck are we gonna do now?" said the one who had closed his knife. Much to my dismay, he clicked it open again and came toward me with his weapon at the ready. "I'm gonna cut the motherfucker," he said.

McVay extended his long arm and stopped the guy's advance. The other guy with the knife said: "Ace, we gotta do something, he can identify us, he'll talk."

"Not here," said McVay. "We'll bring him down into the bushes and take care of him there." With a gun pointed at me, I opted to stay on the ground and avoid any sudden movement that might send me six feet under (those thoughts again). I definitely thought at that moment that my life might end here. I was sorry I had not requested *above* ground burial, but I was fourteen and had not expected my demise so soon.

Suddenly, there was the faint sound of voices borne by the wind— it was the two old men. McVay stuck the pistol down the front of his pants. With any luck, maybe it would fire and blow his balls off, the bastard. He bent down and pulled me violently to my feet. The two old men approached, which seemed to unnerve these shitheads, who hid their knives and assumed a nonchalant pose. Thank God for grown-ups. But why did the two available ones have to be enfeebled and seventy-five?

They stopped briefly. "Everything all right?" one of them said in a European accent. McVay, whose back was toward them, put his hand on his gun and glared at me. "Everything's fine," I said. The men walked on. A thought shot through my mind that the old gentlemen knew exactly what was happening but were too afraid to intercede. Who could blame them? I hoped they would call the police.

"Shit, those fuckin' old geezers saw us now. Too many witnesses, let's bug outta here," said the one who wanted to cut me.

"Bullshit. It's fuckin' dark, they couldn't see us, the nosy fucks. But *he* knows me and that's a problem," said Ace McVay, who withdrew the gun from his pants and pushed it into my belly once again, harder than before. He made the most menacing face he could, a face I would remember for a long, long time. I thought this was it.

Then he said, "This never happened, you understand? You better keep your fuckin' mouth shut. Now, get going and keep walking."

This seemed like an excellent, not to say reasonable, idea. I acceded to it immediately, my prospects for a fifteenth birthday having improved considerably. I could hear the threesome grumbling behind me, then the clack-clump of their boots across the walk, followed by the crackling of the bushes that descended to the playground. I was in a kind of trancelike shock as I hurried away at a respectable medium pace: I did not run. But after a couple of minutes, the reality of my acute humiliation began to set in. The awful thought of having been violated, and my strategically sound but hardly courageous fainting shtick, commenced to haunt me and gnaw at my self-esteem. This feeling became a familiar one in the coming weeks, as omnipresent as the air I breathed: the air of abasement, of shame.

As I passed the old men yet again, they seemed concerned and looked me over. One of them said, "You all right?"

"Yes, I'm fine, thank you. I just fell."

But I was not fine. I was furious and deflated and chagrined. I arrived at rehearsal with forced composure to find three thoroughly jolly TeenTones horsing around and laughing. Sure, nobody had just threatened to kill *them*. When I told them about my experience, I intentionally chose to underplay the intense emotion of the event (again, boyish pride) and emphasize the fortunate outcome: the result of the assailant being my classmate, and of course my fainting ruse, which I recounted humorously. The TeenTones found the story quite funny, and I even pretended to agree, though I could not yet, with the event so fresh in my mind, see much humor in it. I hid my disappointment at their lack of compassion and their failure to acknowledge the seriousness of the affair. Apparently, TeenTones are easily amused, though I had contributed to their attitude with my evasion of emotion.

After rehearsal, for which I had little enthusiasm, I took the longer but well lit and heavily traveled route of Gun Hill Road home. I thought of the future, and of the irony that the very thing that had saved me from physical harm—my acquaintance with my assailant— was also to be my curse. We were schoolmates. Despite the fact that Ace McVay's attendance at DeWitt Clinton High School was becoming sporadic at best, I dreaded encountering him. It was not so much that I feared another physical confrontation, though I did; it was the mortification I dreaded most: the shame of a marked man. He and his goons had been witness to when I was demonstrably the weak lamb to his menacing lion, and he knew it. I fantasized many times about blowing his head off, about punching his ugly face so many times that he would bleed from every pimple. I almost bit my own lower lip just thinking about it. Now it was his smirking countenance on my living room ceiling morning and night, instead of my favorite images of the TeenTones and rock-and-roll stardom. In fact, my enthusiasm for the whole TeenTone enterprise diminished. I had trouble falling asleep, and previously innocuous noises set me on edge: I was not the boy I had been before the outrage.

I did not see him again until a week after the incident. There was McVay, between classes, walking in my direction in one of the long, crowded corridors of the huge building. When he spotted me, I saw an instantaneous change in his demeanor. He toughened his walk as he approached: more resolve, more intimidation, more of a clack from his boots. His steely gray eyes were focused on me, bespeaking the unmistakable message "Keep your fuckin' mouth shut." This behavior was repeated every time he saw me, especially in biology class, where he was, of all things, my lab partner, though he never said a word to me. These encounters precluded any closure to the traumatic event, a constant reminder of my helplessness.

As the weeks went by, McVay continued to glower when he saw me, though he would sometimes throw in a simple, not unfriendly nod of recognition. It began to dawn on me how afraid he was that I would report the incident, which I never did. I didn't even tell my parents, for somehow, in my mind, it was not an attempted armed robbery, as it would be in the grown-up world, but the business of boys, and exempt from the purview of grown-up authority. The thought, however, that I might engender fear of any kind in the likes of Ace McVay gave me mild satisfaction, though the fact remained that he and his buddies had committed a felony and had seen me collapse to the ground believing I had fainted. Which of us had the more dreadful secret about the other?

I continued to daydream about revenge and physical destruction in which I would subjugate my tormentor. I thought of enlisting one or more of the tough rocks who hung out at the fence on Mosholu Parkway and appreciated the TeenTones, like the fearsome Lefty Farrell and the borderline psychotic Roy Drillick, who many years later would kill his father and himself. I had visions of them beating McVay and forcing him to apologize to me in a victory of good over evil akin to the Allies over the Nazis. But with Lefty and Roy, it would be more a case of victory of *evil* over evil, and I concluded that it was nobody's business but my own—and Percy McVay's.

The weeks went by, and McVay's glares began to disappear, replaced by a kind of self-absorption; thoughts, I surmised, that were far from the Reservoir Oval. Perhaps he was contemplating subsequent armed robberies and beatings, or that he was shortly to be expelled from school for nonattendance. The tension in me had abated somewhat as well, but not my desire for vengeance, which I knew realistically would never come.

The TeenTones continued to harmonize and improve, though *Ted Mack's Original Amateur Hour* was still up in the air. We were invited to sing at a couple of local dances, for which we bought red-and-black-striped vests that were cheaper than sport jackets. Though I still enjoyed my involvement, I had developed an ambivalent attitude toward the TeenTones, with whom I made an associative connection to my recent catastrophe. My journey to the rehearsals was now an ordeal, conducted with a vigilance like never before. Every person on the street, every noise and shadow, was cause for alarm, and I did not venture through the gates of the Oval after the daylight hours, preferring the perceived safety of the more populated streets.

One day, sitting with some friends and TeenTones in the huge high school cafeteria, I observed a crowd and potential ruckus at one of the doorways. Arguments and fights in the lunchroom were not uncommon in a building containing several thousand male students, and we were accustomed to watching, fights being more interesting than cafeteria food to teenage boys. I personally hated to fight, as I've said, though I had been in a few that were unavoidable. The strange thing was that I loathed the feeling of my fist connecting to someone's face only slightly less than the feeling of being hit, with its painful, throbbing sting and the need to fight tears.

We ambled over to the tumult, where Bill Haroldson, a lunchroom monitor, was attempting to prevent a boy from ascending the stairs to the halls and classrooms. It was against the rules until one's lunch period was over, and Billy, a spirited but diminutive kid, meant to enforce them. The miscreant was none other than Ace McVay. Twice Billy tried to block the door and twice McVay arrogantly pushed him aside, having sport with Billy. Finally, McVay took a step back, assumed his macho feet-apart stance, put a suspicious hand in his jacket pocket, and said, "Hey, asshole, you looking for trouble?"

Just then a burly figure broke through the crowd and said, "I handle the trouble here." It was said in a most understated manner, but it was a dramatic moment, and the crowd hushed. It was Al Gorden, the chief lunchroom monitor, who did not look the part of a tough guy, with his glasses and preppy clothes, but he was strong.

McVay's smiling face twitched slightly as he observed what seemed to be slightly more even odds. Gorden was a respected guy who would fight only over the proper beef. "Who the fuck are *you*?"

McVay asked with all the confident venom he could muster, and he proceeded to try to exit yet again.

Gorden removed his horn-rims and carefully placed them in his breast pocket as he blocked the door. "I'm in charge here, and you can't go up into the halls."

McVay smiled again, or rather smirked that smirk that I knew so well, and looked down at the floor as a ruse. Suddenly, he released a right-hand roundhouse at Al Gorden, who blocked it with his massive forearm. At the same time, Gorden hit the tall, skinny bastard with a powerful left hook to the stomach, which made him grunt like a pig and took the wind out of him, doubling him over.

There was a tense pause as McVay caught his breath and straightened up. It had looked like it was all over with one punch, but "Fuck you," McVay said, and he put up his dukes to continue. He tried some flailing punches to Al's head but got caught with a stunning combination to his face that made the sound of smacking meat and bone and sent his head crashing into the steel-meshed glass of the door and his body to the ground.

I found myself biting my lip, and my fists were clenched as if it were I, not Al Gorden, delivering the punishment. Blood was pouring out of McVay's nose and several of his multitude of pimples, not unlike my fantasies. My fellow students were screaming the usual "Fight! Fight! Fight! Fight!" like convicts at a prison riot. Gorden stood over McVay, fists at the ready, and prepared to stop fighting, when McVay kicked out at his legs, trying to trip him, then rose, all the while cursing: "You motherfucker, I'll kill you. You're dead, you fucking Jew bastard."

Percival McVay had said the wrong thing. Allen Gorden was the child of holocaust survivors—his parents had in fact met at Dachau— and McVay's words sent the head lunchroom monitor over the top. He grabbed the bleeding, reeling boy by the collar of his black leather jacket and jerked him upright, holding him with his left hand while beating him unmercifully with powerful, true punches with his right fist, grunting loudly with each one like a tennis player on his serve. "*What* am I? You piece of shit! *What* am I?"

Gorden's own lip was bleeding from his teeth biting down on it, and the maniacal look on his face and the intensity of his eyes convinced me that he would kill the boy. A female teacher was screaming for help. McVay was becoming pulp. My fingernails were digging into my palms from the vicarious beating of my archenemy, this villain who had changed my life. Each punch was *my* punch.

Then, as I looked at the scarlet mess that was McVay's face, I realized that the savagery of the attack was becoming too painful for me to watch, and I found myself wanting to shout out for Gorden to stop. I did not. A surprising revulsion overtook me. I could not stand more, and was about to turn away when finally Al Gorden desisted his furious attack. He stepped back, a snarling, sweaty animal, and regained control of himself. He stood for a few moments over McVay, like Hemingway over a slain lion. I looked at the vanquished Percival McVay lying half conscious on the floor and tried to drink it in, wanting so much to enjoy it, thinking that it would at last end my preoccupation with the humiliation that had afflicted me since the incident. What a shitty fighter he was. I had never thought I would see this, though wasn't it what I had hoped for? But the sight gave me no comfort. A tremendous wave of pity replaced the revulsion and the vitriol, and I felt a sudden desire to help McVay up. I did not. I thought of his mother.

A couple of nervous teachers on lunchroom duty, who had sensibly stood back during the fight, helped the pitiful figure to his feet and dabbed his wounds with paper napkins. A few boys taunted him that he had not landed a single punch; perhaps they, too, had been victims of his predatory habits to take such cowardly advantage of his condition. Ding dong the witch was dead. Percy McVay was now off the sociological map at DeWitt Clinton High School. He never returned to school.

With hindsight, I have to admit that his demise afforded me closure of a sort. If I had not seen him so humbled, his power over me— or rather, my *mind*—might have continued. I slept more soundly, and I had more confidence, and I was a more productive TeenTone from then on. I never saw his face in the flesh again, though I cannot say that I have not seen him in my mind's eye from time to time; more as the bleeding heap than the terrifying intimidator.

The TeenTones did appear on the *Original Amateur Hour,* singing an up-tempo version of the Harptones hit "A Sunday Kind of Love." We were up against NBC's *Cinderella,* which had, I'm told, the largest audience up to that time in television history. Only our immediate families watched us, and even that is somewhat doubtful. The TeenTones did not win. We were defeated by a one-armed piano-playing post-office worker from Missouri.

Chapter Four

Push Like You Mean It

Shortly after my fifteenth birthday, I met someone who would change the entire course of my life. We met briefly, and I haven't seen her since, but I will be indebted to her as long as I live.

It was around this time that two high school friends and I, shot through with 110-proof libido, began to contemplate our stifled Bronx teenage life. The notion arose that we had been virgins long enough. Manny and Joe were good guys, reasonably intelligent, fun, and like myself, plenty frustrated and at least tentatively determined to do something about it. Joe was a thickly built blond-headed boy with a wonderful disposition and an appealing tendency to smile a lot. In my upbringing, optimism was not a highly touted concept, and his glass-is-half-full outlook played well with me. He wore his blond hair cropped and reminded me of Moose Skowron, who played first base for the Yankees on those fifties championship teams, though Joe was much better-looking than the first baseman. He was as unneurotic and sanguine as could be, having never wanted for anything in his life, either emotionally or materially. Joe's mother, it was said, had never missed a breast feeding and was known to have been punctual at all times, especially with regard to anything that affected her little Joey.

Manny, on the other hand, was a worrywart, compulsively neat, perpetually washing his hands and in motion: fidgeting, examining objects. He was very smart and had an excellent sense of humor. He was tall and rather handsome, though his black horn-rimmed glasses gave him the stereotypic look of an intellectual, which he was not.

In matters of sex, we were masters of inexperience, figures of futility, impatient, not hopeful. We were not Don Juans or Casanovas. We were horny. The three of us felt overdue and resolved to finally score, hit a home run, go all the way, get laid. To be sure, guys like us all carried a condom in our wallets just in case we got lucky; but no one seemed to get lucky, and in the wallets they stayed—in my case, for years. In fact, it caused a semipermanent impression of a ring in my wallet and on my left buttock, which looked like a miniature three-dimensional schematic of Belmont Racetrack. Never mind that the condom, three years past its expiration date, would have crumbled into dust if removed from the package.

Clearly, the prospects for real sex in my middle-class life at that time were slim, as the neighborhood girls were "good girls" who would not yet engage in such things, repressed as we all were by the prevailing fifties culture. (I use expressions like "prevailing fifties culture" now, though I would not have had a clue about it back then.) There were "bad girls," or so we heard, and rumors of sluts and tramps who would do anything with any guy (God bless them), but I never seemed to run into them. To hear the talk of certain boys, *someone* was getting it, but it sure wasn't me or anyone I knew. At that time, my most advanced sexual experience consisted of a girl and I rubbing against each other fully clothed, the utterly frustrating maneuver known as dry humping. Before my hand was stopped in its tracks, I had experienced a couple of instances of feeling tiny bare breasts, and a glorious but brief digital touch of a vagina, that most divine of body parts, with which I longed to get better acquainted, but which seemed destined to elude me.

All of this aroused me enormously with no orgasmic payoff, which sent me into painful cases of what we called "blue balls" among the boys. I know little or nothing of the male sexual and urological plumbing, but my sense of it as a layman and an individual who possesses this physiological setup, is that the condition is caused by the pressure of intense arousal for long periods of time, with no climax. The pain would result in a limping gait, not to mention much agony, and it reminded me of the pain incurred when trying to jump over a fire hydrant (which we often did as a dangerous macho challenge) but instead landing on *top* of it. A couple of testicles smashing into that hard, steel hexagonal nut at the top of the hydrant—enough said. Blue balls also required torturous explanations to my mother about why I was walking "that way." "What's the matter with your leg? Why are you walking that way?" "I'm all right, I'm all right, it's nothing, Ma, I'm just going to lie down for a minute."

By necessity, expediency was the order of the day, and my main squeeze at the time was my compliant and always reliable right hand, frequently referred to as Mother Palm and Her Five Daughters. Masturbation was the savior of us all: the safety valve, our friend. Some parents panicked upon catching their boys in the act and issued dire warnings about hell, blindness, or worse. My mother had caught me a number of times since the age of five, rubbing myself in the prone position against the living room rug. She told me that my penis would eventually fall off if I did this regularly, but she had a smile on her face, which indicated that her declaration was said in jest, tongue in cheek. While I sensed that it wasn't really true, I was gullible, as small children are, and would frequently check myself for possible penile breakage. All in all, I calculated the risk to be well worth it, which says quite a bit about the joys of orgasm and a risk-averse boy.

Now I was fifteen and knew better, as my sexual organ had survived mightily, and far from having fallen off, had grown and prospered and was playing an increasingly important role in my young life. I knew there was a world out there where people were having sex. My father had a deck of cards from the thirties with black-and-white photos of real people engaging in real sex, confirming all the things I had been imagining. I had found it two years earlier, the consummate bar mitzvah present, and it was, to a hormonal thirteen-year-old, like a paleo-anthropologist discovering the missing link. It was impossible not to share the find with some close friends, who liked to borrow the cards for quick, private games of solitaire in the bathroom. My father hid the French deck, as it was called (since such things were purported to have originated in Paris), in his sock drawer, next to his Trojan prophylactics, which I fiendishly counted to see how often my parents were having sex. The incessant use of these pornographic cards by pubescent boys resulted in a dilemma. When I found them, they were in pristine condition, never used; but now the edges had become frayed, and the box showed considerable wear and tear. If my father knew anything, he pretended not to notice and certainly would have been too embarrassed to bring up the subject. Time after time, the cards were right where I left them. He never removed them from their accustomed place in his sock drawer, since such a move would indicate that he knew that we knew that he owned them.

This deck of cards got a real workout. The image was practically obliterated on the jack of diamonds, an acrobatic ménage à trois that was everybody's favorite. It is not an exaggeration to say that this deck of cards and I went steady for over two years, and the courtship was most educational. I wish I could thank the skanky-looking cast of characters that appeared in these photos: the tough-looking men with greasy hair and black socks, and the homely whores doing the most fantastic things while tempting the wrath of hell and the law. They did a great service for us, these lay professors who risked jail and worse. It was not information generally available to us at that time, except through the hyperbole of older boys, who tended to exaggerate their experience and skill. I feel genuine gratitude when I think that these men and women performed these forbidden acts for the camera in the antiquated nineteen thirties, so that some hapless shleppers under the influence of powerful, natural, and unavoidable urges in the not-so-sexy fifties could get off once in a while. The closest thing to pornography that most of us had was a Marilyn Monroe calendar or a *Playboy* magazine, even though Hugh Hefner had not yet discovered the existence of pubic hair.

And just where could kids like us have enough privacy to even *imitate* having sex? In New York City, no one could drive a car until the age of eighteen, so we had to content ourselves with stolen moments at parentally supervised teenage birthday parties, necking on top of the coats in the bedroom or dancing and groping in a dark room to the music of Johnny Mathis or the Cadillacs. These experiences were so frustrating that it was guaranteed that the boys would be limping home. Yet they were well worth the pain, these first encounters with holding, squeezing, and kissing a female, keeper of the elusive vagina, though not the adored object itself.

Let me say that even though these events happened well before a more permissive, enlightened time, it was not some amorphous person I was attempting to fondle in the dark. It was Susan Gilbert and Suzanne Billitzer and Leona Fleigner and Flo Bierman, girls in my class, friends, whose gender did not make them automatic adversaries or depersonalized objects. They were wonderfully intelligent, positive, spirited girls with the highest self-esteem. The fact that they were mature for their age and in charge of themselves made my intimacy with them, such as it was, all the more exciting. The juxtaposition of a cool, public exterior and those primitive, private, intimate moments on top of the coats in the bedroom was very erotic. The girls, model citizens with first-rate brains, from good families, yet rubbing against me with a passion and loss of inhibition that they exhibited nowhere else in their lives—this was one of the enigmas of sexuality, but I felt no need to figure it out.

Often the quest was just to dance close and slow and maybe explore a little in the darkness. The result was usually the good girl abruptly removing my hand from her breast when I'd gone too far, and saying something like "Robert, do you respect me?" "Yes, I respect you, I just want to touch your breasts." There was plenty of guilt, embarrassment, and regret at having blurted this out; even though it was the truth—an unfortunate utterance of the id—this girl was my friend and was only trying to protect her reputation. I found out years later that she wanted me to touch her breasts as much as I wanted to touch them, but she was constrained by the prevailing pressures of family and decency. Weren't we all? The girls, though, were especially victimized by a double standard. We all wanted to do something with a girl that we wouldn't want our sister to do. When all was said and done, I had a sister at home, and she was a good girl, and I was thankful for that. But if we were to do it with a girl, it had to be with *somebody's* sister: This was another contradiction of sexuality that I felt no obligation to solve. Anyway, why is something as good as sex thought of as bad? And why is the idea that it's naughty so arousing? That's an enigma and a contradiction rolled into one.

In any case, it was clear that for the foreseeable future, what Joe and Manny and I sought to attain would never be accomplished with the girls we knew from the neighborhood. The answer would have to be a professional woman, a prostitute, a whore, or, as it was pronounced in the Bronx street, with two syllables: a hoo-ah. But who knew a hoo-ah? There were occasional "hot" phone numbers of supposed prostitutes bandied about, garnered from lavatory walls. All were hoaxes: the phone numbers of good girls, supplied by rejected boyfriends or demented mischief makers. Joe supplied the number of a "definite hoo-ah" that he got "off a guy" at the Fordham library. We worked up the nerve and called, giggling and goosy, only to hear some pathetic drunk female with a three-pack-a-day voice say, "I don't do that anymore." Surely not with the likes of hysterical teenagers like us.

"Did you really *used* to do it?" I asked, fascinated that I might be talking to an actual hoo-ah.

"Where did you get my number?" she spat, through a spate of bubbly wet coughing right out of the pulmonary ward at Bellevue. I pursued my fascination: "How come you don't do that anymore?"

"I just don't."

"Why don't you do it *once* more? Just *once* more," I pleaded, determined to coax her out of her premature and inconvenient retirement. Manny wanted me to ask her if she would recommend someone else.

"Grow up, you bunch a jerks," she coughed, and abruptly hung up.

The message seemed to be: "Wait till you grow up, jerk," but none of us jerks had the patience to wait that long. We made inquiries in school, and along the fence at Mosholu Parkway, looking for a live clue. Around this time we heard a story from Nicky C., a boy in Manny's biology class who had none too good a reputation. It was said that Nicky could steal your socks while you were wearing them, though his specialty was stolen bus passes. We were sitting in the lunchroom when he told us about a street corner in Harlem where, every Saturday night, twenty or thirty prostitutes of all descriptions would gather and openly solicit their wares. This sounded too good to be true, especially since it was illegal and being done openly, and more especially, since it came from Nicky C. But he stuck to his story, and it actually seemed to have the aura of truth, or so we hoped. Could it be the breakthrough we'd been seeking, the solution to our frustration? No embarrassing telephone calls, no doubts, take your pick . . . a sure thing, whores, tons of them.

"Even the cops walk right by," Nick told us, "as if nothing is going on."

"Wouldn't someone try to jump us?" I asked. I reckoned that three white boys from the Bronx would be rather conspicuous in the middle of Harlem, especially with money on us.

"Yeah, someone might jump you. I got friends down there, so no one would touch me, but for you mooks, it's a different story. They can see a little white boy a mile away, and they could take your money. You gotta watch your ass down there, 'cause they know you don't live there, and they damn well know *why* you're there, capeesh?" said Nick.

We capeeshed all too well. This was discouraging though not unexpected information. I wondered what a mook was. "How much does it cost?" Joe inquired.

"Five bucks for a lay, but anything else is extra."

"Extra?" We were nonplussed.

"You know . . . like blow jobs and shit like that."

"Five bucks each? Jeez. Could they do the three of us for ten bucks?" I asked in the spirit of thrift.

Nicky C. got testy. "I don't know. I ain't no pimp, you'll have to ask the hoo-ah. Mine really liked me. She told me next time she'd do it for free, 'cause she likes me so much." Now, Nicky C. was an ugly unkempt sucker with a first-degree case of underarm odor, whose greasy hoodlum pompadour hadn't been washed for weeks. Somehow I doubted that he had stolen the heart of a streetwalker. Maybe his whole story was bullshit, and maybe it wasn't, but I wanted desperately to believe him, short of his self-aggrandizing embroidery, because what he had told us about that happy street corner had planted an erotic germ in my head, and maybe a determination: a carpe diem mentality. Well, some kind of diem mentality, I think it was carpe.

I began fantasizing about it and nothing else, yet the thought always lingered that there was danger here, real danger, and a good boy in a protected life could get his ass kicked in the pursuit of the forbidden. It almost seemed fair, a kind of righteous symmetry, paying the piper and the price. Was that part of the allure?—the trade-off—that is, pursuing a naughty, forbidden goal in the face of adversity and even danger?

Nick's story became the subject of conversation every chance we got: between classes, in the cafeteria, on the walk to and from school. We talked and talked, and the more we discussed the pros and cons, the more it appeared that there were quite a few cons and a discouraging dearth of pros. Truth be known, there was only one pro: getting off the coital shneid. Among the cons we discussed were the prospects of getting robbed and beaten and horrendous venereal diseases. We mulled over the headlines and the effect on our families of being dragged dead from the East River or shot through the head, and not innocently, mind you. For the shameful fact, the locus of the affair that the bereaved families—indeed, the whole world—would know and be forced to live with was that these boys died *seeking sex*, in pursuit of pussy, in sin. We discussed these weighty scenarios for the better part of three minutes, and decided that they were small risks for such an intensely desired goal. We were ready, for such is the power of teenage lust.

It was decided that the three of us would make a trial run to 112th Street and Lenox Avenue, with the intention of testing the waters: a reconnaissance mission. We chose a Saturday night, our meeting place, and our subway route. The whole thing had the feel of a commando operation, complete with the element of secrecy. All that was missing were the ski masks. Forget about the furious feelings of lust and anticipation and fear that pervaded my thoughts and dreams: This was it. Put up or shut up.

We sat silently on the subway, co-conspirators headed for destiny. I, in my self-consciousness and guilt, could have sworn that everyone on the train knew *exactly* why I was there and where I was headed. Moreover, I felt certain they would tell my parents. I was a victim of both my conventional morality and my New York liberal social conscience. I imagined that I had a large, brightly lit sign on my forehead: THIS UNDERAGE BOY IS TRYING TO GET LAID ON THE BACKS OF OPPRESSED MINORITIES. I was too uptight to make anything but minimal eye contact with the other passengers, so I couldn't detect whether they were reading my forehead or gave a shit about me at all, for that matter. We emerged from the train, the only Caucasians among two hundred brothers and sisters, and as we poured from the

110th Street station, I could have sworn I heard a booming voice: "White boy, what do you want?" I felt conspicuous, to say the least, and I was now certain that everyone had gotten a good gander at me.

We had a brief huddle to get our geographical bearings, having several blocks to walk, but the passengers disgorged with us from the subway station seemed to have been absorbed into the buildings or taken off in other directions very quickly. The three of us were uncomfortably alone on the street. The dark street. At first we walked casually. Then we made a fairly brisk pace to 112th and Lenox, just short of a run, which we thought would attract attention. We adopted the technique of those schmucky-looking Olympic fast-walkers, which must have attracted even more attention in a neighborhood where people ran as a matter of course.

We approached the appointed corner, which, much to our relief, was well lit and crowded with people and loud with conversation. A closer look revealed that the crowd was largely women, many of them pretty, none of them white; most were dressed in evening clothes of bright colors that starkly distinguished them from the drably dressed neighborhood civilians with their shopping bags, on their way home. The scene reminded me of primitive Caribbean paintings that I had seen in a book or museum.

I realized that we had been noticed by the prostitutes, and after some conversation and giggling among them, two of the ladies approached: a buxom one and a thin, light-skinned woman who sounded like a Latina. They walked right up to us, and the one with the big breasts made a proposition—literally: "You goin' up tonight, honey? Huh? Come on, baby, I'll do somethin' nice for you."

Her words surged through my body like an electrical charge. My legs shook. "No thank you," I replied politely as if it were mashed potatoes I was declining. I could have kicked myself, having to refuse the first such offer of my life. Nonetheless, Manny and Joe and I exchanged glances of triumph, though they were couched in embarrassed smiles. After all, what that loser from school had told us was true: namely, that a bevy of loose willing women was there for the taking, albeit for a price. However, we were not prepared to take them yet; not that evening. We had purposely not even brought along enough money, because this trip was considered reconnaissance, and we were determined to stick to the plan.

After a while, we began to feel more at home and at ease in the atmosphere, which was deceptively friendly. As we approached for a closer look at the women, we were even smiling and pointing at the merchandise like three adolescents at FAO Schwarz. It was like some Middle Eastern bazaar, with shady-looking guys—pimps? customers? There were offers and counteroffers and haggling, and one could hear snippets of gossip. Then a stereotypic Irish policeman sauntered by, swinging his nightstick, right out of a Hollywood musical, and spotted us. "Hey, you, get da hell outta here. I know why youse are here, and ya gonna get hoit," he said. We had contemplated the possibility of being murdered, but we had not counted on trouble with the police. Nicky C. had said the cops wouldn't care. Here we were surrounded by criminals, and the cop picked on us. "Let's go! Youse better move it, or I start takin' names!"

"We're not doing anything," I protested mildly. Very mildly, as he had hit the trigger for us, the "taking names" part, which could only lead to family disgrace and irreparably ruined lives for all. Once again, we were slaves to our upbringing.

"Go home, boys. This ain't no place for you. You don't want to have your mudda comin' to the morgue to identify youse." That was all I needed for my already damaged ego, a softhearted family-man cop. Then he said what I *really* didn't want to hear: "If I catch youse down here again, I'm gonna lock youse up." Boys with our level of experience took such a threat seriously indeed. We had now become a criminal-justice problem. Not only did we have to contend with the criminal underworld; worse, if we continued to pursue our rite of passage into manhood, we would have to do it in opposition to the overwhelming force of the NYPD. We retreated to the subway, under the policeman's watchful eye.

The train ride home was pervaded by a definite deflation of mood. I felt stupid and ashamed. The humiliating encounter with the policeman had been the worst part, because it confirmed our true status as powerless children and frightened novices with consciences. I looked at my hapless, unhappy companions. I cannot explain why, for I was in exactly the same situation, but I was overwhelmed with a sense of pity for them. Joe insisted with much bravado that unless the cop actually caught us doing something illegal, we were free to walk anywhere we wanted, but I could tell he didn't believe it. Manny was afraid he might lose the chance of a college scholarship two years down the road because of a criminal record. I contemplated the awful and ever more likely possibility that I would spend my threescore and ten and die, never having had sexual intercourse.

Such was the morale of the dispirited troops, in stark contrast to the weeks of hype and anticipation. That night I dreamed my old recurring forbidden sex dream. Not the one about hot dogs chasing doughnuts through the Lincoln Tunnel. This dream was so psychologically obvious that it came right off page 1 of a Freudian textbook. In the dream, I am at the center of beautifully sculpted bushes, like topiaries, the center of a maze. On a flat pedestal is a naked woman beckoning me to come to her, to make love to her. Not one to argue, I eagerly approach. At the very moment I try to touch her naked body, she turns to bronze, and I am feeling a cold statue. Any questions, students? Thank you, let's move on.

While my dreams tormented me with guilt and shame, my waking thoughts were of the streetwalking women on 112th Street, with their high heels and their pretty dresses, who told me they wanted my body. The cop had not reduced my ardor, so like General MacArthur to the Philippines, I vowed to return.

By midweek the boys and I were still discouraged. We were also still horny, and there were gut decisions to be made. We decided that on the coming Saturday night, we would journey once again to 112th Street and Lenox Avenue. A few strategic adjustments were made, like dressing in jackets and ties to look older. Joe had suggested bringing a knife from his mother's kitchen for protection, but the idea was voted down as ludicrous. Manny put a pipe in his mouth, which fooled nobody, and Joe allowed a five-day growth to mildly suggest a mustache, which made him look like a fifteen-year-old with a mild suggestion of a mustache.

We were certain we needed to use condoms, but were unsure whether we should bring our own or if they would be supplied by the prostitute in an all-inclusive package deal. I pilfered a Trojan from my father's sock drawer and counted the ones that were left. Unless my father was using them for water bombs, my parents were hot as hell. Joe's older cousin supplied Sheiks for him and Manny after I refused to lift a couple more from Ben Klein.

The boys and I had a strategy meeting to discuss our concerns. We were fearful about running into the same meddlesome police officer again, yet his warning about the danger had resonated. Joe talked about hooking up with the buxom brown woman who had approached us the week before. Manny and I planned to take our time and look over the whole lot before selecting the whore of our choice.

In a flash, it was D-day, and there we were on the train again. This time there was less sense of being conspicuous, and we sat on the noisy train like innocent citizens on our way from point A to point B. We seemed to have more confidence, borne of excellent planning, and when those subway doors hissed open, we disembarked as if this were our home station. Once again, out into the Harlem night. We had our bearings and proceeded to the theater of operations, ever watchful of who was around us—ironically, cops *or* robbers. We kept a brisk pace through the semideserted side streets. "What if they're not here tonight? What if they don't come every Saturday?" Manny said.

"What are you talking about? Of course they'll be here. Saturday night has to be the busiest night for whores, wouldn't you say, Robert?"

"Oh, yeah. Saturday night is entertainment night. Movies, theaters, nightclubs, whores. They all must clean up on Saturday night. I mean, I certainly hope so—I didn't come down for the beautiful scenery," I said.

We came around the corner and there it was, the scene from the week before, plenty of chatty women looking for a score. There were a couple of policemen, but they were halfway down the block and walking the other way. I clutched the ten-dollar bill in my right pants pocket and felt for the circular bulge in my wallet, lodged in my buttoned back pocket. I had always been taught by my parents to be aware of pickpockets when in crowds.

We waded into the swarm of women and potential customers and could hear the bargaining going on over the price. A few camels, and it could have been Baghdad. Apparently, everything was negotiable, from what was paid to what was performed, and the sweet smell of cheap perfume permeated the area, which I found exciting and titil- lating. What I really found exciting and titillating was passing through groups of women whose sole intent was sex, possibly with me, who would not metamorphose into statues or slap my hand away or say no. These women were yeses all the way. Joe looked the ladies over like an expert as we cruised through at a moderate pace. He was, at any rate, an expert as to what would satisfy him, looking like a buyer for Bloomingdale's or an inspector from the U.S. Department of Agricul- ture. He also had a one-track mind with respect to locating the busty brown woman from the previous week. Then, bingo, there she was. He spoke up: "Hi, I'm Joe, what's your name?"

"I'm Desiree. You wanna go up tonight, honey?"

"Maybe," he said. I would have been mortified to bring up price just then, but not good old Joe. "How much?" he said.

"Ten dollars. You gonna have a good time, baby." She approached him and put her lips to his right ear. "I'll do things for you, baby, that you don't dream of."

"Ten dollars? Uh-uh. That's too much, way too much," he said, "and besides, there's three of us, so maybe we can make a deal."

I was really impressed with Joe's consumerist pursuit of a good prostitution value, worthy of *Consumer Reports*, but I noticed another woman. She was pretty, in her late twenties, with a tall slen- der figure like a fashion model's. There was something almost classy about her, at least my fifteen-year-old idea of classy. She wore an ele- gant skirt and a blouse with a mink collar, which was very popular in those days, a subdued ensemble that made her look altogether out of place, as if she had mistakenly waded into this mélange by accident. Perhaps, I surmised, she was a student at Columbia University who had fallen on hard times and had to pay for books.

Joe forged on. "How about this, Desiree: I got a deal for you. How about the three of us for ten dollars?"

Desiree gave him a sneer, and as she turned away, she said, "Baby, for that money, you can take it and wrap it around the lamppost." She and some of the other women started laughing hysterically, as if this were the funniest thing they'd ever heard. Clearly these people were easily amused. We stood there with our mouths open, having been made to feel like perfect fools. The lovely thin one with the mink collar did not laugh, for she evidently saw a business opportunity, and the Columbia tuition is known to be heavy. "You boys together?" she said.

"Well, sort of," I replied. I wanted to keep all options open.

"I'll do each of you for five dollars, but no kissing and no French. You understand?"

"Uh . . . sure. Could you give me a minute?" I said.

"Sure, but hurry on up, 'cause you wasting time, and I got to make some money."

"Okay, but don't go anywhere," I blurted out. The three of us stepped to a private space to discuss the proposition. "I don't want that one. She's too skinny," Joe said. "And I think we can do better pricewise."

"Pricewise? She's charging half as much as yours," I pointed out.

"Yeah, but she's got no meat on her bones."

Manny was too intimidated to say anything except "Let's go home. I've got a bad feeling about this."

I could have choked him. "Look, we've come this far, we can't back out now. You want to get laid or don't you?"

"Why don't you guys go with this one, and I'll get the other one," said Joe. "I'm sure I can get her down to eight bucks."

"Jesus Christ, Joe, can't we simplify this thing with one woman?" I whined. "Besides, we agreed not to separate, for safety."

"And what's the thing about no kissing?" Joe said. "For five bucks, you should be able to kiss her."

"Who the hell wants to kiss her?" Manny chimed in. "I guess I'd fuck her, but I wouldn't kiss her. I don't care if she doesn't speak French."

"You idiot, she's not talking about speaking French," I said. At least he no longer wanted to go home.

"Hey, boys, time's a-wasting, and I got things to do," shouted our lady-in-waiting loudly enough to be heard in Yonkers. "What do you want to do?"

"We'll be right with you," I assured her. "Come on, Joe, let's do it. It's now or never, so let's not be choosy. There's no cops in sight, let's make the deal."

"Shit, that Desiree has such a beautiful pair, though," said the boy who always got everything he wanted.

"To hell with her pair," I said, exasperated. "We've got to stick together!"

"Okay, let's do it with her," Joe said. "You in, Manny?"

"I guess so," he mumbled, obviously wishing he'd never come.

We walked over to our woman. "We'll do it," I said. Maybe I expected joy or gratitude, but the news hit her like a ton of feathers. She showed not the slightest satisfaction in the score, from the perspective of either vanity or finance.

"You see that building over there? I'm gonna walk into that building. You follow me about fifty feet behind. I'll meet you at the elevator."

"Hold it," I said. "What's your name?" "What the fuck you want to know my name for?" she snapped. I began to doubt the validity of my Columbia University "needs money for books" scenario. She relented. "Sheree," she said. "My name is Sheree."

"Hi, Sheree," Joe replied, "my name is—" Joe actually put out his hand to shake, but it shook thin air, because she ignored it. She turned and walked toward the apartment building, a walk I imagined she had taken hundreds of times before. I didn't care about her other affairs; tonight she was mine—and theirs.

We estimated the fifty feet and followed her. Joe warned us to be careful when we got into the building: "This is where she could have someone hide to jump us." I began to worry that we would be prey for an easy mugging that the police couldn't see. I even found myself looking for a cop until I realized where I was and what I was doing, then hoped I wouldn't see one. I looked at Manny and was afraid he'd crack up. He looked terrified, and I knew somehow that his terror was more from potential sex than potential slaughter. But his stride was brisk as he continued the quest, brave and horny fellow that he was.

The lobby was a beautifully tiled relic of a bygone era, circa 1917, marred only by an artless, and therefore useless graffiti. To my relief, the three of us and our escort were alone. I could see that there was no one behind the staircase. The elevator came and, as the old-fashioned accordion gate opened and we entered, a huge black man barged through the front door and right into the elevator behind us. I could tell instantly from everyone's looks that we were all thinking the same thing, that this was the payoff of the setup. He rang the button for his floor and pretended to look unobtrusive. This guy was big, and we thought the worst through the longest thirty seconds of our lives. My heart felt like a kettle drum in my chest. The man carried a paper bag under his arm that I'm sure contained a weapon, though he hardly would have needed a weapon to intimidate us. Not a word was spoken; we all looked up or down, like you do in an elevator, but not at each other.

Finally, the elevator stopped with a noisy screech and a lurch, and the gate opened. The mystery man walked out, turned, and removed the package from under his right arm with his left hand. We were frozen. With his right hand, he tipped his hat and said, "Good night to ya'll. God bless." Then the gate closed and we were off and up. We stopped at the next floor, and our hostess disembarked onto a landing with four apartment doors. Like the lobby, the floor had beautiful old tile, and it amazed me that just before the biggest moment of my sexual life, I could notice architectural details of a building.

Sheree put a key in the lock and gave a warning knock: "Evelyn, you in there? You cool?" Could that be the signal for her confederate to jump us when we enter the apartment? We entered with trepidation, but Evelyn didn't jump us. In fact, no one was there. Sheree said, "I'm goin' in here to get ready. I'll let you know when. Who's goin' up first?"

This simple question sent us into shock. We had not thought that part out. "Well . . . uh," I said.

"No matter, I don't care," she said, and closed the door to what seemed to be a bedroom. We were in a small apartment with grandmotherly lace curtains. It was sparsely furnished, as if nobody lived there. It appeared to be a place of business.

"I don't want to go first. Joe, you go first," Manny said.

"You know, it's funny," Joe said, "I don't feel like going first, either."

"For God's sake, somebody's gonna have to go first," I said, stating the obvious. "All right, we'll choose by odd finger. Odd finger goes first." This was the neighborhood method used by children choosing up sides and settling disputes. On the call "Once, twice, three, shoot," the participants put out either one or two fingers. If you put out one finger and the others put out two, you are the odd finger. Likewise if you put out two and the others put out one, while three of the same resulted in a do-over.

We agreed that this would be fair. I checked the bedroom door, and as quietly as we could, being very fearful of having the woman hear us, we said, "Once, twice, three, shoot." Right on the word "shoot," Sheree opened the door and caught us being the children we were. She began to laugh, and we were devastated. Out of humiliation I ripped off my jacket and charged into the bedroom. "I'll go first, for Chrissakes!"

There I was in the room with her. A chair and a night table sat next to the bed. My legs began to shake. "Put your stuff there, on the chair, and put the money on the table." She had a silky robe on, and I could see as she sat on the edge of the bed that she was wearing a red bra. "You got change for a ten?" I asked, too young to be embarrassed by the absurd context of the request. She quickly pulled a five from somewhere and made change, like a proper merchant.

The room smelled of liniment and latex and roselike toilet water. There was a package of condoms, a box of tissues, and a large jar of Vaseline on the night table. I stripped to my socks and my Fruit of the Loom briefs and retrieved the condom from its accustomed place in my wallet. "I brought this," I said, like a seven-year-old doing show-and-tell.

"Okay, we better get started," she said matter-of-factly, and she gestured for me to join her on the bed.

Here was the moment I had waited for forever, the invitation I had hoped I would hear in my lifetime. Perhaps I had daydreamed about a slightly more sexy line than "We better get started," which sounded more like the beginning of a construction job. Nevertheless, there she was, and here I was, and we were almost naked. It was then that I realized I was not sexually aroused. Quite the contrary. All those salacious thoughts had been replaced with dread. What was more, this apprehension was not born of the fear of physical harm, as I was certain that no one would rip us off now. It was manifest because of the business at hand. Could I go through with it?

She took off her robe to reveal a crotchless red garter belt to match the bra, and pale stockings. "This your first time?"

"Yeah."

"Come on, now, take off your underwear," she said.

I reached out and touched her thigh, and while it didn't arouse me, the feel of her lovely copper skin sent through me a shiver of hope. She had, so far at least, not turned to bronze. I noticed that she was indeed very thin, skinny, even, with small breasts under the bra and a bit of wiry black pubic hair surrounded by narrow thighs. It seemed as if I had never known a thin girl or woman in my life; the sexy garter belt and stockings I had seen or imagined were on big women, bursting and Rubenesque. On her, they looked like the working uniform of the day, somehow inappropriate and a little sad.

I lay down next to her and discovered that the pleasant, rosy scent came from her hair; it was a pomade preparation of some sort. I had never felt hair like hers. I reached to remove her bra, but she grabbed my hand. "Uh-uh, the bra stays on," she said.

"Jeez," I said, "can't I just see 'em?"

"No, you can't see 'em, and you can't touch 'em, so let's do what you came up here to do." She appeared impatient: just what I didn't need, and the romance was quickly sliding away here. She took my penis in her hand and looked at it carefully, like a farmer inspecting a cow's udder before milking. Evidently, I passed the inspection, because she started rubbing and manipulating and doing all sorts of things that unfortunately were more painful than arousing. The problem was that *her* right hand didn't have the years of experience and knowledge that *my* right hand had. She did not know when to be gentle and when to be rough.

I moved to kiss her, but she turned away: "Uh-uh, don't do that, neither."

"Why not?" I needed to get started here, and necking was the only way I knew how. "'Cause that's my rules," Sheree said.

"Okay," I said. She knew a guy who would follow rules when she met one. I was just thankful she hadn't said, "Robert, do you respect me?"

I avoided her gaze and closed my eyes until her manual labor yielded some results and I became aroused enough for her to put the condom on and place me inside her. So this was it. It occurred to me that I could stop right there and truthfully tell everyone that I was no longer a virgin. I resolved, however, to stay. The fact that she was real, that she was not a statue or a pornographic playing card, cannot be underestimated. As real as she was, though, it was not she I was thinking of as I struggled to keep in the mood. I was intimidated by her distance and by her treating the whole thing like a business deal or something. I lay on top of her, with my face buried in the pillow next to her fragrant hair, and pumped for all I was worth. An orgasm, however, seemed some considerable distance away, the exact opposite of my previous experience in the world of autoeroticism. I thought of the dirty pictures. That nifty ten of spades and my beloved jack of diamonds. Nudist magazines, my Marilyn Monroe calendar, even *National Geographic.* I did not have the perspective to note that here I was, in my first experience, and already cheating on my lover. As a matter of fact, making love to one woman while thinking of another was to become a well-practiced art in subsequent years, coming in mighty handy in given situations.

Sheree tried to be helpful as she coached me: "Come on, honey, push like you mean it. That's it. Now push."

I pushed faster and faster until my gluteous maximus began to cramp up, but to no avail. She not so gently pushed me off and removed the condom, studying it intensely. "Don't you even feel like you gonna come, honey?" "I don't know," I said, feeling numb, like a mouth-breathing imbecile. She let out a sigh and reached for the package of condoms next to the bed. "Look, I'll give you one more chance, then that's it," she said.

The specter of failure was staring me down, and cold it was. How could I face the guys? Would I lie? Would she tell? She opened her arms and gently enfolded me on top of her, which felt very good, and I began to relax a little. I looked at her face, and she smiled, and it suddenly dawned on me that she was a real live woman, and she was pretty, and her body felt warm, and I didn't need Marilyn Monroe or those loose women from 1938.

"Yeah, that's more like it. Come on, baby, Sheree's gonna make you happy," she whispered in my ear. The tactile sensation of her lips on my ear made me excited. I had a nice rhythm going, headed for the home stretch. "That's it, now. You doin' good. Keep it up, nice and smooth." It was going to happen. I got incredibly hot and . . . there . . . was . . . no . . . stop . . . ping . . . me NOW!

I felt limp and exhausted and sort of happy, but she left little time to ponder the accomplishment. "Good. You did good," she said, pleased, as she pushed me off. At least she seemed to be showing some enthusiasm and satisfaction. Not sexual, necessarily, but certainly in the sense of a professional job well done. I felt a tremendous weight lifted from my shoulders, the proverbial monkey off my back, as I dressed hurriedly. "I need a minute here, honey, then tell the next one to come in. You near wore me out, baby." My mouth opened to reply, but I knew some stupid unintelligible sound would come out, so I said nothing as I exited the room.

My companions looked at me as if I had just journeyed to the moon. "Did you do it? You son of a bitch. You did it, didn't you," Joe said with a huge smile. "Oh, man, I can't wait." But Manny was next, having lost "Once, twice, three, shoot" with Joe. With only two participants, it's evens or odds instead of the odd finger.

Sheree stuck her head out and summoned the next gladiator. Poor Manny looked so intimidated as he slogged through the door that Joe and I looked at each other with some apprehension. "You think he'll make it? He's liable to have a nervous breakdown in there," I said, worried. But there was some condescension in my concern, because I had passed the test and Manny had yet to. "He'll probably have a hard time getting it up," Joe said. "Not me, though. Shit, I could get a hard-on during an H-bomb attack."

"Me, too," I lied.

Joe began to question me about the details of my recent affair, things I never would have thought to ask. He wanted to know the size of the bed, when you paid, how you paid, did she smell good, and did she have nice boobs. He did not take kindly to the fact that Sheree's breasts were off limits. "That's not fair, that's just not fair," he whined, sounding like a guy who might call the Better Business Bureau or complain to the Channel 4 consumer reporter. I told him about the no-kissing rule, and while he didn't like it, he was impressed that she could make change of a ten.

My mind was still so busy sorting out everything that had happened that I couldn't think of what to tell Joe. Indeed, some of what had gone on in there, I might not want to tell anybody.

"So, how was she in the sack?" said the man on deck.

"Oh, I don't know," I said, "she was kind of standoffish."

"'Standoffish'? She just let you fuck her, for Chrissakes! How is that standoffish?"

We heard Sheree giggle and remembered the vulnerable Manny. "I hope she's not humiliating the shit out of him," I said. Joe continued with his "failure to get it up" theme and how it would devastate Manny. Just then, Sheree came out laughing and holding her arms in front of her like a surgeon after the scrub. "Wooeee! Wooeee!" she said, and closed the toilet door behind her.

"Oh, shit, he must have cracked," said Joe as he approached the closed bedroom door. "You all right, Manny?"

"Yeah, I'm fine. Mind your own business, I'm not through yet," came the voice through the door. Contradicting our concern, it seemed that our friend Manny was too good at getting it up and had prematurely ejaculated in three nanoseconds into her hand. In a decent and sporting gesture reminiscent of "the customer is always right" creed, Sheree agreed to continue the procedure and take Manny all the way to a second orgasm. After washing her hands, she returned to the bedroom to satisfy her current lover-customer. He apparently felt no such obligation, for after a few garbled sounds of conversation and the rhythmic squeaking of the bed, a smiling Manny emerged in a minute and a half flat. For a fifteen-year-old, two orgasms in five minutes is no problem, more the rule than the exception. Manny had had a grand time that he couldn't stop talking about, extolling the virtues of the entire experience at a rapid clip. "You knew I was scared shitless, I know you knew. Well, as soon as I got in there and saw her naked, I got a huge boner. She touched me, and two seconds later, I came, I was so hot, it was great. Let's do it again next week." So much for "poor" Manny.

Joe went in totally relaxed for his crack at it, and unfortunately for us, he took his damned time. A full twenty-minute cacophony of groans, yells, and bed squeaks ensued, during which Manny and I exchanged sporadic conversation and tried not to notice. But we had grown antsy. We had been here for the better part of an hour, three horny honkies in a tenement in the middle of Harlem who still had to get to the subway and safely home. "What the hell is he doing in there?" I asked Manny. Just then we heard Sheree let out a bizarre squeal and "Oh baby! Oh baby!" Joe emitted a groaning roar like the *Titanic* breaking up. Complete silence followed. Sheree emerged looking like a dazed hurricane victim, limping noticeably as she made her way to the toilet. Joe came out with his nine-foot patented smile. "She was unbelievable. Just unbelievable," he said.

"What the hell took you so long?" I said, annoyed.

"What do you mean, what took me so long? I could have gone a lot longer, but I didn't want to keep you guys waiting."

Sheree came out and made a parting statement: "Well, you boys ain't virgins no more. You done good. Come and see Sheree again. I'm out there most Saturday nights." It was like a commencement speech without the diplomas.

We each mumbled an embarrassed farewell as we left. I took special care to get a good look at her for my memory bank as she stood there, slightly disheveled, in her red slip. I felt a little guilty; it sure looked like a tough way to make fifteen bucks. We elected to take the stairs down the four flights amid the aroma of curry and bacon and the sounds of television. Out on the street again, we adopted a brisk pace as the dread enfolded us once more. We seemed to be attracting more attention as an assortment of devious-looking characters pointed and whispered, or so it seemed. A pimp right out of central casting, wearing a huge white hat, grabbed Manny by the arm. "You boys looking for something good?" he growled.

"No, man, we're cool," said Joe, haplessly trying to use the vernacular.

"You ain't that cool," said the pimp, and his tone was disturbing. Our path was now blocked by several laughing whores and pimps, and my hand automatically went to my wallet. We were in a crush, and they were toying with us. "You got any money?" said one of the whores.

"No," snapped Joe, and he pushed forward. "Who you pushin,' mutha-fucka!" said the gentleman in the wide-brimmed hat as he grabbed Joe by the collar.

So this was it. My heart was booming, and I could hear the pound-ing of my pulse in my head. Manny looked like he was about to snap.

"Let 'em go, they cool." Everyone turned to see Sheree. She parted her way through the small crowd and calmly took the pimp's hand off of Joe. There was an uncomfortable momentary silence. "Thanks," Joe said. We carefully brushed past the company assem-bled and continued on our way to a chorus of laughing obscenities and catcalls until we were out of earshot with a long block to the sub-way entrance. "Keep your eyes open," warned Joe. He seemed to have assumed the role of guide and protector, which was all right with me. Between us and the subway we could see six men shooting craps in front of a liquor store. They were noisy, surrounded by beer cans and wine bottles. "Just walk like nothing's the matter. Just keep walk-ing," said Joe. But we had been noticed, and two of the men were coming toward us. We stopped dead in our tracks. "Oh shit," Manny said in a dry-throated whisper.

"They don't want anything from us. They won't bother us," assured our leader. The three men were upon us now. "Keep walking," Joe repeated, "they won't bother us, keep walking, they don't want any-thing from us."

The men stopped right in front of us. "You got any money?" one said. So much for Joe's instinct and gift for prophecy. "Run!" Joe screamed, and took off across the street to execute an end around, followed by us in a panic, running along the other side of the street in the direction of the subway. The men were somewhat drunk, and we were somewhat terrified, which gave us a slight advantage as we raced for the finish. I ran as fast as I ever have before or since, but I was thinking they could easily chase us into the subway and trap us there; that we might have a better chance out in the open.

But it was too late to change course now, as Joe was almost to the subterranean stairs, with Manny and me breathless and close behind. Joe disappeared down the hole three steps at a time, while we were out on the street twenty feet from the subway entrance. I could feel the muggers practically breathing down my neck. Manny whizzed by me down the subway stairs. I don't know why, but I stopped and turned to see how close behind our pursuers were. I couldn't find them. I looked past the subway canopy to the left and to the right, but no muggers. Then I looked way down to the next street, where I could see men shooting dice. I could count them. There were six of them, leading me to the inescapable but humiliating conclusion that we were never chased at all.

Suddenly there was a scream from the subway entrance: "Leave him alone, you motherfuckers!" It was Joe, with two cops and Manny close behind. He seemed more disappointed than puzzled that I was unharmed and there were no thugs to be seen. "What's going on here?" asked one of the cops.

"Nothing, Officer," I said.

"Nothing my ass," said the other cop. "Now, get on up to the Bronx, where you belong."

"Yes sir," I said, and we scampered down the stairs like five-year-olds. The ride home was as melancholy and silent as the previous week's; why, I could not say. We had accomplished what we had come for, but at what risk to body and pride?

Manny broke the prolonged silence. He was agitated. "I can't wait to get home so I can take a shower. God knows what diseases she may have."

"We used condoms, and anyway, she was clean," said Joe.

"How do you know? What are you, a doctor? Besides, condoms can leak."

Listening to this, I began to feel itchy, more itchy than I'd ever felt, especially in the groin area. I dared not scratch in a public subway car, so I just sat there imagining the horrendous afflictions possibly brewing in my crotch. I could smell faint traces of Sheree's rosy hair dressing and the clean smell of her skin, and I wondered if my parents would smell anything unusual when I arrived home.

There were the three of us, strangely somber and thoughtful. "It was worth it," Joe said. "Dammit, it was worth it." We looked at one another and smiled in agreement. Manny looked like he hadn't made up his mind yet. Whatever the experience was, it had been a watershed, if only because we thought it so and therefore made it so.

My first sexual intercourse was not all it was cracked up to be, but I felt changed, less innocent, a man of more substance, and a thorough coward. We parted at the Mosholu Parkway station in the Bronx and walked our separate ways home. I turned the key, hoping no one was home, but unfortunately, it was a full house and more. In addition to my parents and sister, several doting aunts and an assortment of uncles and cousins were on the scene and greeted me with excited hugs that I tried unsuccessfully to parry. I felt like I smelled of sex and cheap perfume, and my aim was to get to the shower immediately. I had not counted on a gauntlet of aunts with particularly acute olfactory senses, who could smell an unfresh chicken at the market at twenty yards. "Ooh, Robbie, every time I see you, you get taller," said Aunt Marlena. "You're so handsome, Robbie," said Aunt Bessie. "But most of all, you're such a good boy."

At this, a shot of heavy-duty guilt went through me. I wanted to disappear like Claude Rains. Some good boy, who just had sex with a whore in Harlem. "I have to take a shower, I've been playing basketball, I'll see you when I come out," I said.

"Basketball? Who plays basketball on a Saturday night?" my uncle Henry asked. "Saturday night and no girls?" If he only knew.

I caught a break when my mother merely waved from the kitchen and my father became involved in a torrid conversation on the art of parallel parking. The bathroom was a welcome respite from the tiny and crowded apartment; in fact, it was the only respite. I locked the door and began removing my clothes gingerly, as if they belonged to a leper, having discarded the idea of using my mother's kitchen tongs, whose removal from the kitchen to the bathroom would be difficult to explain.

"Robert, you want some pot roast, darling?" my mother hollered through the door. "Not just now, Ma, wait till I come out, okay?"

"Of course I mean when you come out," she said. "I'm not giving you pot roast in the toilet."

I opened a new bar of soap that I planned to discard after use, in order not to inadvertently infect my family. I then proceeded to take the most thorough shower of my young life. Common sense told me that I hadn't caught any disease, and for what it was worth, Sheree appeared to be a hygienic individual. Yet Manny's obsessive-compulsive ravings on the train, combined with the possibility that my sexual partner had fucked a thousand men before me . . . Well, let's just say I scrubbed myself so hard that the image came to mind of a sandblasted building. I rinsed and then scrubbed again, hid the brush to get rid of it later, and dried and powdered, thoroughly, hoping for the best.

Finally, wearing a terry-cloth robe, I joined the family at the foyer table, which was covered with the remnants of what appeared to be a fine dessert. "So, how's school?" my aunt Bessie inquired.

"Oh, great. Just great," I said.

"One more year and you're in college. I can't believe it, my little Robbie going to college, can you believe it?" No one could believe it. I could make out what people were saying, and I guess I answered appropriately, but it was mainly an amorphous din, and I was on automatic pilot. My head was miles away, sorting out thoughts of shame and triumph and guilt, thinking of Sheree, and the little room with the Vaseline, and the fear in the street, and the man in the elevator who had blessed us.

Chapter Five

Joe College

So I found myself in September 1958 in a college dormitory hundreds of miles from the Bronx. I was a freshman of sixteen, a regular Joe College, and Alfred University had been carefully chosen after prudent scrutiny of two dozen college brochures showing happy students holding test tubes and playing Ping-Pong.

There was much activity in Bartlett Hall, what with the moving in of the flotsam and jetsam of students bent on a four-year stay. There was lots of looking at everybody's name tag, handshaking, and a variety of shy greetings among the boys, who were, after all, strangers. Boys alone occupied the dorm. In 1958 the girls were housed in a different section of the campus, located a safe quarter mile away, and any incursion of boys into the girls' dormitory (aptly called the Brick), beyond the lobby, provided grounds for expulsion.

A number of upperclassmen walking the halls were fraternity guys scrutinizing the freshmen for prospects. Some new boys seemed to know a few of the fraternity members through some kind of connection or other. These were the guys who would be rushed the hardest in the next few weeks by the fraternities. The subject was a main topic of conversation in the dormitory.

In the afternoon most of the parents had left, and those mothers and fathers who lingered had anxious sons wishing them to go, so as not to make a bad first impression. It did little for a boy's reputation to begin his college career with a crying mother clinging to him. My mother was quite nonchalant about the parting. It was my father who looked a bit forlorn as he reminded me, "Don't forget to call your mother. A little call won't hurt once in a while." I was thankful that my parents had gone home early and tearlessly.

I sought out my friend Bob Chaikin, with whom I attended junior and senior high school. He had come up to school alone on the train and had a hell of a time lugging his enormous steamer trunk to its destination. We were grateful for each other's company among all these strangers with funny accents. Many of the students were from western New York State, and their manner of speech was strange to the Bronx ear. It was a hard-R midwestern accent more akin to Ohio than to New York, in contrast to the wide R of New York downstaters and Bostonians. The word "car" could sound like two different languages: "kare" and "cah." Spoken by people from Buffalo or East Aurora, the words "marry" and "merry" sounded exactly like "Mary"; my nickname, Bob, sounded like "Bab," and it took me several months to realize that people were addressing me.

Bartlett Hall was composed of single rooms connected by a door to one's neighbor. My neighbor was Rolando Hoyt, from Monterrey, Mexico, who would be studying ceramic engineering. He was a sympatico fellow of twenty-three, a little old to be a freshman, slightly thick in the middle, with a receding hairline and a widow's peak. He was very open and loquacious, and in short order I knew a lot about him. His father was a wealthy Dutch entrepreneur and his mother was Mexican, and he liked to sing as he unpacked his belongings and hung on the wall a huge picture of Christ on the cross. This was not one of those easygoing crucifixion pictures like you see in a barbershop, with a blondish, movie-star-handsome Jesus. This was a suffering Jesus, a bloody, painful, ethnic Jesus, complete with the trickling blood of the stigmata. It was no doubt favored in *Mexican* barbershops.

I had no objection whatever to Rolando's display of religious fervor, but his singing, occasionally alternating with whistling, concerned me. Though it is pleasant to hear one sing quietly and pleasantly during work, it wears quickly, especially if one is studying or concentrating on something else and the singer is relentlessly mediocre and persistent. Whistling is another story entirely. Exposure to bad whistling in a confined space like an elevator or a dormitory can be

injurious to one's health, practically fatal, and I was concerned about
the possibility of having to endure it for a full year. Totally ebullient
and cheerful though Rolando was, I was for the moment grateful for
the door that separated us.

The whole building reeked of tobacco smoke, including the ample
aroma of cheap, sweet pipe tobacco, the result of pipe-smoking freshmen who embraced it as one aspect of being Joe College. Walking
around with a pipe in your mouth, or using it to gesture, was thought
to give you gravitas and maturity. I observed that most of the pipe
smokers in the dorm looked positively embryonic and did not shave
frequently. The air in the dormitory was as toxic as your average coal
mine, but nobody gave it a thought in Alfred, New York, in 1958.

An odor was beginning to compete with the smoke in Bartlett
Hall—a *human* odor, from two hundred boys in close quarters in a
stifling building on a hot September afternoon. In 1958 deodorant
was merely an option, and taking daily showers was only slowly coming into vogue. I am an olfactory-oriented person, no doubt, but I'll
be damned if the place didn't smell zoological, and no one had even
slept there yet.

I was walking down the hall toward the john when something
shiny and large caught my eye through the open door of a room. It
was hanging from the light fixture as a kind of homemade silver
metallic mobile covered in aluminum foil. It was a form familiar to
me. It was a swastika. Hello, neighbor. I saw from the name on the
door that the swastika belonged to a Harold Mueller, who had written
"Call me Hal" beneath his name, apparently in a gesture of cordiality.
He was not there at the moment, possibly organizing a freshman Nazi
Bund group on the second floor.

In all my childhood on Decatur Avenue, with all the Irish-Jewish ill
will, I never saw a swastika. This one was very disturbing to me, but
the incident could have been predicted, given the social structure at
Alfred. The university tolerated a discriminatory fraternity system in
which four of the six houses did not admit Jews or people of color. To
put further pressure on the situation, each fraternity was allowed to
add no more than twenty-five new members each year. I could not
help but notice that there were a fair number of Jewish freshmen and

a handful of blacks and Hispanics and not enough room for all of them in the fraternities. Anyone could do the math, and it was disquieting.

There was no alternative social life, the student center being a Quonset hut left over from World War II that served Cokes, though the drinking age was eighteen. There was no alcohol for thirteen miles around, either in bars or retail, as the snowbound village lived by the rules of its Seventh Day Baptist founders. But there was plenty of music and fun and all the booze you could drink at the fraternities, and I had my eye on Kappa Nu, which was one of the two nonsectarian houses on campus, famous for its parties and athletes.

Right now I had my eye on Harold Mueller, who had returned to his room. He was a redheaded, unremarkable-looking guy about three inches shorter than I, which was a source of some comfort.

"Hi, I'm Bob Klein from New York."

"Hal Mueller."

"Hey, Hal, what's that thing hanging from your light?"

"What thing?"

"That swastika thing."

"Oh, that? That's not a swastika. That's a Corsican cross. That symbol is hundreds of years old."

"I've seen plenty of swastikas, and it looks like a swastika to me."

"Well, that's too bad, 'cause it's not a swastika, so if you don't mind leaving my room, I got some things to unpack here."

This guy was full of shit, and doubly insulting by denying what was clear to anyone. "Wait a minute. Are you trying to tell me that's not a swastika?"

"Are you hard of hearing? I told you, it's a Corsican cross, and it's none of your business." He nudged me toward the door, a gentle push, really, but I shoved his hands down and pushed him. "Don't push me," he said as he pushed me.

I don't remember who threw the first punch, but we caught each other pretty good in the face and tried to grab each other's hands like hockey players. I wrestled him down to the floor, and the tumult attracted a few boys who came in to break it up. I got in one more nice painful squeeze to Hal's red face before I let go into the arms of the peacemakers and their "Hey take it easy" and "That's enough" and

"Calm down." I made a grab for the Corsican swastika, but I was held back and dragged away.

By this time the ruckus had attracted the dorm's head resident, Norm somebody or other, and he was not pleased. Norm was a twenty-six-year-old graduate student in ceramic engineering who performed his dorm duties in exchange for room and board. He was carrying a slide rule and acted as if he had been rudely interrupted in the middle of a delicious calculus problem. Norm wore the jacket of Lambda Chi Alpha, a fraternity where one would be hard-pressed, shall we say, to find matzos in April. "What happened here?" he said.

Mueller spoke up immediately: "This jerk started a fight with me for no reason."

The head resident entered the room and went right to Mueller, who was eight inches from the swastika. Norm being a taller man, the thing could practically poke him in the eye. "What do you mean, no reason? Did you provoke him?"

"Look! Look! Right by your head," I screamed.

"Pipe down!" he said. "You'll get a chance to explain in a minute. Right now I'm talking to *him*." He turned back to Mueller and continued, "Fighting in the dorm is a punishable offense. We are adults here, not street brawlers. Now, what happened?" This conversation was occurring directly *under* the swastika, like mistletoe at Christmas. Instead of kissing, I expected both of them at any moment to give each other the fascist salute. "I *asked* you, what happened?" said Norm.

"Ask *him*. He's got a problem with my Corsican cross, he tried to pull it down."

"A problem with your what?"

"My Corsican Cross."

"What Corsican cross?"

"*This* Corsican cross," said Harold Mueller. The head resident's neck arched back as he gazed with his half-spectacles at the thing. He took a few seconds, examining the swastika like an archaeologist. "This is a swastika," he said.

"See? See? I told you," I said, overreacting to the first fragment of sanity since the incident began. "The guy is hanging a swastika from his ceiling, for Christ's sa—for God's sake."

Mueller was unmoved. "It is *not* a swastika, it's a Corsican cross."

"I've never heard of a Corsican cross," said Norm, "can you tell me what it is?"

I could not contain myself: "I can tell you what it is, it's a fucking swastika, that's what it is!"

"Hey, control yourself. I'll hear you in a minute, and there's no need to bring that kind of language into the issue." Norm was disturbingly tolerant of this bullshit conversation, which was becoming more and more surreal. "Now, what exactly is a Corsican cross, Harold?"

"It's an ancient figure, religious I think, consisting of a cross with arms of equal length. Each arm, as you can see, is at right angles to the other arm. It's not a swastika. The swastika faces clockwise, the Corsican cross faces counterclockwise."

"Not if you look at it from the other side," I said.

"What do you mean?" said Mueller.

"When I first saw it, it was facing clockwise," I said, "it was a genuine swastika."

"I can't help it if it turns on the string it's hanging from."

"That thing has been turning the whole time," I said, "so are you trying to tell me that it's only a swastika *half* the time?"

"No. It's never a swastika any of the time."

"What about when I saw it clear as day facing clockwise?"

"It rarely turns that way. When it does, it's only temporary."

"I see, so now it's only a *temporary* swastika. It's only a swastika for a few seconds, until it becomes a Corsican cross again, is that what you're telling me?"

This was beginning to confuse Harold Mueller. "Yeah, I guess so."

"So you're admitting that it's at least *part* swastika?"

"No. When it turns, it always comes back to the counterclockwise position."

"That's a load of crap, it definitely seems to favor the swastika side. And anyway, while it's turning, *someone* will see a swastika, at least for a few seconds, depending on where they're sitting in the room."

"Just a minute, hold on here," said Norm. "Harold, you're saying this is a Corsican cross and not a swastika?"

"That's right."

"Is this a religious symbol for you? Some Christian sect?"

"Not exactly," said Mueller. "But it represents gallantry in battle and spirituality from ancient times. Anyway, I like the way it looks, and it's a free country, and the First Amendment protects my right to free expression, you can look it up."

A large young man stepped forward. He had a blond crew cut and the stereotypic look of an offensive lineman. He was angry, and regarding this argument, I somehow didn't think he would side with the angels. He addressed the head resident. "Hey, what's your name—Norm?" He was from Buffalo and pronounced it "Nerm." "Uh, Nerm, this guy is trying to bullshit you. That's a swastika plain and simple, and it means one thing: Nazis. My mother's brother, my uncle Joe Thornquist, was killed in Belgium in 1944 fighting those Nazis, and it isn't right for an American to hang that thing in his dormitory room. He should take it down."

"Absolutely, you're right," I said to this big guy, whose book I had erroneously told by its cover.

"Hold on just a minute," said Norm. "Dean Whitlow will have to decide on this. He's the dean of students. I don't think I have the authority to take down the ornament."

"It's a swastika, not an ornament," I said, "it dishonors everyone who fought in the war, like this guy says, and it's a huge insult to . . . Jews."

"Jews? What do the Jews have to do with it?" said Herr Mueller.

"What do the Jews have to do with it? You're a fucking imbecile," I said.

The big blond boy from Buffalo spoke out again: "And that's another thing: the Jews. We got some of them in this university, and you got to consider their feelings. They had a million killed in the hollycaust."

"Six," I said.

"What?" he said.

"Six million killed" came the refrain from a few of the boys with Berg and Gold and Stein attached to their names.

"He's full of shit. That ain't a Corsican cross, it's a fuckin' swastika, and he should take it down, goddammit," said a boy with a pronounced Brooklyn twang who had walked into the room.

"You wanna try and take it down? Come on, try it," said Mueller.

The boy from Brooklyn went right for Mueller's head with a right-hand roundhouse that just missed, before the general assemblage and Norm could hold him back. It was Steve Murray, who I later would discover was an intelligent, streetwise Jewish tough from the pool halls of Borough Park. He would become a good friend of mine, though he would eventually flunk out of school. Right then, the first time I ever laid eyes on him, he was very pissed off and the veins in his neck were sticking out from his anger, and he wanted to take Mueller's head off: "You fucking Nazi piece of shit, I'm gonna kick your ass, motherfucker!"

"Watch your language. There's no need for such filth," said Norm. "Let's be civil here."

"Filth? You're worrying about filthy language?" said Murray. "*That's* filth: the swastika that's hanging in the room and the asshole who put it there, not my fucking language." His argument exuded a wisdom far more nuanced than one would expect from a freshman.

"Just a minute," said a freshman from Niagara Falls. "This guy has a right to put up anything he wants. It's his room." There was a quiet but approving murmur from some, and a chorus of "You gotta be kidding" and "Take it down" from others.

Finally, Norm turned to me. "You're Klein, right? From 201?"

"Yes."

"First of all, I want you to know that I am reporting both of you to the dean for fighting, and you will both go to his office tomorrow morning. As far as Harold's room decoration is concerned, I will convey your complaint to Dean Whitlow and let him decide."

"It's a room decoration now? You have a problem with the word 'swastika,' Norm? Let's try it together, shall we? S-W-A-S—"

"Don't be a wise guy, Klein. Nobody likes a wise guy. Mueller, would you take that . . . thing down temporarily until the dean decides?"

"No, why should I?"

"I'll tell you what," said Norm with Solomonic wisdom. "At least temporarily, till we get this thing settled, I want you to put it on the wall in the Corsican cross position so it doesn't offend anyone while it's turning, okay?"

"Okay. I wouldn't mind that."

"Why don't you just shove it up your ass instead," said Murray.

"All right, I'm reporting you, too," said Norm. "I will tell you later what time to be at the dean's office tomorrow morning, and you'd better be there."

"Oh, you're really scaring me," said Murray.

"Mueller, take that thing off the light."

Mueller removed it from the light fixture and scotch-taped it to the wall facing counterclockwise. Funny, but it still looked like a swastika to me. Not surprisingly, Norm would prove to be a very unpopular, tight-assed guy with *all* the boys, regardless of creed. At the end of the school year, the entire dorm would carry his Volkswagen Beetle into the lobby and leave it there.

The next day, Mueller, Norm, Steve Murray, and I were in the dean's office, a room cluttered with papers and pictures on the wall of past football teams and track stars and old geezers in caps and gowns. Dean Whitlow was a man of fifty, energetic and fit, who favored bow ties and black glasses. He reminded me of Dennis the Menace's father. The dean seemed friendly enough and made some small talk about the weather before addressing the business at hand. "It will snow in October," he said in an accent that could have been Indiana or western New York. He lit up a Chesterfield with a Zippo, took a deep inhale, and eased back into his leather executive office chair. "What's all this about you guys fighting? Bab, tell me what happened."

"He had a swastika hanging from his light fixture. I don't think that's right."

"It's not a swastika, it's a Corsican cross, Dean."

"It's not a Corsican cross, it's a swastika," Murray groaned.

"What's a Corsican cross?" said the dean.

Mueller went into his bullshit refrain about the angles, and the counterclockwise, and the ancient valor. The dean shook his head affirmatively, as if Mueller's argument was valid history and not the stupid rationalization of a schmuck who hadn't the courage to admit his biases outright. "Nerm, do we have the, uh, cross here?"

Norm produced the thing from a shopping bag, and the dean examined it. After about eight seconds he spoke: "This is a swastika."

"No kidding," said Murray.

"Of course it's a swastika," I said.

"No, Dean, it's a Corsican cross. It was an important symbol," said Mueller.

"But Dean, it's not important what it *once* was, it's what it means now, in 1958," I said.

The Dean was pensive for a few seconds, took a deep drag on the Chesterfield, and began his soliloquy of wisdom. "Harold, I believe in your sincerity, but many people would look at this object and believe it is a swastika, a symbol of our enemy from the war. On the other hand, Bab and Steve, you have no right to hit someone because you disagree with them. I'm sorry, Harold, but you'll have to take it down. Bab, Harold, Steve, you are all confined to the dormitory for two evenings for fighting. Now shake hands and try to start off on the right foot in college."

This was a difficult handshake, and I looked away as I did it. Murray wouldn't shake hands but turned and walked out muttering profanities, much to the dean's puzzlement. Mueller's artwork would come down, but the dean's rationalizing crap ("I believe in your sincerity," "many people would look at this object and believe it is a swastika") was disturbing. Many people would look at a curvy yellow fruit with a peel and believe it is a banana.

Busy busy busy. I was in the flow of things after three weeks in college, the proud possessor of two hundred dollars' worth of spanking-new hefty textbooks. I confess I enjoyed hugging them and smelling the aroma that brand-new books have, that smell that one experiences in anything new, from appliances to automobiles, that signifies it is yours, that you are its first owner. Most of us have had a lot of hand-me-down clothing, toys, and books in our lives; in fact, except for the occasional gift, between the library and school, who owned a book? There is no deprivation in that, but the aura of new resonated with me; all the more because, though my family was not poor, money was scarce. I posed in front of the mirror with several books at my side, as if I were walking across campus exactly like those Joe College guys in the university brochure. I had never owned textbooks before, as the New York City Board of Education supplied them free of charge and expected them to be returned at the end of the term. It was common in college for students to underline in the books, a practice I began against all instinct, since defacing textbooks had always been a cardinal sin in public school. Still, it was one more sign that I was a *college* student, all grown up and far away from what had been.

I was enrolled in a rigorous premed course for which I was poorly prepared, my last year of high school having been loads of fun and totally unchallenging. Furthermore, having attended DeWitt Clinton, an all-boys school, for the previous three years, I could not help paying too much attention to the female students in class, with their bobby socks and calf-length skirts. I found I was distracted by any leg without hair on it. I daydreamed about romance with several of the prettiest and most popular girls, the ones who dated only the alpha-cool males. These were childish, naive Hollywood daydreams of winning the girl with a heroic act like beating up a bully or scoring the winning touchdown. In reality, these girls would never have considered me, a sixteen-year-old kid, a proper date; not to mention the fact that I wouldn't have had the courage or confidence to ask. As a substitute, I worked at winning their platonic friendship by being funny, my old standby.

I was in college at sixteen because I had gained a year by being born in February (only those born in March and April were younger than I). I had skipped the eighth grade in a New York City Board of Education program called Special Progress, or SPs. This program was offered, after an examination, to the students who had excelled from kindergarten through sixth grade. I went from being near the head of my class to near the bottom when I encountered a multitude of geniuses in the SPs. Now, in college, I was the youngest again, with a pitiful deficiency of social experience.

As for any real pre-fraternity social agenda for the freshmen, there were three events pending. First was the Jewish High Holiday service. The second one was the freshman social. The third was the ROTC military ball, which would take place in several weeks. Though I was hardly a regular at synagogues, and my mother had fried more bacon than you could shake a stick at, I was compelled to go to the

Rosh Hashanah service. The reason was more social than spiritual, as it was the general consensus among Jewish guys that the services were a must in order to meet the Jewish girls, among whom the same idea prevailed. There was an obvious dearth of rabbis in Allegheny County, New York, so a distinguished faculty member from the English department, Melvin Bernstein, did the honors. On the way to the services, there was a small, ugly incident in which some anti-Semitic remarks were tossed out by a few members of Lambda Chi, sitting on their front porch as we passed. Subtle remarks, nothing you could put your finger on: "HEY, JEW BOY, WHERE YOU GOIN'? HOOKER, HOOKER." I had never heard the expression "hooker" before. It was explained to me that it referred to the stereotypic size and shape of Jewish noses. A couple of embarrassed Lambda Chi brothers scolded their drunk friends and retreated back into the house. A couple of freshman Jews, led by Steve Murray, wanted to make something of it but were restrained by me and a few others. I had already been involved in one brawl, and I had been here only a few weeks; besides, we were wearing our best suits. The identities of the bigots on the porch were duly noted and we continued on our way.

The service was mercifully brief, in Hebrew and English, with much surveying of the room by the boys and girls assembled. Afterward we had a light meal and time for socializing. The guys with the social gift instantly made their way to the prettiest girls, like iron filings to a magnet, and commenced to charm them into a date. Ironically, some of these guys would fall in love and drop out of circulation, and several marriages would result down the line from this evening. We had seen the crop, and they had seen us.

For better or worse, the Jewish kids were drawn to one another by social habit, and in some cases parental admonition. Even among the nonobservant, there was an unwritten code in 1958 regarding not being serious with a girl who was not Jewish. It was obvious that the gentiles had similar proclivities. This provincialism was much reinforced in the Jewish students' case by the fact that we were far from home and were a distinct minority on campus who were not welcome everywhere. The barrier between religions and cultures would eventually bend for many, as a fair number of interreligious relationships would form over the course of four years, and eventually, some marriages. These were touching liaisons, formed against the counsel of authority, parental and otherwise, in the hope that love would conquer all.

The pending freshman social was causing a lot of discussion in the dorms. Many of the boys would have liked to check out the freshman girls, but the event was touted as a stiff, boring affair. What the hell was a social, anyway? Some guys even suggested that one could lose some crucial status with the fraternity guys if he attended. Most of us decided to go to the social at Howell Hall, which was the place for receptions and ceremonies, a white-pillared, two-story Jeffersonian building, neat as a pin. Various faculty members in a line greeted us as we entered and picked up our name tags. The girls in their Sunday-go-to-meeting dresses ladled a harmless orange punch into stemmed glass cups for the boys in their ties and jackets. There was a formal, nineteenth-century air to the gathering, with the din of polite, quiet conversation: certainly not the sound of two hundred teenagers at a party. I could hear a recording of the Alfred Glee Club singing the school alma mater.

At first there was a distinct physical separation between the genders. Eventually, the commingling began, started as usual by the most confident boys: the hustler-smooth cocksmen, who showed off their stuff and moved in for the kill. Their targets were predictable: The prettiest were swarmed, the plain attracted a few, while the homely were ignored and conversed with one another. I noticed that the girls were not flocking to me in large numbers. I shared a cup of Kool-Aid with a first-year nursing student named Virginia Duncan, from Hamburg, New York, near Buffalo. She was cordial and full of smiles, and it was clear from our conversation that she came from a culture that to me may as well have been Martian. She had always wanted to be a nurse, she told me. She was eighteen, like most of the freshmen, yet she did not flinch when I revealed that I was sixteen: a good sign. She had been to New York once in her life, with her parents, to see the Thanksgiving Day parade, and clearly had no idea of the size of the city. She asked me, "You from New York? Do you know a guy named Tony Johnson?" I couldn't believe my ears. One may as well have asked: "You from the Western Hemisphere? Do you know a guy named Tony Johnson? You're from China? You know a guy named Wong?" It turned out that I did know Tony Johnson, but there is still no excuse for a ridiculous question like that.

Virginia and I strolled outside, and I walked her to the Brick. In the lobby, on couches and easy chairs, boys and girls sat at a discreet distance from each other under the watchful eye of a matronly head resident. Virginia and I had run out of conversation, so we shook hands and parted with no particular sweet sorrow. A few days later, we bumped into each other at the student union, and I asked her to go to the campus movie, Ingmar Bergman's *Wild Strawberries*. We were congenial and going through the motions of what proper boy-and-girl first-year college students did socially.

The movie theater was an ad hoc affair in Alumni Hall, a hundred-year-old wooden auditorium, which was also the location of the eight A.M. Western Civilization lecture that all freshmen had to attend, during which the sound of snoring resonated embarrassingly off the dry, ancient walls.

Virginia and I held hands briefly during the film, which neither of us understood. The difference between us was that she admitted it, while I, on the way back to the Brick, launched into a pretentious, long-winded dissertation on the film's meaning. Reading the subtitles had given her a headache. She allowed a sisterly, closed-lipped kiss good night at the Brick, thus ending the first date of my college career.

Two aspects of college life seemed to dominate our attention at the beginning. One was fraternity rushing, and the other was the Army ROTC program to which all able-bodied male students had to belong for two years.

As regarded the fraternities, the administration had preached as often as possible that each boy should see every house before he made a decision. Six consecutive Sundays were set aside for this purpose, so that each week you saw another house, drank some punch, and met the guys. The hypocrisy was thick as pea soup, yet everyone played along with the rhetoric—"see every house," as if all of us had a choice. It was pretty much an open joke among everyone that certain parties would be wasting their time visiting certain fraternities. There was the gallows humor shared by the Jews: "They say that the snow melts in front of Lambda Chi." "It's probably the ovens inside." "Do you think anyone from Kappa Psi will be attending Yom Kippur services next year? Ha ha ha." Some of us actually visited a couple of the discriminatory houses and were politely treated and courteously ignored. This was institutional anti-Semitism, not the least bit frowned on by the university administration, and it was a creepy experience for me to be standing there in the belly of the beast. The fraternity rushing had begun in earnest, with brothers having coffee with the freshmen they were interested in. Some, like my buddy Bob Chaikin, were courted openly and robustly, while others had to prove they were the guy the house wanted and needed. I seemed to be more in the second group than the first. This amounted to ass kissing, and it was not a pretty sight, but necessary. Exactly what the criteria were, that is, what made a kid acceptable and desirable, were amorphous and difficult to quantify; "dresses well, dates well" was one standard that leaked out among the boys. What the fuck did *that* mean? In the humiliating ass-kissing mode, the freshman candidate had to be extra nice and totally cool to impress a stranger who had a veto over his social status: a stranger who was a relative peer and a mere boy, just like him.

There was a small minority of guys on campus who wouldn't be caught dead in a fraternity. These were largely the avant-garde, English major, ceramic-designer types who would be much more prevalent in the counterculture of the sixties. At sixteen, wanting to be Joe College, I felt that approach was not an option. I was optimistic about getting into Kappa Nu, because Al Uger, my friend since junior high, was a popular sophomore member and the funniest guy I knew. He very much wanted me to get tapped by the fraternity and had worked hard to convince his fellow brothers what a great and funny guy I was. Al instructed me carefully on who to meet and shake hands with, who were the hip brothers and who were the assholes.

I visited Kappa Nu the second week. It was a ramshackle old house with a newer dormitory-style addition, complete with a dining room and living room/parlor. It housed about thirty of the brothers, a little under half the membership. But the highlight that they couldn't wait to show the visitors was in the basement party area. It was a thirty-foot bar, with Carling Black Label and Rolling Rock neon signs lighting the back, and booths and tables like a real bar and restaurant. It had a television room off the main bar area, with dark nooks and crannies for making out during parties. The brothers made sure I noticed the fresh keg on tap, the row of liquor bottles underneath, and everybody's individual beer mug with the fraternity crest and his name on it. Photos of members and parties past lined the walls, as well as an array of varsity athletes, former and present brothers. The house mother, Lynda Alcott—who had her own tiny apartment on the premises—was a pleasant old gray-haired lady with a cane, who smiled at inappropriate times and seemed on the verge of mild dementia. This suited the members well, as her acuity appeared to be very much in question regarding her duties as overseer. It made for a wonderful combination—sixty-five boys with a thirty-foot bar and no supervision—a perfect prescription for delicious anarchy, and I wanted more than anything in the world to be a part of it.

Al introduced me to several key members: some gregarious and friendly, some pompous and distant. I went for a few laughs, and Al and I did a couple of our comedy routines from high school for his friends, who loved them. When we got a chance to talk outside, Al told me that I was making a good impression on a lot of the brothers. There were a few, he said, who were ambivalent about me, including one who had heard that I was a clown and a wise guy. I did not reveal to my friend how much helpless anxiety this caused me, to hear that someone who didn't even know me had already passed judgment. I wanted to know who these people were, but Al demurred on that for the moment, saying he would tell me if it became necessary. He passed on ominous information about the secret voting for new members: four blackballs and you're out, with as many as sixty or seventy brothers voting. He was cautiously optimistic about my prospects, but he had done the math, too, and he reminded me that a lot of guys were going to choose Kappa Nu on preferential day, with a limited amount of space.

The next day Al was coming to my dorm room at seven P.M. to discuss some strategy. When I heard his knock, I quickly lifted my
bathrobe and faced my naked buttocks toward the door, a full moon
for my comrade in humor. The problem was, Al Uger was not alone.
He had brought with him an important and influential member of
Kappa Nu, an officer, in fact, and this guy was not amused by the sight
of my anal sphincter staring at him from close range. He was Steve
Chaleff, an extremely serious fellow who was genuinely nonplussed
by my attempt to get a laugh.

"Oh jeez, I'm sorry. I didn't know you were bringing someone," I
said, pulling up my pants.

"Robert, I want you to meet Steve Chaleff, secretary of Kappa Nu."

Chaleff shook my hand, but cautiously, as if he feared that I would
pull down my pants again, or kiss him, and he made some excuse to
leave immediately. "Nice meeting you," he said with less than total
sincerity. When he closed the door, Al Uger revealed his concern but
tried to make light of it: "I guess it was just bad timing. Well, anyway,
I thought it was funny."

"Holy shit, man, I'm sorry. I didn't know he was coming."

"Steve's a good guy. I think he was just a little shocked, that's all."

"What's the matter, hasn't he ever seen an asshole before?"

But it fell flat and the moment was lost, and I had one more thing
to worry about in addition to my math and chemistry, in which I had
already fallen behind. I was failing algebra and running a D-plus in
General Inorganic Chemistry, which, along with this fraternity business, was causing sleepless nights.

Meanwhile, life at Alfred went on. It turned colder, and the autum-
nal trees made a gorgeous spectacle of the hills surrounding the college. As we walked along the campus, we could see our breath,
shivering in clothing that had not kept up with the weather. Dormitory
life settled into a routine of three meals, lots of studying, pranks, and
incessant bull sessions on any subject that lasted well into the night.
There was much short-sheeting of beds and shaving-cream fights.
Lighting farts with a match became a popular stunt among the freshman, until someone on the first floor accidentally scorched his ass and
had to go to the infirmary with second-degree burns.

The food was terrible; my high school cafeteria had been better. I soon learned to attend breakfast only intermittently, extra sleep being of paramount importance. It was dished out by scholarship football players with dirty hands, wearing white kitchen jackets. The fare was eggs, incredibly greasy bacon, and pancakes that had been prepared hours before, giving them the consistency of birch bark. For whatever reason besides the food—lack of sleep, cold snowy mornings, or cigarette smoking—I had little appetite at that time in my life for breakfast. Lunch was usually canned soup and a sandwich made of commercial luncheon meat, the kind that is an unnatural gray, with large specks of fat embedded in it—surely the kind of meat product that you would never want to witness the manufacture of, à la Upton Sinclair. Dinner was the best of the three, since it was the best-attended and most social meal, and by comparison, the food was slightly better. If you could survive the lousy frozen fish and the mystery Salisbury steak, you got real turkey, roast chicken, and franks and beans with some regularity, though the frankfurters were the synthetic bright pink of a dog toy and looked like they could bounce to the ceiling if you dropped one.

The one dish that confounded me was served every night in the salad section: namely, an orange gelatin mold with specks of celery and carrot inside. Gelatin is a dessert, so why the hell were vegetables in there? But the truly disgusting aspect was that it came with a large dollop of mayonnaise alongside, and never were two ingredients, Jell-O and mayonnaise, more antithetical, at least in *my* culture. It was like putting ketchup on chocolate cake. All too frequently, the gelatin slid into the dollop of mayonnaise. When this happened, I was forced to carefully cut the mayonnaise-contaminated Jell-O like a cancer from the edible part, and get it out of my sight as quickly as possible. We were required to wear jackets and ties to dinner, and dinner for hungry college boys on a day-to-day basis was a messy affair, so it soon became standard procedure for the boys to designate a particular tie, shirt, and jacket as eating clothes. After just a few weeks, everyone's outfit was encrusted with old food in colorful, random blotches and streaks reminiscent of a Jackson Pollock painting. These garments were beginning to develop a pungent odor as well, and a directive soon appeared on the bulletin board regarding more frequent dry cleaning.

In addition, each of the freshmen had to have a turn eating at the table of the house mother of Bartlett Hall, Lita Page Smallbach. Well into her seventies, she walked with a cane and an unusual L-limp, by which she locomoted three small steps forward and one to the side, like the knight on a chessboard. Unlike the benign Mrs. Alcott at Kappa Nu, this old lady was tough, quite formal and demanding, given to teaching unruly boys manners and courtesy, especially while eating. Naturally, while a boy was dining at her table, his buddies were behind her back, pulling the old game by making obscene gestures in order to crack up the unfortunate freshman in front of her. One October evening, a boy from Brooklyn named Mike Wiener could not hold in his laughter, lost control, and ejected a mouthful of peas onto Mrs. Smallbach through his nose. He quickly became a legend in Bartlett Hall.

All in all, there was nothing more ubiquitous on the Alfred campus than the ROTC program. With all the young men in uniform and the frequent marching, on some days one could have mistaken it for a military school. To be truthful, as a sixteen-year-old kid, I loved looking in the mirror while wearing my uniform, which was a khaki marine officer's tunic with a belt and matching overseas cap. After one of these sessions at the mirror, I decided to take a girl to the military ball.

The gymnasium was all decked out for the occasion in purple and gold, sporting a large replica of the crested school pin we wore on our uniforms, with its motto "Fiat Lux"—Let there be light. There were a couple hundred guys in uniform, and the ROTC faculty had on their dress blue-and-whites, with the officers wearing swords at their sides and white gloves. There was a fair amount of saluting and introduction of dates to the officers. All this was really cool. A queen was chosen from six nominees; my date was not among them.

I really didn't mind ROTC. I actually enjoyed learning the manual of the arms with an M1 rifle and responding to marching drill commands: "Right shoulder . . . arms! Left shoulder . . . arms! Forward . . .

harch! To the left, harch! To the right, harch!" We took turns commanding the platoon in marching formation, which is more difficult than it looks. We were novices prone to panic, and to marching thirty guys into the wall of the gymnasium where we drilled in inclement weather, which was most of the time. The guys did not stop of their own accord if you got flustered and didn't give them the proper command: "Company, halt!" They would simply pile into one another and keep their legs marching even as they squashed their faces into the wall to make their fellow cadet look bad as he shouted, "Come on, fellas, stop! Stop already!"

We had classes in military science and tactics twice a week and drill and parades at least once a week. We were taught the assemblage of the M1 rifle. In the first minute, I stuck my thumb in the workings to release a spring that went slamming into my thumb, just as the instructor warned us to be careful about the spring slamming into your thumb. I let out a howl of pain, much to the merriment of my fellow cadets, suggesting a Laurel and Hardy army movie. We also had training in basic marksmanship, but with a lighter gun. I was learning to fire a twenty-two-caliber rifle on the indoor range; in a manner of speaking, that is, for I was making little progress. Sergeant Gemmill, our instructor, was losing patience with my ineptness, having not forgotten the thumb debacle: "Klein, you are the worst marksman I have ever seen in twenty-two years of infantry service. I know you're trying, son, but you are one for the books." This resonated badly because I really wanted to be a good soldier, and my feelings were hurt.

Also, the jovial, alcoholic Sergeant Gemmill, with the forty-six-inch beer belly, was the favorite required faculty chaperone at Kappa Nu parties, as it was more than guaranteed that by nine-thirty, having imbibed a sufficient amount of Kentucky whiskey, he would be somewhere on the planet Pluto, and the party would roar on beyond the rules. He was a buddy of the guys at the house, and I didn't want to get on his bad side. It was well known that inviting faculty chaperones who enjoyed a dram or two in a dry town was a frequent modus operandi of those cool guys at Kappa Nu. Brilliant. One hand washed the other: At the party, the chaperone having a wonderful time at the

well-stocked bar looked the other way, either voluntarily or unconsciously. If the chaperone had a snoot too many, the boys made sure
he got home safely, with no one in the gossipy little village any the
wiser.

In any case, I was humiliating myself on the rifle range, and it was
the talk of the platoon. I was getting advice from everyone, including
rural upstate guys who had been hunting squirrel all their lives, but
none of it helped. At one point I figured it must be the gun, not me,
so I changed rifles, with no discernible difference. It took me five sessions before I even hit my target, much less a bull's eye—though I
seemed to have little trouble hitting the fellow's target next to me. In
fact, I hit a bull's eye, though unfortunately, I was aiming at mine. I
suggested to Sergeant Gemmill that perhaps I had stumbled on a successful system for accurate shooting: Aim for the bull's eye to the
right of me in order to hit my own. The wily veteran considered this
proposition for a few moments. "Well, Klein, that wouldn't be by the
book. I'd have to check with Captain Reese on that."

Finally, the sergeant called in his superiors, Major Davis and Captain Reese, to figure out why I was so hapless. The major watched me
fire two rounds. He was a spit-and-polish officer from the Deep
South. "Klahn, do you shoot raght-haanded or lift-haanded?"

"I shoot right-handed, sir."

"And which ah do you use to look through the sight?"

"My left eye, sir." It turned out that all along, I had been closing
the wrong eye. No wonder he was an officer and Sergeant Gemmill
was only a noncom. The day I hit my target from fifty feet was the
high point of my military career.

It was two days to Preferential Sunday, the day the freshmen indicated the fraternity house of their choice. Al Uger had told me that a
lot of guys were voting for me, but several others were noncommittal
and not revealing their hand—to him, at any rate. He strongly suggested that I target three Kappa Nu brothers whose vote he wasn't
sure of: to be nice to them, to show them my serious, thoughtful side.
The phrase "not sure of" I took to be Al's euphemism for blackballs,
in order to spare my feelings.

I found myself trying to make coffee dates with three guys I assumed didn't like me; worse, there could be no pretense in these requests for a get-together, the reason for the solicitation being so embarrassingly obvious. One gave excuses and demurred, while my meetings with the others provided some of the most uncomfortable moments of my young life. One feigned cordiality, but it was clear that, like me, he wished he were elsewhere. The other, a short ugly twit from Long Island, seemed to relish the opportunity to talk about how great the guys were and how great the house was, the house that I was certain he would do his best to keep me out of. "I would really work hard to be a good brother," I said, the banality of my statement nauseating me. "I get along well with people, I—"

"Well I've got to go, I'll be late for class," said the twit who might ruin my life.

It was down to the wire as Sunday came. The nervousness among the boys was more than palpable; it was seizing everyone's emotional energy. People were edgy, and no one was studying except the guys who knew they were shoo-ins. One idea had permeated the psyche of the dormitory from the beginning. It was a precept we had been taught, and many of the guys had bought into, that can best be summed up this way: If you didn't get into a fraternity, you were nothing.

Evening came, and we went at the appointed time to the fraternity house we had chosen. When we got to the wonderfully dilapidated porch of Kappa Nu, I noticed several boys counting heads, as I was. By my count, there were fifty-six of us, which meant that over half wouldn't get in. Once inside, I noticed that the two coffee dates avoided me altogether, while Al guided me around to several brothers who whispered encouragement. Among them was Steve Chaleff, who had not held against me my attempt at a laugh in the rectal fiasco. There was a brief speech by the president about how "all of you are good guys, and we're sorry everyone can't be tapped for the house." Everyone left with a handshake and a "good luck," and we were sent packing into the chilly night to speculate and hope, while the brothers commenced the all-night task of voting and choosing. Tap night, when the new pledges were revealed, would be a tense twenty-four hours later. We were told to be in our room after eight o'clock.

I couldn't sleep and had difficulty concentrating the whole next day of classes. Around nine o'clock that night, cars with horns honking pulled up to the dorm, and great excitement and shouting were heard in the halls. The fraternity brothers grabbed the chosen and threw blankets and blindfolds on them in the manner of a kidnap, carrying them off to the respective houses with much slapping on their heads, cursing, and roughhousing. Wave after wave came and hauled off their targets. For a half hour to the left and right of me, boys were being tapped until it was all over and there was silence. Finally, those remaining emerged from our rooms to see who were the losers, the outcasts, the unwanted. The feelings of degradation and anguish and loneliness were almost unbearable. I immediately felt as if there were a mark on my forehead indicating that I was inferior, an unworthy boy. It was apparent that several boys had been weeping; someone could actually be heard wailing a lamentation into his pillow in the otherwise quiet, half-empty building. I had never felt so lost, so worthless, and tomorrow morning everyone on the small campus would know who the winners and losers were. My grades, which were in the shithouse, were now joined by my social status to torment me. I felt genuine grief at the death of my college career and I was not at all certain that I could handle it.

Predictably, I called my parents to tell them the bad news. Predictably, because they lived in another universe from me, they could not understand the reason for the depth of my despair or the intensity of my pain. "Why didn't you get in?" my father asked.

"Because a few of them blackballed me—they voted against me."

"Why would they do a thing like that?"

"I don't know. They don't like me."

"Why wouldn't they like you?"

"I don't know."

"The nerve of them," my mother said.

"What's the big deal? Who needs them?" my father said.

"I need them."

"You hold your head up high," my mother said.

I hung up with tears in my eyes, feeling almost angry for their futile encouragement. I even envied them; they had no desire to be in

a fraternity. Then I felt guilty having such thoughts about my loving
parents. It was not their fault. This social catastrophe was the most
terrible thing that had ever happened to me, the beginning of a very
dark and difficult year. How would I survive it?

I would survive it by being the biggest brownnosing ass kisser I could
be toward the brothers of Kappa Nu. Al informed me that a lot of the
guys wanted me in the house, and that I could be tapped later in the
second term or early next year. The Interfraternity Council allowed
such exceptions. He said I should continue to show the brothers how
much I wanted to get in, whatever that meant. I would soon find out.
Al's bit of news gave me a sliver of hope and a modicum of resolve. I
was invited to several of their parties, but my good time was tempered
by my uncomfortable status: outsider, supplicant, and moocher.

One of the brothers, a diminutive cheerleader nicknamed
Munchkin, asked me to be the Alfred Saxon mascot for the homecoming football game. This would involve parading on the field in a
short tunic, a cape, and a Roman-type helmet with matching gold
boots and sword. No wonder he had a difficult time finding a volunteer. Under ordinary circumstances, I would have rather had elec-
trodes placed on my balls by the North Korean secret police than
wear this schmucky costume in thirty-degree weather in front of a
thousand spectators. But I soon found myself freezing my ass off on
the sideline in a purple cotton cape, cheering Alfred on in driving
sleet and rain. Why? Because a Kappa Nu man had asked me to.

Another brother, a soph named Bernie, had approached me a few
days earlier: "Could you do me a tremendous favor, Bob? My girlfriend is coming up with her sister from Long Island, and she needs a
date. I'll pay for everything, pizza, Cokes, everything. And of course
you'd be invited to the party at the house. Okay?"

I looked at the portly guy with the wavy hair and the ready smile
and wondered if he had voted against me. "I may already have a
date," I lied. "I'll let you know tomorrow." The proposition smelled
suspicious. Why had he asked me and not one of his fraternity brothers? I made some subtle inquiries on the matter, and discovered that
he had indeed asked five of his comrades and had received five

emphatic rejections. Steve Murray told me that he heard that the sister was "something from under a rock." Steve was his old belligerent Brooklyn self, though a new pledge of the fraternity. "I wouldn't advise it," he said. "Bernie's a fucking idiot, and his girlfriend is only a slight improvement on her sister. Anyway, he's got a lot of nerve trying to take advantage of you that way. " I was touched by Steve's concern, but I wanted to be a part of homecoming weekend, and I was determined to ingratiate myself with the members of Kappa Nu.

My date turned out as advertised: an ungainly girl who would have been pretty if she were fifteen pounds lighter. She was shy and insecure but agreeable, and seemed grateful to be out and about, even with a reject like me. Because I was loath to dance and raise my profile in the party basement, we struck up a conversation at the table. She was a very bright high school senior who was bucking for Sarah Lawrence and Radcliffe. As I talked to her in that noisy place, with the Marcels' "Blue Moon" blaring, the obvious occurred to me. She was no longer some name being bandied about: "Suzie's sister," a "thing" that Bernie was trying to pass off on someone. She was a kid named Leona. Maybe she had some problems; well, so did I. In fact, she and I had more in common than I cared to think about.

Still, I was among people for whom "dates well, dresses well" was an important criterion for social acceptance. My Ivy League jacket and paisley tie were right in tune, but "dates well" meant "pretty," and I was embarrassed not to have a better-looking date. I was also ashamed of having such thoughts, and of being part of this scheme of Bernie's, and I fervently hoped the girl would never know how, or for what reason, I was there sitting next to her. Furthermore, I could discern several poorly hidden snickers from brothers who knew the circumstances surrounding Bernie's dilemma. Just what I needed, another ego boost. A couple of juniors, Kenny Zwickel and Freddy Linzer, came over to us, drunk and out of control. One of them was wearing a pig nose and gesticulating at the two sisters, who, if they knew what was going on, didn't show it. "Hey, Bernie, introduce me to your girlfriend. Does she have a sister? Oh, you're the sister, nice to meet you." Then Linzer turned to me. "Who are you? You a new pledge?" Finally, he staggered away, laughing, and barfed all over the bar. Bernie pretended to be amused and gave me one of those "Whaddaya gonna do with them?" looks. Classy guys, these Kappa Nu boys. I felt even worse knowing how desperately I wanted to be their brother.

Several guys had seen the incident and angrily dragged the offenders upstairs, leaving a trail of vomit behind. Barfing at the parties was definitely looked down upon, and harassing another brother's date was a serious offense; so was bird-dogging, which was trying to steal someone else's date. How about further humiliating a sixteen-year-old kid who didn't get into your fucking fraternity? What do you call that?

Steve Chaleff came over and told Bernie that he would bring charges against "those two fucking imbeciles." "Pardon my language, ladies," he said to the girls. "Can I talk to you for a minute, Bob?" He gestured for me to follow him to a corner of the bar. He was forced to shout to be heard over the earsplitting music, but the content of his message made his delivery seem gentle. "I want to apologize for the behavior of those guys. You're a guest here, and they were completely out of line. I also want to say that I'm sorry you didn't get in. But keep your chin up, we'll keep fighting, you never know."

This brief exchange buoyed me considerably, to have one of the most respected brothers, considered by one and all a mensch and a big wheel, take the time to intervene in the situation and to comfort me. Still, as I walked back to the table, it struck me how pathetic I had become, to so cherish something as small as an apology from the wrong guy.

Steve Chaleff notwithstanding, there were still a number of enemies among the partying joyous chosen, with their smart, safari-helmet Kappa Nu homecoming hats, and all it took was four blackballs. I had a rough idea who was against me, and there were more than four. To make matters worse, some of them were only sophomores and could happily blackball me for another two years. I hadn't even considered the other guys who were rejected and had backers in the house. I was suddenly homesick.

It had always been assumed by my parents and me that I would be a doctor. To my family, there could be no finer or more prestigious attainment. It had been one of those ideas repeated so often as to never be questioned. I had gone to Alfred University to be a doctor, but a few things had gotten in my way—chemistry, college algebra, zoology, inclination, comprehension, preparation, concentration, aptitude, attitude, perseverance, and depression. The first semester mercifully ended with a D-plus in chemistry, and I failed a subject for the first time in my life—math. The premed course was tough, and the students were first-rate and knew what they were doing, and I didn't. My academic performance so far had pretty much guaranteed that I would more likely be the archbishop of Boston than get into medical school. I decided to go into history and political science. Unfortunately, I couldn't make that change until September, so I had to "buckle down," as my father said, just to stay in school.

The one positive scholastic experience I'd had was the History of Civilization course in which I received a B. I had always liked history, an interest I acquired from my father. In the Civ course, I got my first taste of the satisfaction of college learning taught by knowledgeable experts, in depth and with meaning. This was what college was supposed to be about. I was incredibly impressed with ancient Greece, which, thousands of years before, had developed democracy, philosophy, theater, and architecture. Western history seemed to go downhill from there, a mixture of ignorance and slaughter and corrupt values from the Romans on to the Middle Ages, culminating in me trying to get into Kappa Nu.

Speaking of ignorance and corrupt values, ROTC had become a time-consuming aspect of life at Alfred. It was not the program itself that was beginning to wear on me, it was the people in it: the third- and fourth-year cadets who had entered the optional advanced program. This involved a few weeks of summer boot camp and resulted at graduation in a commission as second lieutenant in the United States Army Reserve, whereupon they did at least a two-year hitch. Some of these guys could be a real pain in the ass.

At the moment, there was quite a soldierly buzz about the place, since a large semiannual military parade was scheduled, in which the entire corps of cadets would march before a few hundred spectators. A delegation of army brass was expected to review the troops. This

had been the cause of several additional ROTC practice drill sessions
in which the nervous student commanders had driven us hard. Several of us were given extra demerits by a few of the fussy upperclassmen superiors, some of whom had seen too many war movies. It was
galling to hear one of these yokels berate me in front of the boys:
"Klein, you'd better learn to shave. Is that hair on your lip, or have
you been eating soup? Do a better job shining those shoes and that
brass, too. Is that clear, Klein?" "Yes sir!" was my only response.

Certain guys protested defiantly in their own way: guys like Howie
Slonim, a dapper Kappa Nu sophomore who hid his long pomaded
hair under his hat on uniform days. At the last drill, he had presented
himself for inspection with his curly blond hair sticking out from his
cap like a Harpo Marx wig. The lovable lunatic Mike Wiener, who
had spewed the peas through his nose, won the prize by showing up
for inspection in full uniform, with no pants. When a senior officer
from Kappa Psi Epsilon told Steve Murray he was on report, Steve
pointed to his crotch and said, "Report *this.*"

In a new development, Major Davis, the faculty commanding officer, asked me to be the drum major, leading the entire corps of cadets
in the military parade. He did not ask me for military reasons. Unfortunately, my reputation as the Alfred Saxon on homecoming weekend
had preceded me. I was recommended for the role by a Kappa Nu
brother, a junior named Brezner who was in the advanced ROTC.
More favors, more of the old tongue up the you-know-what.

Major Walter Davis was a Phi Beta Kappa graduate of the University of the South, whose IQ was about a hundred points higher than
that of his colleagues on the ROTC faculty. He *looked* like a major,
impeccable in his uniform, with the scrambled eggs on the peak of his
hat. I liked him and respected him; his class in military science and
tactics was interesting and well presented. He did not pretend to be a
hero, like some of the other officers, and told us that he had never
been in combat or fired a shot in anger. "Ah spent the war at a sup-
plah depot in Hawaii," he liked to say. He was quite keen on my taking the job. "Klahn, you're musically inclahned. Ah know ya'll can do
it. Ah saw you at homecoming. You were struttin' lahk a real Saxon
warrior."

Such praise from the major was hard to ignore until I saw the getup he wanted me to wear. In addition to my standard uniform, I would have to wear white spats and, worst of all, a busby. This was a huge, cylindrical fur hat about two feet high, like the guards wear at Buckingham Palace. It was the most uncool ensemble I had ever seen, and I found that initially I could not walk two feet wearing that stupid hat without falling over like a toy soldier. Furthermore, the major showed me the high-knee, exaggerated strut step he wished me to use on the parade field, like a Tennessee walking horse or a college band, all the while moving a large baton up and down to the martial music. This was beyond embarrassing, but I did it, and I had to contend with everyone in the dorm imitating my strut step for the rest of the year.

There was a small consolation. Major Davis told me that the brigadier general reviewing the parade gave me excellent notices.

In March, I volunteered along with a few other rejects to make artificial carnations out of tissues for the Kappa Nu St. Patrick's parade float, St. Pat's weekend being a major event on campus. St Patrick was purportedly the patron saint of ceramic engineers, a rather esoteric field of responsibility. This flower making was especially humiliating and took hours that I would much rather have spent elsewhere, but I was a determined boy. I was becoming somewhat of a familiar face around the house, through my invitations to the parties and my voluntary slavery, though my discomfort there had lessened only slightly: I was still far from an equal. Some of the guys ignored me, while the ones who were on my side were a little too nice, a little too guilty, watching me make flowers on the fraternity's behalf, the fraternity that wouldn't accept me as a member.

My grades had improved to respectability, but Kappa Nu continued to be a dead end. The last big weekend of the school year was Parents' Weekend, which I dreaded, since I'd been invited with my folks to the festivities at the house. Sitting with them next to the thirty-foot bar compounded my feelings of being second rate; my parents, too, appeared uncomfortable, as the situation was not lost on them. Somehow I had spread this contagion to my mother and father. Thank God the term was finally over.

Chapter Six

Boy Hero

Somewhere on this earth, there walks a man who owes his life to me. Though few are able to make such an immodest claim, I am not exaggerating in the least.

The summer I graduated from high school, I had a job in the Catskill Mountains at a small, reasonably dumpy resort called the Alamac Hotel and Country Club. "Country club" was an appellation frequently affixed to second-rate hotels in the area, to add the panache so lacking in the rickety buildings and the bumbling staff. But this was hardly the kind of country club where one would expect to see William F. Buckley in whites, brandishing a tennis racquet. This was 1958 in Woodridge, New York, in the heart if not the height of the now defunct Borscht Belt. Resorts tiny and large dotted the landscapes of towns named Woodridge, South Fallsburg, and Liberty: Jewish resorts, all located in the incongruously named Sullivan County. These hotels and bungalow colonies had sprung up earlier in the century, after the huge European migrations. Escape from the sweltering city at affordable cost drew hundreds of thousands to Swan Lake, Monticello, Woodbourne, Ellenville, and all the points between. They came by car, bus, and overloaded over-the-hill limousines that eight people would share, suitcases tied to the roof. Except for a few ritzy giants of the Borscht Belt hotel world, such as the Concord, Kutsher's, and Grossinger's, which were top of the line and expensive, Sullivan County was a truly egalitarian getaway. Bungalow colonies and rooming houses with kitchen privileges offered the urban working class fresh air and green grass. Small hotels like the

Alamac offered their middle-class patrons modest accommodations with maid service, sports, entertainment, and three gargantuan meals a day. The second most popular sport was the sedentary card game, featuring pinochle, gin rummy, and the latest sensation, canasta. The first most popular sport was eating.

Food in these parts and its quantity were legendary, a major facet of a guest's stay. There was no limit on the amount or the portions, no sign on the wall: TAKE ALL YOU WANT BUT EAT ALL YOU TAKE. People took and ate and called for more: prodigious amounts of roast chicken, boiled beef flanken, brisket, and goulash, and enough sour cream to clog an artery the size of the Brooklyn-Battery Tunnel. Though only a minority were religiously observant, kosher customs were observed, making breakfast and lunch dairy, nonmeat meals. Guests gorged themselves at breakfast on eggs, various fruits, berries, and vegetables with sour cream, and an assortment of smoked and marinated fish. Lunch featured strange, delicious concoctions of mushrooms, various vegetables, and grain laden with butter, which were ingeniously designed to imitate meat. These so-called vegetable and protose cutlets and the vegetarian meatloaf were served with fresh creamy mashed potatoes. People frequently extended the gluttony beyond the dining room to avoid personal embarrassment, and many a customer could be seen smuggling the occasional herring away from the table, in a newspaper under his arm, in order to consume it in his room.

Our hotel consisted of a main building, a three-story walk-up. There were several smaller buildings housing guests, along with the casino, which was used for bingo, dance lessons, and live entertainment several times a week. Jugglers, dance teams, magicians, hypnotists, and singers: These were the usual bill of fare. For some unknown reason, there was a special affinity for roller-skating acts, which usually featured a couple from Latvia or somewhere else in Central Europe. The poor things had to put a lot of effort into each brief show, like assembling a roller track and other equipment on the stage, not to mention the expenses for sequined costume maintenance. The highlight of the act would be when the Latvian man would spin his wife around by his teeth so that her body was parallel to the floor and her face was taking five Gs, which made her cheeks flap back like the monkey's in the unmanned rocket test.

Saturday was the big night, the primary-show night, with a singer and the closing act, which was most anticipated of all: the Borscht Belt comedian. The singers, no matter what their nationality, would always include among the show tunes and standards a couple of songs catering to the Jewish clientele. Some might call it pandering when an Italian kid from Brooklyn named Tony Caputo sings "My Yiddishe Mama," but nevertheless, it drew tears. Special material about the Jews without a land of their own: an emotional song, "Tell Me Where Can I Go?" brought the house down, especially after the part where Israel is created, which had happened only ten years earlier: "Now I Know Where to Go." They loved opera arias and light classics, consistently buying into the high schmaltz of pretend opera singers with little talent and too much phony vibrato. The comedians, the stars of the show—Catskills legends like Bernie Burns, Larry Deutsch, and Lou Menchell—strutted their stuff with mock insult and a clipped rhythm with roots in the nineteenth-century East European shtetl.

At times they would throw in jokes with Yiddish punch lines, mystifying and confusing those of us who did not understand the language. "I says to my wife. I says let's make love. She says I can't. So we went to the doctor. You know what happened?" Punch line: "*Echubda echubda chubda chubda shmetzel.*" Those who understood Yiddish would double over in laughter, leaving those of us under sixty to inquire of an old person next to us, laughing hysterically, if he would translate the punch line so that we could laugh, too.

The comedians always did well. They invariably demolished the audience and jumped into their Cadillacs to do one or two more shows that night. Though I loved comedians on television, this was my first opportunity to see live ones and their mastery: getting laughs on demand, fulminating, crackling laughs that seemed to last minutes at a time, that left the audience with aching stomachs and cheeks and teary eyes. These are merely the physiological manifestations of laughter. Though I could not intellectualize it at that young age, the palliative effect of laughter was obvious. People looked happy. For a time they forgot about their mother's cancer or their financial debt or their disappointment in their children, and all because of a skillful comedian.

It resounded like a Chinese gong over my head: Wouldn't that be a wonderful life? Though I had played out such notions before, as in my daydreams about the TeenTones, the possibility was still unreal to me, so I continued my company line—that I would be a doctor.

Though my job was to be the hotel lifeguard, a show-business window opened for two weeks in the middle of the summer when the master of ceremonies/social director quit. I was known as a bit of a cutup who had performed in the staff show, so the management asked if I would introduce the professional acts in addition to my pool duties, until the new MC was hired. I jumped at the opportunity to be on the stage, and they paid me an additional twenty-five dollars a week.

I borrowed a tuxedo from the band, which I hurriedly put on over my wet bathing suit. I had a few impressions of Johnny Mathis and Jimmy Durante up my sleeve, but with a twist. Instead of Durante singing one of his songs, like everyone who imitated him did, I planned to talk about things around the hotel that everyone knew about, using the Durante voice. I also prepared a joke that I had heard some time before and that fit the style of the Borscht Belt comedian: "Two medical interns standing in front of a hospital. Guy walks by with an unusual limp, his feet spread apart like this while he walks. [demonstrate walk] First intern says, 'Looks like acute osteomyelitis.' Second intern says, 'I disagree. Looks to me like aseptic necrosis.' First intern: 'No, no, can't you see the classic limp? It's definitely an osteomyelitis.' Second intern: 'No, it's an infarction of bone, clearly aseptic necrosis.' First intern: 'Why don't we ask him? Sir, excuse me, my friend and I are interns, and we noticed your unusual limp. He thinks you have aseptic necrosis, and I think it's osteomyelitis; could you tell us which it is?' The guy with the limp says, 'Sorry, fellas, I'd like to help you, but I just shit in my pants.'" "Shit" was too strong a word to use at the family hotel, though "crapped" could be substituted.

I decided on a bold step. I got Yetta, one of the hotel housekeepers, to teach me the punch line of the joke in Yiddish, which would probably make it sound funnier and less risque. She came up with "I have made in my pants." I will write it phonetically here: *"Eh chub gemacht in der heusen."* It was a smash with the older folks, and it left the younger members of the audience searching for an elder to explain.

The Durante–Hotel Alamac schpritz got some good laughs. It was the first time I ever made out a list of ideas as an outline, and fleshed them out onstage through improvisation. It was crude, but it worked, and I got quite a bit of encouragement from people who thought I was talented, for a lifeguard. I took some kidding about my age from the comedians I introduced, and all in all had a good time, after which I relinquished my MC duties to the new man: a fortyish guy with a ukulele and a toupee that looked like arugula on his head.

After the shows, the Saturday-night festivities continued with dancing to the house band. Latin music was the rage. The cha-cha, the pachanga, and the mambo were played in long sets, featuring lots of timbales and bongos, with a roomful of dancers and no Fred Astaires, to be sure. The largest and most prestigious hotels, like the Concord, had the best Latin bands in residence, like Tito Puente and Machito. We, at the Alamac, had to be content with the four undergraduates who comprised "the Alamac Quartet, featuring the Accordion of Manny Salmanowitz." The band had mediocre chops but showed great resourcefulness. For example, since they were shorthanded on those big-band arrangements, the saxophone player invented a way to shake the maracas with his feet and hit the wooden claves at the same time, all the while singing in poorly accented Spanish.

The dance floor was filled with guests and staff of all ages, the old-sters stepping to their own slow pace no matter the tempo of the music, while the small children enjoyed placing their feet on Daddy's shoes. The tiny bar in the corner of the casino did very little business among the guests, thus reinforcing the erroneous folklore that Jews don't drink. With the legal drinking age at eighteen, the staff more than made up for the deficit and the faulty stereotype.

That was the night life in a family-type hotel, which was not considered a meeting place for young singles, in contrast to the Concord and Grossinger's, which were hot—1958-style. Many a husband and wife found each other in the sizzling atmosphere of the Catskill Mountains.

❖   ❖   ❖

In the daytime, in any kind of favorable weather, the social center of our hotel was the swimming pool. For those who disdained swimming and the sun, there were plenty of umbrellas and card tables. The pool was large, almost Olympic-sized, and was lined with redwood chaise longues covered with pads. The hotel acreage featured lovely oak, maple, and various pine trees, along with some manicured lawns speckled with green Adirondack chairs. Against the aging white wooden buildings with their green trim, the scene could have been from the nineteen twenties.

To a city boy accustomed to living in an apartment house and playing on concrete, the greenery and fresh air were wonderful. The starry nights, without car horns and tumult, coupled with the long vacation from school, were a happy change. The staff of waiters, busboys, and bellhops was composed entirely of college students trying to earn a few bucks during the summer. The other major goal of every libido-laden kid working in the mountains was sex, and not necessarily in that order. This was my summer before college, and I was the hotel lifeguard, which I considered a plum job and a grand opportunity to impress young women. I had earned a senior lifesaving certificate and wore the familiar red cross sewed to my bathing trunks with great pride. I had admired lifeguards since I was a small child spending the summers in Long Beach, Long Island. The image of these muscular, heroic men diving into the rough surf and manning lifeboats and buoys was a lasting memory. They had a hell of a lot more difficult job fighting the mighty, unpredictable Atlantic Ocean than I would have if I had to rescue someone from the Alamac pool. Still, I was a genuine lifeguard with an important purpose, trained in the various techniques of water rescue and resuscitation.

One of the strangest of these was instruction in how to subdue a panicky drowning person, who, we were taught, had the strength of five men in their mindless flailing. The theory was that two drownings were worse than one. Therefore, we were taught how to assault the victim we were trying to save if he or she could not be calmed by any other reasonable means: a true contradiction in terms for a lifesaver.

There was training in resuscitation, in which the victim was placed facedown in a prone position and pressure was applied rhythmically to the back, to eject the water. Unlike today's technique—"out goes the bad air, in goes the good air, out goes the bad air, in goes the good air"—we were taught "out goes the bad air, out goes the bad air, out goes the bad air." Apparently, the beneficial effect of inhaling had not yet been discovered, and one wonders how many lives may have been lost from the efforts of misguided lifeguards. This was years before the introduction of mouth-to-mouth resuscitation.

That summer, however, at sixteen, I was not interested in mouth-to-mouth resuscitation. I was more interested in mouth-to-*genital* resuscitation, whose existence I knew of from naughty pictures and an occasional lucky friend. I would survey my aquatic domain wearing an army-fatigue cap, a whistle around my neck, and a tight pair of bathing trunks around a slim waist. There were sobering aspects to the job: I had been lectured by the hotel's owners about attention to duty, and the fact that in forty years there had never been an incident at the pool. They even threw in a stern warning about insurance and my personal liability, and the specter of the unthinkable: someone drowning on my watch. This put a scare into me and stiffened my resolve to keep a close eye on my charges, especially the children, who would stay in the water hours at a time, until their skin turned the texture of a fresh prune.

Nevertheless, in the performance of my job, there was no harm if my eyes lingered awhile on the bodies of the scantily clad mothers and their teenage daughters, who provided fantasy material for my off-hours. Wasn't this also one of the perquisites of being a lifeguard? My motto for both work and play was, appropriately, "It doesn't hurt to look—and think."

On my pool watch, I met a pretty sixteen-year-old girl named Marcia, with whom I engaged in long conversations about school and family. She cut a most voluptuous figure in her two-piece bathing suit. She was also unnervingly intelligent, engaging, and seemingly quite virtuous, as she continually refocused my one-track mind. Still, it was fun to dance with her in the casino, hold hands on country walks along the property, and delight in increasingly passionate good-night kisses. Her family were six-week season guests, and her mother kept a close watch on her like a Sicilian chaperone, which required the kissing to be furtive. I guess you could say we were kind of going together, which might have put a crimp in my habit of looking at the women at the pool. But Marcia understood that I had to constantly survey the swimmers, and did not think me rude if my eyes wandered while we talked, even to the half-naked females baking in the sun on the chaise longues across the way.

Early in August, a couple checked into the hotel with a ten-year-old son in tow. Word had gotten around the staff that this kid was trouble. The child had insisted on sitting on the luggage while the bellhops were carrying it, and he had painted another boy's face blue during arts and crafts at the day camp. After he caused a ruckus by throwing oatmeal in the children's dining room, and throwing a screaming fit in the lobby, after which a guest threatened to call the police, the hotel management had a tactful talk with his parents. The next day the family came down to the pool, replete with an array of floating toys and a tire tube. The mother and father, who looked rather old to have a child of ten, took me aside, and he explained that the boy was all they had and would I please keep a special eye on him. "You look like a nice young man. I want my little Oscar to grow up just like you, so please keep a good eye on him in the pool, and I'll take care of you."

"Of course I'll watch him, don't you worry." They had begun to walk away when the father turned and said, "Oh by the way, he can't swim. Maybe you can teach him. He's a smart boy."

I told them he had to stay in the shallow water and out of the deep end, and to obey my instructions at all times. They gave him these provisos in my presence, followed by a few of my own stipulations with regard to proper behavior at the pool. Oscar seemed to accept these rules and promised to abide by them. He was a skinny nervous kid, with extremely thick glasses that gave him an owlish look. Though he was apparently a healthy child, he was forever fidgeting and seemed to have the attention span of a two-year-old. This brought to my mind the need for a yet-to-be-invented product: Saint Joseph Valium for Children.

His reputation having preceded him, I watched carefully as he sat in the tube and proceeded to kick his way around the pool, all the while keeping a close eye on me. In under two minutes, he was in the deep end, which was eight feet down, and I whistled him to come back, but he continued on his merry way. Ten whistles later, I grabbed his tube with a pool net, lifted him out of the water, and delivered a warning in a courteous tone (arguments with guests were frowned upon) about the danger of drowning and the inconvenience his death would cause. "Do you realize how your parents would feel if you drowned?" I asked him.

"Who cares?" he said. "They'd probably laugh." Nice kid. He behaved for a while, if one doesn't count smacking a girl in the face, but soon had to be rebuked again after taunting and vexing me from the deep end of the pool. "Let's go, Oscar! I told you to stay in the shallow end."

"You can't tell me what to do. We're guests here. We pay a lot of money to stay here," he told me. "You just work here."

I silently prayed that the child I might have someday would not be like him. In a fit of anger and frustration, I forgot myself and blurted out, "I'm going to ban you from the pool, would you like that, you little bastard?"

"You called me a dirty word," he said. "I'm going to tell my father on you." He exited the pool and ran up to the main building, shouting, "Mommy, Daddy, the lifeguard called me a dirty name!" This attracted enough attention so that people looked up from their magazines and began buzzing among themselves. The Mephistophelian Oscar was a known pest, but nonetheless I got odd, questioning looks from some of the guests.

I became a little nervous. The thought occurred to me that I was expendable, with a host of young men waiting to take my coveted job. Five minutes later, Oscar returned with both parents. The father was furious and the mother seemed passive and embarrassed, as if she had seen this all before and knew that she had unleashed from her womb an adolescent plague on the earth. The kid seemed to be crying, but I could swear he was faking it. "Hey, lifeguard, my son says you used dirty language to him. That's not right. You don't talk to him that way." The kid's sobbing turned to a celebratory smirk, as if he had something on me—which he did.

"Sir, Oscar will not listen to me when I tell him to keep in the shallow end."

"He's only a child. Oscar, you listen to the man or you can't go in swimming. Do you hear me?"

"Yes, I hear you, Daddy."

The parents went back up to the lobby to play cards, and Oscar threw his tube into the deep end and jumped in on top of it. This went on for several days. One afternoon he arrived with his favorite tube and entered the pool at the shallow end. The day was somewhat cloudy, and pool attendance was down, as many of the adults, including his parents, were engaged in a gin-rummy tournament. I was brushing off the chaise-longue pads and sweeping the pool area as I kept an eye on Oscar. A couple of people were reading the paper and chatting while the loudspeaker blared the original cast album of *Guys and Dolls*. I could see the boy watching me as he trolled the shallow end, looking for a chance to make his move into forbidden territory. When he did, I whistled him back, and he complied, but slowly; just slowly enough to piss me off. This was repeated several times, and it became apparent that he was enjoying this game and the sound of the whistle. Tormenting me was his aim, and I cursed him under my breath, making a mental note to think long and hard before having children at all.

As I performed my other tasks, I made sure to look up frequently, to see Oscar kicking in his tube before I returned to the broom or folding the towels. Then I looked up, and my heart dropped to my stomach and began to beat like a timpani. He was not there. There was only an empty tube. I screamed, "OSCAR!" at the top of my lungs as I took off running full speed toward the deep end, trying to see where he had gone under.

I saw the telltale disturbance beneath the surface of the pool. I dove, arms outstretched like Superman, into the water, grabbed him across the chest, as I had been trained to, and sidestroked him to safety. Unfortunately, there was no need to assault him. He had taken water and was coughing and vomiting voluminously as I carried him to a chaise lounge and proceeded to expel his bad air and a good portion of the pool.

By this time, a small crowd had gathered, and there was some tumult and screaming, but the boy began bawling heartily; to my immense relief, I knew he was all right. At this point, the whole Alamac Hotel and Country Club was on the scene, and I heard several people ask what had happened. "This boy was drowning, and Robert the lifeguard saved his life." How I loved that moment when everyone was looking toward me, a hero, just like in the movies. Marcia was there and ran her cool hand over my bare back in a gesture of affirmation, then clasped me to her in a hug and asked, "Are you all right?" What would a heroic rescue be without a girl to show her appreciation? Even her wary mother gave me a hug.

The boy's parents came running through the crowd, his mother sobbing hysterically: "Oscar! Oscar! *Gott in himmel!* Where's my Oscar!" I had to admit that it was a touching sight to behold when the little shit clutched his mother. I was congratulated all around, and Oscar's mother gave me a huge hug as the father carried his child away in his arms, the child whose life I had saved.

That is the official story, but there is a postscript. The next day Oscar's parents approached me and tipped me five dollars. It wasn't that I was ungrateful, but there is a philosophical question here: Namely, how did they come up with the figure? You know how much to tip the waiter or the bellhop, but how much when someone saves your kid's life? How did the conversation go about the amount? The mother: "I don't know, how much should we give him? Twenty-five?" The father: "Twenty-five? What am I, Rockefeller? We're on a budget here. Let's see. [*counts on his fingers*] How long have we *had* the boy? Okay, here you are, young man, *five* dollars. You can use that for college."

He stuffed the five into my pocket as if it were a Mafia payoff. I don't want to seem callous, but I was trying to earn tuition here. Five dollars to save his life? I could have gotten *fifteen* from the bellhops to let him drown.

Chapter Seven

New Passions

I returned in the fall to a new dorm and a new roommate. He was an easygoing premed from New Jersey named Stan Friedman; we had developed a strong friendship and chosen each other to live with. He studied hard, bucking for medical school, and had not gotten into Kappa Nu, either, which, among other things, gave us something in common. Stan was not quite as aggressive as I with respect to the fraternity, but that was his nature.

On my second day back at school, Al Uger and Bob Chaikin told me they were going to bring up my name for a vote. I received this news with mixed emotions. The summer had, to some extent, tempered my anger and shame, and I wasn't thrilled about the prospect of more hope followed by more disappointment.

A week later, one unforgettable night, five of my best Kappa Nu friends busted through my door cursing, with big smiles on their faces. They covered me with a blanket and pounded on me all the way to the car and the fraternity house. Under the blanket, I was free to shed a tear as one of the guys squeezed my hand. At the house, the hazing began immediately as someone shoved a huge pitcher of beer at me. "Chug it down, pledge! All of it!" I did and was given another, halfway through which I barfed all over the front lawn and passed out.

When I came to, I could hardly believe this new state of affairs. Suddenly, I remembered Stan Friedman standing in our room, witness to the whole thing: Now I was in and he wasn't. Al Uger, Steve Murray, Bob Chaikin, and others were ecstatic. I learned later with what emotion they had taken up my cause. All this good news notwithstanding, the hurt would not easily fade, and it would take quite a while before I felt like I really belonged. When I called my parents, my mother was happy because I was. My father was grudging and resentful in his approval: "What took them so long?"

Because I was a sophomore, my pledge period was brief, though there was some hazing, like forced drinking, paddling, and foolish errands. I was required to eat fried ants (which I found delicious), and some asshole forced me to make his bed a few times. Not surprisingly, it was Freddy Linzer, the moron from the pig-nose barfing incident. I had to be tolerant of him for another few weeks.

Now that my social standing had improved, my academic life had taken a turn for the better as well. Compared to the previous year, it was a joy to study history, political science, and international relations, to actually be interested in and adept at my studies for a change. I did not wish to think too far ahead, but law school had been suggested as a possible future consideration. My father had never approved of paying heavy tuition to learn for learning's sake, thinking that a college education should be a means to an end. Now that I wouldn't be going into medicine, he wanted my new courses to be practical, subjects that I could actually use in a career. I got the impression that he would have preferred me to be taking Shoe Making 101 or Watch Fixing 104 rather than American Diplomatic History or Philosophy. He loved history, but he said, "You think you're gonna make a living because you know about the War of 1812?"

No matter, those days even my ROTC brass was shinier, sitting upon my newly issued modern army greens, and my marksmanship had improved considerably. Maybe I was imagining it, but people on campus seemed to look at me differently, as I did myself. Now I felt like—I don't know—a real Joe College.

I had a new interest. Up to then, I'd had no curiosity about the plays presented by the Footlight Club, as either participant or spectator. My theatrical experience, apart from making people laugh, had so far been confined to grade school and summer camp shows.

One frosty October day, I saw a posted notice announcing tryouts for *The Brothers Karamazov*, a stage adaptation of the Dostoyevsky novel. I read for the part of the youngest brother, Alexey, a monk. I not only got the part, but the two professors who made up the drama department, Duryea Smith and Ronald Brown, raved about my reading. I hadn't received such adulation since Major Davis and the schmucky hat.

The rehearsals were fun but demanding. The direction by Smith, and the set design and technical work by Brown, were at a much higher level than the general acting talent. Nonetheless, these guys forged on as if Olivier and Brando were members of the cast.

My new involvement was making me new friendships, for the most part with people who weren't conventional fraternity types: English majors and ceramic designers, campus Bohemians à la 1959. Sam Chororos was a literate twenty-five-year-old army vet with a hip sense of humor, who always wore his old military fatigue jacket and a four-day beard. Joanne Wendover was a talented actress, mysterious and delicately pretty. Sandra Sherman was a brilliant yet quiet intellectual, who loved—and more importantly, understood—William Faulkner. She was too shy to perform, but she loved the theater and lent her talents to all things offstage. She was a "techie," with paint all over her jeans, exhaling the smoke from her Pall Malls thoughtfully. I was accepted right away into their community, which was a refreshingly different world from the Alfred I had known up till then.

Smith, who was called "Prof," deftly guided me during rehearsal from corn and phoniness into a genuine performance. I found I had a knack for it. He was as energized by my work as I was by his, like a football coach who has found a talented quarterback. I had never encountered such an association before. Brown, whom we called "Rod," was less formal than his colleague, more accessible, and a wonderful source of theatrical know-how. He was a handsome tweed-clad redheaded former World War II bombardier with a charming British war bride, June, who was the college librarian. Rod was an aficionado of Scotch whiskey, and of course an honorary faculty member of Kappa Nu.

I was damned nervous about the opening of the play, but not for the conventional reasons. I was still insecure about my status among my peers on campus, especially my fraternity brothers. Was being in a play cool? I was afraid of being an object of derision: another home-coming mascot, another drum major. But that didn't happen. I received a fine ovation and a good notice in the college newspaper, *The Alfred Saxon*. People complimented me and offered congratulations. I had found a new passion and purpose. You got it: the theater.

We were rehearsing a staged reading of *Antigone* at an apartment just off campus. It was the residence of a cast member, a drama volunteer named Charlotte, who was playing Eurydice. I was playing Haemon, her son, who ultimately defies his father and, among other things, commits suicide. It was a good role and the only one appropriate for me, but I wished Haemon had more to say and died later in the play. It was the first of many times that I would count lines. I was becoming a real actor.

Charlotte's husband was an assistant professor, and they had two small children. The rehearsal was over, the coffee and cake consumed, everyone was leaving, and I was just about to go out the door when Charlotte said, "Bob, wait a minute, I want to ask you something." She gestured me to the couch, sat down, opened her script to Eurydice's speech, and said, "I'm not sure of this section where I enter, could you help me? Here, you read the Greek-chorus part just before my entrance."

I was about to open my script to the proper page, a scene in which she learns of her son's death, when she took it from my hand. "No, let's just use *my* script. You begin right here." So I did.

HAEMON

Eurydice is with us now, I see. Creon's poor wife. She may have come by chance. She may have heard something about her son.

EURYDICE

I heard your talk as I was coming out to greet the goddess Pallas with my prayer. And as I moved the bolts that held the door, I heard of my own sorrow. I fell back fainting in my woman's arms. But say again just what news you bring. I, whom you speak to, have known grief before.

As she spoke the line about the bolts holding her door, I was aware that she was moving closer to me so I could feel her leg and thigh touching mine. On the word "sorrow," she looked at me, but not in sorrow. I made a mental note to remind her of the sorrowful content of the speech, which she was playing all wrong, unlike her more logical approach during rehearsal. When she reached the part about "fainting in my woman's arms," she took a strange five-second pause, then leaped on top of me, grabbed my crotch, and pushed her tongue down my throat. She was breathing hard, like a miler at the end of the race.

"Charlotte, what are you doing?"

"I want you," she said.

"But you're married, for God's sake."

"My husband's at a conference this week, and the children are with their grandmother." She began to take off her sweater. She was rubbing herself against me with all her weight, and I was becoming impaled on the metal clasp from the script underneath my back, which hurt like hell. Being impaled on a script may have been an appropriate death for some actors, but I was not among them. I wrestled myself free and ran to the other end of the room. She was persistent, though, and pinned my hand against the wall, trying to kiss me again, while putting my other hand under her bra.

Many things were going through my mind at once. I had never been seduced before, not to mention by a married woman. I pictured her husband, whom I did not know but had seen on campus. He was a tall, gaunt man with glasses, and I wondered what he was doing right then at the conference. I hoped he was actually there and wouldn't suddenly come through the door.

Even with my vivid imagination, which could see sexuality in almost any woman, I had never even remotely thought of Charlotte in that way. She was the epitome of plain, a thirty-six-year-old who wore no makeup, had a nifty wart near her upper lip, and favored dresses and a haircut that reminded me of the Amish. She must have had bad feet, because I had never seen her without orthopedic shoes, the kind that old ladies wore. Yet here she was, in full passion mode, with a kid half her age: Who knew? In any case, I was more intimidated than hot, and I finally pushed myself free.

"Relax Bob, nobody's here. I want to make love to you. Come on, no one will ever know."

"I'll know," I said. Even though I was innocent and practically a child—well, sort of, anyway—I felt guilty. I didn't know what to say. I, the sexual novice, had had many fantasies of seduction by older women, but this was not what I had in mind. "Uh . . . I have to go now, got a test tomorrow."

"You won't tell anybody about this, will you?" she said.

"No, I won't tell anybody."

She tried to kiss me good night at the door, but I was out of there. However, the image of her face coming toward mine, that zoom shot of the wart getting closer and larger, would stay with me for quite a while.

The walk home was an emotional mix. My heart was still racing. I couldn't believe what had just happened. Intellectually, I was appalled at her behavior, but I found to my surprise that I was aroused after the fact. I was quite the man now; my new world of the theater was one adventure after another.

Charlotte's presence at subsequent rehearsals made me uncomfortable at first, but we carried on as if nothing had happened. I was most awkward meeting her husband on opening night, and I sincerely hoped he would never know that his wife had jumped on top of me and that I had accidentally touched her breast.

The ever welcome spring arrived, the snow melted, and the major Footlight Club production was Molière's comedy *The Imaginary Invalid,* in which I played the male juvenile lover. A cute fireman's daughter from Staten Island named Gwen Kegley played the ingenue opposite me. Our stilted seventeenth-century love scenes were lots of fun, though my long wig kept getting in my mouth when we kissed. Gwen and I enjoyed it so much that we carried the spirit of the lovers offstage and dated a few times twentieth-century-style, without wigs and knee breeches. It was my first stage romance. There was a good deal of making out, but it went no further. For a few weeks, we held hands, went to the movies, and attended the parties; however, as with so many romances between actors, the feeling faded shortly after the production was over, though we remained friends. Nonetheless, I'd had meaningful feelings toward her, shared real kisses with her; it had not been going through the pleasant motions, as had been the case with Virginia Duncan.

Spring break brought an exciting prospect. I, who had never been farther from New York than Washington, D.C., had been given funds and permission to go to Fort Lauderdale, a spectacularly desirable destination for vacationing college students. I had just seen *Where the Boys Are,* a Connie Francis movie about the college-Florida phenomenon, which sure gave the impression that there was a lot of fun going on in Fort Lauderdale. And though it was 1960, and movies had to adhere to a code of decency, there was a certain amount of vaginal-penile contact implied in those torrid South Florida parts.

I was still too young to have a New York driver's license, so my two Alfred companions did the driving, and I shared gas expenses. William Wadsworth was a junior engineer and the owner of the '58 Buick two-door coupe that would carry us to the eternal land of collegiate girls out of control. The other guy was John Wilkinson, a quiet chemistry major from Pittsburgh. Wadsworth was a transfer from Duke University who couldn't stop praising his two years there. "It's the Harvard of the South," he would say.

The trip was long, sitting in the back seat of the Buick, but I absorbed it all like the travel-deprived provincial I was. I even went radical in southern Virginia and put gravy on my grits instead of sugar.

We stopped in Durham so Billy Wadsworth could say hello to his Duke buddies. The grounds were gorgeous and made Alfred look like a trailer camp. We entered the fortress-like building and knocked with the pure brass knocker on the proper door with the gentleman student's name on a brass name plate below. "Heeeey, Billy! We thought you'd be here later. You son of a bitch. If we knew you were comin' sooner, we'da had the nigger polish your name on the brass plate." Yeah, the Harvard of the South.

Billy had some matters to attend to, so John and I took the Liggett & Myers tobacco-factory tour. And there they were, those things I had seen in the newspapers as long as I could remember: the water fountains in the factories marked "colored" and "white." I wanted to drink from the colored fountain, but I was afraid to, because this racist outrage was sanctioned by the sovereign state of North Carolina, and I was less than keen about winding up on a chain gang.

The best was yet to come. Just south of the Georgia border was the town of Yulee, Florida. There was a crowd along the side of the road, watching a spectacle of hooded men with a fifteen-foot-tall cross. In an homage to modernity, the cross was lit with electric lightbulbs. My companions were so amused that they turned the car around and came back for a second pass. One of these hooded yokels noticed the New York license plates on our second pass and said, "Get on outta here!" As the only Hebrew in attendance, and quite convinced by the tone and ugly face of this idiot, whose skin reminded me of an expensive handbag from Bonwit Teller, I took this to be a sound idea. It seemed that on my journey south in 1960, I was destined to experience every stereotypic, negative aspect of the South. But that's the way it was.

Fort Lauderdale was sunny and hot, a novelty for boys who had just left two feet of snow thirty-six hours earlier. Its hotels and motels, including ours, all had prominent signs saying RESTRICTED CLIENTELE, which, it was explained to me, meant no Jews. It did not mean blacks, who made the beds and cleaned. That *they* could not stay in these places was a given. Socially, the trip was a bust. *Where the Boys Are* was an appropriate description. I would guess there were seven boys to one girl, an unfortunate ratio, especially as the boys all seemed to be morons from Mississippi State who roved around the streets yahooing Confederate battle yells and vomiting. I was delighted to get back to school.

Meanwhile, back at Kappa Nu, I was experiencing being on the inside of things for a change. I voted to accept every new freshman who wanted admission, vowing never to blackball anyone, though once again boys were rejected and scarred. I also refrained from hazing the pledges, though many others did not. On the whole, the guys in the house were a good bunch. There were about a dozen gentiles, among whom were a couple of blacks and a Chinese guy named William Louie. Louie was a wonderful guy, a talented artist and potter whose parents owned a Chinese laundry in my neighborhood in the Bronx.

The brothers were justly proud of this diversity, and miles ahead of the college administration, which still allowed a rotten, bigoted, hypocritical system that hurt boys. In fact, this humanism paid its own dividends to all concerned, few of us having spent so much intimate time with people so different from ourselves. However, the boys wanted so much to make the minority members feel at home that they sometimes overdid it and unwittingly became patronizing. Ricky Sampson, a black member from Long Island who was a running back on the football team, was everybody's favorite. Everyone was so anxious to show him they weren't prejudiced that the subject came up too often, accentuating rather than obliterating the difference. The guys meant well, but they were far from subtle while raving about Harry Belafonte and Sidney Poitier.

Chapter Eight

Tales of a Busboy

As it turned out, it was the worst job I'd ever had. A summer-hotel busboy, three meals a day seven days a week, unending nightmare of a job; with an incredibly hot one-hundred-and-ten-Fahrenheit kitchen, appropriately staffed with dubious vindictive characters from hell. People can get very cranky in a commercial kitchen in July at a hundred and ten degrees.

My fellow inmates and I—for that's what it felt like—were college boys working for tips, hoping to buy a used car or contribute to tuition from the summer's labor. Other jobs around the small old hotel were easier, and some were even fun, like day-camp counselor or lifeguard; but, to paraphrase the bank robber Willie Sutton, the dining room is where the money is. Though we had looked forward to a lucrative summer (an ambitious and lucky busboy could earn eight hundred dollars), none of us had anticipated being prisoners in the gulag. The problem was that we were bourgeoisie: sheltered children, every mother's son of us, who didn't even make our own beds, much less cope with such rigorous and stressful labor, especially with no days off.

The bitching and groaning of the dining room staff became an accepted way of life, and the sight of all these exhausted and misused future internists and periodontists was both funny and sad at the same time. These were the apples of their families' eye, princes every one, yet living a life more akin to Oliver Twist and Cinderella before the slipper. The fact that one could not look forward to even an occasional day off was particularly depressing. We served big breakfasts, which ran into huge lunches, which slammed into gargantuan dinners with no respite, only to be repeated again and again and again. Set up, serve, and clean up in the dining room, amid the never-ending noise of the kitchen, which I could not wait to get out of: I could never stand the heat. We all wore standard uniforms of black pants, white shirt, bow tie, and cummerbund, which were perpetually wet with perspiration and reeked of every soup and sauce we served. We were constantly screamed at by the demented kitchen personnel, with their heavy accents and short tempers and stench of alcohol.

In the dining room, many of the guests, who could have been our parents, demanded impeccable service worthy of Michelin, and immediately. People who would otherwise be considerate and patient in their everyday lives became imperious tyrants once they signed the hotel register and were assigned a table, as if checking into a joint like this conferred on them the perquisites of aristocracy. A new woman at my station beckoned me over to her, and grabbed me by the bow tie—yes—grabbed me by the bow tie. She jerked my head down to face her like an errant dog on a leash. She was about fifty and taking no shit. "Listen, dolling. I like my cawfee burning hot—so hot that it burns my lips. You undahstand? This cawfee is ice cold. Now, go get me a cup of hot cawfee, and make sure the cup is hot when you paw the hot cawfee into it." She pulled my bow tie and me even closer, as if she had some great secret to share. "You take care of me, and I'll take care of you. Okay?" She then released me from the stranglehold. As I removed the "ice-cold" cup of coffee, it burned several layers of skin off the tips of my fingers. She was going to be a tough one, but not atypical of some of the guests, who were doggedly determined to get their vacation money's worth, civility and common courtesy be damned. For those of us on the receiving end of this determination, it was an object lesson in humility.

We spent a certain amount of time feeling sorry for ourselves, lying on cots lined up in our dank, dark quarters. Many of the boys were prideful, and many of the guests were rude. This was a bad equation from our point of view, because the customer was always right and the busboy was expendable and had to stuff it. We were teenagers barely out of adolescence, for whom summers had always meant freedom, and now we were tethered to two months' hard labor.

There was a most interesting and enigmatic character on the scene that summer named Morris Landsman. Born in Poland, he was the headwaiter and the undisputed boss of the dining room. On the other side of the kitchen door, the chef was in charge, but in the dining room, Moish, as he was called, commanded the waiters and busboys like a culinary Captain Queeg. Moish did his share of yelling, mostly about clearing the livestock, which was the name given to perishables like milk and butter, retrieved from the tables to live another day. He had an excellent, sardonic sense of humor, and while he occasionally sounded harsh and strident and impatient with the boys, many of whom were learning on the job, he was fair as long as you tried. Moish was not a student; he was a professional waiter who had survived the holocaust but seemed to barely survive the summer's agita.

In August, an improbable event occurred at the hotel involving Morris Landsman. A middle-aged couple checked in, with European accents and no children: Mr. and Mrs. Von Cherbourg. The husband was exceedingly handsome, with a full head of gray hair, and his wife looked like an older movie star. Moish met them at the casino bar, and the three engaged in ordinary conversation. Herr and Frau Von Cherbourg were natives of Hamburg, Germany, who were now living in New York. Then Moish recognized the gold pin in the new guest's lapel. He had seen these pins many times in his postwar debriefing days for the U.S. occupation forces in Europe: They signified an honorable discharge from the Luftwaffe. Von Cherbourg was, it turned out, an ex–German fighter pilot. Why such a couple would check into a hotel in the Borscht Belt just fourteen years after the war is an interesting question.

The guy took a liking to Moish, who spoke some German, but the headwaiter skillfully brushed him off, just short of rudeness. When some of the boys would kick around a soccer ball after breakfast outside the kitchen door, Herr Von Cherbourg would gesture from a distance for the ball to be kicked to him, to be included. Moish, about to kick the ball, would display a broad smile for the fellow while muttering profanities under his breath that we could hear but the German could not: "You cocksucker, find your own game, you piece of Nazi shit." He would then kick it to someone else. This occurred practically on a daily basis, with the German gesturing "Hey, over here!" in two languages and then walking away rejected.

The Von Cherbourgs had befriended a young Jewish couple with two children. Both couples were looking to buy vacation property in the area and planned to stay at the hotel at least three weeks. Von Cherbourg would intermittently ease off of his unrequited courtship of Morris Landsman, but after a day or so, he was back trying to get in on the boys' soccer catch, but always at a respectful long distance. "Hey, here here!" he would shout, but no one would kick him the ball. Moish would dribble it awhile from his head to his knee and look tantalizingly in the direction of the Luftwaffe. "Kiss Hitler's ass, you putz," again said so that only we could hear, which was cause for some satisfied giggling. This soccer ritual, a sort of revenge for World War II on a playground, continued for the better part of the three-week stay. But despite the laughs, there was a sobering aspect to it as we watched Herr Von Cherbourg: none of us had ever seen a German officer in person before.

Moish was an angel compared to the staff on the other side of the kitchen door. Nothing could have prepared the boys for the dark, amoral characters who worked in the kitchen. The chef was a Hungarian named Henry, a stocky balding man with tortoise-shell glasses and a sour countenance who had emigrated during the 1956 uprising in Hungary. He worked in Miami during the winter months and drove up from Florida to work at the Fieldston Hotel every summer. To be sure, Henry was far from a first-class chef, but earning seven hundred dollars a week in 1959 at a hotel that featured its food made him pretty important to the operation. The hotel owners fawned over him, desperate to keep him happy, though he grumbled incessantly behind their backs. Like everyone else in the kitchen, screaming was his specialty, especially "PICK UP!," which he pronounced "PEEK OP!," followed by a slew of Hungarian curse words.

The other key people in the kitchen were the assistant chef, the baker, and the salad man. Henry's assistant was an alcoholic Slav named Johnny, with a paucity of teeth and a wet-lipped Chesterfield perpetually dangling from his crooked mouth. It was repulsive to watch him working over food, with his ashes and his runny nose. He stood over six feet tall but weighed only about 135, giving him a dissipated, tubercular look. He had a hefty underarm odor straight out of 1943 Paris, and an assortment of obligatory tattoos covering his hairy forearms. The tattoos were snakes curling their way up from his wrists to his biceps, and their greenish color was fading. With a large knife in his hand, and a bone-chilling stare, he promptly got anyone's attention. He was mean and fearless and probably crazy, and it was clear that Henry was afraid of him, just like the rest of us. It was said that upon receiving a complaint that a dish of mashed potatoes was cold, he heated it up, spit in it, and sent it back out to the dining room. Unfortunately, he was indispensable. What Johnny lacked as a cook he made up for in speed, which was at a premium in the job, and even semireliable help was difficult to find in the middle of the summer, ashes and mucus notwithstanding.

The baker was a temperamental Romanian who pretended when convenient that he did not understand English. He had an odd sense of humor, as when he invited me to smell "something delicious" that I thought was a fresh pastry, and then he thrust a pan of pure ammonia under my nose. As I coughed and gagged, he laughed hysterically; it was the only time I ever saw him enjoy anything.

The salad man was a Taiwanese named Chen with an assistant called Lee. They gambled heavily at cards, craps, and harness racing at Monticello Raceway, and they yelled the loudest of anyone in the kitchen, albeit in Cantonese. God knows what they were calling us. They had an excellent grasp of English words that were useful to their everyday lives: words relevant to salads and gambling. They could say "lettuce," "tomato," "I raise you," and "six is your point" like Oxford scholars, but they couldn't carry on a conversation outside of those subjects.

The rest of the kitchen workers—the unskilled lower echelon, like the dishwashers and the pot washer—were pickups and drifters from everywhere, who would gravitate to the Sullivan County resort area for work. For a bunch of sheltered college boys, these people represented the authentic underside of society best known to us from literature or strolling through the Bowery. For the most part, folks like us had never interacted with folks like them. Nevertheless, we were largely the children of liberal New Yorkers, readers of the *New York Post* back when it was ennobled, full of Eleanor Roosevelt and John Steinbeck; so it was natural for us to ascribe to these misanthropic strangers a fair amount of that good old "dignity of man" we'd read so much about. Spending a summer with them, however, tended to confirm that there are bad and good among all classes of people, and the experience pushed our progressive political beliefs to their absolute limit.

We all liked the mildly retarded pot washer named Guy, who was big and gentle and central casting for Lenny in *Of Mice and Men*. There was a sweetness, an earnestness, about him. Pot washing is the most difficult and least desirable physical task in the kitchen, and it suited the man to a T. Always eager to please, he would scrub the huge soiled pots compulsively until they shone. For him, no job in the world was more important, and Picasso himself could not have derived more satisfaction from a work well completed, than Guy did from a well-cleaned pot. Such, I suppose, is one blessing of simplicity of mind. The downside was that his colleagues, knowing his docility and lack of guile, mistreated, cheated, and scorned him.

The key dynamic in the frenzied kitchen was that everyone hated everyone else. When they weren't hurling multilingual invective, they were saving their most vituperative stuff for the waiters and bus-boys—especially the busboys. Neither the chef nor his colleagues ever memorized the waiters' or busboys' names, so they would habitually refer to us by screaming what our order was: "Hey, tuna salad, pick up already! You, too, pickled herring!" If the retort was not to their liking, they would surge into a rage. "Hey, don't gimme no lip, tuna salad, you asshole! That goes for you, too, potato pancakes! I kick your ass, too! Hey, tuna salad, tell your friend pickled herring I kick his ass, too!—PEEK OP!"

This was how it went for eight hours. Every day. When the Fieldston was operating at full capacity, we didn't have enough time between breakfast and lunch to go back to the hovel where we slept, so we would gather outside the kitchen door, exchange complaints, and smoke. A few Israeli and European boys, along with Moish, might kick a soccer ball, though it beats me how they had the energy.

Some of the Americans would play catch with a Spaulding rubber ball. I had never appreciated such simple things as fresh air and relative quiet, a wonderful relief from the torrid kitchen. It was also the zenith of my love affair with tobacco, a death grip that I have continued to battle for the rest of my life. The cigarette with morning coffee was great, and the cigarette after eating was splendid. But nothing compared to that first inhale after three hours of sweaty, breakfast madness, stinking of smoked fish and spilled milk. Though many of the dishes prepared in the kitchen were delicious, the aggregate odor was not: a commercial-kitchen stench of food, garbage, disinfectant, and sweating human bodies. I have never eaten in a restaurant since without thinking of it.

About twenty of us slept in an ancient wooden building that we called the Waldorf, not much more than a large shack, which also housed the hotel casino above. The creaky structure was built on a hill, so we lived and slept *underneath* the casino. The rooms had few windows, a communal toilet, and smelled of mildew and old mattresses, as befitting a cellar. Above us, there were calisthenics, Simon Says, and dancing several times a week with live music provided by the house band called the Fieldston Four. The combo was led by an accordionist who was a third-year NYU dental student named Herbert Schwam. He was the prototype that would come to prominence thirty years later in *Revenge of the Nerds*. The sound of two hundred klutzes doing the cha-cha on a dry, groaning wooden floor reverberated through our humble rooms and shook our beds until eleven P.M. So we, who were exhausted after a long day of kitchen and dining room abuse, could not even expect proper repose at night. We were expected to be in the dining room for breakfast no later than six-fifteen A.M. (the tables having been set after the evening meal) or we were denied our own breakfast. Most of us didn't have much of a morning appetite and preferred to sleep. The guests could stroll in from seven to ten, which made for a less hectic meal but also a time-consuming marathon. The food was the thing here, the selling point, the star. It was an all-you-can-eat jubilee. Can't make up your mind between pickled herring, scrambled eggs, pancakes, blueberries with sour cream, or lox with cream cheese? No problem, have all five.

Lunch and dinner for the hotel patrons, arguably the two most important events of the day, were heralded with a loudspeaker announcement from the owner's sister-in-law. She had a thick Brooklyn brogue that she attempted to enhance with a pompous affectation in the form of a bad British accent. She spoke slowly and deliberately, with all the dignity she could muster, like a Jewish duchess of York, but Flatbush came through loud and clear: "Yaw attention, please, ladies and gentlemen. The doining room is now open, and dinnah is soived." On the words "your attention, please," the veritable stampede of guests would commence. Many of these hungry people would congregate near the dining room doors, salivating. After all, it had been a full two hours since breakfast. The five-hour fast between lunch and dinner was difficult for many, so the small hotel coffee shop did a tremendous business in late-afternoon snacks.

The staff ate lunch and dinner at our stations, forty-five minutes before the doors opened. These meals consisted of the leftovers from the previous day or days, and the selections were limited. We were forbidden any expensive cuts of meat or the wonderful European pastries, which made us covet them all the more, so that stealing food and consuming it surreptitiously became the order of the day. I can recall eyeing a half-eaten steak on a plate I was clearing, going through the swinging doors of the kitchen, finding a secluded spot, and devouring it like a feral dog. Or seeing two honor students arguing over a lamb chop in true Dickensian spirit. One could detect bits of meat or pie or gravy on the mouths of dining room staff who had sneaked a quick bite and returned to work, attempting to conceal the chewing. A busboy named Charlie Abrams, a Boston University prelaw student, was wearing sunglasses to hide a minor case of pinkeye. He had evidently scarfed an entire slice of Boston cream pie in one quick bite, because his sunglass lenses were covered in whipped cream. Temporarily blinded, he crashed into a tray stand filled with aluminum meal covers, which collapsed and jangled for what seemed like five minutes, just like a vaudeville joke. He got off without serious consequences because he looked so stupid that none of us could stop laughing. Even the mysterious Moish got a kick out of it.

Thus for a salary of twenty-five dollars and a three-dollar tip per week per head, we, whose mothers might scrimp on anything but food, suffered these indignities like ragamuffin children of 1850 London. Only subsequent history would tell if these travails would be in any way beneficial to the boys, but at that time "a good learning experience" was the furthest thing from our minds. Besides food, money, sleep, and bullshit sessions, the other major pursuit of the collegiate staff was sex, though this pursuit was often an exercise in futility. We had at this stage of our lives varying degrees of experience in such matters, the busboys less than the waiters. The scuttlebutt was rife with stories of summers past, of lusty girls who went all the way, and a few of their mothers, too. This raised the expectations considerably in early July, with lots of optimistic bravado. But after weeks of life in the real world, of girls too young and girls too old and girls too good and girls who paid not the slightest attention to me, the summer was waning, and those stories of Catskill sexual conquests seemed like bitter pipe-dream fantasies. I was, as usual, left to my own devices on my prison cot at night. There were visions of the women I'd seen that day in the dining room, or half clad at the pool, dancing in my head like sugarplums but out of my reach. Then something happened to shake up the routine and drudgery and the sexual doldrums. Some delicious gossip: word of a notorious woman checking in for her annual stay at the hotel. How much of what I heard is true and accurate, I cannot say. But from the moment she arrived, rumors crackled through the staff like an electrical storm, and this is what I heard.

"Diamond Lil" was the staff nickname (no one dared use it to address her) given to a Miss Dora Pincus. She was an unmarried career woman (that was what they called it then) in her fifties, with a penchant for expensive jewelry, who had booked a three-week reservation at the hotel every summer for ten years straight. She took the only two-room suite the place had to offer, tipped all personnel generously from a fistful of bills, ran up a tab equivalent to a family of ten, and was the most important guest of the season from the management perspective. Word was she could have afforded Paris or Newport but chose a small hotel in the Catskills, apparently choosing to be a big fish in an extremely small pond.

An excellent dancer, she had a special affinity for doing the cha-

cha with the young men of the staff, picking out one or two each summer, and lavishing gifts on them. She bought a few ties for our handsome master of ceremonies with the nice tenor voice, Paul Sorvino,
but he backed away as charmingly as he could from any further
involvement. Lil was given to sexy, strapless mule shoes, and summer
dresses that carefully accentuated her excellent legs and breasts,
while attempting to hide a fairly wide load on the hips and buttocks.
The quid pro quo in her annual summer adventure was that the particular waiter or musician or busboy would be obligated to be an
attentive lover. She would be discreet in front of people, not wanting
to cross the middle-class sensibilities of the hotel clientele by appearing to be a cradle-snatcher. No hand holding or stolen kisses. In the
daytime she was Dora Pincus, middle-class straight.

Lil was a dyed redhead with high-fashion clothes and a Cadillac
convertible who, through the years, had no trouble turning the head
of one aroused Oedipal college boy or another. But this summer she
was having a problem finding the increasingly elusive gigolo-in-
training. According to a few hotel waiters who had seen her over the
years, she was never a beauty to begin with, but over the winter, her
aging process had evidently taken a geometric leap, and she had
metamorphosed from a vivacious middle-aged woman into an old
lady. The situation had become so serious that Lil, feigning the flu, let
it be known that she was contemplating checking out of the hotel
after only five days. This was bad news to management, who proceeded to shower her with attention and free limousines to the Monticello shops and the racetrack, not to mention a hundred-dollar bill
to bet with. But it wasn't limousines or cash that Lil needed. It was
the high hard one from some delectable young man that she craved.
It was a little sad to see her tickling the chin of some college sophomore sitting at the bar, to no avail, though the staff had a few cruel
giggles.

In a desperation move, Mr. Grunwald, the owner of the hotel, dis-
patched his sister-in-law Myrna, the famed public address announcer,
to find a lover for the valued guest. Choice number one was Shelly,
the dark curly-haired trumpet player, a favorite of the ladies at the
hotel. Myrna offered him fifty dollars to make old Lil happy. He was

appalled. She offered a hundred, and he was twice as appalled. In his eyes, Myrna, a religiously observant homemaker and mother of three, had become a pimp. She didn't see it that way. "Come on, Shelly. A good-lookin' boy like you, what do you have to lose? A little toss in the hay. I hear you do your fair share of that for free. Why not make a nice woman happy and satisfy our best customer?" She pressed Diamond Lil's room key into his palm. He replied, "I'll keep this under my pillow for the next time I feel like shtupping my aunt. Let me ask you something, Myrna. Would you like this offer to be made to *your* son when he's a little older?" Myrna gave him a "why are you busting my balls" look, but she had no answer for that one. She swept the ethical concerns effortlessly under the rug and proceeded on her way to proposition some other mother's son.

I had a particular fondness for Shelly. The house musicians were all pretty good guys, older than I by two to six years, which was a lot back then. Two were graduate students, and Shelly was a Korean War veteran. No Dizzy Gillespie, he had fair chops on the trumpet, but his calm maturity, and the sense that he had been there and back, set him apart from the rest of the flakes in the band. He was a mensch through and through: an ethical mensch, a real person. The band was extremely cordial and occasionally invited me to sing a tune or shake the maracas during their set. Maybe my latent aspirations drew me to them, the closest thing to show business at the Fieldston Hotel. In my eyes, their job had the most panache of all, and of course I loved music.

They also seemed to attract the most girls and not a few women. With few exceptions, they kept their sexual escapades to themselves out of discretion and a fear of embarrassing any guests and thereby incurring the wrath of management. However, Shelly couldn't resist telling a few of us about Myrna's offer and how repulsed he was by it. He considered the proposition an insult to both him *and* Diamond Lil. Nonetheless, my inexperience, not to mention a 0.00 batting average for the summer, made the story exciting and inflamed my imagination. The idea of a woman who was such a sure thing that another woman was offering money to any willing person with a penis to have sex with her—that was my kind of offer. The money seemed strangely unimportant.

"I'd do it," I blurted out.

"You'd do what?"

"I'd shtup her," I said.

"Have you seen her? She's old enough to be your grandmother. You must be a gerontophile," said the erudite Shelly.

"A what?" I said.

"Someone who likes old people."

"Of course I like old people," I said.

"No, someone who likes to *have sex* with old people," he said to general laughter. Shelly tossed Lil's room key to me. "Here you go, sport. Good luck." Suddenly, I was surrounded by assorted kibbitzers egging me on. "Yeah, Bobby Klein, stud extraordinaire." "He's gonna make it all the way with the famous temptress Diamond Lil." "Let's hope she doesn't have a heart attack while he's humping her." "Next he's gonna make a play for my tonta Bessie and my bubbe."

These taunts notwithstanding, the fact was that my earliest sexual fantasies were about the adult women who lived in my crowded apartment building on Decatur Avenue. They were elaborate if naive fantasies, based, among other things, on my observations of these women in very close quarters. Even as a very small boy, I noticed the way their housedresses clung to their bodies; I noticed their lips, their breasts, their perfume—natural and not—their clothes, their shoes. As I grew older, they never could have imagined how often I thrilled to them secretly in my bed, during my nightly date with myself. All of this preoccupation with adult women was no doubt a safe, acceptable Oedipal expression—I hope. True, these women were younger than Miss Pincus, who was on the edge of being downright old, but it turned me on that this normal-looking middle-aged grown-up woman could be so naughty.

The next night in the casino, I got a perfect observation spot at the bar and watched Lil doing the mambo, an impeccable pachanga, and her specialty, the cha-cha. She flung her arms about and moved her generous hips back and forth gaily and gracefully, like someone who knew she was the best dancer in the room. Of course, to be truthful, most of her competition on the dance floor was, shall we say, uninsurable. Yet the Arthur Murray Dance Studio would have been proud of her this night. I watched from the relative darkness of the bar, with a mouth-breathing grin from three Scotch and sodas, which provided the rose-colored glasses for everything I saw and heard. The musicians were riffing better than ever, with those intoxicating, surging Latin rhythms. The casino, the bane of my existence, with its noisy wooden floors above where I slept, actually looked elegant, enhanced by theatrical spinning glass reflecting lights.

As I watched Diamond Lil from the anonymous darkness, I thought of her thrilling proclivities. "She loves to fuck young boys," I repeated to myself several times, and oh that Scotch whiskey. I began to get secretly excited. She was dancing with such passion, well at least for the Fieldston Hotel. Damned if she didn't look hot to me. Nice big breasts. She was wearing a kelly-green chiffon dress cinched at her waist; it spread into a wide hoop skirt, favored by fashionable women in the fifties, designed to hide a fairly ample tuchas. She wore matching satin five-inch heels. She wasn't young and couldn't be mistaken for a teenager, yet . . . I took a hefty sip of whiskey and focused on the feminine way her feet melded into the strappy, high heels. During the mambo, she grabbed the dress with her right hand and raised her left hand into the air, thrusting her head back in the Latin style like a regular Carmen Miranda, without the fruit-bowl hat.

I dared not ask her to dance; I would have been much too embarrassed, and subject to ridicule from the guys. I told them all that I had been kidding about making a play for Lil, but the more I watched her, with the Scotch whiskey pumping through my bloodstream, the better she looked, and the prospect of realizing my long-held fantasy of making it with an older woman took hold of me. She was there for the taking, wasn't she? She may have been a little nuts, but she was still that rarest of women who never said no.

The evening wore down, the band packed up, and there were good nights all around as a few of us drifted to the coffee shop. I noticed that Diamond Lil had left the casino alone and gone up to her second-floor rooms in the main building, just above the lobby and the coffee shop. After about a half hour, the bullshit session broke up, and I pretended to use the men's room off the lobby, waiting until everyone was gone. I was shaking a little, because at that moment, I knew I was going to do it. I had no plan as I ascended the staircase to the second floor. It was quiet. Most of the guests were asleep, it being midnight on a weeknight. I could hear snoring through the thin wood walls of the old building, and a mother soothing a crying baby. How sweet: an innocent mother and an innocent baby, and here I skulked, drunk no less, in pursuit of debauchery.

When I got to the second floor, I sat down on the step to think this through. What the hell was I doing? Could I really go through with this? Strange scenarios began creeping into my head, paranoid and improbable. What if this was an elaborate practical joke being played on me by the guys? What if Diamond Lil was actually just plain old Dora Pincus, an aunt or a grandmother, who served dried fruit and nuts? What if I made a play for her and she smacked my face and scolded me like the buxom women I fantasized about on Decatur Avenue probably would have? Shelly and the boys would have a good laugh on me. Worse, what if she screamed and called the police? My family . . . disgrace. Headlines in the *New York Post:* GERONTOPHILE RAPIST ARRESTED. But these were unlikely contingencies, as the hotel, according to Shelly, was offering money. And ooh, how she danced that mambo in those high-heeled shoes, and she was right down the hall. Now what was I going to do, knock on her door? I was not used to drinking, and the whiskey was beginning to take its toll, giving me the intermittent feeling that the hallway was spinning. I was afraid I might puke, which would be the ultimate capper to my attempted sexual adventure. I decided to walk down the hall and see if I had the nerve to knock on her door. I passed it, and it was wide open, and she saw me. I kept walking down the hall, pretending to be looking for another room. As I returned the way I came, she was at the door wearing a bathrobe with a newspaper under her arm and a highball in her hand.

"You looking for someone, darling?"

"Uh, yeah. I think I'm on the wrong floor, though," I said.

"I'm just reading the paper. Come on in," she said. I stood there like a sphinx. "Come in, come in, I won't bite you," she said gently, seductively, as if she would like to bite me.

I entered the parlor of her suite, which, like the hallway, was spinning a little. I could see the bedroom adjacent to the parlor; there was a half-full bottle of Haig and Haig Pinch Scotch on the night table, right next to a bottle of Chanel No. 5. The room was suffused with it, which smelled wonderful and, of course, expensive. She seemed eager to have company as she closed and locked the door. "Have some candy, read the paper. You can learn a lot from the paper. I have the *Post* and the *Mirror.* I didn't get the *Times* today. What college do you go to?"

"Me? Uh, Alfred University."

"Oh my God, Alfred University. What a coincidence. My nephew just graduated. Of course you'll plotz when I tell you who he is. You ready? My nephew is Bernie Pitkin."

This news about Bernie Pitkin was less than the lightning rod Miss Pincus was counting on. I had never heard of Bernie Pitkin. "Uh . . . Bernie Pitkin? I don't think I know him."

"What? You must be kidding, he was president of Tau Delta. He was on the golf team, a sociology major. You really don't know Bernie Pitkin?"

"No, I don't think so," I said.

"He's about five foot six, dark hair, very popular?"

This mundane discussion, this Jewish geography, was hardly good presex banter. "I can't believe you don't know him. He was such a big man on campus." I decided to meet her halfway. "Wait a minute—Tau Delt? Golfer? Yeah, I remember him, but I didn't know him well."

Lil, in a fancy red bathrobe with a slit up the side, offered me a piece of candy from a Whitman's sampler. She lit a Lucky Strike and took a sip of her drink. "The square ones have hard centers, and the light ones have soft centers. You like nougat?"

"Yes. Thank you."

"You want a drink?"

"No, thank you."

She took a seat in an easy chair. As she crossed her legs, the bathrobe rode up enough to reveal her leg and thigh and a complex pattern of varicose veins. They reminded me of a diagram of the jet stream on a weather map. The room was well lit. *Too* well lit. Lil had removed her makeup and eyelashes for bed, having contemplated

sleeping alone once again. There were bags under her eyes and wrinkles around her mouth, and I could see that she had a slight mustache. God bless her, these were all quite normal for a woman of her
age, but not for the prospective lover of a boy of seventeen. She looks
so old, I thought. Gone was the flamboyant mambo dancer/nympho-
maniac. I was in the presence of a nice, talkative old woman in a
bathrobe and slippers who was an excellent hostess but not the slightest bit appealing to me sexually. I was feeling a surge of my old pal,
guilt, for having entertained this whole notion to begin with. Suddenly, I wanted out of that room more than anything in the world. I
would have been happier clearing two dozen plates of brisket or hearing the bone-jarring screams of the chef than sitting there with her.

She continued with her newspaper gambit, sounding like a yenta
cliché at the mah-jongg table: "Did you read that they broke ground
for the Verrazano-Narrows Bridge? Two bam. That's gonna fire up
Staten Island real estate for sure. Three crack. I already bought
twenty-five acres in New Dorp. That's in Staten Island, you know."
She put her hand on my cheek and looked me over. "I don't recognize
you. Are you a waiter? A busboy?"

"I'm a busboy, station six. You know, I better be going. I have to
work breakfast. It's been nice chatting."

"What's your hurry? You're young, you got plenty of energy." She
went into a sort of nostalgic reverie: just what I needed. "When I was
your age, I never slept. I never got tired. There was plenty of time for
sleep. Having a good time—that was the important thing. I find it
very hard to sleep. The night the war in Europe was over, we had a
party for three days and three nights." Tears came to her eyes. "I had
a sweetheart who was killed in the war . . . in Italy. Did you know
that?"

"No, I didn't. I'm very sorry. Look, I better go now. Thanks for the
candy. I'll see you around the hotel."

"You're a very nice, very sweet young man." She reminded me of a
Hebraic Blanche DuBois from *A Streetcar Named Desire,* trying to
seduce the newsboy. I went for the door. She arose quickly, blocking
my way. "Are you sure you have to go? I have some dried apricots and
pistachio nuts."

I mean, did she actually think that offer would be the clincher to keep me there? That I would suddenly say: "Dried apricots and pistachio nuts? Wow! Well in that case of course I'll stay a few minutes. Throw in some prunes and halvah, and I'll stay all night." A gigantic wave of nausea descended on me, mixed with shame. "I really have to go now," I said.

She cupped my chin and looked steadfastly into my eyes. "Yes, darling, I know you do. Good night." She unlatched the chain and opened the door and gave me a tiny peck on the cheek. "You're a sweet boy. Best of luck in college. I *still* can't believe you don't know him. *Everybody* knows Bernie Pitkin."

So much for my foray into the land of older women. *Much* older women. I felt like shit. I returned to my quarters at the Waldorf and vomited vigorously for five minutes.

In lieu of the real thing, the majority of the sexual stimulation among the busboys was talk, fantasy and stories of sexual conquests from colleagues, dripping with braggadocio that was largely bullshit. One rainy August night I was in the musicians' quarters, called the Taj, and listening intently as Herbert, the accordion-playing dental student, told a few of the busboys of his encounter with a girl named Sheila. She was not a guest at the hotel, but her family had a summer home nearby and paid a fee for the seasonal privilege of doing the cha-cha and enjoying the shows at the casino. Herbert was short, with tortoise-shell glasses, and looked like a well-read chipmunk. He certainly didn't strike me as a cocksman, and despite my eager, vicarious interest in the story, I was simultaneously and, come to think of it, hypocritically put off by his telling it—his failure of discretion. He may have been kissing and telling, but I could tell that he was being truthful in his account, as he could never be that good at improvisation. In his high voice and meticulous diction, he told how the girl kept coming up to him at the bandstand to request various numbers, all the while dancing.

I knew who Sheila was, having seen her around the casino, but at nineteen or twenty, she was in my category of "older woman" and would not be interested in me. She was not pretty, more of the intellectual type from City College, but with huge "mammaries," as Herbert called them. (He enjoyed demonstrating his knowledge of gross-anatomy terms learned in dental school.) Sheila's favorite tunes were "Embraceable You" and "The Cuban Mambo," which the band had played three times at her request. Herbert spoke to a captive audience of horny would-be-Casanova busboys: "She kept doing these wild gesticulations during the mambo, thrusting out her mammaries and grinding and wiggling her ass."

Shelly, the oldest member of the band, interjected a question with mock solemnity: "But at what moment did you know she was coming on to you in particular? Was there a hint?"

"Fair question," said Herbert pompously. "Every time she looked my way, her tongue would dart in and out, and she kept winking at me. How's that for a hint? I could tell she was hot to trot." He recounted how they got to talking after the band was through, when the two of them had a few drinks at the bar. After all the salacious hinting, and much to Herbert's surprise and disappointment, Sheila launched into a spirited discussion of philosophy and political theory. It took a while for him to plod through Voltaire and Thomas Hobbes and get her into talking about sex. He came up with Freud, which was the perfect segue, because it presented an opportunity for him to intellectualize the conversation right into what was on his mind.

Here was where Herbert's story really started to percolate. I could swear we busboys moved closer so as not to miss a word. "We were sitting on bar stools, and our knees were touching. She was chatting on nonstop about Freud's *The Interpretation of Dreams*. Then she very deliberately maneuvered her knee right into my crotch and began to move it—very knowledgeably, I might add. I moved my stool closer. A few deep kisses, and I began stroking her knee and gyrating my pelvis against it. Slowly at first, then faster and faster and faster and faster until—Modesty prevents me from telling you the exciting conclusion of the evening."

There was a chorus of "Oh shit" and "Oh no" and groans. I protested: "Come on, Herbert, don't leave us hanging. Did you go all the way with her?"

"None of your business. I'll tell you when you're twenty-one."

Then Mitch, the drummer/law student who always needed a haircut, spoke up: "Uh, Herbert, aren't you forgetting something? Don't forget to tell these kids the best part. You're not going to leave it out, are you?"

Herbert glared at Mitch as if he had a strong desire to place the drummer's head between his cymbals and play a Sousa march. Mitch continued, "Yes, it's true, Herbert did invent a new position for lovemaking that night: sex on a bar stool. Then, in the middle of his hot and heavy intercourse with her knee, he got a little carried away and fell off the stool and banged his head. His glasses were bent like a Calder mobile." We all broke out laughing.

Herbert protested, "Will you shut up already, you're exaggerating."

"Exaggerating? Everyone came running to help. All this in the middle of a torrid knee-humping session with a boner that wouldn't quit." More laughter; even Herbert couldn't suppress a smile.

"All right, all right, let me tell my own story, if you don't mind, Mitch. He thinks he's Mr. Comedian." Herbert continued, and the story came out more or less like this. After three seconds of limp groaning and a quick, tactile search for blood, the hearty horny boy picked himself up in a masculine display of recuperative power. This played well with Sheila, who had initially wanted to call for an ambulance. In fact, she began fussing over him, straightening his jacket and bending his glasses back into shape. Herbert seized the opportunity to invite her to the Taj, but the episode seemed to have cooled her off, and she refused. She said that was way too far to go for two people who hardly knew each other. He tried to kiss her, but she presented only a cheek, in contrast to the tonsil-depth kisses of a few minutes before. She said she'd better get home or her folks might worry. All of a sudden she had gone from steamer to dutiful daughter. "I thought, who needs this? She's a cockteaser," said Herbert.

"Would you mind walking me home? It's late," was the girl's request. Herbert Schwam was nothing if not a gentleman, so though he now expected no payoff, he could not refuse her, and they began to walk the half mile or so to her parents' vacation home. The conversation was sparse, with a slightly sullen Herbert contributing little, especially when she had the nerve to regress back to Voltaire. He was cold in his perspiration-soaked tuxedo, and he thought he could see his breath. To add to this, the poor fellow was experiencing the first sign of male excitement interruptus; his testicles were exceedingly painful as he walked. Finally, they arrived at a small white summer cottage with a 1956 Chrysler parked adjacent to it. "This is the house. My parents are sleeping. Thanks for a really nice evening," she said. No kiss. No nothing. Then she looked at him strangely and took his hand and said, "You know, I like talking to you, but it's kind of chilly out here. Why don't we go into the car?" They did, and she was all over him. "Bingo! That was it. I was home free," Herbert told us. When she said: "You know, I like talking to you, but it's kind of chilly out here. Why don't we go into the car?," the dentist-to-be knew he would find the cavity of his dreams.

What a story, I thought. I should be so lucky. For several nights after, I looked for Sheila, though I didn't see her. I wasn't sure what I might have said to her, since at that stage of my academic career, Thomas Hobbes could have played third base for the Chicago Cubs and a Calder mobile might have been a car. But I kept visualizing Sheila performing acrobatic sexual feats in the backseat of a Chrysler. The vision was a mixed blessing, as it was difficult to eliminate the nerdy Herbert from the mind's eye.

"PEEK OP, YOU COCKSUCKER! IT'S GETTING COLD!" The gentle voice of Henry the chef pierced my reverie. I had been caught daydreaming, and a hotel kitchen is a mighty bad place to daydream, especially with those maniacs behind the counter. I hurriedly picked up two side orders of stuffed derma, or kishke, a tasty compote of flour and fat stuffed into the intestinal tract of a cow. If they could eat this stuff and survive, small wonder that Jews had survived for over three thousand years.

Just then a vicious argument broke out in front of the chef's station between two waiters in dispute over whose main dishes were sitting on the counter. The kitchen can do that to people. There was only one denizen of the kitchen without a care: the childlike pot washer, Guy. He was showing everyone his new construction boots, of which he was very proud, and he told anyone who would listen how he had hitched a ride into Monticello and bought them for twenty dollars "all by myself." At twenty-four, he had never purchased a pair of shoes on his own. The kitchen staff, especially the dishwashers, teased him about his boots and said he had paid too much and got taken by the store clerk. But Guy didn't care. He would interrupt his pot-washing rhythm only to look down at his precious new boots, whistling and smiling. This was a happy man.

Twelve hours later, during the next morning's breakfast, there was a silent, sullen Guy, scrubbing at half speed. He was not wearing his new boots. In fact, one of the furtive dishwashers was wearing Guy's new boots, while Guy had on a pair of used, trashy, pointy stiletto loafers from some Tijuana tag sale, which, to add to the insult, had been *sold* to him by the dishwasher, who was wearing *his* boots. It seemed that Guy had lost the boots in a dice game with the two dish-washers, and when we found out about it, a certain amount of extra tension began to build in the already volcanic environment. To the chef, the salad man, and the lunatic baker, Guy's misfortune was a source of entertainment. They showed not the slightest pity for the man's loss, smirking and exchanging remarks about it in two or three Central European languages with a dash of Cantonese. However, the humanistic collegians of the dining room staff were outraged, because everyone knew that Guy had been cheated, that he couldn't negotiate his way through a dice game if his life depended on it. Though he kept muttering something about losing his boots "fair and square," we knew he didn't understand the rules of craps.

Davy, one of the Israeli waiters on summer leave from a kibbutz, approached the dishwasher, who was a Panamanian. The dishwasher was small but scary, wiry and muscular, and had a bumblebee tat-tooed on the tip of his penis. He was quite proud of this tattoo and would often show it upon request, given a sufficient amount of cheap wine. He also had T-R-U-E L-O-V-E tattooed on eight of his knuckles; the two remaining knuckles bore red hearts.

"*Amigo mio,*" Davy said in a thick Israeli accent, "give the poor guy his boots back."

"Fuck you" came the quick retort. The dishwasher tensed his body in preparation for battle, producing from under his apron a switch-blade knife which he did not open.

The Israeli proceeded more warily. "I'm not looking to fight you. Look, here's five dollars. Take your shoes and give him his boots, and everyone will be happy."

At this the Panamanian let out a rapid stream of Spanish words that were undoubtedly opprobrious, lots of *putas* and *madres* and *maricones*. He had a crazy look in his eye, and Davy backed off. The chef and his gang got a kick out of the confrontation and seemed disappointed that it was over, screaming, "Whatsamatta, you scared to fight him? Fight him! Fight him!"

Davy looked at them contemptuously and hurled some insults in Hebrew, which I found out later were about whores and mothers and fags. He had been in the Israeli army in the Sinai in 1956 and was no coward. But perhaps because he had seen bloodshed up close, he seemed little interested in engaging in a knife fight in a kitchen with a psychopath over a pair of boots. He took his tray, turning to leave, and playfully hit Guy on the head. "Meshuggenah! Don't play no dice no more with these charming gentlemen in the back here. Okay?" Guy just muttered and scrubbed and occasionally looked forlornly at his beloved boots on someone else's feet.

All day everybody talked about poor Guy and his boots, but nobody dared confront the thief. Joel, a political-science major from City College, gathered a petition and presented it to Henry the chef, demanding that he intervene in the matter. We all signed it. The theory was that the chef's ego would be stroked by this acknowledgment of his power, and in the interest of justice, he would act. When the petition was presented to Henry, he looked at it for five seconds, uttered a Hungarian expletive, contemptuously blew his nose on the document, and threw it in the garbage. So much for the theories of political-science majors.

At the Waldorf that night, a lively discussion about Guy's boots took place, and much anger and indignation were vented. Billy Fink, a liberal-arts guy from NYU, gave an impassioned speech about "the dignity of man" and how "the workers must be protected from exploitation." This stuff seemed to make sense, but then he veered way left, comparing the stolen boots to "the hideous execution of the Rosenbergs," which was a bit of a stretch. Fink, though a good speaker, was a Commie through and through whose bullshit no one took seriously, and he was booed heartily to sit down.

Kendall Haynes, the gentle Episcopalian from the Yale Divinity School who could imitate a calliope, talked quietly, in the manner characteristic of modest people who have something important to say. Kendall thought before he spoke and considered his words carefully, framing the question in the simplest ethical terms. There was right and there was wrong, justice and injustice, right before our eyes. He invoked the holocaust as an example of people seeing injustice and doing nothing, but he counseled against violence. I think some of the boys had tears in their eyes upon hearing the gentle gentile espouse such a reasonable treatise. Kendall had nailed the problem admirably, but he offered no solution for correcting the matter beyond vagaries about "moral suasion." How are you going to exercise moral suasion over a maniac with a switchblade knife and a bumblebee tattooed on his penis?

Charlie Abrams, the prelaw from Boston University, said that the owner of the hotel, Mr. Grunwald, should fire the Panamanian forthwith. He suggested an "executive committee" to approach Grunwald and hope that he would do "the decent thing." Larry Zwick, a dental student from the University of Maryland, revealed that he had already talked to Mr. Grunwald, who was his uncle, and he could not have cared less about a pair of boots. "The Panamanian does a good job cleaning the dishes. That's all that concerns me," Mr. Grunwald had said.

Grunwald had inherited the Fieldston Hotel from his father, the late and much venerated (by the immediate family) Israel Grunwald. An amateurish portrait of Grunwald the elder was prominently displayed in the hotel lobby. Several penciled-in mustaches had obviously been painted over in a futile attempt to maintain the dignity of the portrait, whose quality brought to mind paint-by-numbers. It looked as if number seventeen, the lower jaw, had not been fully filled in. Mr. Grunwald was a hands-on boss who endlessly nagged the boys about wasting food in the dining room; it was crucial that the butter and the cream be collected and refrigerated. Surviving hard-boiled eggs would become tomorrow's egg salad. He liked to make inspections of the dining room stations to see that they had been properly swept and maintained. One of his main preoccupations was reminding the male staff to dance with guests who had no one to dance with, especially elderly widows. This was considered part of the job, so no cash was offered, as in the special case of Diamond Lil. This duty was avoided whenever possible. When one of the busboys was locked on the dance floor in the embrace of an elderly guest (more for balance than passion), the others would position themselves behind the widow and try to make the boy laugh by making unearthly, repulsive faces—that is, until Grunwald caught a few. He lectured them, saying that this was a test of their maturity and they were failing.

However, the moral dilemma about Guy's boots was a more sobering, important test, and *Grunwald* was failing. Steven Stern, a basketball jock from Syracuse, suggested that we all surround the Panamanian and threaten to beat the shit out of him unless he returned the boots. "He's only five feet tall, for Chrissakes!" This appealed to a fair amount of the boys, thanks to the old strength-in-numbers concept.

"What if he pulls a knife?" I said.

"We just rush him, and we can have knives, too," said the basketball jock. He was addressing a group of boys whose experience with a knife was largely confined to buttering bread. Somebody pointed out intelligently that our trays would make excellent shields. But the question to me was who would be in the front row and most vulnerable to a nice knife in the belly? If there were fifteen of us, should we confront him in three rows five deep? Five rows three deep? Or the most egalitarian, share-the-risk mode of a circle of fifteen? The latter suggestion appealed most to the group, and everyone agreed we would do it the next morning before we served breakfast.

When morning came, no one involved in the plan bothered to eat the two-day-old blintzes or the oatmeal that was offered, preferring coffee and cigarettes. A certain jumpiness pervaded the room as we looked around conspiratorially like cons about to break out of Sing Sing. Stern, the jock, gave a signal with his head, and we all grabbed our trays and proceeded to the kitchen. It was apparent that the squadron was in a highly defensive mode; no one picked up a knife.

We formed at the dishwasher's station, a hodgepodge of nervous volunteers holding trays at our sides at the ready, like a phalanx of Roman soldiers. The dishwasher was in a position near the wall, where we couldn't get behind him, so we had to make do with a semicircle of varying depth. Stern put his money where his mouth was and gamely, if nervously, stood at the front.

The dishwasher looked confused. "What the fuck *you* want?" he said.

"We want you to give Guy back his boots," said Stern.

The Panamanian smiled, revealing ugly gold teeth barely hanging on to rotten bone and diseased gums. He put down some cups and saucers very slowly and deliberately, and in an instant, he produced a switchblade that opened with a CLICK. On that sound, fifteen trays snapped up with absolute precision to the shield position, worthy of a scene from *Ben-Hur.* It is amazing what the instinct of self-survival can accomplish for even inexperienced warriors.

The Panamanian slowly waved the knife at us, from left to right in a semicircle, still with that terrifying smile. I worried. Unlike a Roman shield, my tray had no handle, and my fingers were exposed. Suddenly, the venomous bastard took a menacing step toward the group, which promptly retreated five steps. One of the boys screamed, having backed into a griddle and burned his buttocks. A couple of warriors tiptoed through the swinging door and returned to the dining room, being more discreet than valorous. I had more or less held my ground, though I have to admit that the dishwasher's advance had caused me a heart palpitation. While he continued to menace, I inched toward the chef for sanctuary, figuring the dishwasher would never attack in that direction. He kept smiling that sinister smile and, with the knife in his hand, totally belied the tattooed message on his knuckles.

He had stabbed the air a few times for effect when the chef screamed at the top of his lungs: "WHAT THE FUCK YOU DOING, YOU JOIK!" At last, I thought, the chef will end the madness and disarm this asshole. But no. It quickly became apparent that it was *us* he was screaming at. "GET THE FUCK OUT OF MY KEECHIN, YOU COCKSUCKERS!" He grabbed an eighteen-inch cleaver out of a chopping block and charged the company assembled, waving the thing within inches of us, all the while spewing a torrent of Hungarian curses. He looked like he meant it this time, sporting a nice homicidal glaze in his eyes. "BOZMEG UNYUCA! BOZMEG AZUPATA! YOY ISHTANEM, I KILL YOU ALL!" My parents spoke fluent Hungarian, and I can tell you that the incantation was vile indeed. "THIS EES *MY* KEECHIN! DOSE BOOTS EES NOBODY'S BEEZNESS! GET THE FUCK OUT OF MY KEECHIN, OR I FIRE YOU AND YOU GO HOME TO YOUR MOTHERS!" At this, the plan collapsed in a humiliating dash as the busboys cut and ran back into the dining room and proceeded to prepare their tables.

Moish sat at his station picking his teeth with a wry smile on his face, absorbing the scene. He always smiled, but most of the time it wasn't a warm smile, signifying pleasure. It was more of a cynical smile, a tormented smile, born of his year in the Auschwitz concentration camp where his family was murdered. We would hear whispered accounts of his misfortune and subsequent exploits. There apparently had been an escape and four years spent running from the Nazis. Morris Landsman had even been awarded a medal from the Polish government, a bizarre irony, because he loathed that country since it was his Polish neighbors who had turned the family in to the Germans. He was a legendary figure at the Fieldston, having worked there for ten summers, and it was said that he had a deal that guaranteed him four thousand dollars for the season. Not your ordinary waiter, he had the best station, with the most generous customers, as well as administrative duties as the boss of the dining room.

Moish rarely spoke to any of us about his war experiences or his loss. Davy, however, had known him for years and told as much as he dared about the arcane past without violating his friendship. The stories had a mythic quality about them, short on details, which stimulated the listener all the more to imagine just how dangerous and horrifying it all had been. In any case, Morris Landsman was portrayed as a man with tremendous inner discipline who did not much savor recounting the past. We were told he had escaped from the concentration camp by killing a guard with a knife, followed by a stint sabotaging trains with the Polish underground, some of whose operatives were as anti-Semitic as the Nazis. Davy implied that Moish knew how to kill a man in ways unimagined.

He certainly didn't look the part of a killer. He was sort of handsome and compact and, well, Jewish, with a nice head of prematurely graying wavy hair. Though he was quite muscular and sinewy, he looked older than his forty years and seemed to take a certain pride in the numbers tattooed on his arm. One wondered what he thought behind that inscrutable smile. He had an excellent sense of humor and timing, speaking English with a Yiddish accent that's almost gone from the culture now, the one associated with Jewish jokes. He often made us laugh. But there was sorrow in his eyes, and more than a tinge of Pagliacci about him.

Occasionally, if Morris Landsman had enough Scotch in him, he would let loose with some stories to the boys sitting at the bar. Just after the war, the American army had hired him as a translator to communicate with the Germans. He was a Pole, and his German was scanty, so he would speak to the enemy in Yiddish, which was an exquisitely nonviolent revenge with a comedic twist. He recounted how they all understood him perfectly, and how "nice and normal" and polite and humble these Nazis were, sitting there as captives being spoken to in the language of the people they had just been slaughtering. I loved that one.

Yet after my vicarious gloating, it occurred to me that the emotional implications were stark. How much satisfaction could Moish derive from a little humiliation of these "pieces of shit," as he called them. They had slaughtered his family, for God's sake. He told about playing cards with his comrades while hungry young German women under the table sucked chocolate off the men's penises for money. As he told it through his smile, and the kaleidoscope of time, he shook his head, seemingly as regretful of that war memory as he was of the others. It was probably true that in his past, both the triumphs and the tragedies were tinged with shame. But as a holocaust survivor who had seen and suffered the ultimate in terror and degradation, there was a mystical aura about him. He had not been just a passive victim of the Nazis; he had fought back, and bravely, so the aura earned him respect and a little distance, and maybe just a bit of fear.

Though all in all, if you got your butter and cream off your table in a timely fashion, cleared the dishes promptly, and gave good service, Moish was not hard to deal with in the dining room.

To our surprise, he said nothing after the breakfast-knife fiasco. The dispirited busboys worked the meal with glum faces and no snap in their step, too disgusted and embarrassed to talk about it. Reporting for lunch, we were instructed to gather in the corner of the dining room nearest the kitchen doors. Moish entered from the kitchen with Mr. Grunwald behind him. As headwaiter, he wore a waist-length white jacket with epaulets on the shoulder suggesting rank. He paced back and forth with his hands behind his back and delivered a talk. His subject was the failed insurrection against the Panamanian. He delivered a quick admonition about not disturbing the kitchen, but it seemed halfhearted, reluctant. It seemed that Henry the chef and his gang had threatened to walk out over the knife–tray fiasco.

Grunwald stepped forward, looking calm, even smiling. "Look, fellas, here's the thing. If my kitchen staff leaves, nobody eats, and the hotel closes down. What am I gonna do, send out for three hundred corned-beef sandwiches?" There was some nervous laughter from the boys. "To replace a whole kitchen staff is impossible." Then his tone got ugly and foreboding. "On the other hand, I can call Harold's Agency in Monticello and replace every fucking one of you with some other nice college boys in forty-five minutes. Every fucking one of you. Capeesh?"

The Communist muttered something about union busting. Grunwald continued, "I'll give you union busting, you little pinko snot nose. Mind your own business. You could have gotten knifed in there, I'd have a big lawsuit on my hands, and what would I tell your parents? Now, get back to work or pack your bags and get the hell out of here."

There was a long, still pause. We took it like sheep. Apparently, management had taken the side of the felonious scumbag dishwasher for strategic reasons, never mind right and wrong. So the issue of the boots was put to rest for the moment, though we were reminded of it on every trip to the kitchen, where the amiable pot washer struggled uncomfortably to stand in ill-fitting shoes while the smirking shit who had cheated him displayed the goods.

A few nights after Mr. Grunwald's speech, some of the guys were playing cards and preparing for bed at the Waldorf. A massive mambo lesson was happening above us, sounding like a stampede of buffalo. Suddenly, Guy walked in on the way to his shack, and he was wearing his boots and was happy as a ten-year-old at Christmas. "Hey, fellas, look what *I* got," he said proudly.

"How did you get them back?" someone asked.

"I don't know," he replied. "I woke up from a nap, and the dishwasher was putting on his shoes, and my boots was under my bed. He didn't fuss none when I put on the boots. He even give me a Life Saver."

"Holy shit!" said Mickey Newman, the English major from Queens College, "this is fucking unbelievable! The dishwasher must have had a revelation like Scrooge had—a dream, a vision, that made him atone for his wicked deed!"

"Bullshit," I said. "Like that dishwasher would atone for anything in ten lifetimes without a thirty-eight pointed at his head."

A lively speculative discussion ensued about the turn of events, with some of the boys assuming that Mr. Grunwald had made things right by giving the Panamanian money or threatening to fire him. Some of us didn't think so. Grunwald wouldn't bother to open another can of worms, and neither would Henry, who didn't care in the first place. It had to be Moish. He became the prime suspect, though he had never shown the slightest interest in the case and always made it a point to mind his own business. Some of us could not wait until morning for an answer, so we went upstairs to the casino bar, where the headwaiter had his nightly drinks. Unfortunately, Grunwald's sister-in-law was there and cajoled a few of the boys into dancing with some single female guests, a few of whom were widows, while others were unmarried daughters looking to hook on to a dentist or lawyer in the hope of someday *becoming* widows.

There was Moish, sitting at the bar with his usual smile that really wasn't a smile. When the "Cherry Pink and Apple Blossom White" cha-cha was over, we approached him. He seemed disinterested in the news of Guy's good fortune and denied having had any part in it. Maybe I was imagining things, but the tension of his facial muscles seemed to suggest that he knew something. Anyone who could kill a Nazi face-to-face could convince a small-time diminutive thief to give back what he had stolen, I reasoned; that is, if he cared to.

"Moish, did you get him good? That slimy thief. You showed him, didn't you?" I said.

"Enough already with these noodnik questions. The boy got his shoes back, so that's that. Go to sleep, and don't be late for breakfast."

The next morning everyone pumped Davy for information, but he seemed reluctant to talk about it, which only made us more suspicious. Later, he told Kendall Haynes that he had seen Moish talking to the Panamanian on a wooded path behind the kitchen. The Panamanian was not at his station for breakfast, lunch, or dinner. His silent partner washed the dishes alone. This piqued our curiosity all the more. Johnny the cook said that the dishwasher had a sore throat and needed to take the day off. When he returned to work the next breakfast, he seemed like a different man, remarkably not the least bit hostile to the busboys who had threatened him and now dumped hundreds of dirty dishes at his stand. Nor was he unfriendly toward Guy, who was scrubbing burned eggs and onions out of huge frying pans. Guy was at full speed once again and whistling "Get Me to the Church on Time" from *My Fair Lady*, which was played endlessly on the hotel public address system.

Everyone noticed the source of the "sore throat" on the dishwasher, who wore a three-inch-square bandage on his throat, just above the collarbone. Some blood had seeped through the bandage. One of the boys asked him what the bandage was for, and he said he had cut himself shaving. Nobody grows hair that far down their throat short of a gorilla, so we knew he was full of shit, though none of us dared pursue the subject further.

We could only imagine what Moish might have done to the dishwasher. Tuli, an Israeli business major from City College, suggested that Moish had bitten the guy's neck like a vampire. I thought he had grabbed the son of a bitch by the throat and dug his nails in. Most figured it was a knife, his purported weapon of choice in killing German soldiers. Throughout the entire meal, all of us kept glancing over at the headwaiter, though he revealed nothing, carrying twelve main dishes with aluminum covers on one tray, like a circus juggler. He yelled at Steven Stern for dropping two plates of sour cream and bananas on the dining room floor, but other than that, he seemed on an even keel.

Nobody ever asked him about the incident again. Not knowing exactly what had happened, I filled in the blanks and probably romanticized the issue. I hoped that Moish had seen the injustice done to a poor, helpless retarded man, and that it had affected him, and that this caring had cut through the thick callus of cynicism. That this was a small part of his healing the unhealable, a sign that Morris Landsman could feel again, hope again; so much so that he would intercede like a hero to right a wrong.

Between breakfast and dinner, the European and Israeli soccer boys played harder than usual, far less casually. Moish spun and faked better than I'd ever seen him; he was tireless. Then there was Klaus Von Cherbourg a hundred feet across the green, beckoning for the ball. Moish stopped and looked at him. "You want the ball? You want it?"

"Ya, ya, Morris, kick it to me," he yelled.

Moish muttered in Yiddish, *"Eh chubisen drerd"* (go to hell). "I'll make you run like you made me run for four years," and he kicked the ball way over the head of the huffing and puffing German. Moish seemed to experience some release from his long kick and began to laugh. None of us had ever seen him laugh so long and hard. The German smiled, waved, kicked the ball back to Morris Landsman, and proceeded to check out of the hotel.

Labor Day weekend was just around the corner, and I had accumulated around four hundred dollars. The affair of the purloined boots and the kitchen insurrection were over. The kitchen staff had become a little nicer, probably because they would soon miss not having some jerky college boys to scream at. Financially, my summer had been nothing to write home about. Socially, it was a disaster, without even a hint of sex, not to mention my brief attack of gerontophilia. There were some flirtatious fifteen-year-old girls running around the hotel, but no serious prospects.

Then, in the casino on the next-to-last night of the summer, there was Sheila of the infamous "You know, it's kind of chilly out here, why don't we go into the car." She was wearing a red cocktail dress and dancing every dance with men who could have been her father, while totally ignoring Herbert, who hadn't called her since their encounter in the Chrysler. I assumed that she didn't know that *we* knew about her and Herbert and was therefore spared any humiliation. She certainly didn't look humiliated on the dance floor, throwing her ample body around like a whirling dervish. I worked up the courage to ask her to dance. When Herbert and the boys broke into Bill Haley's "Rock Around the Clock," I pushed my way through a horde of suntanned elders and took Sheila's hand for a spirited Lindy. But she paid no attention to me and danced off in a frenzy by herself, leaving me embarrassed, with my hand extended in midair. The event did not go unnoticed by the drummer and Shelly the trumpet player, who was laughing so hard that he couldn't play. Thanks. Like it's not difficult enough having a confidence level of zero. Shelly had been a bit of a summer mentor in social matters, and I guess I expected more from him than ridicule.

The next tune was a slow fox-trot, "My Funny Valentine." Shelly had a fancy solo at the top of the tune. He held the trumpet with his right hand, while gesturing with his left for me to ask Sheila to dance. I ambled over and presented myself to Sheila for a take two, and this time she smiled, displaying a hideous set of crooked teeth that the dental student had oddly failed to mention. To my surprise, she followed my lead excellently, dancing close to me. I mean bone-close. I thought of Groucho Marx's line when the woman says "Hold me closer, closer": "If I was any closer, I'd be in back of you." Sheila's dress had a luxurious silky texture that was unfamiliar to my hands, and the fabric fit her loosely, which made it slide against her skin. She kept looking at me, as if to gauge my reaction to her teasing. I could feel her large breasts as she rubbed against me, not accidentally. She smelled of the mildest perfume, more like soap, and her skin was the pristine pale white of someone who kept out of the sun. I kept remembering her in Herbert's story, though once again I tried like hell to blot out the image of the accordion player with his pants down in the backseat of a car.

With the band's eyes on me, I would have a new problem when the dance was over: how to hide a rather obvious erection that you could hang a suit of clothes on. At the end of the tune, instead of applauding, I pretended to be warm and took off my jacket, carrying it in front of me, but I don't think I fooled Shelly, and Sheila had to know. In fact, she seemed quite pleased.

We sat at the bar with her back toward the bandstand and me facing it. As she talked about the brilliance of James Joyce and *Ulysses,* the band made an assortment of obscene gestures behind her back for my benefit. I could feel Sheila's knee inching toward me. I had never read any James Joyce, which I wisely admitted, so I went to my strengths. I declared that John Steinbeck's *In Dubious Battle* was a better book than people thought, and that it had been overshadowed by *The Grapes of Wrath.* She agreed that might be true as her knee kept progressing closer. I told her how I cried reading Thomas Hardy's *Tess of the D'Urbervilles,* and she said she had cried, too, as her knee made contact. I instinctively looked around to see if anyone was watching, but the casino had emptied considerably, and our little corner was not well lit. I was beginning to like my chances in the world of romance when Sheila popped off the stool and said, "Well, it was nice talking to you, you certainly are a smart boy." She shook my hand and walked out the door, leaving me sitting there like the world's biggest schmuck.

The trumpet player gestured for me to go after her, but I was numb and so let down that I just stood there. Fuck it, I thought, the summer's over already, and this is my last chance.

I trotted out the door after her. "You want me to walk you home?" I asked.

She continued walking. "No thanks, it isn't far."

"I don't mind," I said.

"Look, you're a nice boy, but you're too young for me, you understand? I know what you're after, but you're not going to get it."

That old refrain once again. She had busted me, all right, and I was embarrassed. I kept walking alongside her. "All right, walk me home, but that's all, okay?" At this, she nudged me under the chin like a kid brother, and she took my arm. I wanted to bring up the subject of her grinding her body into mine, but she began talking about her impending senior year at City College. I had mixed feelings about entering my sophomore year at Alfred, and I mumbled a few words about changing my major, though it was the last fucking subject in the world I wanted to talk about. She advised against changing my major and gave me an earful of reasons why. I was sorry I had even brought it up, as I had unwittingly turned the woman I wanted to have sex with into a guidance counselor.

The whole thing was becoming a fiasco of meaningless conversation. I got the feeling I was being played with, perhaps mocked. She was older and, Lord knows, more experienced. Then the thought occurred to me: What if she really didn't want to have sex with me? Just because Herbert had scored didn't mean *I* would. She had wanted to walk home alone, hadn't she? I could be the tagalong jerk I appeared to be, though she did seem to enjoy the conversation. Maybe she really did think I was too young. Maybe the accordion player had broken her heart.

In any case, it seemed that the sexual highlight of my summer was going to be a knee-in-the-groin bar-stool quickie interruptus. I could feel in my pants that there was nothing to hide anymore, and I became petulant, sorry I had volunteered to escort her home. I couldn't wait until we got to her house so I could turn around and go back to the Waldorf. What would I tell my curious colleagues, many of whom knew that I had left with Sheila? None of their collective business.

The more she talked, the more annoying the whole thing became. On that unpaved country path, it was dark between the occasional porch lights of homes, and practically moonless, so she was unable to see my expression. I began making outrageous juvenile faces, mimicking her silently, amused that I could get away with it. I was only seventeen and pissed off.

"This is it," she said, "good night."

Sure enough, there was the dimly lit little cottage and the famous '56 Chrysler. Too bad I would never see the inside of it. I felt thoroughly crushed and ineffectual, like a little boy. We turned in opposite directions, and I had begun to walk back when I heard: "You want to talk a little more? You can't come in the house, 'cause my parents are sleeping."

Slowly I turned, step by step. "What did you say?"

There was a slight pause. "I said if you want, we can talk a little more, but you can't come in the house, 'cause my parents are sleeping." I began to tremble, and it wasn't that cold. "You know, it's kind of chilly out here," she said, "why don't we go into the car."

My slumbering penis shot up like a railroad semaphore. I couldn't believe what I was hearing. She opened the car door and guided me into the generous backseat of the big Chrysler, where we slumped in ardent glory.

I won't go into details. I can say only that it was worth every humiliating minute of the roller-coaster evening, the first of many such evenings in the course of my youth. She was not the best nor the worst lover I can remember, and I suppose in retrospect she was a homely girl. But why is it that I can still remember the thrill of it? She was lusty and passionate and uninhibited, and she gave to me, the neophyte, an experience I had never had before. She happened to be also highly intelligent, which I could not fully appreciate at seventeen and in heat. In all honesty, had she been the lowliest of dunces, my quest would have been just as vigorous. Considering my sexual scorecard at the time, I was too much of a beggar to be a chooser.

I was still in a trance on the walk home, thinking that sex was the greatest thing in the world. Yet I was so thoroughly sated that I believed I'd never want it again. This belief was short-lived, and in about five minutes I began to feel like I could have another go at it. Was this really ever possible? Sex, I came to discover, is a lot like eating, in that after a full meal, one feels, fallaciously, that he may never need to eat again.

My clothing was rumpled and sweaty as I walked in the darkness. I kept lifting my upper lip to my nose to smell Sheila's smell, to remind myself that it had all been real. Some dogs barked and howled, and tiny animals rustled the bushes in the increasing distance behind me. I found myself smiling, fulfilled, amid the cacophonous crickets rubbing their legs together, and the noisy August cicadas, all of whom were celebrating with me. I could swear I saw not one but *two* shooting stars as I strolled in a contented daze down the country road to the end of summer and back to school. I was smoking a cigarette and coughing, exhausted, drained, hungry as hell, ebullient and yet a little bit ashamed. Then again . . .

Chapter Nine

Ducks in a Row

I chose to live in the fraternity house my junior year. Happily, Mrs. Alcott, the house mother, was more out of touch with reality than ever, and the boys living there were totally unrestrained. Thanks to several sensible upperclassmen, it was still possible to study there, but it could be difficult, and more and more guys headed to the library.

My roommate was Bob Matolka, one of eleven children, from Endicott, New York. He was an engineering student with excellent grades, who became the steward of the house, in charge of meals and snacks. Before coming to Alfred, the closest he had ever been to Jews was when he ate a kosher pickle from a jar in 1956 in Binghamton. Yet for all his bucolic upbringing, he proved incredibly sophisticated and wise, and he had the respect of one and all. He was a serious type, but the zany and nonsensical carried the day at the house, with wild practical jokes planned and executed nonstop. Bobby Chaikin continually rolled an automobile tire down the stairs from his room in the attic, which would smash open the door below with an explosive sound and pin the occupant to the wall. He liked the element of surprise, like four in the morning. Not surprisingly, he became a dentist.

At supper one night, the main-course platter came out of the kitchen, the lid was removed, and on a lovely decorative bed of lettuce sat the head of a dead cat that Steve Levine had purloined from the zoology lab. Mrs. Alcott, whose sight was not much better than her mind, had to be restrained from taking a portion. "Oh, I love hash," she said as Levine swiped the platter away. At the end of the meal, she was still slightly perturbed that the main course had been removed before she could taste it. On another occasion, Mike Wiener put flour all over his naked body and hid himself in the large industrial-size freezer in the kitchen. Munchkin, the house scaredy-cat, was induced by some of the guys to open the freezer. Wiener fell out like a corpse, and Munchkin almost had a cardiac arrest.

Bessie Hurd, the elderly churchgoing local farm woman who cooked five nights a week for the brothers and had never met a Jew until she took the job, was unfazed by any of this. Naked boys popping out of freezers did not deter her from preparing her hearty farm fare, which was frequently delicious and featured outlandish peach and blueberry pies. The guys treated her like some eccentric aunt, but unlike the house mother, whom she disliked, her perspicacity was intact, and she was unlikely to mistake a cat's head for hash. I did a fair imitation of Bessie, who was prone to saying "God bless you," even to people who hadn't sneezed. She meant well.

I had become the court jester of Kappa Nu, the house comic. I had developed somewhat of a repertoire, which included several accurate impersonations of faculty members. The guys loved sitting around the living room hearing their reserved, scholarly teachers say incongruous things: cursing, soliciting sex, and telling dirty jokes, the more vulgar the better. My imitation of Professor Russell, a Yankee American-history specialist with a down-east Maine accent, was my best. Henry Liederman, a sweet, gullible basketball jock in one of Russell's classes, was busy studying for the midterm exam and had in his possession several old tests. This was quite common among the students and entirely legal and aboveboard. I called the house from another phone and asked for Liederman. The whole house was in on the caper, and everybody gravitated toward Henry as he took the call. "Mr. Liederman?"

"Yes."

"This is Professor Russell. Mr. Liederman, it has come to my attention that you have acquired an advance copy of my midterm examination. As you know, this could be grounds for expulsion."

"What? Oh, no, sir, I don't have the test. I have some old ones, but not the one you're going to give. I swear."

"That's not what I hear, Mr. Liederman. I'm afraid I'm going to have to report this to Dean Whitlow."

Henry believed it completely and was in a panic. I kept it going for a couple of more minutes and then decided to give up the ruse by saying something that Willis Cleaves Russell would never say in a million years: "Mr. Liederman, I'll let you off the hook on one condition."

"What, sir? Anything."

"I want you to come to my Pesach seder and eat three helpings of gefilte fish. Is that clear, Mr. Liederman?"

"Oh yes, sir, I'd love to come."

"And Mr. Liederman, bring a little sponge cake with you, if you don't mind. Goodbye, Mr. Liederman."

"Goodbye."

"Hey, guys I'm in big trouble unless I go to Russell's seder. I didn't even know he was Jewish." Henry was almost in tears. Everyone was cracking up, but he still didn't get it. Finally, I burst through the door and went right to him and spoke in the professor's voice: "Mr. Liederman, it has come to my attention . . ." He finally got it and chased me around the house, too relieved to be angry.

There were some attempts at practical jokes that were loathsome, and fittingly backfired on the perpetrators. One such circumstance occurred at the annual Valentine's Day blast, a highlight of the Kappa Nu social season and a very wild night. Warren Shamansky, a witless senior pre-dental student, hatched a secret plan to hide a tape recorder in the bathroom of the new wing, which on party nights became the ladies' room. It had showers, sinks, and was a three-bowl affair with no partitions. Only Shamansky knew about his plan. He was hoping to hear comments from the girls about the boys as they powdered their noses. He wound up hearing plenty. He revealed his stunt the next evening, which appalled some of the guys, but *everyone* wanted to hear the tape, so ethics took a backseat.

The boys gathered around the tape recorder, and Shamansky turned it on with a flourish. The sound quality wasn't great, but it was good enough to hear an assortment of tinkles and flushes and an occasional fart, all of which cracked up the listeners, some of whom clinked their beer mugs. Several happy girls sang while they urinated.

One hummed while she defecated. A few of the voices were recognizable as the steady girlfriends of brothers, and these boys were not pleased, since an intimate line had been crossed, and the entire house had heard their sweethearts fart. If word of this got out, they would have a lot of explaining to do.

So far, the toilet conversation had been innocuous chatter, but it slowly dawned on the listeners that the caper could prove highly embarrassing to the boys as well. We heard Billy Gildner's date tell her friend about what a lousy kisser he was, and then she complained about "the stench of his breath." A few guys roared, but Billy wasn't laughing. Joel Belson was one of the house drunks, and we learned that his date was disgusted by his drinking, was afraid of him, and wanted to leave early without him. Shamansky's date, who was going out with him for the first time, couldn't stand him and delivered a monologue that was the hit of the evening. It was as if she knew the tape recorder was on. "He's such a creep, Madeline. Boring, self-centered. He never stops talking about his two-point-six average. He thinks he's God's gift to women. Can you imagine? An ugly jerk like that. He makes my skin crawl. He's asked me out four times, and I always turned him down. He's not even nice. Ugh. I'm sorry I said yes. I can't wait till the night is over. I'm telling you, he positively makes my skin crawl. Can I borrow your lipstick?"

Then she flushed, and Shamansky's social standing went right down the toilet. He put on a weak front of amused nonchalance that no one believed. There were some snickers, but the mood had changed to a more somber tone. There were a few who said "I told you so," and someone said something about Shamansky being hoisted on his own petard. A few of the guys were remorseful about the disrespect accorded their girlfriends, some of whom they were pinned to. In any case, Shamansky got what he asked for.

One evening Ricky Sampson, Bob Chaikin, and Mike Benedict were sitting on the front porch of Kappa Nu when a customized 1952 Ford with loud mufflers and a continental kit pulled up in front of the house. The driver revved the noisy engine a few times as five guys got out of the car holding beer bottles. They stood there looking at the guys on the porch until one of them finally spoke. "Hey, Sambo, how come you're hanging around with those Jew boys?" Another one, good and drunk, said, "Hey, you fuckin' Jew bastards! Jew boys! Christ killers!"

Immediately, Ricky the halfback leaped over the porch railing and grabbed one of the shouters before he could get back into the car, with Chaikin and Benedict right behind him. He was pummeling the shit out of the guy by the time the rest of us, twenty strong, poured out of the house. The look on the faces of those guys when they saw a horde of angry Jews coming at them was worth remembering. A brief melee ensued, but after each of the cretins had taken a few good blows, cooler heads prevailed, as a homicide would look bad for the house.

The intruders were all subdued, some of them bloodied, and then came the beauty part. Ricky had the guy who'd called him Sambo by the hair and on his knees. The guy had a look like he's about to be killed, but instead of punching him again, Ricky made him apologize like a kindergarten kid. "Say 'I'm sorry and I will never do that again.'" When the guy hesitated, Ricky pulled his hair. "Say it, asshole."

"Okay, okay. I'm sorry and I'll never do it again."

Ricky released him. The driver tried to make nice and blamed it on too much beer. "We didn't mean anything by it, we were drinkin', just kiddin' around," he said.

Steve Murray stepped forward. "You were just kiddin' around? I like kiddin' around." He ran his hand along the '52 Ford. "Nice car," he said. Then he took a baseball bat and smashed the rear window. "Now you got air-conditioning in it."

Ricky's stock among the boys rose threefold after the incident, and Mike Benedict, a popular Methodist basketball player from Syracuse, was eventually elected president of the fraternity, though not for his fighting prowess. Unfortunately, there were three or four more such fights in my time at Alfred. Drive-by shouting was more frequent than the brawls. The miscreants were stupid enough to scream obscenities and peel out, yet prudent enough not to get out of their cars.

An odd confluence of two aspects of my life at Alfred occurred one day. I was cast as Shylock in the university production of *The Merchant of Venice*, thus combining theater and anti-Semitism in one enterprise. I wondered how certain segments of the audience would react to the play. Shylock was an actor's dream, my grandest role thus far. In rehearsal, I developed certain affectations of old age, like stooped posture and trembling of the hands and head. This was a hard sell, as I was only nineteen and Shylock was about seventy, though a gray wig and lots of makeup wrinkles were planned to aid in the effort toward authenticity.

The play involves itself, among other things, in the abstractions of obligation, revenge, and mercy. The way the sixteenth-century author has written the part, Shylock is a vengeful, unpleasant man; certainly not Mr. Nice Guy. Nevertheless, he is a human being vilified for his beliefs who has been wronged, and Shakespeare cannot resist dealing with all sides of the human issue: even expressing, persuasively, the logic of the apparently villainous Jew.

Twentieth-century history being what it is, contemporary productions tend to give Shylock a more sympathetic interpretation than perhaps Shakespeare intended. Given the Elizabethan context, it is unlikely that the Bard was crazy about Jews or even knew many, yet there is a brilliant speech in the third act that is as eloquent a statement on prejudice as has ever been written. It is in the form of a series of questions which I performed in front of a packed Alumni Hall, with all appropriate dramatic pauses and quasi-authentic trembling. "Hath not a Jew eyes? Hath not a Jew hands, organs, dimensions, senses, affections, passions? Fed with the same food, hurt with the same weapons, subject to the same diseases, healed by the same means, warmed and cooled by the same winter and summer as a Christian is? If you prick us, do we not bleed? If you tickle us, do we not laugh?"

"NO!" came the answer from the Alfred audience. Then they charged the stage, coming at me like a murderous mob, some with growling German shepherds straining at the leashes. I was forced to flee, blowing through the stage door with hundreds of people chasing me, screaming "JEW BOY! JEW BOY! KILL HIM!" They pursued me all over the campus, carrying torches and homemade weapons. I sought refuge everywhere, knocking on doors and pleading, but even the ethics professor, after considering the matter, wouldn't let me in.

Then I woke up. The nightmare reminded me that the issue was a sensitive one around here, certainly to me, and that this portrayal would not be just another role. It would be a mission much larger and more momentous than merely playing the role; a mission with sociological implications and real-life meaning.

Still, this was such an obvious dream—too obvious. Most of the time, the meaning is hidden and the dream is not about what it appears to be. The one I had was right on the money . . . too right on the money. I began to suspect that it was not what it seemed. I mentioned it to Sam Chororos at the final dress rehearsal, after which I came to an amusing conclusion. The dream was not about anti-Semitism at all; it was about the fear of failure. I was terrified that the old-man act wouldn't go over. Despite their words, the people were chasing me not because I was a Jew; they were chasing me because I was giving a lousy performance. Regarding the play, I was scared, plain and simple. This revelation cleared my mind and allowed me to concentrate on the role in a new and unfettered way. I gave the passages a lot of thought and made decisions that I applied in rehearsal, which was, after all, its purpose.

Smith and Brown and the other actors noted the progress, which resulted in my confidence shooting way up. When I performed the speech on opening night, I heard not a "no" in the joint, the attentive silence a testament to the veracity of the words and, dare I say it, a hell of a performance. Everybody bought into my old-man act; no one laughed; people were touched. One of the best compliments I received was from James Knox, an associate professor in the philosophy and religion department. He was a bespectacled Lutheran minister, about forty, with a wonderful sense of humor, who always had a good joke or two and told them well. He wore a beret and rode his bicycle around the place, and his secular-oriented course on the Old Testament was one of my favorite classes. He was also one of the few faculty members who was outspoken against the university-approved exclusionary policy of the fraternities. Late in the term, word got out that Dr. Knox had been denied tenure and would not return next year. Everybody in the community knew why, to the shame of half the faculty. There was a small protest, but it was to no avail, and life at Alfred, good and bad, went on.

*   *   *

The Phoenix Theater Company, a professional bus and truck touring group, came to the campus doing George Bernard Shaw's *Androcles and the Lion* in the afternoon and *Hamlet* in the evening. I had seen a few Broadway shows from the cheap seats, but I had never seen a professional production at such close range. With their additional lights and expert sets, they transmuted Alumni Hall into a real theater. I got to mingle all day with the actors, since we campus thespians acted as hospitality volunteers, and it reminded me of meeting big-league ballplayers close up. They were not stars, but they were otherworldly; somehow not like us. They looked different; they *were* different. They didn't have a typical job. I had always disliked routine, with a particular disdain for getting up every day at the same time for school, putting my underwear on the radiator to warm on cold winter mornings, or egging the classroom clock on to that three o'clock bell. To know for the next ten years exactly where you will be, and when you will be there, struck me as wearisome. Every adult I knew had a conventional job. Was that what I wanted? We observed these actors closely, especially interested in their preparation, how they applied makeup and put on their costumes and got ready to do the play. Then we went out front and watched the very people we had been socializing with transform themselves into exciting characters of the imagination onstage. The performances were thrilling and alive: the attack of their speech crisp, so you could see tiny sprays of spittle going over the footlights into the first row. It was an excellent lesson in craft.

What a wonderful life, I thought: traveling around to different places and performing plays; a sense of freedom, doing something they love. I liked everything about the actors: their nonconformist clothing, hair slightly long, and their self-assured manner, even if it was only acting. Law school seemed a dull prospect compared to this. I was especially fond of John Heffernan, who played Androcles and Polonius: a tall, willowy gentleman who cordially answered a barrage of questions from the members of the Footlight Club. Eight years later, I would appear in a Broadway show with him: *Morning, Noon and Night.*

Shortly after the Phoenix Theater visit, I had a momentous encounter with Sandra Sherman, Footlight Club member and English scholar. This event was not like the cold, anxiety-ridden episode with the prostitute when I was fifteen; nor was it a matter of grabbing what I could in the back of a car in the Catskills. Though we were not in love, this was real lovemaking, starting with intelligent conversation, into kissing and caressing, all the way to home plate. It took place at an off-campus apartment that had been generously lent by a stage-manager graduate student. There was danger here, because such behavior even away from campus was forbidden and severely punished. Furthermore, all female students, regardless of age, had a curfew, though after freshman year the boys did not, at forward-thinking Alfred University in 1960. We couldn't stay the night together, but the time we did have was well spent and unhurried, thanks to her calm confidence, which mitigated my deep fear of being caught.

Among other things, Sandra first removed her hornrimmed glasses, then let down her red hair. I had never seen her like this. It was like one of those Hollywood movies in which the secretary takes off her spectacles, undoes her conservative hairdo, and her boss suddenly realizes, "Why, Miss Jones, you're beautiful." Miss Sherman was not beautiful, but she had fine facial features; she was gentle, affectionate, mature; and her intellectual nature made her all the more appealing. After sex, I lay in bed with her, and we had intelligent conversation, sort of like a French movie. I was not the first Footlighter to take pleasure from intimacy with her, but that was no matter. She was an independent thinker, a woman ahead of her time on whom I had no claim.

We had several repeat performances, to our mutual delight, and there was no discomfort in chancing upon her around the little community; in fact, we were adults and friends. I told almost no one about it, it was entirely my affair and hers. This was part of my other life away from the fraternity, where such information instantly would have become public, like the announcements at Grand Central Station. The sexual relationship was brief, but the friendship continued, and I thought of this experience as a breakthrough into adulthood.

Then love struck. Not with Sandra Sherman. I was smitten with a freshman named Judith Silverman. This should have been a wonderful development, except for one thing: She was the girlfriend of my fraternity brother. I had noticed her from the beginning, but Andy Ruby, a sophomore, had moved in early, and they had been going together for a couple of months. I tingled every time I saw her, though it was a kind of torment. Judy and I liked each other, I made her laugh, though I took care not to reveal how I felt about her. I liked Andy, too; he was one of the guys, he even looked up to me. Andy was intense, to be sure: good-looking, physical, a basketball player, not an intellectual type. He seemed to be totally in love with Judy. He even asked me for advice about Judy, like a big brother, and confided in me that they were leaning toward having intercourse soon.

This was a conversation I could have done without, so like a good friend, I told him it was a bad idea. I found myself cautioning him like somebody's grandmother: "Of course it's up to you and Judy. But will you like yourselves in the morning? She's a good girl, and you love her." Some of this may have been valid, but for the most part, I was spouting disingenuous bullshit for which I felt a little guilty. Anyway, I could tell by the look in his eye when he talked about it that sex between them was a foregone conclusion.

Going all the way was no small matter between students in love in 1961. It was often a particularly wrenching decision for the girl, given the prevailing mores, one's reputation, and the fear of pregnancy. Pregnancy presented few options, as abortions were illegal, and the lives of unwed mothers were generally considered ruined. Once in a while, we heard of a girl taking a semester off or leaving school, with fuzzy reasons given, and sometimes there were whispers that she was pregnant. There were many instances in which a guy became suddenly and opportunistically religious. It was usually manifested in praying for his overdue girlfriend to get her period. When it occurred, it provided a happy rationale for tapping a keg at the thirty-foot bar; there were more than a few of these menstruation celebrations.

This was a pivotal time I was living in, when more and more of the good girls were defying what they had been taught and took a chance because they were in love. That seemed to be the assumption, anyway—that love was the reason, the quid pro quo, and that they were mainly doing it for the guy.

Among the boys, the girls' hormones and natural desires remained subjects unspoken and never seemed to enter the equation. If she liked sex too much, she well could move into another category in the mind of a guy. But love, and the sincerity of a boy, made it almost all right, palliating the seriousness of the situation, easing the conscience. When love was over, however, there could still be a taint in the minds of some, including the girl, because she had given herself before marriage in a relationship that didn't last. Maybe half the young women would still be virgins when they graduated, though that's not a scientific assessment. There would be quite a few young men in that category as well, though a lot of talk to the contrary.

The Kappa Nu boys liked to congregate in the living room in the evening, talking, smoking, and snacking. After parties and taking the girls home, the half-drunk, exhausted brothers would come in one by one. Among the guys who had girlfriends, there were those who were really in love but whose relationship had become routine, like a couple married for twenty years. For others, love was still fresh, and they would linger in their girls' arms for as long as they could till the curfew, when the house mother would come out and tell them they must go. Good-night kisses were exchanged on the sidewalk or in the many cars with fogged-up windows lined up outside wherever the girls lived. Guys who were serious got pinned to the girl, which often was the preliminary step to an engagement. It involved an elaborate ceremony in front of the girl's residence, in which the brothers serenaded her with the special pinning song. She would come out, and her boyfriend would pin to her chest a gold pin with the fraternity logo on it. All the girls would be looking out the window, a few with tears of joy for their lucky friend. The song was sung slowly—ironically, like a dirge, with the rhythm of the slow beat of a drum before an execution, and it went something like this: "The pin. The pin. The Kappa Nu pin. She wears it for her love." The serenade duty was supposed to be compulsory, to show solemn respect for a brother's commitment. But if the couple wasn't especially popular or the weather was bad, the turnout was small and the singing was terrible. Standing in the twenty-degree night for a guy people didn't care about made for a lot of grumbling and vulgar, denigrating jokes about what kind of children would come from this union.

One Saturday night after a party, Andy Ruby came into the living room slightly tipsy, with a gigantic grin on his face: He and my beloved Judy had gone all the way. Amid the buzz in the living room, he did not exactly treat the event confidentially. A couple of his pals gave him the old thumbs-up and a slap on the back, though there were no salacious snickers, as would have occurred if the girl was one of those kind who put out for a lot of guys. Yet this was small comfort to me, the unrequited lover. The conjugal venue, Andy revealed, was the back of his '57 Impala. I was learning much more than I cared to and went upstairs to a sleepless night.

For a while after that, I saw Judy differently. Intellectually, I knew that she hadn't done anything wrong, that she was just as likable and sweet as ever. Yet I was haunted by the vision of her and Andy in sweaty intimate passion. She was stunningly beautiful but comported herself like someone who wasn't, and I found it agreeable that she was not self-assured like other pretty girls seemed to be. Though she had a wonderful laugh, there was a seriousness about her, sometimes a sadness in her lovely brown eyes. All of the things that I loved about her were the same as before, and she was still not my girl, but something was different now: She was flawed. I was still a captive of the social values and moral attitudes of my time. I somehow knew there was hypocrisy here, but I couldn't help it. Andrew Ruby had fucked her, the girl I loved.

Maybe this question of mores, this code, was starting to crack. As the weeks went by, I found that I was still in love from a distance. I had begun to think differently on the matter; maybe it had to do with growing up and seeing things in a more mature light. She and Andy were a couple, and as such, it seemed more and more natural that they would do what comes naturally. Yet I had begun to notice something about Andy—he no longer had stars in his eyes, that transcendental look of the lover; and maybe I was imagining it, but the couple seemed less affectionate in public. Also, Andy was in trouble academically and didn't seem to care, the opposite of Judy. He had become irritable and gotten into a couple of near-fights at the house. At a party, I observed them in a mild argument. She huffed off to the ladies' room, and he seemed not to give a damn. Could this be a sign that love was fading? I unequivocally hoped so.

Sure enough, they broke up shortly thereafter. What would I do now? Protocol dictated that I couldn't just make a move immediately, before the body was cold, so to speak. It could be the last thing she wanted right then was to date some other guy. Andy was my friend and fraternity brother, and the situation was exceedingly awkward. Apparently, other fellows both inside and outside the house did not share this concern, as Judy was immediately besieged by two or three of them right off the bat. What was more, she went out with a couple of guys without hesitation, while I was sitting like a schmuck on the sidelines, crazy about her. I had to get her attention without revealing my intentions, but it seemed impossible to find her without fifty people around.

An opportunity presented itself at the Campus Center one afternoon between classes, when I saw her go into the building with another girl. I went in shortly after and met her "by chance." I was welcomed to sit down by a bubbly Judy who was delighted to see me. It was a relief to be able to look at her without having to steal furtive glances from a distance, and she looked wonderful. The three of us chatted amiably, and I got some good laughs imitating Dr. Vasquez, the head of the romance-languages department, who was known to raise the grades of those students who "volunteered" to mow his lawn. It was such a pleasure to see her laugh so heartily, and to know, at least for those moments, that it was I who had made her happy.

I don't know if the other girl sensed something or had somewhere to go, but after a few minutes, she got up and left, God bless her. I got two cups of coffee at the counter and rejoined Judith at the table. It was four o'clock in the afternoon. By the time we stopped talking, it was eight o'clock, the fastest four hours of my life. I had no sense of time or place; there was only Judy. As profound as this meeting was for me, its importance was not so much in the words we exchanged about parents, future plans, and all that. Not that we hadn't been listening to each other, but for me, her presence—being near her, absorbing her—was more important. I loved her scent of soap and a trace of Maja perfume. We didn't yet know each other well and therefore did not exchange intimacies or venture into delicate subjects like her recent relationship.

I walked her back to the Brick, wanting desperately to hold her hand, but I didn't dare. So I said good night and extended my hand, and we shook. "I really enjoyed our talk," she said, "and I want to see you again."

"Me, too."

Our hands were still clasped in the shake position when she planted a gentle kiss on my lips. "I want you to know something," she said. "I like you a lot. I've liked you for a while, and it was nice to spend time with you. I want to get to know you better."

My mouth turned dry, and I had difficulty getting words out. There was so much I wanted to say, and it was two minutes to curfew, so I went to a joke: "I don't exactly hate *you*, either." I could feel my knees shaking. "Judy, if you only knew. Well, what the hell. I've liked you from the first time I saw you. I more than like you—this word 'like' is really a substitute, because I'm sort of scared—to tell you how I really feel."

"How do you really feel?" she said without hesitation.

"I'm crazy about you," I said, too scared to use the proper word, "love," and deciding against "adore."

"Oh," she said, and threw her arms around me. We had the most wonderful kiss, the unattainable kiss I had been longing for, that happy-ending kiss from the movies; only this was the beginning. "I've got to go now," she said, running her index finger gently along my lip. "I got a little lipstick on you."

"One more, please," I said, like a man dying of thirst who has been given only one sip of water. She smiled and we kissed again, shorter but better, and she ran into the dorm, and I watched until the last fragment of her coat disappeared from view.

I stood there in the ten-degree cold that I did not feel; heard voices but could not hear words and paid no attention to them. I was numb, under a spell. I had never felt like this before. "Happy" hardly described my mood: It was more like supreme elation, exhilaration.

"Hey, Bob, what's with the new girlfriend? You and Judy?" It was Roger Lang of Kappa Nu, one of Andy Ruby's best friends. Just what

I needed. He was soon joined by a few others as we all walked back to the house. "Is this the new couple on campus? That kiss sure looked like it," said Howie Horowitz, whose date was a good friend of Judy's.

"Howie, you should have been kissing your girl instead of watching me," I said.

"This is out of the clear blue sky, how long has it been going on? Are you two an item?" said Howie.

This exchange was annoying because it was transporting me from the clouds back to earth, and I wanted to enjoy the heights a bit longer.

Earth called soon enough. I had not been back at the house ten minutes when Andrew Ruby approached me with a forced smile. He was known to be a fighter, and it flashed through my mind for a brief moment that he wanted to hit me. He seemed to be a little tense. "I heard about you and Judy. Is it true?"

"Is what true?"

"You know, you two."

"It's true that we talked."

"I heard it was more than that."

"What?"

"I heard you kissed."

"Did we? Oh yes, we had a little kiss good night."

"I heard it wasn't so little."

"Maybe so. Little, big, I don't know."

"There's no hard feelings, but it's a little uncomfortable," he told me.

"You're not still in love with her, are you?" I envisioned one of those "I still love you, take me back, darling" scenarios. Maybe he really did still love her. I loved her. How could anyone not love her?

"Nah, I'm not in love with her. I thought I was in love with her," he said. "We had a good time, though."

What did he mean by that? Quickly, that unpleasant image again, of he and Judy doing it. It was clear to me that his displeasure had more to do with proprietary rights than his heart, as if I had taken something that was his. The hell with him. I could not sleep, waiting for the next day to come; to see her, to be assured that she had not changed her mind, to kiss her again.

I arranged another chance encounter outside the Foreign Languages Building. I didn't want to wave or attract attention, so I waited on a plowed snowbank until she saw me. Her eyes lit up and told me everything I wanted to know. She carried several textbooks in her right arm and gave me a half-hug with her left.

I carried her books like a proper Joe College while we walked. "Where are you headed?" I asked.

"To the library. I have a math exam Wednesday, and I'm sick of the dorm. I can't get enough studying done there with all the noise and the gossip. Speaking of gossip," she said, "we caused quite a stir last night."

"Yeah, I know. I took a little razzing, but it was worth it," I said, not wanting to mention Andy just yet. It was too early to discuss him, but I reckoned if we were to be true lovers, the subject would be broached sometime. "You're not sorry, are you?" I said.

She smiled the most beautiful smile. "No, I'm not sorry at all."

We got to the library, and I decided to study, too, though I had no exams pending; I had only Judy pending. We sat opposite each other at a long table with a fair number of others, all studying. There was a large sign that said QUIET in the middle of the room, and there was only the sound of pages turning and an occasional cough. I opened my textbook on state and local government and began reading, but from the start, I was thinking about when and how I might look at the lovely Judy. I looked up, and she was reading and underlining. I looked up again, and our eyes met. We were a little embarrassed and went right back to our books.

This went on for about an hour. I found that I had gone over the same paragraph fifteen times and didn't have the foggiest idea what I'd read. I stopped the pretense, put down the book, and gazed unabashedly across the table, having had enough of stolen glances; I wanted to look to my heart's content. In short order, she noticed me looking at her and put down her book, and we were staring at each other straight in the eye. It was a look that I had seen in others, a gooey hearts-and-flowers look that previously made me want to puke. But I had never been a lover, and this new perspective eliminated all such negative feelings.

I couldn't stand not touching her for one more minute, so I gestured with my head for her to follow me, and I stood up and pushed back my chair. I was trying to be surreptitious, but the chair made a loud noise against the floor, like a dinosaur fart, and the whole room looked up. I ambled into the maze of library shelves, pretending to be looking for something, with Judy close behind me. I found a dusty corner and beckoned for her to join me. We looked at the same book, holding it together so that our hands were touching and I could feel and smell her sweet breath. We looked around like a couple of bandits and then crushed each other in a mad kiss.

It was not enough. We returned to the table, collected our books, and got the hell out of there as fast as we could. Where to? Privacy was so difficult to find without a car, and it was December in the snow belt, making the outdoors an option for only the hardiest of lovers. It had gotten dark, and as usual, it was snowing, and the famous Alfred carillon bells were playing a beautiful rendition of "The First Nöel." We walked along a path up the hill toward the bell tower, to a spot behind the Steinheim, an old and picturesque building that looked like a tiny castle. It was traditionally a lovers' place, and there were two or three kissing couples obscured by the scant light and the blowing snow. We put our books down on the stone steps, Judy leaned against the wall, I removed my gloves and took her face in my hands and kissed it all over. I could not see her well, but feeling her face was enough: her breathing, her holding me and squeezing me. She was far from a passive kisser—we were both hungry, and there was much that had been held back for so long. I could feel her body against mine through the dense winter clothing; Loden coats, but with our hoods on, the whole thing was cozy beyond belief. I had my arms around my girl, protecting her from the cold and snow.

It came out of my mouth before I even realized it: "I love you, Judy."

"I love you, too," she said. I took off her glove and kissed her hand, but this was not the vicarious experience of a movie; it was the real thing, to which I was unaccustomed, and it was so much better.

I gathered our books, and we returned down the dark path through flakes and mounds of white, walking so close together that we could have been participants in a three-legged race, while above us the carillon played "Joy to the World."

Christmas vacation was upon us. Judy and I would be going home together via the eight-hour Erie Lackawanna train ride, a raucous trip with dozens of reveling college students, lots of beer, singing and laughter, merry train conductors, and smiling black car porters. Minus the raccoon coats and ukuleles, it was the epitome of, dare I say it again, a Hollywood college movie. Sitting next to Judy, with rustic winter scenes of upstate New York whizzing by the window, I hoped the journey would last forever. We held, we clutched, we kissed every two minutes and kept each other warm in the chilly car.

It had been ten days since my rebirth as a man in requited love, and I had been making up for lost time. The only moments of trepidation had come during especially heavy necking sessions outside the Steinheim when it became a question of how far we would go. At these moments she gently calmed us down. The last thing I wanted to do was push it; I was content to kiss, hug, and hold; to do the virtuous thing—this despite my aching gonads, eager for release and an end to their agony after each session. My gonads notwithstanding, it was I who may not have been ready to go further.

Somewhere passing Binghamton, Judy and I were holding hands, watching the silos and telephone poles whiz by. She turned her head and leaned in to my ear. "There's something I need to tell you," she said.

"What?"

"Kiss me first."

And I did. "I know it's all so new. But I want you to know that I love you very much, and I want to know that you love me, no matter what," she said. For the first time, I realized that we were surrounded by forty noisy people, though a quick check revealed that they were not paying the slightest attention to us.

"I love you so much I can't even tell you how much," I said.

"I want to tell you . . . I need to tell you . . . that when I was going with Andy, we made love. We had sex."

Hearing it directly from her own lips, the lips that had kissed

Andy's, was an emotional jolt, but I didn't show it. "I sort of expected you would. You loved him, didn't you?"

"I thought I did. But I know now that I didn't, and I'm sorry that we went that far."

"It doesn't matter, that's over now," I said, because I couldn't think of anything else to say. Quickly, the wound that was disappearing was opened again, and those images flooded in.

"I don't want us to make the same mistake," she said.

"Are you saying it's a mistake to ever have sex until you're married?"

"No, no. It's just that it should happen at the right time. Not yet, when it's too early. It should happen when we feel sure about it."

"How will we know?"

She brushed my hair off my forehead and looked at me. "I'll know."

"You will?"

"Oh yes, I'll know. So I want you to promise me that you'll wait and be patient. Because I want to make love to you very much already, and if we do it too soon, it could—well, ruin things or . . . hurt our relationship."

Everything she said made consummate sense and was expressed in a heartfelt way. Yet this was bittersweet, in that I now felt guilty for my desire, and goddammit, Andrew Ruby had slept with her and I hadn't. Despite how close I felt to Judy, he had been intimate with her tenfold. Why couldn't I shake this crap from my mind? Because I was nineteen years old and living in December 1960, that's why.

"Does it bother you a lot? About Andy?" she said.

I cast my eyes down, then out the window, taking a long time to answer. "I know I have no right to object. It was your business—and, I guess, his. Anyway, it's over and done with."

"You're not answering my question. Does it bother you?"

"It's just that I care so much, that the thought of you and—"

She took my head to her breast and stroked my hair and said, "Don't worry. We'll be fine. I love you."

"I love you, too, Judy. Maybe it's a little painful, but I'm glad we talked about it."

"Me, too."

The train groaned to a brief stop in Hancock, New York, and we poked our noses out the door amid the loud roar of the big Lackawanna diesel. The arctic air was a shock and practically burned the lungs, but it was fresh and cleansing, like the conversation we had just had. About two hours from home, I felt comfortable enough to bring up the matter again, with a kind of mischievous smile, to tell her that I was not uptight about it. "Did you like it?"

"What?"

"Sex with Andy."

She was a little embarrassed but not offended. "I guess so, initially."

"Whaddaya mean, you guess so?"

"Should I have *not* liked it?"

She laughed and I laughed and the rest of the ride was carefree and we could talk about it easily, and it was back to the clouds. By the time we pulled into the terminal in New Jersey, I had matured by ten years: a new man, confident and in love.

Judy and I made plans to see each other as much as possible during vacation, though she lived on Long Island and I was in the Bronx. I had a driver's license, and I was sure I could get my father to lend me his huge '59 Pontiac Bonneville a few times. Then the next day, as if we hadn't seen enough snow at Alfred, there was a major blizzard in the metropolitan area, and driving was out of the question. I had to content myself with the telephone. One, two, three calls a day were not enough, until conversation was exhausted and I found myself calling just to hear the sound of her voice.

After three days I could stand it no longer and planned a trip to her home by subway and Long Island Rail Road. I had a nagging cough that had been going on for two weeks, which I had neglected through the chimera of love. My father had told me to go to the doctor several times, but I felt fine, so I dismissed the idea. The cough persisted, and my father insisted, so I promised to stop by Dr. Rosenstein's office, which was next to the subway entrance, on my way to see Judy.

Our family doctor, my old inspiration for pursuing a career in medicine, was a caring practitioner worshiped by the neighborhood. Catholics and Jews both prayed for him. He was also a little absent-minded, as when he was doing a gynecological examination on my mother and took a phone call in the next room and forgot about her, leaving her in the stirrups for a half hour—with her hat on, yet.

As someone who had known and treated me since the age of five, he wanted to know everything about what was happening with me in college while he looked into my throat and ears and poked around in my nose. All I could talk about was the anticipation of seeing Judy in a couple of hours, but as he listened to my chest, he shushed me and his expression changed. "You got that walking pneumonia again, kid. I want you to go right home to bed. Your mother can get this prescription filled."

"Go right home? You gotta be kidding, Doctor. I gotta see this girl, I've been waiting for three days, snowed in."

"No, go home, we don't want this to get serious."

"But I feel okay."

"You're not well now, but you'll be all right in a few days, and guess what, your girlfriend will still be there. Go home."

I went out on to Bainbridge Avenue and right into the subway, determined that nothing would prevent my visit. I would tell my parents that I went to the doctor and had a cold and would take care of the pneumonia later, though I very much hoped that my father would not find out about my deception.

The trip seemed to last a year, but I would have hitchhiked to Nebraska to see her, and see her I did. It was an added novelty to be out of the college setting and with her in the simple, tidy house where she was brought up. Her mother and kid sister were home, which confined our initial greeting to a small peck of a kiss, until we found a corner in the finished basement to do the job properly. It went with the territory, having to look over our shoulders every time we wanted to embrace.

Her sister was shy but her mother was not, and she got right to the point: "So, I hear you two are cuckoo about each other."

"Mother, please," Judy said, blushing.

"Uh . . . I guess 'cuckoo' could describe it," I said.

Judy's mother was a pretty, self-confident woman with a competitive twinkle in her eye, who enjoyed giving us the needle, and she continued with playful gems like "Judy is gaga over you" and "Are you gaga over her?" It was a difficult gauntlet for a first visit, but I was game for her game and as charming as I could be, which calmed Judy, who was not amused by her mother's audacity. If it was some sort of test, I think I passed, but I understood why Judy had said they didn't get along.

Her father came home, a quiet, gentle man who greeted me warmly and with dignity. He was prematurely gray, tall and thin, and looked like Judy. Like love itself, meeting the parents was a new experience for me, and slightly unnerving, because there was the incongruity of their being strangers and my passion for their daughter.

After a nice chicken dinner, we found a few moments of privacy to talk. Her parents had noticed my cough, as had she, and I let slip the doctor's admonition. Much to my chagrin, she immediately told her parents, saying that my health was more important than pride. Her father then insisted on driving the fifty-minute trip to the Bronx and would not take no for an answer. I was terribly embarrassed, but Judy came along with us, so the extra time with her was compensation, though she sat up front with her father while I sat in the back.

In front of my building, I gave her a measly buss good night, with her father looking on. After my twentieth apology, I went up to our apartment, my head in the clouds once again. I opened the door and could see my father from the back, watching live television news of the aircraft carrier *Forrestal* on fire. He did not turn around to greet me. My mother came out of the kitchen wiping her hands on a dish cloth with a concerned look that I knew well. I crashed back to earth with a bang. They had called the doctor and knew everything, and my mother's worried countenance told me that my father was livid. He turned around with that curling of his upper lip that had terrified me all my life. I was too old to smack across the face (I thought), but he was as angry as I'd seen him in a long time, and he began a tirade at the top of his lungs. "YOU HAVE PNEUMONIA, AND YOU GO TO LONG ISLAND? TO LONG ISLAND! YOU STUPID IDIOT!"

"Dad, I feel fine. I just had to see this girl. I love her, and I couldn't wait any longer."

"A GIRL! YOU WENT BECAUSE OF A GIRL! YOU LOVE HER! DON'T TALK TO ME, I DON'T WANT TO TALK TO YOU! GET OUT OF MY SIGHT!"

The television was blaring casualty reports from the carrier fire as my mother gingerly tried to intercede on my behalf. "Benny, stop yelling, the neighbors can hear. He likes this girl, he couldn't help it, he'll go right to bed now."

"YOU BUTT OUT AND MIND YOUR OWN BUSINESS!"

"Don't talk to Mother that way, it—"

"SHUT UP AND LEAVE ME ALONE!"

This was humiliating, sending me right back to my guilt-ridden, futile childhood quest to please him. I was a helpless boy again, descended rapidly from the firmament of love, which for the moment seemed very far away indeed. My father gave me the silent treatment, his ultimate punishment, for six days, and it took its toll every second that we were together in the small apartment. I could understand parental concern, but his anger was vicious. Couldn't he let up, knowing that my action was a foible of youth and for the sweetest of reasons? I found myself as angry at him as he was with me, since he had put a sizable dent in my manly romantic euphoria. Worse, Judy and I would have to wait until we went back to school before we saw each other again, So, housebound, I counted the hours until I could flee the close quarters of this, at the moment, unhappy place.

As my junior year rolled by, I was having a grand time, what with my academic studies, the theater, and my social life all ducks in a row. I truly enjoyed my classes, especially International Relations, taught by an intellectual World War II marine combat veteran named David Leach. I loved his lack of pretense, the absence of elitism in his style, though he was eminent in his field and sought after by Yale and Harvard. I also had the privilege of studying under Frederick Engelmann, the brilliant Austrian-born political scientist. He displayed all the eccentricities of the genius professor as he lectured, complete with an assortment of fidgets, tugging at his trousers, and weird facial expressions, all of which I had down pat. He replaced Professor Russell as the premier faculty imitation in my living room shtick.

My participation in the Footlight Club was marching on. We put on a production of a recent Broadway hit called *A Majority of One,* which was about an old couple, a Japanese and a Jew, who fall in love against the wishes of their families. For a change, I did not play the old Jew. The honor fell to Sara Calvalli, a vivacious English major who was the first woman I ever knew to wear black tights every day as outerwear: These Bohemians were ahead of their time. I played the old Japanese gentleman, once again using makeup and acting tricks to depict age, and an accent borrowed from a World War II movie.

A Majority of One is a fluffy piece, a little too cute for its own good, and neither Smith nor Brown was in favor of doing it. It's the sweet culture-clash idea in which the audience is charmed and amused to hear a Japanese pronounce Yiddish words and vice versa; but the professors acceded to the kids' wishes and put on the play, which was a success.

I was now the biggest star of stage in Allegheny County, New York. Judy and I were a solid couple, as steady as any on campus, and were almost always seen together. One spring afternoon in 1961, we were photographed strolling along a scenic walk and were told it might be used for the college brochure: Joe and Judy College, documented at last.

There was an important development regarding the issues of privacy and mobility: I had been given a new car. My father surprised me during spring break with a four-door Ford Galaxie sedan, a leftover 1960 model (yes, Pop had his good points, too). He presented it to me dramatically, enjoying the occasion as much as I did. It was not a flashy rich boy's car, like a number of the sports cars and convertibles parked outside the fraternity house, but who was complaining? It was brand-new and smelled like it, and it was mine. Never mind the two-hundred-horsepower engine that could push your head back when you stepped on the gas, or the stylish whitewalls; the roomy six-passenger interior was the feature I most coveted, since it would serve as a romantic refuge for my girl and me. Soon enough, we joined the motorized fogged-window throng for all we were worth.

It was all so grown up: I had my woman, my job of college, and my car. At the end of the term, it appeared that I might have an enticing future as well. The two-man drama department, the talented, tasteful, wonderful Smith and Brown, had cornered my father on Parents' Weekend and suggested that I go for graduate work in drama upon graduation. The stereotypic contrast between my New York Jewish father and these two professorial gentlemen was quite amusing. Professor C. Duryea Smith, replete with suede patches on his tweed jacket, fiddled with his pipe and very politely said, "Mr. Klein, Robert has a good deal of talent, and he should study at the Yale School of Drama." Professor Brown concurred: "Yes, indeed. Yale would be best."

My incredulous father replied, "Yale? You mean the Ivy League Yale—boolah-boolah and all that? To be an actor? A person goes to graduate school to be an *actor*? Did Eddie Cantor go to Yale to be an actor?"

Dad had an excellent point. But as I would be graduating college at only twenty, it seemed a good idea to stay in school, to pursue and immerse myself in what would now become, legitimately, my chosen field—one my father viewed with a worried eye. To his way of thinking, it would have been safer to take his suggestion and somnambulate into law school. That pretense, faint as it was, would now be cast aside, thank goodness.

There was a symmetry, in that most of my buddies would be going on to graduate school, mostly for medicine, dentistry, and law. For them there was no equivocation: It had been their goal for years, their pursuit of which had never wavered; they belonged there. What, then, could be more appropriate for me than to go where *I* belonged, to pursue my true ambition, sheltered by the comforting structure of academia? Yale, yet.

The summer was full of beaches, picnics, movies, bowling, and the deepening maturation of a loving couple. Judy came on a picnic with my extended family of cousins and aunts, and I was invited to her cousin's wedding. We had developed a good relationship with each other's parents, who approved of the courtship. We had also become

adept at stealing intimate moments at her house and in the beloved
Ford, yet not going all the way.

I was working in a Pepsi-Cola plant in Long Island City for the
summer: eight hours a day of clanging machines and intense heat.
They hired temporary additional help for the season, a few of whom
were college boys, at eighty-five dollars a week. I was an American
assembly-line worker, pride of the proletariat and a bona fide member of the Teamsters. The veteran workers, most of them grizzled tattoo types, really laid it on the novices: "Hey, college boy this" and
"Hey, college boy that." When the midmorning ten-minute-break
whistle blew, I was chastised by one of the Teamsters for not leaving
my workstation promptly enough: a union transgression I would not
commit again.

I ate my lunch on the East River pier every day and was fascinated
to watch the unloading of sugar from Filipino and German freighters.
I also enjoyed watching one of the forklift operators (the plant
bookie) scoot about the huge building and around the dock, taking
numbers and racing bets. My sandwich was always accompanied by a
Pepsi, as there happened to be about a million bottles handy, and the
company rules permitted you to drink all you wanted as long as you
did not remove any from the plant—a transgression which could get
you fired. You could just grab a cold bottle from the assembly line
before it was capped and take a swig and put the bottle in the
unwashed-bottle box.

Drinking all the free Pepsi I wanted would have been a dream
when I was eleven, but these moving lines of it were endless, and I
wondered if people would ever stop drinking it and give me a rest
from the deafening noise and repetitive routine. The place was always
two inches deep in the stuff, which was somewhat corrosive, so by
summer's end, my tough, thick work boots had turned into Egyptian
sandals. The old-timers at the plant drank soda by the ton and, not
surprisingly, had severe dental problems. Inversely, you could tell
how long someone had worked there by how few teeth he had.

I was in the bottling department, and one of my jobs was taking
flat-folded cardboard six-packs designed to hold bottles, pushing
them open, and placing them four at a time into wooden cases going

by on the assembly line. It was sometimes difficult to keep up, which made me feel like Charlie Chaplin in *Modern Times,* or Lucy in the chocolate factory. I repeated this motion over a thousand times a day for days on end, so that I could feel my hands forming the six-pack for years afterward and in my dreams.

Another job was watching clean empty bottles go by in front of a light, making sure they weren't dirty or broken before they were filled. Watching bottles go by for long periods of time is a soporific of the first order, so there were periods of dozing in which broken and contaminated ones passed my station. Odd objects frequently turned up in the previously used bottles, from bracelets and condoms to love notes between Juan and Matilda. Many of the empties had spent months in the basements of Bronx candy stores, and the occasional dead mouse presented itself: a collector's item. For some time afterward, I would thoroughly inspect any Pepsi before I drank it, fearing that it had been produced on my watch.

All in all, I had never wanted so badly for school to start. Seeing Judy only on weekends, the rivers of Pepsi, and the routine of getting up every day at six A.M. and counting the minutes to that five o'clock whistle made me long for college life.

I purchased a suit on my own for the first time, from Paul Sargents in Greenwich Village: a banker's double-breasted stripe, but far from conservative in cut. It was called a Continental suit and was very hip; the jacket was short and barely covered my buttocks. It cost $69.95, most of a week's salary, and I brought it home knowing my father would scrutinize it thoroughly, as an expert on garments and fabrics. He had always accompanied me and paid for clothing, and I was prepared for him to nitpick, though I vowed to shrug it off.

He took it out of the box and rubbed the lapels, the shoulder pads, and the lining. "How much did you pay for this?"

"Sixty-nine ninety-five."

"Yoy ishtanem! They saw you coming! They saw you coming! [He imitated a moron with a funny walk.] They said here's someone coming with money who doesn't know anything about suits. It's garbage, this suit. A piece of crap."

"What's wrong with it?"

"Look at this lapel stitching: cheap. Crappy buckram in the shoulder pads, probably reprocessed wool."

"What's buckram?"

"The stuff in shoulder pads."

"Who cares? I like the suit."

"Who cares? Who cares? You spent seventy dollars on a piece of shit."

"But it's *my* seventy dollars."

"Don't be a wise guy."

He'd gotten my dander up once again, a little reminder of who was the grown-up and who was the child. Once again, he couldn't accept the mistakes made in another rite of passage for a young man. Was I being unfair? Maybe. Of course I loved him, but I couldn't wait to get the hell out of there.

Ah, sweet autumn in the country, the bracing air, the sentimental carillon bells playing the alma mater, and everyone reading *Franny and Zooey*. College life fit me like an old glove now; I, the big wheel. I was elected social chairman of Kappa Nu, which meant that I would plan the parties, buy the kegs and booze, and hire those great black musicians from Buffalo for the big weekends.

I got a fair number of accolades for my performances in the plays from people who had never attended them before; the kind of respect usually accorded a good campus athlete. My schoolwork was well under control, with excellent grades, and I shortly got some fine news: Yale had accepted me. And of course there was Judy. Stan Friedman and I took an off-campus apartment together. I tried my hand at directing a one-act play, *Crawling Arnold*, by Jules Feiffer. It was the American premiere of the work, about a neurotic man clinging to his childhood. For years afterward, it would be the opening topic with the wonderful Jules at New York cocktail parties, that I had directed his premiere. The experience was enlightening, but I found that I couldn't shake my actor's instinct, so while watching the performance, I found myself wanting to take the stage and play all the parts myself. The Footlight Club concluded its season with *Rashomon*, the story of a Japanese bandit from ancient times. In a continuation of my Japanese specialty, I portrayed the bandit: There were no Jews in this play. I almost poked someone's eye out during the sword fight, but the production was well received.

It was inevitable. In March, Judy and I were pinned. In contrast to my experiences at previous ceremonies, I didn't find this one the least bit funny. The turnout was good, the singing as usual left much to be desired, and I went for the whole thing emotionally, hook, line, and sinker. As I put the pin on her chest, looking into her eyes, I thought the boys sounded like the Mormon Tabernacle Choir. A definite bridge had been crossed in our relationship, which was now more sanctified, the commitment more firm.

Meanwhile, Stan Friedman, my roommate, had gotten himself a nice girlfriend, a math-major Theta Chi sorority sister of Judy's named Karen Cummings. She was from Endicott, like my friend Bob Matolka, and she and Stan really hit it off. She was also a Roman Catholic, so Stan dared not tell his mother, who, to put it mildly, would have vigorously objected and disowned him.

An idea popped up among the four of us, a daring exciting notion to go to Niagara Falls for a weekend. It would require courage, secrecy, careful strategic planning, and lying through our teeth. Any way you looked at it, this was heavy stuff for all of us, very much against the rules, with potentially serious consequences. Nevertheless, we were all keen, besotted with romance, and decided to do it, picking a weekend in April.

In the weeks before D-day, the four of us were all smiles and conspiratorial winks. The plan was for the girls to sign out for the weekend, pretending to be going home in order to circumvent curfew; Stan and I would pick them up in my car at a secluded place near campus. Unmarried couples did not rent motel rooms without questions and opprobrious glances in 1962, so we planned to buy cheap wedding bands at a Woolworth's on the way. The night before, Judy and I talked about the trip as if it were a honeymoon, but left unspoken was what sleeping in the same room and marriage bands implied. There was a nervous anticipation, like the feeling one must get before parachuting from a plane (a feeling there was little chance *I* would ever experience).

After class on Friday at about one o'clock, we gathered in the car and successfully scooted out of town without being seen (the girls in the backseat crouched down out of sight), west toward Niagara. Once we were safely on the road, Stan joined Karen in the backseat, and my honey sat shotgun for the two-hour journey. In Scio, New York, a tiny town that looked like it had been built in frontier times, we spotted a five-and-dime. We discovered that we had not discussed the logistics of the ring purchase, a crucial element of the operation. Should one of us go in or a couple? Either way, we could arouse suspicion in a clerk or a nosy customer. Why was a young man buying a fifty-cent imitation gold wedding band? Would a young couple, even in Scio, have bought such a sacred keepsake in a Woolworth's?

My car was amply stickered with the Alfred University name and logo: Some snooping prude might put two and two together and report us. It had happened before. "All right, you kids hold it right there. Hello? Operator, get me Alfred University. Hello, Dean Whitlow? I've got four of your students here trying to buy phony wedding bands. Yeah, that's right. Probably trying to shack up out of wedlock."

Karen made a suggestion: "Why don't you or Stan tell them you're getting married tomorrow and the real ring has been misplaced?"

"Why would I be getting two of them?" I asked.

Karen said, "You've been so careless that you want an extra ring in case you lose another one."

"Too complicated, they won't believe that," said Stan.

"Maybe we only need one ring," said Karen. "We could check in to the motel separately, and once a couple is inside, they can pass the ring to the other couple."

"Too complicated," said Stan. "We need two rings."

"Absolutely," I said. "Anyway, we'll have to go in and out of the motel. What if one of the girls is seen without a wedding ring?"

"Maybe we should get four rings and you boys wear them, too," said Judy.

"Is that necessary?" I said. "My father doesn't wear one."

"Mine does," said Judy.

"So does mine," said Karen.

"Mine, too," said Stan.

It was decided that I would go in alone and purchase four wedding rings, the explanation for which was up to my improvisational mind, if indeed an explanation was needed. There was always the happy possibility that I would see what I want, take it to the cashier, and leave without comment, sneer, or confrontation.

I entered the store with the mentality of a criminal pulling off a job, and soon located a counter with dozens of rings: diamonds, rubies, and emeralds, all under two dollars. There were many engagement rings, but being engaged wouldn't do us any good, we had to be married. I looked and looked, but there were no wedding bands. Then I heard those dreaded words: "Can I help you, sir?" The woman was speaking in a Scio accent, so I decided to answer her in the same dialect, to avoid being downstate conspicuous. "Oh, hi, yeah. We're heeaving a castume perty, and I'm looking fer those . . . what do you coll thim . . . those little rings theat people put an ther fingers when they're merried?"

"YOU MEAN WEDDING BANDS?" she said, a little too loudly.

"Uh, yeah, but nat real ones, for goodness sake, just cheap fake ones. Lerd, we're nat married, we're just pretending for the castume perty."

"What ere you going eas?" she asked.

"Oh, Romeo and Juliet . . . and her parents."

"Theat's vury original," she said as she pulled out a tray with phony wedding bands. "You wahnt diamonds er gold?" she said.

This was getting complicated and I glanced around to make sure no one was watching me. "Anything. How about diamonds fer Juliet and Mrs. Capulet and gold for the men?" I said, anxious to get moving.

"Wull, in theat case, you better take two diamond engagement rings, too. Girls nermally wear engagement rings with diamond wedding bands like these," she said.

"Good idea. I'll take these two, and these and those. That's six, right?"

"Yeah. But eren't these diamond ones too madern for Romeo eand Juliet?"

"No, I don't think so, they're fine. I'll take um."

"Okeydoke."

She rang up the rings on the noisy cash register. "Sex dallers eand sex cents." She put them in a bag and I was off. "I hope you win fer best castume," she said as I darted out the door to the getaway car.

On the road again, we divided up the loot like the John Dillinger gang. "These engagement rings are the phoniest-looking things I ever saw," said Judy.

Karen agreed. "They don't look real. They'll attract more attention and suspicion if we wear them," she said.

"Why don't they just wear the wedding bands?" said Stan.

"The girl in the store said this kind of band is always worn with a ring like those," I said.

"Why didn't you get all gold ones?" Judy asked.

"I thought it would look suspicious if we all had on exactly the same band."

"I don't think what she said is necessarily true, that we have to wear two rings," said Karen.

"Maybe in Scio it's the custom that if you have a fifty-cent wedding band, you have to wear a two-dollar engagement ring," I said.

It was decided that the girls would go with the bands only. There was much self-conscious giggling as we put on the rings and contemplated our fingers, though none of them fit properly and were jerry-rigged with Band-Aids to stay on.

Before long, we were in the vicinity of Niagara, though still a few miles from the falls. Much to my surprise, it was an incredibly ugly area of industrial sites, some abandoned, that were built to take advantage of the cheap power source. Somehow I did not expect such eyesores so close to one of the most beautiful places on earth. Then we saw an assortment of motels advertising vacancies and had to decide on which one and how to pass as married. "Just look bored with each other," I quipped.

"That's not funny," Judy said. "You won't be bored," and she gave me a little kiss.

We pulled up in front of a decent-looking place with "Niagara" in the name and gave one another an "Are you ready?" look. We decided to enter together; going in as separate couples could raise a red flag if someone noticed that we came in one car. The lobby was done up in rustic wood, with a large American flag and an appropriate deer head staring at us as we approached. At least *he* wouldn't tell. The place smelled a little damp, like wood that had survived another ferocious western New York winter, and the unsmiling survivor behind the desk looked like just the kind of son of a bitch who would turn us in. He was about fifty, American Gothic, with a cowboy string tie. "Good afternoon, checking in?"

"Yes, uh . . . the four of us," I said. "That is, two couples."

"Newlyweds?"

Karen was about to say yes when I cut her off: "No. We've been married for two years, and they've been married for one. We're just getting away, you know, for the weekend . . . see the falls . . . left the kid with my mother-in-law."

Judy and Stan were about to choke, while Karen, an incessant giggler, almost broke out laughing. But the guy pushed the register forward for me to sign. I signed the predecided "Mr. and Mrs. Robert Henry, New York City." Stan signed "Mr. and Mrs. Charles MacDonald, Hackensack, New Jersey." He looked like a Charles MacDonald like I looked like a Wong Fong, but the guy paid no mind and gave us the keys. We felt an urge to run to the rooms and private sanctuary, but we walked nonchalantly, to look normal and unassuming. We split up, and I closed and locked the door behind Judy and me, forgoing the urge to carry her over the threshold. Alone at last, we fell down on the bed, clenching and grabbing. Judy suddenly interrupted: "Let's see the falls first. I really want to see the falls."

"You're right, I want to see them, too. But we have to wait until this bulge in my pants goes down before I'm presentable in public."

I knocked on the MacDonalds' door, and they had the same desire to see Niagara Falls that the Henrys did, so off we went. The beauty and power of these falls was beyond unbelievable, beyond stunning. Judy and I wrapped around each other in the chilly spray and wind, against the incessant roar. Standing there together amid such majesty, I felt like the cascades were performing just for us, like a thunderous cosmic show; and when we left, they would rest until we returned. It was small wonder that honeymoon couples came here to feel alone even among people.

We went to the Canadian side, whose vista was even more gorgeous, and saw a couple of red-clad Royal Canadian Mounted Police, which made me realize that this was my first trip outside the United States. We had a nice dinner in Ontario and, broadened by travel to a foreign land, we returned to our new home, the lovely Room 120 at the Niagara Something Motel.

Upon locking the door, we looked in each other's eyes. We kissed, we lay down together, and slowly, we removed each other's clothing in the semidarkness. "We'd better hurry, it's close to curfew," I whispered as I kissed her breasts.

"Yes, the house mother's coming to get me. She ought to see me now," Judy whispered back as she ran her hand down my thigh. For a while, we could hear only our breathing and the little slurping sounds made by eager lips and tongues. A few cars whizzed by on the road, their headlights sending momentary dancing pools of light across the window shade. It was all so gentle, taking our time like this, and while I was hot as could be, I was in no hurry. We were naked, entwined like a kudzu vine around a slender tree. I had to speak, I simply had to speak: "Judy, I love you."

"I love you very much," she whispered back. "Do you have protection?"

"Of course, that was in the plan," I said as I leaped out of bed, looking like the letter L, and grabbed a package of prophylactics from my bag. My hands were a little unsteady as I unwrapped the thing and tried to put it on. She assisted me, taking care that it was rolled as high as possible. She lay down and beckoned me with outstretched arms and the most beautiful look on her face: part smile, with the slightest glistening of moisture in her eyes.

I was inside her now, though we were really inside each other. I was in a new place, a place I belonged, and it felt like home. How do I describe it? I had enough trouble describing Niagara Falls. The two experiences were similar in grandeur and emotion, power and permanence; I felt that a monumental event had occurred, and that I would be making love like this to her for the rest of my life. Though the sex by itself was exciting, I had never experienced the awesome combination of love *and* sex that I'd heard about all my life. Before Judy, sex as a concept had been naughty, lacking in romance, and romance as a concept had been sexless. It occurred to me that before we began dating, when I was worshiping Judy from afar, I had never even had a sexual fantasy about her, but rather a vision of us married, with adorable kids bouncing on our knees. Making love to Judy was tender and sexy at the same time: the perfect combination of naughty and nice.

We lay together on the queen-size bed, looking at the sprinting headlights on the ceiling, exhausted, secure, happy. "Thank you, my darling," I said. I had never used the word "darling" before, but I used it unself-consciously. Love makes you say things like "darling" and "I adore you" and "I love you" and not be embarrassed.

"Thank *you*," she said as we maneuvered our bodies around each other like a couple of mating pythons. "Oh, Judith." "Oh, Robert."

Then it was morning, and she was next to me, facing me. I had never seen her sleeping before, so I took advantage of the opportunity to drink her in, unseen. I was careful not to move, since I did not want her to awaken just yet. Her face was perfectly serene, with none of the drooling, openmouthed facial contortions or snoring common to sleepers. Her eyes opened and met mine, a big smile from both of us, a kiss. "Well, here we are," I said. "Do we hate ourselves in the morning?"

"Uh-uh," she said. We not only didn't hate ourselves in the morning, we positively *loved* ourselves in the morning and were soon entangled in a blissful way again. The Niagara Falls adventure was a great success, and there were four happy people in the car going home.

Knowing where I would be the next year, and looking forward to it, made the rest of the term a pleasant coast to graduation. Judy decided to transfer to Hofstra University to be nearer to me. I would come home from New Haven on weekends, and she would live at home; there lay the only serious rub, because she and her mother were less than harmonious.

When classes and finals were at last over, only the seniors were left until the ceremony, which would occur in five days. It was the first

week of June, and there was a heat wave, and the boys took to fre-
quenting an old local swimming hole right out of Tom Sawyer. The
portable radio blared out our rock-and-roll favorites as we bebopped
around, singing along: "Ooh, baby . . . I want to know, will you be my
girl?" Beer cans in hand, future doctors, dentists, lawyers, actors, not
a care in the world. Then caps and gowns, long boring speeches in the
summer heat, proud parents, handshakes, and hugs, and it was over.

Chapter Ten

Yale and Beyond

It was my first day of classes at Yale, and I was walking down York Street amid the ivy and the bicycles, in my tweed jacket and plaid tie, once again right out of the school brochure. As if the lovely scene were not stereotypic enough, I suddenly heard men's voices singing "The Whiffenpoof Song": "From the tables down at Mory's / To the place where Louie dwells." For a second, I thought I was hallucinating a cliché, but I backed up a few steps and the sign said Mory's: the very place they were singing about. I took this to be a good omen.

The campus was mighty impressive, with a mixture of traditional and modern architecture and excellent facilities, in contrast to tiny Alfred. The water fountains were offered to all races, but the undergraduate colleges were still all-male.

The School of Drama was different from the rest of the university, however, with a student body that included women and Bohemian theater types. It had a brilliant reputation, which was well deserved in areas like playwriting, directing, and scenic and costume design; for actors at that time, it was a mixed bag. I did learn a few basics of the acting craft, and most importantly, this was no longer an extracurricular activity. I found myself steeped in the world of theater. Constance Welch, the school's acting coach—who had previously taught Julie Harris and Paul Newman—was a melancholy septuagenarian given to tearful reveries about having seen a 1927 Gielgud *Hamlet*. She no longer possessed the good communication skills she once had regarding what she was trying to convey and who she was trying to instruct. We watched her work on scenes with our classmates, but her remarks and suggestions were murky, abstract, frequently personal. On those rare occasions when she worked on my practice scenes at all, her comments seemed out of touch, and I would inject humor into the serious proceedings, which got big laughs from the class. She invariably said the same thing: "Klein, you ought to do a one-man show." Maybe she was a better prophet than an acting teacher.

She seemed to take little interest in the majority of the students, all of whom had been vetted from college programs around the country and had obvious talent. Her efforts were directed mainly at her favorites, Robin Strasser and Louise Schaefer (who undoubtedly showed great promise), while the rest of the class looked on longingly like neglected puppies in the litter. Every week, after my Saturday-morning Theater History class with Professor Alois Nagler (who wrote the definitive book on Shakespeare's Globe Theater), I drove home to the Bronx and then, in the evening, to Malvern for my date with Judy.

As the fall progressed, she was, as expected, becoming more and more unhappy living at home in conflict with her mother. She was surrounded by girlfriends who were getting married one by one, and she put the subject of engagement and marriage on the table, which scared the hell out of me. I think she saw it as some sort of solution to her problems and had not thought it out clearly. I was a twenty-year-old schoolboy supported by my father, who himself had no money: a perfect candidate for marriage. Yet I had begun to feel guilty about her unhappiness, feeling that I was the cause for her transfer from Alfred, where she had thrived. All this was beginning to affect the way we felt during our time together: less happy, not as optimistic.

I brought up the subject of marriage with my father, in a hypothetical way, of course, and he replied with hearty, derisive laughter that was in no way hypothetical. "You? How you gonna support a wife?"

"I know, Dad. I'm just talking in theoretical terms."

"Theoretical, my tuchas. Just study in school, and let's pray you can make a living as an actor."

I knew he was right, but I couldn't help going through some of the motions, like looking at engagement rings in jewelry-store windows in New Haven, or daydreaming of marital privacy and sex somewhere other than a car. Judy and I had settled into a routine, and we had begun taking each other for granted. The Saturday-night bowling and movies, capped by some stolen sexual moments while looking over our shoulders for her parents to walk through the door, were losing their luster. There was an incident in which her mother gave her a hard time about a stain on the couch that we made while having sex. This threw a nice dignified monkey wrench into the already strained situation and caused a giant fight between Judy and her mother. Maybe Judy resented me a little, and maybe I resented her for resenting me; in any case, we rolled right along like nothing had happened.

That is, until early December, when Judy called me on a Saturday afternoon and broke our date for that night. She said she didn't feel well, but I could sense that something was wrong, so I pursued the matter. "I think we should cool it for a while," she said.

"What do you mean, cool it?" I asked.

"I mean . . . not see each other for a while."

A chill ran down my spine. "How long are you talking about? A week? A month?"

"I'm not sure," she said.

"Can I call you during that time?"

"It's best if you don't," she said.

"Did you meet another guy?"

"No."

I hung up the phone, stunned. She was breaking up with me, I was sure of it. Suddenly, the doldrums I had begun to feel with Judy disappeared, and I forgot any little negative thought I had ever had about her. I could only remember the good things. She was perfect and I loved her and wanted her more than ever. I could not raise even the slightest feeling of anger toward her, only adoration. The thought of not seeing her, not being with her, losing her, seemed unthinkable, unbearable. I tried to comfort myself with the possibility that she really meant what she said about cooling it for "a while," but I didn't really believe deep down that that was what she meant.

Thus began five months of torture for the once-again-unrequited lover. I was obsessed with thoughts of Judy morning through night, hoping she'd call, wanting to call her but waiting for a while, whatever a while meant. With every ring of the telephone, I hoped it was she, calling to tell me that everything was all right. Every song on the radio had profound meaning again, just as they had when I fell in love. I was filled with heartache when I heard a favorite song we had danced to, like "The Closer You Are" or "Earth Angel," and every lyric seemed to have a new and deeper significance, no matter how banal or corny. It seemed that in breaking up I was paying attention to all the same things I had done when I fell in love, though the feeling was no longer ecstasy. Maybe if I proposed to her, it would set things straight. No, I couldn't do that.

After four weeks and with trembling hands, I called her. She was surprised but did not sound particularly enthusiastic. "Look, have we cooled it long enough?" I asked. "I feel so terrible, I want to get back with you."

"I don't think that would be good," she said.

"Why not?"

"Because I'm not ready to get back together. I'm not sure I want to."

"What do you mean?"

There was a pause. "I've met someone," she said. When I had recovered from the lightning bolts that struck me and the sledgehammers that pounded me and the bullets that ripped through my chest, I spoke: "Who?"

"No one you know, he goes to Hofstra."

"I guess that's that, then," I said, hoping that that wasn't really that.

"I'm sorry about this, I didn't plan it this way," she said.

"Can we ever talk?" I asked, attempting to hold on to some fragment of her.

"We'll talk sometime," she said.

And it was over, two years after it had started. My depression became unrelenting. I was carrying a torch for the first time in my life, and it was a desperate and helpless feeling. At that point I definitely did not feel that it was better to have loved and lost than never to have loved at all. Fuck Shakespeare. I was sorry that I had ever met Judy. I was obsessive about the breakup, talking endlessly about it to my friends, who were patient and sympathetic, but up to their ears in it. Jim Burrows, my Yale buddy, bore the brunt of my moaning at school, while Al Uger, my oldest friend, who was at Columbia studying dentistry, helped me handle the blues at home. Minus the true misery, I presented a rather comic figure: moping like a hound dog, sighing at the moon, depressive body language, yearning for something I could never have again, day after day.

I turned to my father for advice and found him understanding but firm, in his usual blunt way. I explained that I wanted to telephone Judy, even if I only talked to her mother, who was fond of me, and left a message. "You're trying to go through the back door," he said. "It's her you want, not her mother, and she found someone else, so forget about it."

Life went on, but barely. When the spring thaw came, Jim Burrows tried to distract me with golf in New Haven, but I perfected the game quickly and became bored. The challenge was gone when I could consistently get the ball through the elephant's trunk and onto the water wheel. Radios all over were playing the hit song: "If you want to be happy for the rest of your life / Never make a pretty woman your wife." It broke my heart, because I had thought I would never again be happy for the rest of my life—without Judy.

Surprisingly, school provided a welcome respite from my ruminating. I was busy performing and directing scenes, appearing in a major production, and of course there were classes: in elocution, directing, theater history, and acting. There was a compulsory course for actors called Movement for the Theater, which was really a class in modern dance. It was taught by Pearl Lang, who was a direct disciple of Martha Graham, one of the premier names in modern dance. Miss Lang rarely smiled and was a taskmaster, expecting hard work and positive results from a group composed largely of actors with no dance training whatsoever.

I had been instructed to buy tights and a device whose existence I was unaware of: a dance belt. After trying it on in my room, I concluded that the thing caused a fair amount of pain to the male genitals, as its purpose seemed to be to make all dancers, male or female, look the same from the waist down—neutered. I opted for my familiar jock strap for the first class, but a simple look at everyone else's flat groin told me that I had made the wrong choice. "You are improperly dressed for class, you must wear a dance belt," Miss Lang told me sternly.

"But it's too painful, Miss Lang," I whined, which got a hoot from the others.

"You'll get used to it," she said with the blithe ignorance of someone who doesn't have testicles.

In the course of my brief dancing career, she asked my body to do things that it had never done before. I had been a ballplayer all my life, but learning the five ballet positions, leaping and contracting across the room to bizarre piano music, barefoot in tights, was a lesson in humility. I hid in the back of the group, hoping she wouldn't see me make a mess of her art. I counted my lucky stars that the old gang in the Bronx couldn't see me now. I enjoyed watching Pearl do the various moves, the flow of the diaphanous fabric she wore, her grace and strength; it was a truly formidable thing to watch, my eye-opening introduction to dance as art. But doing it myself was another matter, an exercise in futility.

My classmates at the School of Drama were an interesting, often eccentric bunch: a combination of actors, directors, playwrights, lighting, and set designers ranging from the super-serious to the kidders. One of the directing students was a talented nun from Washington University in St. Louis named Sister Wilma. I had never known a nun before. She was friendly, outgoing, and seemingly too hip to be a nun, so I asked her a lot of questions about why she had become one, which she answered patiently. She wore the full habit at all times, though I could tell she was an attractive woman. She told me that she had been a girl who enjoyed parties and the company of men and had planned to get married, like most young women, but then came the revelation of her life. In any case, she was considered a hell of a directing prospect and one of the best in our class, taught by Nikos Psacharopoulos. We each got to direct scenes and then listened to the critiques from the teacher and our classmates. Sister Wilma directed a scene from *A Streetcar Named Desire* and presented it one day. Some guy in the class had several criticisms and called the direction "vulgar." She was very offended by his characterization and answered,

"I have been called a lot of things in my time, but 'vulgar' isn't one of them." Then she lifted her skirt to her shins and did a brief jig while saying, "Boop-oopy-doop, the vulgarest nun in showbiz." It brought the house down with applause.

Another classmate was a Franciscan priest named Crispin McGuire, who sometimes wore his collar, chain-smoked Luckys, and loved to go out for brewskies with the boys. He was a fun-loving man from a prominent, wealthy Connecticut family and had entered the priesthood in his mid-thirties. If nothing else, I learned that nuns and priests, these mysterious, costumed characters, could be multidimensional, interesting people and friends.

The acting students came to Yale having been the stars of their college productions and now had to prove themselves in a more competitive, advanced setting, starting at the bottom rung. Jim Burrows, a directing student, was my pal in comedy. It was in his genes, given that his father was Abe Burrows, the great Broadway writer, director, and illustrious wit who then had the biggest hit in New York: *How to Succeed in Business Without Really Trying*. Jimmy took me to the show about ten times, and we sat in the aisle, stood, or watched from the wings. I met Bobby Morse, Michelle Lee, Donna McKechnie, and a bevy of beautiful dancers smelling of perfume and makeup. I met Charles Nelson Reilly smelling of perfume and makeup. He had a comical feud going with Jim: "Ding-dong, Jimmy, the school bells are ringing, go back to college already."

I couldn't get enough of Morse and his virtuoso performance, which, as far as I could tell, broke all of Miss Welch's acting rules. He mugged, he went over the top, then he brought down the house with a simple turn of his head or the subtlest gesture. His performance was perfect for this delightful cartoonish musical, and I'd never heard such laughter. He had the timing down pat, total command, and he made it look easy, as if he was enjoying it as much as the audience.

I got the backstage opportunity to see how the Broadway magic was made, how the scenery changes went up and down, in and out, like clockwork. It turned out it was all the work of cigar-chomping, third-generation-on-the-job Irish stagehands who all had the *Daily News* in their back pockets.

I did know *this*. I wanted to do what Bobby Morse did. I didn't think of Judy when I had these hopeful theater daydreams, except that I envisioned her coming to my star Broadway dressing room one day with her boring insurance-salesman husband, sorry she hadn't married me. Jimmy had a beautiful sister named Laurie, who was my first date since I had gone into mourning. Come to think of it, the cloud *had* lifted a bit. The Drama School scene felt eons removed from falling in love at Alfred. Also, I had tasted big-time show business and the life of the rich and celebrated. I spent time with Jimmy and his father at Abe's beautiful apartment at the Beresford on Central Park West. He took us in a stretch limousine with Bobby Morse to the Giants championship football game at Yankee Stadium, where I heard some inside show-business tidbits.

During the ride, Morse angrily complained to Abe about how the choreographer Bob Fosse had taunted him during the pre-Broadway run in Philadelphia. "You can't do it," Fosse had told him. Abe soothed him with diplomacy: "I know he was tough on you, but it's not personal, he just wants excellence." They both had a laugh about how cheap Rudy Vallee was; he was one of the show's stars. For the six-degree temperature at the game, Abe had purchased expensive special shoes at Abercrombie & Fitch: just for a football game! If you could afford it, why not keep your feet warm?

I was invited to several parties at the Beresford, where the elevator came right to the foyer of the apartment and there were rooms and rooms without end. I was thrilled to meet John Steinbeck, Sidney Kingsley, and Madge Evans, who played with W. C. Fields in the film *David Copperfield*. The place smelled of expensive vanilla candles, and men with short white jackets carried around trays of caviar and champagne. The great composer Frank Loesser, who wrote the music and lyrics for *How to Succeed* and *Guys and Dolls,* entertained at the piano and was especially warm to Jimmy, his collaborator's son, and to me, a kid trying not to gawk. Abe did a turn at the piano as well, the way he had in the living rooms of Hollywood stars when he'd been a premier radio writer of *Duffy's Tavern* and a funny must-invite guest at the best parties. I especially loved his hilarious titles for songs, like "How You Gonna Keep 'Em Down on the Farm After They've Seen the Farm." Bob Fosse and his wife, Gwen Verdon, made an elegant grand entrance in matching formal suede slippers, with dancers' grace, as if the whole thing had been choreographed.

I hoped that this life might await me in the future, but in the meantime, I was a student with a long way to go. I was getting good experience in the major productions in school, though in two out of the three plays, my roles were small. The acting course continued to be an enigma, so, ever the performer, I took it upon myself to entertain my classmates, fulfilling the spirit if not always the letter of the assignment. I was a very funny loaded pistol and an amusing mute in two of the exercises. My pièce de résistance was created for an exercise in the use of makeup, and to parody Miss Welch's one-man-show remarks. As was the custom, everyone did a two-person scene from a well-known play, but I chose to create an original scene (a monologue, of course). I applied a reddish-brown makeup with war paint to the right side of my face to portray a sort of clichéd American Indian, and I glued a little feather to my right ear. I applied an exaggerated pale color to the other half of my face to portray the white man. I cut a cowboy hat in half and wore the left half on the left side of my head. I sat in a swivel chair with my profile to the audience, so that with a push of my legs, I could turn 180 degrees, expose one side or the other of my face, and have a conversation with myself. The text of the dialogue was out of a grade-B Western, about making peace with the Great White Father, while the Indian spouted something about the white man speaking with forked tongue. I played both roles, though with a deadly seriousness, quite dramatically. Indian side facing audience: "You speak of peace and staying on the reservation, but squaws are starving." Swivel chair to White Man facing audience: "Blackhawk, you are brave and a great leader, but you cannot defeat the blue coats." Swivel chair to Indian facing audience: "We will die before we lose the pride that has made us." Swivel to White Man: "Please, Blackhawk . . ." Swivel to Indian: "Speak no more, Long Knife."

The class loved it, big laughs, and even Miss Welch managed a confused smile before telling me again that I ought to do a one-man show. After a year of this, I felt that I'd had enough training, that I wanted to go out in the world and work. I thought my formal education was over.

Chapter Eleven

Summer Stock and Hard Knocks

Not surprisingly, starting on June 21, summer came. A few weeks later, I was in South Hadley, Massachusetts, working in summer stock, living in a dormitory room on the campus of Mount Holyoke College, which was and is an all-female school. Unfortunately, the women were gone for the summer, but I made it a point to leave the toilet seats up at the end of my stay in order to cause a controversy when the girls returned in the fall.

Curtis Canfield, the dean of the School of Drama, was coming to Holyoke to reprise his Yale production of *Fashion,* a nineteenth-century American melodrama in which I played the very good role of a villain named Joseph Snobson. I did not look forward to his visit, as I had a slight sense that I was betraying him by not returning to school, the school at which he had accepted me, and where he expected to see me in a few weeks. Though I had mixed feelings about the School of Drama, I was considered a talented prospect whom they wanted back.

I was no longer depressed about Judy, but I sometimes wondered where she was and if she ever thought of me. There were a lot of young women in and around the summer theater community, including actresses and cute college apprentices covered with paint, whose presence was intriguing to a recovering boy officially on the loose. I was little interested in getting into a love affair; I was more interested in getting into them. It felt odd the first time I made out with one of them, as if I were cheating on Judy; but, as with riding a bicycle, I reacquired the hang of it in about a nanosecond and drowned my previous sorrow in their charms.

There were plenty of parties and opportunities to socialize, and in general, the energy and enthusiasm generated around the Casino in the Park Playhouse, in work *and* play, was exhilarating. The "park" in question was unfortunately an amusement park, in whose center the theater was located. Among the more ambitious productions was *Romeo and Juliet*. The weird juxtaposition of Shakespeare with the accompaniment of roller coasters, calliopes, and people hawking cotton candy left much to the audience's imagination. "Ah, sweet Mercutio is dead. That gallant spirit hath—" "Hey, cotton candy here! Hey, guess your weight for fifty cents!"—"aspired the clouds, which all too soon did know his grace."

My character, Benvolio, had a sword fight with Tybalt, which was carefully choreographed by a fencing master. In dress rehearsal it was perfect and believably authentic, but on opening night James Dodson, the Tybalt, forgot all the choreography in his nervousness and came at me with a maniacal look in his eyes, swinging his sword wildly. Forget about avenging Mercutio's death, I was forced to run for my life: a less than Shakepearean moment.

The interaction, though, with professional actors, many with Broadway experience, was invaluable to the novice; and some praiseworthy performances in George Bernard Shaw, James Thurber, and Bertolt Brecht plays made me believe that I had a future on the stage. The general word was that I was good, especially for a beginner. Ted Mann, of the Circle in the Square Theatre in New York, had come up to Holyoke to direct George Bernard Shaw's *Pygmalion,* in which I played Freddy Eynsford Hill. I told him that I did not want to return to Yale. He had long talks with me about my ambiguous year there and came to the same conclusion. This would be a monumental move, as I was only twenty-one and had been going to school all my life, so the concurrence of an expert comforted me in my decision.

There was an actress named Georgia Parks, who seemed a distant personage. We had hardly spoken, though I admired her work, which was acknowledged to be among the very best in the company. She was about twenty-six years old, not a beautiful woman in the conventional way, but her smile, her dark eyes, and the magnetic power she projected onstage made her very appealing indeed, and very sensual. She quickly became my number one fantasy, though the reality seemed re-mote, since I was nobody and she was in an exalted position.

During rehearsal for *A Thurber Carnival*, we became friends. It turned out that Georgia was not remote at all, but quite a friendly woman and a terrific laugher whose nostrils flared when she got excited. She called me Bobby, and we found a lot to laugh about. I recounted to her the saga of Judy, which by now had become more historical than emotional, with only the slightest twinge of regret. The story had the patina of many tellings, and for the first time I was actu-ally bored by my discourse on the subject. Georgia was a sympathetic ear, but she was a thoroughly optimistic person who emphasized look-ing forward, moving on: "You've got a wonderful life ahead of you." She wasn't just repeating jargon for my sake; she actually believed it.

The common cold had been going around the company two days before the opening of the Thurber piece, but Georgia wasn't worried. "I have no time for a cold," she said as I sneezed.

"What if you had time for a cold?"

"Then the cold would have to make an appointment, and I would decide whether or not to have it." She laughed, and her nostrils flared, and she posed like a flamenco dancer but without the stomping.

Though Georgia and I had no claim on the other, I began to be self-conscious about pairing off with young women around her. We were platonic friends, but I thought of her sexually in my private moments, though I made no move to change things. She seemed to have no negative feelings about my social life, even teasing me a few times with a slap on the back like a big sister: "Hiya, lover boy." Yet we were physical with each other, with hugs, little kisses, and shoulder rubbing. My unforgivably licentious thoughts were held in check because Georgia was such a decent person, and some part of me still considered a sexual overture to be wrong. She was far from prudish, but she was a proper and accomplished young woman: a good girl who had never behaved in a provocative manner toward me.

One night after rehearsal, we were playing gin rummy in her room in the quaint New England bed-and-breakfast where she was living for the summer. We had played for an hour, and I got up to leave, and at the door I delivered my usual peck on the lips and a hug. Only this time, I was more aware that our bodies were touching, and the hug was extending, and our hands began rubbing on our backs sensually, as opposed to the comforting taps of friends.

Before I knew it, we were in a mad, wild, groping kiss. In five seconds, we were on the bed, ripping our clothes off, sending the deck of cards everywhere, releasing what had been pent up for weeks. She said things in my ear: sensual things, naughty things, things she'd wanted to do to me. Uninhibited now, I released a torrent of words about what *I'd* been thinking about. It was the hottest, most spontaneous episode of my brief sexual life to that point, and it felt quite natural and right—though in a bow to my pragmatism, we took care not to make too much noise and alert the neighbors. We decided that even though we were single, we would keep our liaison a secret (we also vowed to have as many liaisons as possible, whenever and wherever). Georgia had been in several summer-stock theaters and suggested it was best for all concerned that it be nobody's business but our own. "Everyone knows we're friends, but there's an awful lot of gossip in a place like this. I like it being our secret, don't you? It kind of makes me more horny," she said.

"Yes it's true, it makes it even hotter," I said.

We looked at each other, so close that our eyes were out of focus. "I can't believe I'm lying here naked with Georgia Parks," I said.

"I can't believe it, either. My little Bobby."

"What do you mean, *little?*" We laughed. "Now I'd like to make love to Georgia Parks again."

"I hope you're not waiting for a printed invitation," she said as she pulled me to her.

I would like to state officially that I was no longer in the doldrums. I was no longer depressed or sorrowful, as it was turning into a hell of a summer: professionally satisfying, and a sexual dream. My only enemy was exhaustion, held at bay by youth and ardor. Georgia, it seemed, hadn't had much sexual experience, either; but, like me, she was a sensual individual given to fantasy. Our sexual relationship became a learning process, with a lot of exploration of things we'd thought about and wanted to do. Of course, the term "learning process," while true, is somewhat cold and misses the mark in describing what Georgia and I did together. She was a sexual soul mate who was on the same page, and it was such a good page that I didn't want to turn it.

The dean came and directed his play, but I didn't have the courage to tell him my decision then. I would write him a letter. "Bobby, I'll see you back at school in four weeks," he said before he left. I nodded and smiled guiltily, knowing the scary truth.

I was sorry the summer was over. No longer a schoolboy, I had to make a career from scratch, with little knowledge of how it was done. From here, it looked like I'd be scaling Mount Everest, while I had trained only on the Poconos. I had studied how to speak, to move, and to pretend, but no one had taught me the business end of the actor's life—how to get a job.

What was worse, I would be living at home in the Bronx for the first time in five years, on my Castro convertible ottoman in the living room. Georgia had an apartment on the Upper East Side, which I visited regularly for hanky-panky, though, in all honesty, more panky than hanky. Professionally, she had options popping up daily, as her agent got her several auditions, one of which resulted in an offer for a decent part in a road company. She turned it down because she was up for a Broadway show, and her agent felt there was a good chance she would get it. Sure enough, she did.

Ted Mann, the director of the Circle in the Square Theatre, whom I had met in Holyoke, gave me a tiny replacement part in *Six Characters in Search of an Author,* a successful off-Broadway production that was being performed at the Martinique Theater, a two-hundred-seat three-sided arena. Pirandello's play is a unique take on reality in which an acting company is starting rehearsal and is interrupted by a family of six strange people (played by the featured actors) who take over the stage. There was no curtain or light cue, so the play starts seamlessly when the acting company begins drifting onto the stage like ordinary people showing up for work, chatting quietly. I was one of them, not yet a member of Actors' Equity, at fifteen dollars a week. I had two lines in the play, though that didn't count the improvisations required of us during tumultuous scenes, like: "Hey, watch it there!" or "What do you people think you're doing!"

During one matinee, I stepped onto the stage with the others, the audience began to hush, and a guy came out of the audience and said, "Robert, how you doing? I just saw your name in the program, I didn't know you were in this play." It was Larry Resnick, a guy from Alfred, and he was talking to me on the stage, not realizing the play had started. "You went to the Yale Drama, right? That's so great." I tried to walk away from him, sending a message as subtly as I could through my teeth, without moving my lips, like a ventriloquist: "Larry, the play has started. What the hell are you doing? Go back to your seat."

"WHAT?" he said.

"I'm acting here. The play is on, get the hell out of here."

He looked around as the spotlights came up and finally realized what he'd done. "Oh, jeez," he said, and scurried, embarrassed, to his seat.

The proximity of the first row of seats to the foot-high stage was two feet, and for all the intimacy it provided, it was a problem. We "actors" in the play spent quite a bit of time in that tiny space, elbows on the stage platform, practically sitting on the shoes of the first row as we watched "the family" act out their lives. One evening in the middle of the performance, I inadvertently let out a fart, inches from a couple in the first row. I had expected this release of gas to be one of those almost silent, imperceptible hisses, or I never would have allowed the sphincter muscles to relax. Unfortunately, it came out in the middle of a dramatic silence in the theater during which one could hear a pin drop. It was a moderately noisy ripper, reminiscent of a Times Square novelty toy. I froze like a camouflaged lizard, turned slightly, and from the corner of my eye, I saw the husband behind me shaking his head in disbelief, saying to the wife, "No, I don't think so. Can't be." This was theater at its most spontaneous, up front and up close.

One night the leading lady, a wonderful actress named Eileen Fowler, came into work and informed us that she had ptomaine poisoning from bad mushrooms. She looked quite awful and cautioned her colleagues not to jostle her too hard when certain physical scenes were played. Midway through the second act, Daniel Keyes, who played her stepfather, was removing her shoes during a seduction scene while she reclined on her back on a divan. "This is her scene," he said, "she cannot give it up." On the P of "give it up," she gave up an explosive torrent of projectile vomit that practically hit the overhead lights and drenched poor Keyes and several other actors around her. David Margulies, in the featured role of the stage manager, instantly launched into a clever ad lib about how "we never should have allowed these people in here in the first place" as he shook some of her dinner off his sleeve. The play was so well done and the audience so into it that it took a full six seconds and the smell of vomit before they realized that her throwing up was not part of the play. If that is not effective theater, then I don't know what is.

The mother in the family was played by Joan Croyden, who had played Miss Ferncliffe the schoolteacher in both the stage and film productions of *The Bad Seed.* She was a tall, angular woman of about sixty-five, with gray hair and long, veiny arms and fingers, whose costume was a shapeless black dress—one could almost say witchlike. There were an eight-year-old boy and girl in the family who were mute throughout but spent almost the entire show onstage. After a performance, while the actors were filing back to the dressing rooms, I saw Miss Croyden grab the little girl hard by the arm and yell at her in a mocking, contemptuous tone: "I saw you mugging during my speech. You think I didn't see you? I saw you with your cute little eyes trying to upstage me, steal my scene. You keep still during that speech, do you hear me?" This was mighty scary to the little girl, who was already a little delicate, and she broke into hysterical sobs and ran into the women's dressing room and the arms of Eileen Fowler. The child, required to stand still for minutes on end, had merely shown a fidget or two, like any normal eight-year-old might have under the circumstance. She was adorable, though, with a matching beret and cape, and knew it and was not unaware of the audience. The gnarly Miss Croyden entered the dressing room, looked at the girl, still crying, and said with grandeur: "If she can't take it, she shouldn't be in the theater!"

❁   ❁   ❁

Meanwhile, Georgia was performing on Broadway and doing an excellent job in a modest role. She continually encouraged me to knock on agents' doors and keep abreast of casting opportunities by reading *Backstage*, the casting newspaper. "Be positive," she would say. I found it hard to push myself like an aspiring actor had to: I was an exhibitionist onstage yet shy as hell about trying to get there. I was terrified of rejection, a negative attribute for a professional actor. It would take me a while to realize that tenacity was as important as talent.

Georgia and I had lunch together one day at a little Italian place on Second Avenue. I was in a good mood, excited about her first Broadway show.

"I have something to tell you," she said.

"You got a movie?" I said.

"No. I'm pregnant."

"What?"

"I'm pregnant. It's for sure, Bobby, I found out today."

In my stunned silence, I thought of the menstruation celebrations from college—no opening a keg here. In fact, our passion and enjoyment had turned to serious business. I thought of my parents and saw the absurd image of bouncing a baby on my knee. I thought of Georgia's career and the Broadway show: So did she. "I can't have a baby now. It wouldn't be right for the baby's sake, either. Maybe someday I'll be a mother, but not now. I'm not ready to have a baby, nor are you. Don't you agree?" she said.

"Of course. But what do we do now?" We held each other and hugged, this time with the gentle, sexually neutral pats of assurance on the back.

"Are you mad at me?" I said.

"Why should I be mad at you? It's not anybody's fault. Maybe the diaphragm wasn't in right. Maybe it was that time we fooled around a little too much without it. In any case, don't worry. We'll just have to find someone. Do you know anyone who knows where to get an abortion?"

This was a question I'd had no practice for. "No."

"There's a doctor in Pennsylvania I've heard about. I'll find out what I can and call you tomorrow," she said.

I felt quite useless in my shock: no helpful information and no money. Going to my father for help was out of the question, so I confided in Rhoda, my wonderful, always protective sister. She generously offered money and kept my secret from our parents. She had no admonitions or "I told you sos," only concern for Georgia and comfort for me.

I asked my closest friends, with discouraging results. Abortions of course, were illegal. It was said that some Park Avenue doctors performed them for the rich for thousands of dollars, but other than that or going on an expensive trip abroad, the options seemed to be few. That doctor in Pennsylvania was out of commission, possibly in jail, but somebody suggested someone else who would answer to the name of Mike.

I called the number in order to establish a masculine, threatening, don't-fuck-with-this-helpless-female, intimidating character. Then I put Georgia on. After she had answered a few questions, she was given another number to call. In this call, she was able to ask some questions about what the whole thing would entail. She was assured that they had done the procedure safely many times, but they were vague as to whether it would be performed in a doctor's office or whether a licensed doctor would perform it. Georgia made it clear that she would be bringing someone with her, to which they had no objection. She made the arrangement, making several notes on a pad.

In three days we were to meet a guy called Tony at a gas station on Route 46 in New Jersey at three P.M. sharp. He knew the color and make of my car and would identify himself when he saw it. The abortion would cost five hundred dollars in cash, which Georgia was to bring with her, and she was not to eat anything for five hours before the appointment. The whole thing seemed laden with danger and not a little sleazy, but Georgia wanted to go through with it, in her typically positive, decisive way. Her courage gave me the resolve I needed, because I was afraid of what lay ahead. I had no control over matters, being an impotent string-along who had unfortunately not been impotent enough to avoid this situation.

On the appointed day, we drove to Jersey, and I gave Georgia the two hundred and fifty dollars my sister had given me. We were both understandably nervous, but in the interest of morale, we kept up an optimistic front, especially Georgia. She spent a lot of time comforting me, which I needed; I had to take care that I didn't become an additional burden to her. We found the correct gas station and pulled off to a side of it to await Tony. Twenty minutes passed, and doubts about whether we'd found the right place began creeping in. I was about to suggest that we leave when a man, appearing out of nowhere, tapped on my window, scaring the shit out of us. I rolled it down: "Tony?"

"Yeah."

I unlocked the rear door, and he got in. He offered a handshake to each of us, and I held Georgia's other hand in mine. We did not tell him our names. The look and sound of him intensified my greatest fear, since he was central casting for a mobster, with his suit, overcoat, and obligatory fedora. He had a "dis dem and dose" manner of speech, though he spoke softly and was polite, apparently sensitive to Georgia's exigency. I noticed that his hands were not rough, and his fingernails were clean. "You ever been in a family way before, dear?" he said.

"No."

Then he proceeded to ask several questions, like a doctor would— that is, if your gynecologist was Carlo Gambino. "How old are you? How long since your last period? Any health problems? Allergies? Have you got the money with you?"

I had a flash that he would steal the money and take off. I could have sworn there was a strange bulge in his coat that I took to be a gun. He explained that they didn't use a scalpel; the procedure was done by inserting a drug, he called it, into the uterus, which would precipitate the bleeding in a few hours. It was the method used by the unfortunate physician in Pennsylvania who was currently indisposed.

"Are you ready to go?" he asked.

"I guess so. Should I follow your car?" I said.

"No, you stay here and wait for her. The young lady will have to come with me alone."

"Oh no, we can't do that. Why can't I come?"

"That's the way it has to be. I'm takin' a chance here. Don't worry, I'll bring her back here, and she'll be fine."

"How long will she be gone?"

"Maybe an hour, hour and a half."

"Is that all right with you?" I said to Georgia.

"Yes, it's okay," she said, squeezing my hand.

They left my car, and he took her to a late-model Cadillac coupe thirty feet away. He courteously opened the door for her, and they headed off for parts unknown.

I sat there numb and forlorn, with the terrible thought that I would never see her again. I had a tremendous urge to follow them, because her going off alone was a new wrinkle and very disturbing to me. They could rob her, beat her; and even if they intended to fulfill their part of the agreement, they could botch the procedure, which I had heard was a common enough occurrence in clandestine abortions. I envisioned Georgia in critical condition with uneducated louts who wouldn't know what to do, who would run for it while she died of blood poisoning and hemorrhage.

I looked at my watch, and only thirty minutes had gone by. Holy shit, I was sorry we had done this. My mind drifted to other scenarios, including the horrible thought of sweet Georgia turning up dead, dumped somewhere. I hadn't even gotten this guy's license plate, and there was no chance that his name was really Tony.

I tried to be optimistic, a characteristic uncommon to me, having come from a worrying home. Maybe Tony was actually a medical doctor risen from the streets by his own bootstraps, a visionary who performed abortions as a public service, because he was appalled that women couldn't get them legally. Right, and he probably ran the numbers racket in his medical school. He was a doctor like Hitler was a rabbinical student.

An hour went by. I began looking anxiously for the Caddie. What if she didn't come back in an hour and a half? He had given that as an outside figure. He said an hour or an hour and a half. How long would I wait before I called the police? I never in my life wanted to see someone's face the way I wanted to see Georgia's. Then it had been an hour and forty-five minutes, with no sign of them. I fought with all my might not to panic; she would be here any minute now, I knew it.

After two and a half hours, with what felt like permanent damage to my coronary arteries, the Caddie pulled up, and Georgia got out and walked toward me. Thank God she could walk. I helped her into my Ford, feeling more relief than I could hold in. I had been alone with my fears so long that I felt the need to tell her how worried I'd been—until I realized that I didn't have my priorities straight. "Georgia, are you all right?"

"Yes, I'm fine. Everything went okay."

"But you look a little pale. Are you in pain?"

"Not really. I want some tea. He suggested warm tea right away."

We stopped at a diner. Georgia was still a little shaken but looked remarkably well, with her welcome smiling face. "What happened? Where did you go?"

"I was thinking about you, Bobby, how worried you must have been."

"Me? No, I wasn't worried, not at all. I was about to take a cyanide pill, but I wasn't worried."

She took a couple of sips of tea and looked out the window at the passing traffic.

"What happened? Where did he take you?"

"We went to a house about fifteen minutes' ride from the gas station. There was a woman there who was very nice, very comforting."

"Who actually did it?"

"Tony did it. They had the equipment, the stirrups, just like my gynecologist has. He scrubbed, he put on sterile gloves, everything. He seemed to know exactly what he was doing."

"It must have felt awkward."

"'Awkward' hardly describes it. I was terrified. But he did his best to put me at ease, and somehow I had confidence in him. Actually, I had no choice." She put her hand on mine. "Bobby, honey, *we* had no choice."

I dropped her off at her apartment with a long, grateful, tearful hug. She had been so determined and so courageous. I had been in quasi-panic when in fact it was she who had taken such a risk. It was obvious that if a boy were to get in trouble with a girl in this way, he could count his blessings that the woman in question was as kind and clear-thinking and purposeful as Georgia Parks.

I checked all afternoon by phone to see how she was. She said she felt fine. She had begun to bleed, and though the flow was light, it was a welcome sign and painless. It lasted about four days, with all the characteristics of a menstrual period, and then it was over. She felt better almost immediately and didn't miss a performance of her Broadway show. Despite the worrisome sojourn to Route 46, everything had apparently worked out fine.

Ten days later, onstage, she began bleeding profusely and almost fainted. Determined, and wanting to keep private a profoundly personal secret, she managed to finish the performance and went immediately to Roosevelt Hospital, where she was kept overnight after undergoing the D and C procedure that was required to complete and correct the job Tony had botched. She was all right, thank God, my sweet but resolute friend, but it was never the same between us again.

That day I received a wedding announcement in the mail. "Mr. and Mrs. Charles Silverman are pleased to announce the marriage of their daughter Judith to Mr. William Carney, Jr." I felt an emotionless finality. Given what had transpired since my breakup with the future Mrs. William Carney, Jr., this was small potatoes. You could fold up your scorecards right there and then. My childhood was officially over.

Chapter Twelve

Foreign Affair

She was a knockout, a beautiful brainy blond multilingual piece of work. She was four years older than I, twenty-six to my twenty-two when we met, which put her in the fascinating category of older woman. Also, she was European and bright and opinionated, and spoke with an accent that was exotic to my Bronx ear.

It was June 1964, the first of the two years of the New York World's Fair. The Motown Supremes' "Baby Love" emanated from every radio, along with those sensational British imports who were named, in a clever double entendre, after an insect group, singing "I Want to Hold Your Hand." My relationship with Georgia had become distant and platonic. Americans were beginning to heal, coming out of the shock and depression from the murder of John F. Kennedy the previous November. The Mets, those darling New York losers, had a spanking-new modern stadium adjacent to the World's Fair grounds and the brand-new gleaming screaming jets at La Guardia. The Grand Central Parkway had even been widened, and had acquired snazzy space-age lamps and signs to accommodate the multitudes flocking to the area. Things were definitely looking up for New York and me that warming season.

I had a small studio apartment on 153rd Street, near Riverside Drive, shared only with members of the old, even prehistoric, family Blattidae, who thrived marvelously inside the walls and my garbage. But it was mine, my first New York apartment. After the liberties of five years away at college, graduate school, and summer stock, habits and sensibilities had changed; and for me, jobless and no longer a stu-

dent for the first time since I was five, that previous fall of 1963, at
home in the Bronx, had been a particularly excruciating time to feel
like a failure. I had grown unused to my parents and being in such
close quarters with them: independent, one might say. Independent
though I may have been, I had hardly been hopping freight trains
during my years away, having been a student and not financially self-
sufficient. However, I had lived free of parental supervision for so
long that the difficulty of the adjustment added fuel to my already dismal circumstances. Though I had just spent a year at the Yale School
of Drama, I was down on myself, feeling lost, having no connections
nor a clue as to how to break into the theater and show business. The
look of disappointment in my father's eyes told it all. Worse than that,
pity, as my theatrical résumé after graduate school was pitifully brief.

After *Six Characters,* Nikos Psacharopoulos gave me a two-week
spear-carrying role as one of Herod's soldiers in a lavish, expensive
New York Pro Musica production of *The Play of Herod,* an eleventh-
century liturgical church musical underwritten by the Ford Founda-
tion. I got two hundred dollars a week as one of Herod's soldiers
whose job it was to slaughter innocents at The Cloisters museum in
New York and the Rockefeller Chapel at the University of Chicago. I
had a great incentive in the acting job, such as it was. The nasty little
prank-pulling choirboys who portrayed the innocents *deserved* to be
slaughtered, or at the very least remain in the castrati section of the
choir for the rest of their lives. Beware of child performers, and do
not be fooled by words like "choirboy." My chain mail costume made
of heavy wool was like a sauna.

To pass the time between my brief appearances as a slaughterer, I
had marvelous chats with Patty Robbins, who played the Virgin Mary,
interrupted only occasionally by her obligatory appearances in which
curtains would part revealing her in an ark holding the infant Jesus.
She was also an avid reader during her rather lengthy waits in a rather
lengthy presentation. Upon hearing her cue, four struck chimes, she
would put down Freud's *The Psychotherapy of Everyday Life* and
pick up the wrapped doll who portrayed Jesus while the Pro Musica
singers broke into her theme song, a lovely Gregorian chant. She
would assume a silent, adoring pose until the curtains of the ark

closed again, and then put down the doll or throw it, depending on her mood. Not a word was spoken in the play. Well, it was sort of show business, as it might have been in the eleventh century, and I got to see Chicago for the first time.

Since I had left graduate school, my father was concerned about me being able to fall back on teaching, the catchall safety-net phrase that had reassured him and had been the palliative, the very lubricant for his acquiescence in my pursuit of this career as an actor. I of course had no intention of teaching. I cannot help but notice that the patronizing phrase "you can always fall back on teaching," something heard frequently in those days, was and is an accurate barometer of American priorities, despite rhetoric to the contrary. Too little homage and money paid to the teaching profession and too many unqualified people falling back on it. Lenny Bruce's nineteen-sixties observation that Vegas blackjack dealers are paid more than teachers is unfortunately still largely valid.

So there I was in the Bronx, sitting on my ass in the middle of a November day, no school, no work, feeling like a piece of shit, and my father called to tell me that the president had been shot. This event characterized that whole period for me, with the general American pall seeming to feed my personal melancholy and deepen my rut. There had also been the humiliating and scary events with Georgia.

As the theater world wasn't happening, I had to find some steadier and more lucrative employment, with the aim of moving out of the family apartment and getting a few bucks in my pocket. My myopic father reasoned that "you have a perfect place to sleep and eat right here at no charge." I realized in subsequent years that his argument was a screen, that he wanted me to stay at home because he would miss me and had difficulty with those rites of passage. When I was thirteen, I was developing a good deal of hair on my upper lip that I desperately wanted to shave. My father had warned me sternly not to shave yet, because "It'll grow back twice as fast. Leave it alone." One day I shaved it off, and when he noticed it at the dinner table, he went into one of his tantrums, screaming, unforgiving. In retrospect, I can see that his reasoning was the angst of a father who couldn't bear to see his baby zooming through puberty. Unfortunately, Benny was

unable to communicate any of that. My mother, though not eager to
see me go, understood my need to fly the coop and, as ever, gave me
her blessing.

There was an available job that required a college degree and
nothing more, so I fell back on teaching, though I saw the job as a
"great leap forward" (I rather admired Mao then) in terms of self-
esteem and respect. As a substitute teacher, I worked on average
three days a week for twenty-six dollars a day through the winter and
spring, which afforded me just enough money for rent and food and a
modicum of everything else. I had a wonderful circle of friends,
mostly City College graduates whom I'd known since junior high
school. They were a smart, eclectic group of five, with some ancillary
guys thrown in, who read good books and loved good music from
blues to baroque. The politics were decidedly left-wing, with a couple
taking such matters seriously and contributing time and effort to the
cause of socialism. There were thoughtful, mind-opening discussions
of politics, books, and music, with the political exchanges sometimes
reaching screaming crescendos. There was much laughter, intellectual vigor, and sarcasm, with a minimum of sentimentality. Through
them I acquired a lifelong devotion to W. C. Fields, the Marx Brothers, Charlie Chaplin, Laurel and Hardy, and the great Lenny Bruce.
We read everything by Herman Hesse, John Steinbeck, George
Orwell, Aldous Huxley, F. Scott Fitzgerald, and on and on. Comedy
and music were the most important connective tissue in our gather-
ings, which included guitar and harmonica folksy-blues musicales, in
which those who could not play an instrument simply banged on furniture or blew across the mouth of a jug. We detested alcohol, preferring cannabis sativa, which we were certain would be legal any day.
We thought of our parents as completely out of the loop, beings from
another planet.

My association with these friends changed the course of my life,
especially in my appreciation for music. I had been raised on Broadway show tunes and fallen in love with doo-wop at fourteen. An early
rebellion? My parents respected the light classics (my mother played
piano beautifully by ear), but it was the so-called heavy stuff, which
my friends introduced me to, which I had never heard at home, that

took flight in me. While I couldn't afford to buy records, I could borrow anything I wanted from the Fordham library to play on my primitive, scratchy Webcor record player. What I wanted then was all the Johann Sebastian Bach I could get my hands on—the wonderful, esoteric, expensive performances on the best European labels, like Deutsche Grammophon, Erato, and Odeon—and the library had them all. I was especially captivated by the vocal music: the cantatas, *The Magnificat,* and *The Mass in B Minor.* My father referred to them as "that German crap," but the sound of them brought me goose bumps and sometimes tears of exhilaration. The Jewish boy from the Bronx had definitely fallen for German Christian liturgical music, though by no means in the religious sense. I largely ignored the text, except in those instances where Bach matched his music deliberately and splendidly to the words in the libretto. For example, when an angel or Christ ascended to heaven, the musical notes would go up accordingly and quite subtly.

I was hardly religious; my piety at the time was largely confined to asking occasional favors of God, like for me not to fail algebra, or to get this stuck elevator moving again. Perhaps I was an agnostic, but I was grateful for Bach's spiritual fervor. His music seemed to prove the presence of godliness presumed by many to be in each of us, Christian or otherwise. Listening, I would often think that only God could compose this, or create the genius that could.

There was a contradiction for me in that the great Bach was German. I had, as a matter of culture and upbringing, developed in my life a healthy repugnance for all things Teutonic. I was inundated, like many Americans of that era, with stereotypes. The language had a guttural, displeasing sound reminiscent of gestapo officers in Hollywood depictions of the recent war, not to mention the newsreel speeches of the little prick who had started it all. Charlie Chaplin's linguistic imitation in *The Great Dictator* was right on the money. Yet the composer had died in 1750, well before Nazism was conceived. I remembered that Dante, in *The Inferno,* had sort of excused Plato and Aristotle from the worst damnation, even though they weren't Christians, their having lived well before Jesus Christ. Mercy with an asterisk. Certainly old Bach deserved no less an acquittal. As I grew to love the music, the sound of the German words did not intrude on the beauty of the compositions. They seemed less guttural and more soothing the more I listened to them, especially when sung legato or in a long note. Through Bach, they began to sound like a fuzzier, friendlier German; at times I imagined I was hearing Yiddish.

I even loved to play this music during sex, on those rare wonderful occasions when the roaches and I had a female visitor. The feelings about this were never mutual; alas, there was not a Bachophile among them. These young women were invariably baffled by my choice of music to make love by, despite my best efforts to enthuse and infuse them with its glory. As I rapturously conducted and hummed the exquisite trumpet and choral sections of *The Magnificat*, they looked at me like I was deranged. Couldn't they hear the beauty and brilliance and yes . . . *sensuality* of it? For far too many American girls, classical music apparently reminded them of church and boring music-appreciation classes. I must have been an annoying proselytizer at times, especially during sex. I got reactions ranging from "Can't you put on some more appropriate music?" to "Turn off that classical shit." At twenty-two and no fool, with an eager legal-age naked woman in my bed, musical principles took on a more trivial aspect, and compromise, or even outright deference, seemed like an excellent trade-off. I was quite content to have sex accompanied by Little Richard or Dylan, or garbage trucks clanging on 153rd Street for that matter. There was a new concept in my life since my Bronx exodus: privacy. I meant to make up for lost time. I had always lived in a small, crowded apartment or a dormitory with hundreds of people around. I had never had a room of my own, having spent much of my childhood on the Castro convertible ottoman in the living room, not even love-seat-sized, which folded out into a single, narrow bed. Bear in mind that an ottoman is supposed to go with a chair. It is a footrest. My room was a footrest. How one recovers from such a stigma I do not know, but it was an extraordinary feeling to now be *in* my own room and not *on* my own room: free to entertain as I chose, and to feed my infatuation with music composed over two centuries earlier.

Listening to it exhilarated me and gave me hope, and I felt richer hearing it. Eventually, my veneration of this work opened the way to my understanding that German did not equal Nazism (in fact, Bach was much less frequently performed in the Third Reich). A whole generation of young Germans had grown up in democracy, and they were our grateful allies. I had even been profoundly touched by John F. Kennedy's "Ich bin ein Berliner" speech. But there was no forgiveness for Nazis or their sympathizers, and any German over forty was suspect.

So here I was in June 1964 with an apartment of my own, several passions and high hopes, but no job until the fall school year and no prospects in my chosen field. Then something turned up, as *David Copperfield*'s Mr. Micawber would say. My buddy from Yale Jim Burrows called and asked if I might be interested in a job on an NBC television project he was involved with at the World's Fair. The show was called *Ford Presents the New Christy Minstrels,* who were a popular folk-pop singing group. He asked if I might go to the various foreign pavilions at the fair and have them send their representatives in uniform or native dress to appear in the audience of the eight weekly summer tapings. The fair had been garnering all kinds of media attention, and I jumped at the chance to participate in the excitement. Besides, though there was no pay, it was at least in a tangential way show business, and almost a thousand years more current than my previous gig.

I put on my best suit and made the rounds of the many pavilions, identifying myself as Robert Klein from NBC, complete with an official badge-credential. This introduction seemed to impress, and before long I got many commitments of attendance, each pavilion wanting to be included in what seemed an excellent opportunity to publicize themselves. The job was delightful, and afforded a perfect way to see the fair as an insider. Best of all, the people actually thought I was important, something I needed desperately in my comeback spring.

Along the way I met dozens of charming people, many of them attractive young women from all over the world, wearing uniforms and other exotic clothing, with whom I would dawdle and shoot the breeze. There was Samina from Pakistan, who was an authentic princess bedecked in the traditional sari, though she had gone to high

school in Kansas on an exchange program and spoke perfect colloquial American English. There was Angelique from France, a beautiful, gregarious flirty six-footer who wore a size-twelve shoe. There
was Myoshi, the gorgeous and friendly staff member from the Japanese pavilion. These unwitting admirers did not look at me as an
overeducated nonsuccess who had a gofer job with no salary. On the
contrary, they considered me a distinguished visitor representing the
big-time American entertainment industry, which was surely one of
the most powerful cultural influences in the world. I, Robert Klein,
associated with and represented the power and influence of American show business.

One day on my rounds, it was time to approach the Berlin pavilion, and I felt some uneasiness. Perhaps it was a bit immature of me,
but I couldn't shake the notion that despite nineteen years since victory, here was the enemy personified. As I entered the ultramodern
structure, I fortified myself with Johann Sebastian in my head, along
with the comforting thought that *we* had won the fucking war. The
building was a sort of futuristic tent, reminiscent of Eero Saarinen's
imaginative TWA terminal at JFK Airport. I heard the strains of
Bach's *Musical Offering,* one of my favorite instrumental pieces, playing over the loudspeakers. How bad can these people be? I thought.

The inside of the pavilion was full of huge photos of the rebuild-
ing, dynamic city of West Berlin, with tons of John F. Kennedy, Kon-
rad Adenauer, and Willy Brandt, and not a Hitler in sight. There were
photographs of the ruins of the city after the war, to contrast its smart
new rebuilt look, as well as scenes of a moribund East Berlin, with
lots of jackbooted Communist guards. Everywhere was a veritable
plethora of economic charts. I went to the information desk and was
met by a petite, fair-haired woman in a smartly tailored pink suit,
which was the uniform of the pavilion. Her name was Inge, and she
spoke in a shy accented English, eager to please. A real authentic
German, I thought, though this sweetly smiling young woman did not
seem the genocidal type. In fact, she was kind of cute.

I explained the purpose of my visit, which she took to be of consummate importance, and she immediately summoned Herr Haufner,
her superior. He was a portly, neatly dressed man of fifty, with wire

spectacles, the kind favored by Himmler, and a heavy German accent right out of a Sid Caesar professor sketch. He was polite though not particularly cordial, a real bureaucrat, and I had an overwhelming desire, which I thwarted, to ask what he had done during the war. It was a strange feeling to be exchanging conversation with someone who had definitely fought against us. What if he knew I was Jewish? The bastard. I flashed for a second on blurting out "Revenge!" in a kind of uncontrolled Tourette's episode, and then strangling him.

He said the proposal sounded good. "Sank you. Vee vill get beck to you, Meesta Klein," declared Herr Haufner. We were joined by a striking blond woman with her name, Elizabeth, written on a badge on her pink uniform. My mind flashed for a second on having sex with her, and disregarded historical-political differences for the time being. She took over the desk as Inge and Herr Haufner retreated to an office behind it. She asked if she could be of any service, and while she could not, I contrived some reason or other to stay and chat with her. She was lovely and shapely, with wonderful imperfections in her features; she had a rather prominent, aquiline nose, large feet, and gorgeous blue eyes. She spoke perfect grammatical English, though with a pronounced accent, and she projected a palpable warmth, with a glint of mischief in her eyes: eyes that looked right into mine as she spoke and listened.

The Bach piece was still coming through the loudspeakers, and I instantly associated her with the beautiful music, as one might associate a woman with a certain perfume. I told her that he was my favorite composer. "Ach, me, too," she said, smiling with genuine enthusiasm. She suggested that Bach was the greatest thing to ever come out of Germany, a premise that I heartily agreed with. Perhaps it was a bit premature for me to feel this way, but I was in love.

"You are from New York, Mr.—"

"Klein. Robert Klein. Call me Robert. Yes, born and raised in New York," I answered. "And you?"

"I am Elizabeth Schmidt. I am from Munich." Munich, I thought, where Hitler started his climb to power, the land of lederhosen, beer, Oktoberfest, and smacking Jews around. "Klein, this is a German name, no?" she said as I shook her lovely, soft hand.

"Yes, all four of my grandparents came from Hungary at the turn of the century. Of course, it was *Austria* Hungary then," I said, pretending to be a little more German.

"Klein means little in German, but you are not little," she laughed. Two more of her colleagues appeared behind the desk, Goetje and Helge. Goetje, who had a gorgeous face, was curious to know about the television tapings. Helge was a bit more stocky and serious, and though she was from Düsseldorf, she spoke English with no accent whatever; she could have been from Cleveland. Soon they left to perform their office duties. Elizabeth and I continued our chatter, though she kept a wary eye out for Herr Haufner, whom she referred to as "that pompous little German man." She explained that he was always on the lookout for "goofing off." The incongruity of this jazzy American colloquial expression and her German accent made me laugh.

But it was no laughing matter when I saw Herr Haufner exit the office, and I dashed away like a thief toward a photo montage of the old versus the new Berlin and, most difficult of all, pretended to be interested in it. Running like a thief was not the image I would have chosen to impress a woman, but I saw the positive side—it was good acting practice.

Haufner appeared to give Fräulein Schmidt some last-minute instructions with vigorous gestures and, after wiping a bit of dust off a statistical graph of the 1963 foreign investment in Berlin, he proceeded out the door.

Elizabeth looked at me and laughed. "Komm, Ro-behrt, it's uh-kay, he won't be beck, thank Gott." Her smile was amused, but she didn't mock me, which minimized my embarrassment. She rested her face between her hands, elbows on the counter, framing her pretty and fascinating countenance with a much more relaxed demeanor. She looked like she was studying me. Then she asked me to tell her the story of my life.

This is a good question to hear from a girl you're interested in. To begin with, it's flattering, and there is so much room for beneficial manipulation in the storytelling that one must fight the urge to bullshit too much. "My goodness, where should I begin?"

It was a more or less rhetorical question, but she took it at face value and wrinkled her forehead in contemplation. "At the beginning," she said.

The next time I looked at the clock, an hour and a half had passed, and we had exchanged much information about relationships with parents—her father was a German officer killed in the war—aspirations, and experiences. Unfortunately, there were many interruptions: mostly annoying visitors to the pavilion, morons who made outrageous requests for such things as information about what they were looking at. Weren't those photos and charts self-explanatory? At these moments, Elizabeth would slide away and politely engage the curious visitors in English, German, and very proficient French, giving me an opportunity to study her.

As a matter of fact, I couldn't take my eyes and ears off her. Her sweet-voiced trilingual conversation was like music, like *The Brandenburg Concerto #2,* playing on the pavilion sound system. How clever, I thought, to speak so many languages. From the increasing frequency of interruptions and a look at my watch, it was apparent that both Elizabeth and I had a job to do. I still had to go to the Pakistani and British pavilions. I dared not ask for her telephone number but told her that I would surely drop by again, which she took to be a good idea. We shook hands and, somewhat smitten, I floated out into the World's Fair sunshine wanting to dance like Gene Kelly in an MGM musical.

In the course of the next week, I visited Elizabeth daily and learned more about the new Berlin than I cared to while dodging Herr Haufner on his occasional forays around the exhibition. Here I was, hiding from a German authority. Perhaps it was genetic. What did you do between 1935 and 1945, eh, Herr Haufner? I'm sure you had no idea about the concentration camps, you swine, I thought as I peeked from behind a display at his obviously cruel, unfeeling face. This was a difficult courtship, if that was what it was to be.

After two weeks and many visits, Elizabeth's colleagues began teasing me about my frequent appearances, and Helge dubbed me an honorary Berliner, an accolade that, for me, was a million-to-one shot at birth. Around this time, I was sure that Herr Haufner was beginning to notice me. My whistling and looking innocent while reading about the history of Checkpoint Charlie for the fourteenth time were beginning to look transparent. Though I wanted to very much, I still couldn't find the nerve to mention going out with Elizabeth, unsure whether she would be interested in seeing me in some other environment. "Unsure" gravely understates the matter. I had experienced a tremendous loss of confidence. I suspected that she thought I was just a kid with whom she passed some time at work. She was a woman of the world, literally, having lived and worked in Hong Kong, Paris, and other exotic parts. I had been to New Jersey. I envisioned a worst-possible scenario in which I asked her out and she laughed in my face.

I have always been somewhat fearful of rejection; no doubt many people are, to some degree. Yet there are those, whom I envy in a way, who push the envelope, are often rewarded with success, and deal with rejection with a minimum of emotional capital, if any.

Elizabeth had seemed pleased with the time I spent with her, and I had allowed myself to think of, dare I say it, romance. An opportunity presented itself for me to pique her interest and test my prospects. An ad in *The New York Times* music section indicated that a prominent Park Avenue church was presenting a concert of Bach's *Cantata #147* and some motets. It was the kind of evening my friends and I wouldn't miss, but I had never taken a date. With some apprehension, I entered the Berlin pavilion, did my usual search for that ubiquitous Germanic pest Herr Haufner, and was relieved to see Elizabeth at the desk conversing with some yokel from North Dakota who had a cousin in Stuttgart. "His name is Manheim, Helmut Manheim. Would you know him?"

"I am from Munich, I am sorry, but I do not know him," she answered patiently.

"I figured since Germany was a small country, you might know him." At the utter stupidity of his question, it occurred to me that the guy was trying to make time with *my girl*. It seemed an eternity while the cretin went on and on about his family in Germany. Finally, he moved on, and it was my turn at the information desk. I broached the subject of the concert, and Elizabeth replied that she had to work on the evening in question. She muttered something to herself in German that did not contain the only German words I knew, "sauerkraut" and "schweinhund," which left me very much in the dark. Suddenly, she said: "Maybe with me Inge will make the exchange." She darted back into the office for ten seconds and came out smiling. "Yes, Robert, I will come. It will be wonderful."

Inge came out and said, "She will have a good time, no? A better time than she has here. You will both think of me when you have a good time, no?" Good old Inge.

On the appointed evening, I insisted on picking up Litzabet (the German pronunciation) at the Lefrak City apartment she shared with the three other women. Elizabeth suggested that I come up and see the apartment. Walking down the hall, I noticed that almost every door had a mezuzah on it, indicating to my amusement that the four fräuleins from Berlin were living in a very Jewish neighborhood.

Elizabeth greeted me with a European double-cheek kiss, leaving me with my hand extended, and led me into the living room, decorated with rented Danish modern furniture and abstract reproductions. It was a four-bedroom apartment that the Berlin Chamber of Commerce had rented for the duration of the fair.

On cue, Goetje and Helge came out of their respective rooms to say hello. It was a novelty to see three of the girls (Inge was holding the fort at Checkpoint Charlie) in something other than their uniforms. Goetje was even in a bathrobe, looking no less gorgeous for it, and Helge wore pin curlers and gaily showed me around the place. Next to each bed were picture postcards and family photos, including old German faces, and I wondered if the ancestors of these adorable and perfectly agreeable young women had been tormentors of my kinsmen.

Elizabeth looked radiant, in a bright summer dress that high-lighted her dramatic blue eyes and apparently beautiful breasts.

On the way into Manhattan in my Ford Galaxie, I pointed out every landmark like an expert tour guide. After a life of Volkswagen Beetles, Elizabeth couldn't believe how big my car was. The skyline was glimmering, looking its absolute best in the late dusk, and I had a story for every building and point of interest. It was my city, the city of my birth, the city that I loved, and seated next to my foreign companion, I waxed rapturous and romantic. If the guys could only see me now, with a beautiful, bright German woman who loved Bach. If my *parents* could only see me now, going to a church with the daughter of a Nazi.

As a matter of fact, some of my friends would meet her shortly, several of them having planned to attend the concert. Twenty minutes later, there they were, in front of the entrance steps on Park Avenue: Roland Rofkin and the fraternal twins Fred and Frank Casden, the heaviest into Bach of the guys in our group. I was suddenly aware of their Beatnik, long-haired, whiskered counterculture look, to which my *schoene matjen* paid no attention, greeting them warmly. Roland, the bearded Marxist and linguistic dilettante, began conversing in German with her about his sojourns in her native land. As we entered the ornate Episcopal church and sat down, the twins gave me the high sign of approval behind her back from the next pew. We were psyched and ready as the small orchestra and solo trumpet opened the exquisite *Cantata #147*, "Herz und Mund und Tat und Leben," joined by an excellent chorus. There is something so beautiful about the first ethereal sound of music cutting through the silence that precedes it, the acoustics of the impressive church enhancing it all.

Elizabeth seemed to be excited and thoroughly involved in the spirit of the moment; taking my hand in hers, she squeezed it twice, sending an express train of nerve impulses directly to the synapses of every inch of my body, penis not excluded. This was decidedly different from the handshakes we had exchanged up to now, and after a few moments, as if on cue, we looked at each other simultaneously. Though she was smiling, I could see glistening tears in her eyes, but *good* tears, if you know what I mean. I could feel a lightness in my chest and shoulders and a sense of well-being and fulfillment. Forgive the cliché, but my heart was soaring. I was in exactly the place I wanted to be, with exactly the person I wanted to be there, accompanied by as magnificent a musical score as has ever been created. I felt then that this was one of the greatest moments of my life, and I still feel that today as I write this and hear the music in my mind, a gorgeous melange of trumpet and violins and rousing human voices.

There were a couple of motets and a solo harpsichord piece and the performance was over all too soon.

I feared that the magical mood—more precisely, the spell—would end. After a long round of applause from the aficionados assembled, and the well-deserved bows of the singers and musicians, people from the church passed around large donation plates. My euphoric appreciation drew a twenty-dollar bill out of me—after all, singers and musicians, my fellow artists, had performed mightily and must eat. Of course, the Communists behind me sneered contemptuously at the plates. Their point of view on the matter was entirely different; they extolled the virtues of the arts and appreciated the creative talent, but they insisted that the proletariat was *entitled* to enjoy such talent free of charge; anyway, they wouldn't give money to the opiate of the masses.

With the music still in our heads, Elizabeth and I made our way past the oak pews and elaborate stained-glass windows out to Park Avenue, holding hands tightly, suspended, silent.

The boys were thrilled and loquacious about the music. "Did you believe that singer? She was off the wall," Frank said. Roland shook his head. "Beyond belief," he said, "beyond all possible human concept of belief." Fred, ever fidgety, rubbed his fingers together nervously, which he did when upset or ecstatic.

I was about to say goodbye and go for the car when Roland suggested that we all get something to eat. I hadn't planned for that eventuality, and I looked to Elizabeth, who instantly acceded. We walked over to Lexington, it being an impossibility to get a cup of coffee on Park Avenue between Forty-second Street and Harlem. Elizabeth and I found ourselves swinging our joined hands in the rhythm of happy children. We found a coffee shop, and as the boys went in, Elizabeth pulled me to her on the sidewalk and looked into my eyes. "Robert, I want to thank you with my heart for this beautiful experience," she said sweetly. Suddenly, I felt like I might bust if I didn't kiss her right there in front of the coffee shop on Lexington Avenue and she didn't kiss me back. I did and she did and if that wasn't Gene Kelly and MGM I was in the middle of, then I don't know what is. A long kiss it was.

While sipping her tea and pecking at her bread and butter (who but a European would order bread and butter?), Elizabeth squeezed my hand under the table as we all recounted our impressions of the divine concert. Then, as was inevitable with these guys, politics came up, and I became apprehensive, knowing the tenacity and depth of commitment these boys had to their fucking socialist revolution and the peaceful overthrow of the United States government. The usual suspects—fascism, imperialism, proletariat, workers, exploitation, et al, rained over the table like a cannonade of howitzers, yet a good-humored Fräulein Schmidt withstood the barrage and the test of fire. I felt a certain pride as she charmed them and parried their ideology at the same time. It so happened that she lived in a country that was divided by electronic fences and machine guns. These middle-class City College Trotskyites seemed oblivious to the pragmatic side of the issue, the fact that this woman risked death to visit relatives in the eastern sector of her own country. Yet she was gracious and cheerful in the debate. The boys talked glibly at the safe distance of student theorists and intellectuals. She countered patiently, without bitterness, with first-person accounts of the difficult experiences of the individual who must live in the actual world these theories helped create. While she showed some pride in the strides taken by West Germany, she made it a constant point that Germany's behavior during the Nazi era was cause for shame and retribution by the Allies, and that Germany must prove it had a place again in the civilized postwar world. This was good news to the four Jews assembled, though none of us took her for a Nazi. The real beauty of her affable behavior was her forbearance in a social situation that would be considered difficult by any objective person: the first encounter with my friends.

In the next several weeks, Elizabeth and I saw a good deal of each other, with much fervent hugging and long, sensuous kisses and, fairly soon, much more. She took to calling me endearing German names like Herzilein and Robertzien, who was a lovable character from German children's books. She enjoyed pushing my hair from my eyes to a place behind my ear, and kissing me on the nose in public. I took great pleasure in everything, including no longer having to steal furtive moments at the Berlin pavilion and hide behind displays from a possible war criminal.

I had little money to spend, which did not faze Elizabeth in the least. We went to movies; she loved the Peter Sellers British comedies, as I did, and she adored the Marx Brothers at first sight—the pseudo-political farce *Duck Soup* hooked her. She was crazy about Chaplin, though it was taking a little longer to break her in to Laurel and Hardy and W. C. Fields, given the splendid stupidity in the one and the wry American subtlety in the other. We both liked the Supremes and the Beatles; in fact, "Baby Love" was her favorite pop tune, and she sang it in a southern German Munich twang.

We saw the sights of Manhattan arm in arm: the Empire State Building, the Circle Line, and the banjo pickers at Gerdes Folk City. Also included was some of my favorite Gotham esoteria, like the New-York Historical Society and the fabulous Cloisters monastery, scene of my recent triumph as a spear carrier and slaughterer of innocents. My tour-guide commentary, frequently so annoying to my friends—"Did you know that Aaron Burr had a farm on what is now the Upper West Side?"—pleased her immensely. We were so happy, we must have looked like a fashion ad in the Sunday *Times*.

She became a regular visitor to my minuscule pad on 153rd Street, where we held endless conversations. I had been in love with Judy in college, and I had felt deeply then, more than I had ever felt before. But I was older now, and out in the world, and those same feelings were surging through me once again. I felt excited and scared, awed by the power of my emotion; alternating with a blissful confidence, optimism, and pride.

The Bach played on and on whenever we were together, which was more and more. I loved making love while looking into her eyes to the accompaniment of the music: coitus and cunnilingus to cantatas, fellatio to fugues. Beyond satisfied, yet no desire to part our bodies, and hungry for an encore in twenty minutes. We did it tenderly and lovingly slow, and we did it fast and hot, and we did it every chance we got.

Leaving well enough alone has never been one of my strong points, so ever present in my mind was the anomaly of her being German and I being a Jew from the Bronx. I thought of my parents' reaction to the relationship; there could be extremely rough sailing with my father. At the same time, I began to realize that this facet of Elizabeth, rather than a detriment, was powerfully attractive to me. In the shallower sense, it was a refreshing departure from my previous female companionship. In this difference I saw something deeper, even ennobling. It was a case of seeing the humanity of the enemy, of seeing and judging an individual on her own merits and not by ancestral baggage. But dammit, she was *not* the enemy. She had been an innocent baby during the war and the holocaust, and the sins of the fathers and the fatherland should not be blamed on the children, yet—those fucking Nazi bastards. How could they be close kin to a kind, considerate woman with such empathy and longing in her eyes?

We spent our nights together on my single bed, hardly big enough for one adult, and after ardent lovemaking, we would fall asleep entwined in each other's arms and often wake up that way. I, the fitful sleeper who needed space to toss and turn, slept softly and, after the first few nights, had nary a dream of gassing and death. There was a prevalent cliché at that time, long before Betty Friedan, that European women "knew how to take care of a man." Elizabeth, while no cliché, seemed to confirm this idea by insisting on cutting my nails, scrubbing me in the bathtub, and massaging my feet, which took a little getting used to.

She disdained only one aspect of my lifestyle—the smoking of cannabis sativa, which frightened and alarmed her. She had seen drug addicts in Hong Kong and France, she explained, and the fact that pot and heroin were at opposite ends of a wide spectrum did not dissuade her. "Robert, don't take that poison into you," she would say, truly concerned, even angry. It got to the point that I desisted from smoking the weed in her presence to placate her, sneaking an occasional toke in the bathroom. Still hiding from German authority? One evening she discovered me and became very upset, but she did not rebuke me. Instead, she began to weep. I thought she was mourning my downfall, but this was not the case. "Oh, my dear Robert. My dear dear man. This is your house, and I am interfering with your life and what you do, and I am so ashamed of having been discourteous," she said through some profound weeping.

I took her in my arms. "No, not at all. Please don't feel that way. I want you to feel at home here. You're welcome here," I insisted.

"No, my Herzilein, I do not have the right to intrude. It is difficult for me to feel at home . . . anywhere. I have worked so much all over that I have seldom been home. I do not even *have* a home; even in my mother's house in Munich, I do not feel at home, as you say. It is not *my* house, and my mother reminds me of this with her behavior. She is not warm; I think sometimes she would rather not see me at all." She stopped crying, though her eyes were glistening and red. "Remember, Robert, you told me about how when you were sick your mother would, how do you say, *pamper* you? Bring you chicken soup, make you comfortable? I was in Munich for three weeks before coming to New York. My mother had not seen me for nearly a year. I had caught a terrible flu in Hong Kong and was sick for a week in my mother's house. She gave me no special treatment, no chicken soup, no hot tea. Barely a hug, a kind word, from one's own mother. Can you imagine?"

In the course of our conversations about family and childhood, we each produced photos of our parents. I showed a wrinkled picture from my wallet of Ben and Frieda Klein, taken at my bar mitzvah. She showed a picture of her mother and sisters, who looked not a whit like her. Then she presented a snapshot of her father, Captain Schmidt, taken on the eastern front shortly before his death from Russian shrapnel. The picture shocked me once again into the realization that we were descended from disparate stock indeed. Captain Schmidt had Aryan good looks, an ornate uniform, and an arrogant, determined pose. The most disconcerting thing was that he looked like Elizabeth incarnate, though she hardly knew the man, since he died before her third birthday. Elizabeth told me that her striking resemblance to him was a huge emotional issue for her less than affectionate mother, for whom it was a painful reminder of happiness and future lost. The mother favored the other two daughters, who had more of her own temperament and looks.

It was an emotional issue for me, too, though I did not reveal immediately to what extent the picture was so disturbing. Our relationship was already groundbreaking for me, an inexperienced provincial boy, and all too captive of well-founded prejudices. It was an exercise in acrobatics without a net, and I felt that I was growing up in a hurry. "Your father was a very handsome man," I offered, visions of documentary holocaust footage dancing in my head. "It's hard for me to imagine him being your flesh and blood. I'm so conditioned to hating that uniform and what it stands for. Is it hurtful for you to hear that?"

"No, Robert, I don't wonder that you have this feeling. But he also had no choice in the matter. He had to be a soldier."

He vas obeyink awdahs, I thought. Then again, what the hell was I so shocked about, anyway? Every man the age of Elizabeth's father in World War II Germany would have had to serve in the military. What did I expect him to be wearing, a yarmulke with sideburns? I looked from my sweet Elizabeth to the Nazi officer and back again—that darling, gorgeous, passionate Elizabeth who had not a discernible trace of prejudice. I looked again at her father. "He might have killed me if I had been alive," I laughed, trying to break the tension I alone had created. She took my face in her hands and tenderly looked into my eyes. I looked right back, into those blue eyes, those incredible, sincere blue eyes. I was so unfamiliar with women who had blue eyes.

"Ach, my Robert, my Robertzien, my darling. What a tragedy that would have been, for you to be killed. I never would have met my Herzilein." She kissed me, and then again, advancing in tiny, almost imperceptible footsteps, nudging me onto the small bed, whereby we proceeded to join, harmoniously, two dissonant worlds.

One evening I sounded out my sister on the subject of my growing connection with Elizabeth. It wasn't yet like this was a serious consideration of marriage. I was too young and too penniless, not to mention too jobless, to think ahead more than twenty-four hours. But for all the rationalizations I could make, this woman and I had exchanged intimacies and emotions, and for better or worse, I was crazy about her. I was practically *living* with the woman. An *older* woman. A *German* woman. My wonderful sister, Rhoda, the teacher, four and a half years older than I, had always been my tolerant protector and confidante.

After a little teasing goose step while holding a black comb under her nose, and a quick rendition of "Deutschland Uber Alles" (Rhoda always had a good sense of humor), she suggested that our mother would not be a problem but our father was another story. In fact, she could not control her hysterical laughter at the prospect of my bringing Fräulein Schmidt home to meet Daddy. That larger-than-life daddy whom I had been aiming to please forever. That daddy who ranged from the funniest person I'd ever known to a brooding, angry, extremely stubborn man, who could remember a slight from thirty years ago and get angry all over again. That daddy who hated Germany and Germans. Who'd sooner see me bring home a Zulu maiden than one of *them*. "You've got to be kidding, pussycat," my sister said, without missing the humor in the, to say the least, incongruous equation. "They'd never turn you and a friend down for dinner, but . . ." She began to laugh again.

"Rhoda, have a heart, for Chrissakes!"

"Okay, okay, I'm sorry. I'm sorry."

I suddenly flashed on Elizabeth's beautiful eyes and how tightly she would embrace me and I her. She was so grateful to be hugged and held, she needed it so. Bone-crushing hugs that were reassuring and carnal at the same time, followed by deep kisses, a feast in themselves. I had forgotten how profound and exciting kissing could be. All this followed by copulation for sometimes record-breaking lengths of time. Jesus, I was twenty-two . . .

Rhoda continued: "It could be very uncomfortable, especially for Daddy. Mother will be ostentatiously kind and call her 'dahling,' and Daddy will pretend the whole thing is not happening."

Our father, as was the case with many of his generation, was still transfixed by the war and, more specifically, the slaughter of the Jews in Europe. The newsreel image of millions of Germans *seig-heil*ing at Hitler with adoration etched on their faces did not fade easily and, for him, was proof that the German people were "one hundred percent behind Hitler" and the atrocities he carried out. He saw no nuances, here, of new, innocent generations and recent allies. While stopped at red lights, he still cursed quietly at the drivers of Mercedeses and Volkswagens, and continued his enmity toward any and all who had opposed America's entry into the war. Though they had met many survivors of the holocaust, and had friends who fought in its battles, it is safe to say that Ben and Frieda Klein had never exchanged a word with a postwar German and might feel awkward doing so. They were nonreligious—one could say secular—Jews, who probably envisioned having a Jewish daughter-in-law someday but had never made a big deal about the religion of anyone I dated. So how about a nice, homey tête-à-tête with the totally Teutonic blond, blue-eyed daughter of Captain Schmidt? I reckoned there was a first time for everything.

It occurred to me that I might be forcing this whole issue in a kind of "yank my parents' chain, tell it like it is" truthfulness campaign. Needling my father, who could needle with the best of them, had a kind of appeal; but I had in mind to show him, up close and personal, that the sins of the fathers should not be visited upon the sons or daughters. That Elizabeth, despite her forebears, was an ethical, even wonderful, human being. On the other hand, who was I to moralize, lecture, and correct him? Sweet Papa, who had lived those trying, horrific days of war, which were full of uncertainty: What if America had lost the war; would we have been slaughtered like the European Jews? He did his turn as an air-raid warden in the Bronx, since he was thirty-four, with a child, at the war's commencement and therefore too old to be drafted.

I decided to bring up the subject of the dinner guest during one of my weekly phone calls to my parents. "You wanna bring a girl home for dinner?"

"Yes, Dad."

"This Joiman girl?" He pronounced German as "Joiman" in the manner of New Yorkers like Groucho Marx and people from Georgia like Oliver Hardy.

"You wanna bring a Joiman girl home? Here? For dinner?"

"Yes, she's a friend of mine, and I think you and Mother would enjoy meeting her. Besides, she's a long way from home and her family, and I really think she'd like to meet you."

"Is she a Jewish girl?"

"Hardly," I replied.

"What's the matter with you, Benny?" my mother chimed in with that exasperated tone she had perfected during thirty-two years of marriage. "Robert told us about this young lady, she's a German girl from Germany, right, darling?"

"That's right, Ma," I said, resisting the urge to point out that a German girl might well be expected to come from Germany.

"Very nice," my father said in a slow, disgusted, sarcastic way that I knew well. "Very nice."

"Oh, Benny stop. She's just a friend, right, darling?"

"Right, Ma."

"Maybe I'll make sauerbraten," my mother said thoughtfully, without a trace of humor.

"Ma, that'll make her feel right at home, I'm sure."

"You want me to make her feel right at home?" my father said. "I'll make her feel right at home. I'll show her pictures of *Auschwitz,* then she'll feel right at home."

"Oh, Benny, *ma elleg vote,*" she said in Hungarian (enough already). "Would she like a goulash or maybe a nice knockwurst?"

"I'll get on that with her right away, Ma."

On the appointed evening, Elizabeth and I transited the Henry Hudson Parkway north to the Bronx in my Ford Galaxie. I was uncharacteristically quiet, trying to be nonchalant, hiding my apprehension, having purposefully underplayed my anxiety about the meeting so as not to upset Elizabeth. I had, to be sure, made some weak jokes in the previous few days about Elizabeth meeting my parents, but I dared not let on as to my true feelings in the matter. But the reality never left my mind for a second that I was bringing home Captain Schmidt's daughter to my parents' apartment in the Bronx for dinner. Elizabeth was, don't you know, genuinely looking *forward* to the parental encounter. Was she a totally mature, worldly woman, unfazed by such events? Or was she obtuse and not thinking this through?

She cradled a bouquet of flowers in her arms for my mother and a set of mini screwdrivers, purchased from an African street vendor, for my father. I smiled: The screwdrivers seemed to me a stereotypic German gift, and my father enjoyed such gadgets yet had not the slightest idea how to use them.

I got a beautiful parking space right in front of my parents' building, which I took to be a good omen: Perfect parking spots always are.

We were about to be buzzed in when Nanette Newman from Apartment 2F came into the outer lobby and let us in with her key. We entered the art deco inner lobby with its silver stripes on steel doors and elegant black lines and circles made of marble on the floor. "So, Robert, long time no see, where you been hiding?" Nanette had been my den mother when I was a Cub Scout, and I had known her all my life, but I would have preferred to enter the building anonymously. I felt like I had something to hide—like sneaking a Nazi officer's daughter into 3525 Decatur Avenue.

"Hi, Nanette, I've been busy working in television for the summer."

"Television, what channel are you on? We'll tune in," she said, sneaking more than casual glances at Elizabeth.

"I'm not on camera, it's more of a production job," I said. Her eyes met Elizabeth's, and they smiled, making an introduction unavoidable. "Nanette Newman, this is Elizabeth Schmidt," I said, covering my mouth on her last name.

"Smith?" Mrs. Newman said.

"Oh, did I say Smith? No, it's Schmidt," I said, almost inaudibly.

"How do you do, young lady," she said. They did not shake hands, as Elizabeth's were full, but Fräulein Schmidt bowed slightly and said; "My pleasure." I suddenly had one of those Teutonic flashes. That was exactly the way the gestapo officers had behaved in Rick's club in the movie *Casablanca*, except they clicked their heels as they bowed.

We watched the lighted progress of the original-equipment, groaning elevator. It had passed us and gone to the basement. Of all the times to have a yearlong elevator wait. Finally, the elevator doors parted to reveal an assortment of women with their laundry baskets, all of whom were high on my list of people I'd least like to deal with at the moment, much less in a slow, crowded elevator. We joined Selma Abramowitz from 6H, Lil Weinberg from 4C, and Barbara Goldstein from the fifth floor. "Robbie boy, what are you doin' slummin' on Decatur Avenue," said Barbara Goldstein, whose ample breasts and curvaceous hips had been the object of my strongest childhood sexual fantasies. "You never visit, your mother and father won't recognize you." She gave me a kiss on the cheek. She was still beautiful but much the worse for wear and weight.

"Elizabeth, these are some of my neighbors, Barbara and Lilian and Selma."

"Oh, a friend from college?" asked Selma.

"No, vee deed nut go to college togezzah, vee are friends from aftah college," Elizabeth volunteered cheerfully.

"You're not from around here, are you?" said Nanette. The doors opened on the second floor, the den mother got off, and the doors closed again.

"I bet you're from Israel. Huh? Am I right?" Selma said.

"Nah, she's not from Israel," said Lil, "you're from Sweden, right?"

"No, I am from Germany. Munich, in fact."

"That's nice," said Lil. The enthusiastic geography quiz ended abruptly, and except for a few stolen glances at Elizabeth, the women's heads were down for the rest of the ride. Selma had never in her life been quiet for that length of time.

The door to Apartment 6F opened, and there was Benny, sporting a slight smile, which I read as strained and apprehensive. "Come in, come in," he said in a forced tone. So far, so good. He could have been flashing photos of Himmler at Bergen-Belsen. Frieda ambled in from the kitchen drying a dish, untroubled, and looking more beautiful than usual. She had clearly spent extra time on hair and makeup.

"Hello, Ma, Dad, this is Elizabeth," I said. There was a good deal more mirth and energy in my voice than was called for, but let's face it, this visit was taking its toll on me, too.

"How do you do?" my father said with all the detached grace of a prince of Hapsburg, while my mother simultaneously said, "Hello, dear," and shook her hand.

Elizabeth charged right into the spirit of the evening. "Oh, I am very heppy to meet you, Meesta and Meeses Klein." I made a quick check of Benny's face to see if the German accent had freaked him, but I could not tell. He had the countenance of a boxer about to encounter an adversary he believes he can handle. "These are for you," Elizabeth said, handing the flowers to Frieda and the gaily wrapped screwdrivers to my father.

"No, no, why did you do that? I can't accept this," my father complained. He had always been incapable of receiving gifts or the largesse of others graciously, perhaps because he imagined he would be in their debt. Though this was a gift from a stranger, he would have reacted the same way had the giver been his sister. It reflected insensitivity on his part, it never having occurred to him that the giver of the gift is deriving pleasure from the act as he himself did on occasion.

"Oh, thank you, dear, these are beautiful," my mother said, quite unaccustomed to receiving flowers. She smelled them, obviously pleased.

Elizabeth hesitated in the foyer, and Benny grabbed her arm and led her past the formally set dinner table and into the living room, past my ottoman-room combo to the couch located next to Frieda's baby grand.

"Oh, a piano. Do you play, Mr. Klein?"

"No, he plays the violin. I play the piano," my mother said as, in one sweeping motion, she handed me the bouquet, sat down at the baby grand, and played an arpeggio with a flourish of her hands. One could never tell what tune Frieda would choose, but the leading candidates were usually "Small Hotel," "Falling in Love with Love," or "Every Little Breeze Seems to Whisper Louise." She broke into "Liebestraum," a piece she had never before played, thus displaying a by-ear virtuosity and a musical Freudian slip at the same time. I was grateful that at least "Ach, Du Lieber Augustine" had not occurred to her, and I hoped that sauerkraut was not on the evening's menu, as much as I loved sauerkraut.

Elizabeth, who was enthralled by Frieda's piano playing, wouldn't have cared in the least. She seemed to be quite moved by my warm, gregarious, talented mother, which might have triggered thoughts of the less than ideal relationship she had with hers.

Benny could not take his eyes off Elizabeth. I could sense him noting her Aryan blondeness, but couldn't he see the tears in her eyes as Frieda, feeling like Vladimir Horowitz at Carnegie Hall, gave it her smashing, shmaltzy best? Benny's concentration permitted me strategic peeks at his reactions. He still looked like someone who had decidedly not melted, who was planning his debating strategy.

Frieda ended her piece with a dramatic two-hand, two-foot-high flourish that elicited a handsome ovation from the two of us. My father ignored Frieda's triumph, and when the applause ended, he said to Elizabeth, "So, let me ask you something, honey. Do you think all those people in the street cheering him, you think someone was twisting their arms?"

"I beg your pardon, Mr. Klein?"

"All those people I saw in the streets, with their hands up cheering him, were they *forced* to do it?"

"All *what* people cheering *whom*?" Elizabeth smiled, not having a clue.

"Hitler," my father said.

"Hitler?" Elizabeth said.

"I'm not talking about Frank Sinatra," Benny said.

"Dad, please, this is not the time for that stuff. Come on."

"What's wrong? I'm just asking a question. She doesn't mind, do you?"

"Well I—No, I don't mind, Mr. Klein."

"But *I* do," I said.

"Bela . . . meckholuk . . . bulonvudge," my mother said in Hungarian, which, roughly translated, means: Benny . . . I'm going to drop dead . . . you're crazy.

"She says she doesn't mind. I just want her opinion on a few things, that's all. What are you making such a big *megillah* about?" my father said with an innocent-mischievous look.

"What is a *megillah*?" Elizabeth asked.

"It's nothing. It's a big deal about nothing. Ma, play another song," I said, visions of patricide dancing in my head.

Frieda instantly launched into her opening arpeggio and a spirited version of "Falling in Love with Love." To my relief, Elizabeth appeared entirely unfazed by the exchange and once again fascinated by Frieda and her music, smiling and swaying with the waltz.

"Look, I'm not meaning to insult you, miss, you don't have to talk about the Nazis or the holocaust," my father said to Elizabeth. Frieda was playing the piano, but hardly pianissimo, and Elizabeth could not understand what Benny was saying. He replied slightly more fortissimo, and I immediately broke into "Falling in Love with Love" quite loudly, in my best phony operatic baritone. As I'd hoped, Elizabeth loved it, and Frieda was always thrilled to have her baby boy sing along. Most importantly, Benny gave up, at least temporarily, on his inquisition.

In certain ways, his behavior at this dinner was typical. Both my mother and father were talented extroverts who needed an audience while entertaining company at home. This was usually manifested in her piano playing and his clowning with violin. There was at times a palpable competition between them for attention, particularly on his part.

Frieda wrapped up with yet another grand gesture and immediately shouted, "Let's eat!" She led the way back the fifteen feet to the foyer—this was a small apartment. We always ate in the foyer when there was company, as opposed to the tiny kitchen, which was so intimate that from any one of the four seats one could reach stove, sink, or refrigerator. Indeed, my father often enjoyed sticking his hand up my mother's dress and goosing her as she mashed potatoes at the stove. She would laugh and admonish at the same time. But now, at the foyer table, she was angry and asked him to come to the kitchen to help with the soup.

"Please let me help you," Elizabeth said to my mother.

"No dear, you just relax, we don't need any help, everything's under control. Benny," she said, with a withering look. When the kitchen door had closed behind them, a mere eight feet away, I could hear their angry voices. They attempted to suppress the volume of the argument, like they had as long as I could remember, considering the two children and the limited space and the fact that they had at least one argument every day of their lives. I do not recommend this as a modus operandi for couples, but there was great passion between them, and despite the fights, they engaged each other like the gears of a well-oiled machine; they seldom bored each other. These are not small attributes in a marriage.

"I'm sorry, Elizabeth. My father is so pigheaded and insensitive sometimes," I said.

"Not at all, my darling. He is a little nervous; he is even cute. And this question about Hitler"—she began to laugh and covered her mouth—"this question was a little early in the evening, no? I know him for three minutes, and he wants me to answer questions about Hitler." I laughed with her because it really was funny, and out of relief for the fact that my sweetheart was wise and temperate and still speaking to me.

Ben and Frieda returned with four bowls of matzo-ball soup, good and hot. Elizabeth had already nibbled on some of the delicious rye bread, and her eyes lit up at the soup. Dear Frieda. I *had* told her Elizabeth's story about being sick in her mother's house with no nurturing or chicken soup. "How divine is this soup," Elizabeth said.

"Enjoy it, dahling," said Frieda.

"*Essen gut, du bist ein kluges matjen,*" said Benny in reasonable German.

"Ah, *spreckinze deutch,* Herr Klein?"

"*Ein bissel,*" he replied in an accent that sounded suspiciously Yiddish. Between hearty slurps, he told her of his childhood in the Yorkville section of Manhattan, about the Germans and the Irish and the Jews and of swimming on hot days off a pier in the East River. My mother told her of how she and Benny had met in that neighborhood when he was eleven and she was ten, through their sisters, who were friends. "Mein Gott, such a long time you know each other and still married!" Elizabeth said and regretted it immediately. "Oh, Mrs. Klein . . . I did not mean it exactly that way, it's just so rare that I have met people like you, together so long. You must know each other well."

Frieda looked at Benny, rolled her eyes, and said, "Please don't remind me, dear."

I helped my mother clear the soup plates, giving us a chance to talk alone. When we were safely inside the kitchen, Frieda let loose: "*Yoy ishtunem,* I thought I would die," she said, her right hand over her heart for emphasis. Then she began wringing her hands furiously: "The girl walks in the house, and he asks her if she likes Hitler. Did you ever? He's crazy, I know this for years now."

"I don't know, Ma, she seems none the worse for wear. She actually laughed about it, even said he was cute."

"Yeah, cute *a shegedbeh*," Frieda said, which in Hungarian means "cute, my ass."

"She's very understanding, Ma. It's like this European thing. I don't know, she's just more mature than the American girls I know. She's been through more, taken more risks. You know what I mean? She's a real woman."

"Let's take these plates in, because he's probably chewing her ear off," she said. We returned to the foyer with plates of chopped chicken livers and eggs on a bed of lettuce and tomato. Since she was entertaining, Frieda had even used an ice-cream scoop to give the chopped liver an even, well-rounded appearance, and had placed a garnish of parsley on each. Parsley was not an everyday thing in the Klein household.

Benny was in the middle of his "how worried I am about my son wanting to be an actor" routine, which included the "fall back on teaching" theory. His nonstop conversation at least afforded the famished girl a chance to eat. "Oh, Mrs. Klein, this pâté is delicious," she said. "Oh, 'pâté,'" Benny said, as his pinky went up in a crude, faggy high-society shtick. "Fancy-shmancy name for chopped liver."

"Which kind of liver, pork liver, or from a cow?" said our guest in earnest.

"Pork liver? Ecch, fuy. Nah, this is chicken livers with chopped egg," said Benny, eating voraciously, and leaving a nice dollop of liver on his upper lip. "Delicious, *oyon feenum*," he said to Frieda. She loved it so when people enjoyed her cooking, most particularly because she did not like to cook. Of course, we knew that praise from Benny was infrequent at best; and for him to acknowledge her culinary accomplishment, or *any* accomplishment, was one of her little victories in the saga of their marriage. "My wife makes the best chopped liver I ever tasted. It's not too livery, you know what I mean? You go and have other people's liver—or in a restaurant—it's too, I don't know . . . livery. She puts in just enough egg."

"Couldn't that make it too eggy?" I asked.

"Nah, it's never too eggy."

"But Pop, if you don't like the taste of liver, why eat it?" I said.

"Who said I don't like the taste of liver?"

"*You* did. You complimented Mother's liver by saying it's not too livery. And you only eat filet of sole burned to a crisp because it's not too *fishy*. Elizabeth, listen to this, the only fresh vegetable he eats is tomatoes. Can you believe it? He's never eaten a salad in his life, he thinks lettuce is for cows." Elizabeth laughed, but it was true. Benny ate only meat and potatoes, disdained any and all greens, and couldn't figure out why he moved his bowels once every two weeks. Perhaps it was because he had the diet of the average adult puma.

Frieda removed the appetizer plates, including the one lonely lettuce leaf, and I assisted by getting a pitcher of water to refill the glasses. "Please let me help," Elizabeth said, and again Frieda demurred: "No, darling, you just sit and eat, we're fine." Once in the kitchen, Frieda placed a huge amount of her stuffed cabbage on a platter and a good-size pot roast on another, then mashed the fried onions with paprika into the potatoes, which made a lovely orange color punctuated with black polka dots of charred onion. The old standby canned peas, having been poured from the can into a pot, were now poured from the pot into a decorative (for company only) bowl. Some sour pickles and, yes, sauerkraut were placed on a relish dish. The whole thing smelled wonderful.

We returned with the main course unnoticed, due to Benny's intense and persistent verbal barrage, which, to my horror, had turned once again to World War II. "I say to you they *had* to know people were being murdered. I say to you: What did they think was happening to all those families who were being loaded onto trucks and taken away? Where were they going, a Ping-Pong match?" My father would often preface an opinionated statement with "I say to you," to give it more gravitas. True, he could also be found using it in less important contexts, in a kind of pompous pretense of knowledge. For example: "I say to you, that the *Birds Eye* canned peaches are *superior* to the Del Monte and got them beat a mile." But on this occasion Benny was really rolling, and he wasn't talking about canned fruit. He was engaged in a crusade to win the ethical debate of World War II. Unfortunately, he was debating himself, his would-be opponent being reticent to argue, and entirely sympathetic to his point of view.

"I say to you, the German people were one hundred percent behind him."

Elizabeth did not immediately respond, but she let out a quiet sigh. "Dad, cut it out. She doesn't have to answer for Germany, for Chrissakes, she was three years old."

"No, Robert, don't be angry. I cannot speak for Germany, but I can speak for myself. Your father has asked honest questions . . . emotional questions." Elizabeth took Benny's hands in hers and looked into his eyes, much to his discomfort. "What the Nazis did to millions of people can never be forgiven. It can never be forgotten, though some Germans would like to, I know. Believe me when I say that there are many Germans, particularly the young, who believe this, as I do, Mr. Klein. We Germans—we must do everything to prove we are worthy of redemption in the future. In my heart, there is so much sadness and guilt for what happened . . . never mind that I was a child. There is a collective feeling of guilt, even among the innocent, because one is German. Do you believe me?"

Benny would not relent—he was a man who had something to get off his chest. He had always made these points to an audience of the convinced: relatives and friends 99 percent of whom were Jews. Here he was being given the never-to-be-imagined opportunity to tell it to a German. "It's not you, it's not your fault. It's *them*," he said. "There's plenty of them walking around in Germany—criminals, murderers— they claim they never knew anything about what was going on."

"This may be true, but please believe me that there are more Germans who are not that way."

"Eh, what's the use of talkin'," my father said with disgust. I had heard this expression all my life, in my father's disagreements with his wife and children. It was what he said when futile anger and a kind of fatigue came over him and defeated him, and the argument was over.

There was a long silence in the room. A *very* long silence. Finally, I could hear my mother inhale, about to speak. I put my finger to my lips and silenced her. Then something happened that I still can't figure out to this day. Benny put his head down and began to sob. I could see a tear under Elizabeth's eye as well. My mother and I looked at each other, decided not to be embarrassed, put down the platters of food we had been holding all this time, which were heavy in more ways than one, and proceeded to put a comforting hand on the shoulder of our respective mates. Both recovered quickly in the spirit of moving on and not wanting to make a big deal out of it.

My father spoke first to Elizabeth: "I'm sorry, honey, I felt so sad for a minute there. I'm sorry. Let's eat."

"I also felt emotional, I can tell you. So do not apologize, Mr. Klein."

"Call me Benny."

"You do not need to be sorry, Benny."

"All right," I said. "Let the world war be over and let the eating war begin."

The tears had put a temporary crimp in some appetites, but soon enough, the stuffed cabbage and pot roast were heavily dented, and Elizabeth couldn't stop raving about the Hungarian potatoes. After a dessert of pastries and coffee, Elizabeth asked my mother to play some more piano. Benny's spirits were sufficiently improved that he took out his violin and did an assortment of shticks and funny faces that had the patina of many years of performance, though some were improvised. His horrible violin playing by itself was hilarious, and he was a big living room hit, as usual. He directed most of his comedy toward our guest. One could almost say he was flirting with her, and who could blame him? "You know something, honey? You're a real mensch," Benny said to Elizabeth. It was one of his highest compliments.

"That is a *good* thing, no?" she said.

"Are you kiddin'? Of course it's a good thing."

Frieda played her last song—"Small Hotel"—followed by the procession to the front door. Elizabeth said, "Thank you so much for your kindness and hospitality, and Benny, thank you for the vigorous conversation. Ach, you are such a talented family. God bless you."

In the elevator on the way down, we caught it lucky and were alone, a situation I took full advantage of. I could not wait to put my hands on her, to kiss her, this wonderful girl: a first for me, by the way, kissing in the elevator I had spent so much of my life in.

Later, in the narrow bed, squished delightfully together, we spoke less than usual but were communicating more. The day's events had made us more thoughtful, more confident, as if something important had been accomplished, a hurdle overcome. It was not the conventional idea of seeking parental approval or bringing home one's intended to meet the folks. It was more the feeling of a huge object— a glacier comes to mind—being moved a short distance when no one believed it could be done. This was really good stuff. "Good night, Robertzien," she said. "Good night, my darling mensch," I said. There was a giggle and a squeeze, and the harpsichord played *The Well-Tempered Clavier*, and that's all I remember.

Chapter Thirteen

The Second City

Sometimes in a life and career, there is a conjunction of events and circumstances that couldn't be better timed. This was the case when I was cast in The Second City, the Chicago-based theater group whose stock in trade was and is the improvised word and movement. By the time I left the company in May 1966, after a tenure of fourteen months, my skills as a performer had blossomed geometrically.

In the fall of 1964, after the first summer of the World's Fair, I had resumed substitute teaching to pay the rent. Elizabeth had gone back to Germany, planning to return when the fair reopened in the spring; we were busy and content to write to each other. Once again, I received a call from James Burrows, this time asking if I would like to perform in a music and comedy review he was directing. It was being performed on weekends at the Hofbrau House, a restaurant in New Haven, and I would be replacing a Yale undergrad who, Jimmy explained, had suffered a nervous breakdown. After assurances that the young man's breakdown had not been caused by his participation in this show, I jumped at the chance to participate in anything resembling show business; unlike my gofer job at the fair, this Hofbrau gig paid thirty-five dollars a weekend, plus some excellent sauerbraten and red cabbage. It required a tuxedo, which I did not have, so Jimmy lent me his for the performances, though the sleeves and pants were embarrassingly short.

I stayed at Jimmy's apartment on the weekends, and I remember listening to a lot of Charles Aznavour and Edith Piaf, whose high-drama approach to singing held some appeal for me then, the post

Drama School boy. I also remember that after a while, a Piaf over-
dose could begin to sound like an eighth-inch drill screaming into a
hunk of tempered steel. My favorite Aznavour cut was "I Saw Venice
Turn Blue," which, in his heavily accented English, emerged as "I
Saw Veneeese Turn Blue."

The cast in the review consisted of two guys in tuxes and two girls
in gowns, with piano accompaniment, and material that was Julius
Monk and the Upstairs at the Downstairs stuff so popular in New
York at the time: largely liberal political satire whacking Lyndon
Johnson, much of it sung. The pall on political humor following JFK's
murder was lifting, and a president with huge ears and a profound
cartoon honker, who had an affinity for receiving important people
while he sat on the toilet, was a satirist's dream.

This show was right in my wheelhouse: jokes with sharp punch
lines that required timing, and snappy songs with funny choreographed body movements just this side of dancing. And ooh, those
dumplings and red cabbage with schnitzels all around.

After about four weekends, Jimmy announced that an agent from
the William Morris Agency would attend our show. Jimmy's father,
Abe, had been a client for over thirty years and wanted them to see
what the next Burrows generation was up to. If the agent happened to
notice one of the actors, what was the harm in that? I thought of it as
a golden opportunity, and I vowed to make an impression. I had never
doubted my talent in the year and a half since Yale; I had doubted
myself and my ability to self-promote. Of course, I had not had a role
significant enough for an agent or producer to be invited to see me.
Even if I'd had a decent role, who knew agents or producers to ask?

The Saturday-night show that the agent attended was very well
received, with lots of laughs and curtain calls. Jimmy Burrows complimented the cast on such a good show. Afterward, the agent took
me aside, and I anticipated the beginning of the road to stardom.
Instead of complimenting me, he began raving about the goulash
soup and the dumplings. I was terribly disappointed, thinking he
hadn't liked my performance and was making small talk to avoid discussing it. Suddenly, as he looked into my crestfallen face, he broke
out laughing. "Just kidding," he said. "You were good, very good."

His name was Bernie Sohn (most William Morris agents seemed to be named Bernie then). He had signed Alan Arkin and Barbara Harris out of The Second City a few years earlier, and they were becoming stars. He explained that the producers were coming to New York to find actors for their company, which at that time operated exclusively in Chicago and occasionally on tour. He thought I'd be perfect for them. So did I. I had seen them perform on *The David Susskind Show:* Alan, Barbara, Severn Darden, Andrew Duncan, Mina Kolb, and Anthony Holland. I'd also seen an article about them in *Life* magazine. They were sometimes political, always cutting-edge on the culture, with an emphasis on improvising initially, the set material they performed onstage. And they were funny. Oh, they were smart funny. Members of the troupe were already being snatched up by the movies and television. Mike Nichols, Elaine May, and Shelley Berman, who emerged from a precursor of The Second City called the Compass, were being deservedly hailed as comedy geniuses.

While I desperately wanted a career in show business, I did not much care for what I perceived to be the gaudy, hyped, mindless side of it. I wanted a hipper, more enlightened approach, *if* I had my druthers. At that point in time, I had no druthers and would have been fortunate to be booked as a costumed mascot at a supermarket opening, dressed as an onion roll. The Second City represented to me a kind of thoughtful show business with brains, and the maximum application of imagination. I was a bit radicalized politically then as well, though not as much as a few of my Trotskyite friends. I wanted, if possible, to do interesting and meaningful work, to be more than a song-and-dance man. There was some youthful, idealized, have-your-cake-and-eat-it arrogance in all of this; but if you don't reach for the moon when you're twenty-two, when will you? In any case, if I could have planned it out for myself on paper, The Second City would have been my first choice for my first significant theatrical job: a superb training ground in which to learn, flower, be discovered, and, not incidentally, go on to become a star.

Sometime in February 1965, I arrived in the large conference room at William Morris, where about thirty-five actors were gathered to vie for the four jobs pending. Bernie Sahlins and Sheldon Patinkin, the owner-producer and director, respectively, ran the audition. The participants suggested subjects for improvisation to two actors, who would come up with something on the spot. Thus, we found ourselves working with a total stranger in front of an audience composed of our desperate competition, with every incentive not to laugh and with, therefore, a pronounced tendency to put forth the most ball-busting ideas for improvisations that they could conceive.

Though I was improvising with a stranger, it was my good fortune that *my* stranger was an original: a brilliant, enigmatic comedic actor named Fred Willard. He didn't look like a comedian, with his matinee-idol good looks and fit physique. There was, at first blush, a wholesome, straight quality about him. He looked ready to play ball at a moment's notice, like a guy who had never smoked a joint in his life. We introduced ourselves to the group and to each other and proceeded to perform a scene based on their suggestion about a folksinger auditioning for a club owner. First I was the singer and Fred was the proprietor. He suggested weird prerequisites for my getting the job, like wearing gray and singing songs about cow punching and roping hogs. I played a middle-class boy who tries to convince the boss that despite his protected upbringing and college degree, his music of pain, suffering, and deprivation, and his denim work shirt, are totally authentic. I mimed an air guitar and wailed blues and Kingston Trio riffs about hopping freight trains and working on chain gangs, a theme I would return to in my first album, *Child of the Fifties*, with the song "Middle Class Educated Blues." We switched roles, and I became a hustling New York nightclub owner to Fred's cowboy singer: a study in contrasts, a culture clash. He was cornpone and horse manure, and I was a progressive Jewish folk-song fan. "Woody Guthrie and me was like brothers. He sang at my kid's bar mitzvah, for Chrissakes," I said. The avaricious little bastards watching us were laughing in spite of themselves. I could hardly keep from cracking up at times myself, looking at Fred's earnest face and listening to his deceptive mid-America delivery.

We were clearly the hit of the afternoon, but I assumed nothing until I was summoned into an office where Sahlins and Patinkin asked me if I could be in Chicago by April 1. I told them I was getting a haircut on that day, but there was a chance I could break the appointment.

Happily, I discovered that Willard had gotten the nod as well, though his decision was more difficult, as he had to consider the welfare of his partner in a comedy act, Billy Braver, who was not chosen. I could not help but think that these boys had hired just the right guys for the job.

In the next few weeks, I wrapped up my affairs, so to speak, at the cockroach-infested pad on 153rd Street. The William Morris Agency informed me that they wished to sign me to a two-year contract. I was thrilled to get an agent: that magical, must-have, elusive commodity for the just-beginning actor. It seemed fitting for such an important episode, the legitimization of my entry into show business, that I take my father to the offices in the Mutual of New York Building for the official signing. Pop and I were ushered into the plush office of Lee Stevens, an important agent who was on the rise in the company. He was six foot three, with piercing eyes and lots of charm. There were several eight-by-ten glossies of stars on the wall, particularly Walter Matthau, one of Mr. Stevens's clients. Benny was impressed, looking around, shaking his head in admiration at the expensive decor and the beautiful view of Manhattan, as he clutched his fedora.

A beaming Bernie Sohn was there and greeted me warmly, but it was Lee Stevens who was in charge in that room. He recounted a story about his Russian immigrant father. Lee was an attorney and a wealthy, accomplished businessman and theatrical agent. Yet, he said, his father was most proud of one of Lee's lesser accomplishments: the fact that he was a notary. In an old Russian village, that position was the pinnacle of respect. I sensed that he was patronizing Benny, who had been born in New York and knew the difference between a law degree and a notary, which was usually found in a drug store. There was some back-and-forth small talk, and then Mr. Stevens came to the point. "Robert, we see a bright future for you. We are the oldest and best agency in the business. We would like to sign you to the William Morris Agency."

There was a pause. "How many floors do you have in this building?" my father asked.

"I beg your pardon?" said Lee Stevens.

"How many floors does your firm occupy in this building?" my father repeated.

"Four," said Mr. Stevens.

My father turned to me. "Sign," he said.

Thus began a tenuous, sometimes bumpy thirty-nine-year relationship. My nervous, skeptical father staked me to the tune of six hundred dollars for my journey to Chicago. He gave me a few words of encouragement, no doubt impressed by my hundred-and-fifty-dollar-a-week salary, and I promised to pay him back, which, happily, I wound up doing many times over.

Elizabeth and I had spoken several times, New York to Munich. These were the conversations not of lovers but of friends. I, for one, was so focused on my impending career move that when she told me she had met a man and "he reminds me of you, Robertzien," I was both jealous and flattered. His name was John Vinocur, and he was the *New York Times* Bonn correspondent, who eventually would run the *International Herald Tribune*. Jimmy Burrows had gone to Oberlin with Vinocur and assured me he was a good guy. For whatever reasons, I was not the classic torch case. We each seemed preoccupied with important life events, and that seemed to be that.

So it was that I crossed the George Washington Bridge in fair weather, headed for points west in the Ford Galaxie, full of a positive spirit that bordered on exhilaration. I fully realized my fortuitous turn of events. I took nothing for granted and savored what was happening to me as much as at any time in my life. I had just finished reading Moss Hart's *Act One*, and his experience seemed to perfectly parallel mine. In fact, the whole signing episode had reminded me of the book. Sudden success; the big time, or at least my idea of it; the prosperous good life; the well-deserved "all is well" chill of contentment down the spine.

I arrived in Chicago and checked into the Lincoln Hotel on Wells Street. I called the Second City Theater and got Sheldon Patinkin, the director. "Where are you?" he asked.

"At the Lincoln Hotel, Room 1102. Where is The Second City?"

"Look out the window and down," he said. And there it was, with the ornate decorations, ball-shaped objects, and sculpted faces salvaged from the old Chicago opera house. In a short while, we new members of the cast met at the club, as it was often called: Fred Willard, Alex Canaan, Joan Bassie, and myself. Bassie was a sweet but serious actress who had been classically trained at the Royal Academy. She had a British affect to her excellent diction, though she was a product of Chicago. Canaan was a tall, handsome leading-man type, and rather a surprising choice for Second City; he proved to be a good straight man. We watched the performance of the English troupe the Oxford Cambridge Revue, then performing at the theater, while the regular Second City company, including David Steinberg and Judy Graubart, was on a tour sponsored by the Theater Guild. Everything English was all the rage, since the Beatles had descended on North America the year before. This revue was reminiscent of *Beyond the Fringe,* the British comedy entry that had been a recent hit on Broadway. It wasn't quite in *Fringe*'s class, but it was funny and intelligent and political, and the English accents seemed to highlight all of those qualities.

There was an actress in the company, a tall, curvy-hipped woman with short blond hair and blue eyes, named Gaye Brown. She was descended from a theatrical London family and somewhat bigger than life. When we were introduced to her after the show, she greeted the three tall, young, male new arrivals with eyes that drank us in, and said in a perfect put-on cockney: "Ain't they lovely." She was irresistible. Gaye (her real name was Gabriella) was subletting David Steinberg's neat little apartment on Wells Street, a block down from the theater. I would spend much time there with her.

Steinberg was then the undisputed leading actor at Second City, and he was soon to return from the tour. I looked forward to meeting him. I would quickly regret that his tour did not last indefinitely. Sheldon Patinkin was generous with answers to my many questions, from finding a place to live, to how the company worked, its history, and the relationship among the actors in such close, intimate, highly competitive confines. The one subject that seemed to halt him was David Steinberg. It was not that David wasn't brilliant or didn't deliver on his well-earned reputation for intelligent comedy. It was that Sheldon feared that David, whom he knew very well, would see the new cast members as fodder for his nimble stage machinations, in which, more often than not, he performed a kind of monologue with his fellow actor as a handball wall to bounce off of. "Watch out for Steinberg," Sheldon said.

"You've got to watch out for Sheldon," Steinberg said as I looked north at Lake Michigan and Lincoln Park from the floor-to-ceiling windows on the twenty-fifth floor of his new, return-to-Chicago apartment in the Constellation, an exquisitely elegant luxury building. He had invited me for lunch. He was subletting from Chad Mitchell, whose trio was on tour and had been at the top of the charts in a kind of Kingston Trio redux mode. Mitchell was the same guy who later did hard time for a grand marijuana scheme.

David was as charming as could be, and our politics seemed to coincide, as well as our love for Chaplin and the Marx Brothers. He was highly intelligent and funny as hell and keen on flaunting his Jewishness. He struck me as a total mensch. "Sheldon is a great guy, but he can be manipulative," he said. "I'll bet he warned you about me."

"As a matter of fact, he did," I said, astounded.

"Don't believe any of that stuff. We'll be just fine."

Steinberg soon proved a better improviser than a prognosticator. From the start, he hustled to get the best parts in the best scenes. He had several brilliant, *prepared* monologues and characters that he would work into our improvisation session that followed the regular show. His "sermons" were a staple. He had one for each of several well-known biblical characters, his knowledge of the Bible reflecting his orthodox Jewish upbringing in Winnipeg. The trouble was that they were set, polished comedy pieces that were not being improvised on the spot as advertised, and we all knew it. I resented having to introduce such scenes with "David Steinberg will now do an improvisation based on your suggestion, Moses." When he worked with other actors, he dominated the scene. He would maneuver his colleague into a chair and proceed to pace back and forth behind him or her, shouting and cutting them off. Aside from the Marx Brothers, he worshiped the eccentric brilliance of Severn Darden, one of our illustrious predecessors at Second City. Severn had developed a weird professorial character who spouted Wittgenstein and Kierkegaard and was reminiscent of Groucho but with Harpo's rubber squeeze horn. David liked to do *his* version.

In a scene with him, dialogue was difficult; when you tried to speak, he would cut you off with a horn ten times louder than Harpo's. It turned out that Joan Bassie, Alex Canaan, and I were the stooges. For some strange artistic reason, Fred Willard and Judy Graubart (who was going with Steinberg at the time) were able to perform perfectly good scenes with David, while I and the others were mincemeat. Despite his ego, Steinberg recognized Willard's talent immediately, as I did. In fact, our admiration for Fred was one of the things we agreed on completely.

I was frustrated but played to my strengths, among which was improvising music. They called it "make a song" at the theater. Bill Mathieu, the music director, accompanist to the group since its inception, was a wonderful improvisational game player with a golden ear and fine instincts. Like me, he was a devotee of baroque music in general and Bach in particular. We would take a suggestion from the audience of some news event or book title and cook up a Bach cantata or Handel oratorio. We did Broadway musicals and jazz riffs and folk songs, all right off the top of our heads, or, more properly, from the depths of our brains.

Bill Mathieu's brain was deep indeed. He turned me on to books like *Psychotherapy East and West*, pointing out that there were other explanations for human behavior than those of Freud and other Western thinkers. He was especially interested in religions of the East. He made me hear that music went beyond my beloved Bach, so that I could appreciate Thelonious Monk, Beethoven, the Romantics, and even the unconventional work of Stockhausen and John Cage and Ravi Shankar. My passion for Bach, however, reminded Bill that he had neglected the old master, and his ardor was reignited. Before long he was practicing sonatas and partitas and *The Well-Tempered Clavier*, which he would play for me privately. I had heard only recordings of these pieces. It was my first chance to hear an accomplished player from a few feet away, where I could touch the instrument and feel the vibrations, the way the music was designed to be heard, as opposed to in a large concert hall.

Despite my breaking-in problems with Steinberg, I was happy to be in the company, which was clearly respected in Chicago. It was a

bastion of liberalism on the north side, and was visited by the likes of
Studs Terkel, Mike Royko, and Dick Gregory, while the powerful office of Mayor Richard Daley looked upon it with a wary eye. Though
we nailed Lyndon Johnson plenty onstage, the dictatorial mayor took
his share of hits as well. I enjoyed imitating Daley's plodding Chicago
accent, especially in a popular blackout scene (a short scene that ends
with a joke and the blackout of the lights for emphasis) called "No Pictures." In this blackout, Mayor Daley would come out of a building or
off a plane, waving away the news photographers with "No pictures, no
pictures, sorry, no pictures." The photographers immediately say,
"Okay, okay," and walk away, leaving the surprised mayor standing
there like a jerk. The primary political character of the scene was in-
terchangeable: It could be Daley or Lyndon Johnson or Governor
George Wallace of Alabama, anyone we hated.

After the show, the bar downstairs was a lively place, with constantly running silent comedies, Chaplin and Laurel and Hardy, projected onto a screen on the wall. A good many of the regulars were
old intellectuals, leftists, and general Chicago eccentrics. I noticed a
fair number of youthful patrons, some of whom were bright young
women and Second City fans.

Knowing my musical proclivities, Sheldon introduced me to a young
musician named Helen Razeur. She was an attractive girl of Russian
Jewish stock, with an enormous head of thick, dark hair and expressive
hands. She was, most impressive to me, a cellist with one of the finest
orchestras in the world: the Chicago Symphony. Helen invited me to
hear chamber music at the Lincoln Park West apartment of a wealthy
patron of the orchestra, who would serve a hearty pasta dinner to the
players and listeners. I was in awe, as if I had been invited into the Yankee dugout to meet the guys. These musicians were among the best in
the world, and participating for the sheer joy of playing. To hear the
richness of these violins, violas, and cellos, plus a nine-foot grand piano,
in a wood-paneled library room was ear-opening, as with my experience listening to Bill Mathieu. I couldn't take my eyes off Helen as she
bowed her way through a Beethoven quartet, eyes flashing, head bob-
bing expressively with the emotion of the piece. I envied the magnificent eighteenth-century cello her legs were wrapped around.

Later, to her immense amusement, I revealed my jealousy, and she put such thoughts to rest by suggesting that while I could not properly produce the sound of her cello, I was, in the main, more versatile. She could play me very well indeed, in the best sense, this passionate woman. The ultimate convergence of art and sensuality was achieved when she played, impeccably, Bach's sonatas and partitas for unaccompanied cello for me, alone, in *her* chamber. She was naked. The encore was magnificent. This private concert is one of the lasting, wonderful memories of my life.

It was announced that David Steinberg and Judy Graubart were going to London to do a run of The Second City on the West End. I felt happy enough to give him a going-away party.

With some experience under my belt, and Steinberg safely across the Atlantic Ocean, I became more confident onstage and proceeded to flower at The Second City. Fred and I improvised a slew of scenes, including one of my favorites, the war-movie sketch. In this scene, Fred plays a gung ho colonel who comes to me, the general, to bitterly complain that his outfit will *not* be in the *first* wave to hit the beach in the impending attack. We played it dead seriously. "These boys have trained for months, General, you can't throw them in to mop up after the attack. They belong in that first wave."

I point to an imaginary chart on the wall. "This is not about your boys, Colonel, this is about winning a war. You will do as ordered and come in with Fourth Battalion in the *third* wave." The exchange becomes more emotional, with raised voices and tempers. No war-movie cliché is missed. Fred says, "Can we forget about rank for a moment, *Bill*? Take off the stars and talk man-to-man?"

"Sure, Biff. Man-to-man. Smoke?"

"Thanks."

A tense pause ensues as we mime lighting and smoking cigarettes, followed by a rapid-fire exchange: "Hell, Bill, you and I were together at the Point."

"That's not the point."

"What *is* the point?"

"The point is this." Than Bill Mathieu begins playing the navy hymn or some other inspirational martial music under our dialogue. The courageous colonel makes his last plea: "My men are chomping at the bit, Bill. They are a primed, razor-edged outfit, ready for that first wave."

"I'm sorry, Biff. The orders stand. Fourth Battalion will go in the third wave."

Fred gets into my face angrily. "Dammit, is that your final word, Bill?"

"Yes . . . *Colonel*! Your outfit will go in the third wave." I salute and turn my back to the audience to look at my chart.

Fred is on his way out when he suddenly stops, faces the audience, and does a silent jump for joy, while wiping his brow with a cowardly "Phew, that was a close one" expression. Huge laugh. Blackout. Right on the money.

Speaking of money, I had begun a ritual every Friday of going to the Aetna State Bank on Fullerton Avenue and depositing ninety bucks from my pay of $150. My "take no chances" father was constantly warning me to take my money and "salt it away." "You never know when a rainy day might come. A penny saved is a penny earned." He was a man who never earned quite enough, like Mr. Micawber; though, unlike the Dickens character, Ben Klein owed nobody. He had even passed up the opportunity in the late thirties to buy a beautiful home, because he refused to owe the bank money. He preferred to pay thousands over a lifetime to rent a small apartment, and in the end, he owned nothing.

In any case, it became a satisfying hobby to watch my bank account grow. When it got to about $750, I proudly told my father that I would be returning the money he had staked me for my Chicago adventure. "Nah, nah, nah. You keep the money. This is small potatoes. Eventually, I'm looking for you to *support* me. Then we'll talk about the six hundred dollars." Sweet and funny.

I was a working professional actor, and I'd become entirely comfortable with my surroundings. It was a relentless schedule of performing, six nights a week, Mondays off. Saturday nights were brutal, with two shows plus the improvs. Lots of young couples attended the performances, and occasionally I envied them their Saturday date while I labored and sweated in a funny hat like a court jester. Fred Willard and I had a running gag seconds before we would start the show, bedecked in some of the primitive costumes and props taken from the box backstage. We would say things like "Look at us, standing here on a Saturday night in funny hats, entertaining these people for money. What's wrong with us?"

But there was no way we would have changed places with anyone in our audience, even the great-looking, self-confident guy at the table in the second row with the beautiful woman all over him who was laughing at us. At that moment, I was sure she would have preferred us to him. It was a wonderful, productive existence, and Chicago was the perfect setting for it. It was not New York, but it was a bustling, vibrant city nonetheless, enough of an adventure for a twenty-three-year-old boy with one of the best jobs in town.

Eventually, David Steinberg and Judy Graubart returned from London, Sheldon Patinkin took some time off, and Paul Sills, the company's original director and guru of improvisation, directed our new show, called *Through the Eyes of the Inmates, or God Is Only Sleeping.* This was an unexpected opportunity to work with one of the pioneers who had started it all. In David Steinberg's absence, I had blossomed into a much more confident performer. Paul was the epitome of the genius behind the stars: the guy who didn't sell out, who stayed in the Chicago-Wisconsin axis, exploring his theatrical ideas to the fullest, regardless of commercial considerations. His mother, Viola Spolin, had literally written the book on improvisation, called *Improvisation for the Theater.* There was a story about the two nuns who taught drama at a college in St. Louis, who showed up at the theater one afternoon, on a pilgrimage to meet Viola. Viola's improvisation hypothesis was this: When you are improvising with another actor, the only thing that counts is what is here and now and immediate. What you see and hear and smell and touch is the essence of the improvisation. Paul discouraged us from playwriting, that is, talking about your kid brother in Dallas or what you used to do when you were in college. Onstage, your fellow actor's hat or birthmark or smile is much more important to the scene, and this keen tuning in to what you're facing keeps actors alert and creative. If you're stuck, you can always mime taking a round object out of an imaginary cabinet and begin a whole new discussion on what it is. With great difficulty, I got Paul Sills's point, though he was a tough taskmaster. He may well have been a genius, but he was an impatient one. What ticked me off was that he was constantly praising Steinberg (and he was not a praise kind of guy), while he seemed to have no patience with the rest of us. I was jealous. He seemed to be mysteriously tolerant of David's technique of using his fellow actors as lampposts.

Then there was Fred Willard. Fred had no intention of changing his style for Sills or anybody else. He improvised the wrong way, he was guilty of constant playwriting, and the results were, more often than not, brilliant and hilarious. Paul Sills was confounded by Willard, so scolding and lectures were ineffective. Paul even exhibited some rude behavior toward Fred when he intentionally held a loud conversation with the pianist while Fred performed onstage. I have had a modicum of experience with geniuses. The term, of course, is a somewhat subjective matter, and unhappily, it has been too frivolously applied to individuals of modest accomplishment—like Yanni. Paul Sills's ideas and techniques were imaginative, original, and opened the way for rich improvisations that were developed into theatrical scenes of substance. The problem was that Paul's ability to communicate these ideas as a director of actors—what we call, in the twenty-first century, communication skills—was inversely proportional to his prowess as a theatrical master. He would gesticulate with his hands like a Talmudic scholar, fingers closed at the tips, his body would sway, and one would hear a torrent of words in a Jewish Wisconsin lilt, impatient about why we couldn't understand a simple direction or find "the truth" onstage. All I remember is: "The ting wid da ting wid the ting you're doin' here. You take the ting here, and what's your relationship with this girl? Why would she care about you if you're not truthful, isn't that da ting?"

Slowly and a bit painfully, I caught on to the idea. To this day, it is the technique through which I improvise my stand-up comedy material. Instead of another actor, I use the audience, the room, the theater, a noise. It is all in the now. I may begin speaking about something I saw in the paper, and the audience reaction will cause some more thoughts and observations to pop out of me spontaneously. The point is that except for a few lines I may have thought of in advance, it is the "now" part that creates the most dynamic improvisation.

Viola Spolin was a gray-haired woman in her fifties, a free spirit who favored hoop earrings, shawls, and jeans. She was a middle-aged Bohemian, an avant-garde hippie type who enjoyed a few pops at the bar between tokes of cannabis sativa. She was a Second City icon who had invented a complex set of improvisational games and exercises that, passed on to her son, had created a revolutionary approach to theater. She never worked with the company, though she was active in the Second City community, working with talented novices who were future Second City performers and mega–movie stars. The problem for me was that Viola had taken a shine to me, less than half her age, and had begun running her hand up and down my thigh as we sat at the bar, going dangerously close to my genitals. This seduction continued for a few nights until it became necessary to check the bar to see that she was not there before I entered. In retrospect (since I am older now than Viola was then), I do not blame her in any way; nor, actually, did I blame her then. I was simply incapable of dealing with it. Visions of Diamond Lil danced in my head. Viola continued to be touchy-feely with me, even while discussing improvisation. I decided to take it up with Paul Sills. In bringing up the subject, I would have to ask as peculiar a question of a colleague as one could ever imagine.

"Paul, can we talk for a minute privately? Uh. Your mother—and you know how much I respect Viola's work—has uh . . . been coming . . . well, on to me physically. On a number of occasions, she's had a few belts of brandy and well . . . rubbed my thigh at the bar. It's a little embarrassing. I don't know what to do."

He looked at me, not the slightest bit embarrassed, with amusement. "That's Viola," he said.

I could not have imagined saying, "That's Frieda," were I in Paul's shoes, but he had a point. His mother was not some incompetent ancient but a brilliant and imaginative woman. It was *her* business, he reckoned. When I told this story to a female acquaintance, she rebuked me for not dealing directly with Viola. The problem was that I was twenty-three, and she was an idol to the Second City community, a person in authority. Still, my friend's take was acknowledged and absorbed. Today, how would *I* feel if a woman went to my son, Allie, to complain that I was behaving improperly?

My life in Chicago went on, in a wonderful atmosphere of vitality, a sense of freedom mixed with professional discipline and the opportunity to interact with creative people. Avery Schreiber, Jack Burns, Severn Darden, Dell Close, John Brent, and others stopped by the theater and improvised scenes with us. I also met a host of smart, lovely women drawn to the Second City flame. I met Northwestern students, aspiring actresses, improvisers, and waitresses just one paper away from a Ph.D. who were biding their time. There were Republican Evanston debutantes who talked politics over dry martinis in the bar, while Charlie Chaplin, on the wall just behind them, championed the poor and mocked the rich. In my perceived deprivation in the matter of sex, I was ideologically neutral. There was no way that I, playing the politically progressive, hip actor whom the girls perceived as cute, would throw Muffy or Sissy or any of these pretty young women of privilege out of bed merely because of strong political differences. In this new situation of relative promiscuity, I had the feeling that I was making up for lost time, since I had been a slow starter in the sexual-experience department: a geek with fantasies of naked women who turned to bronze when I touched them.

At that point in my life, I never met a sexual experience I didn't like. There were twelve women during my thirteen-month tenure in Chicago with whom I was intimate. I was not in love with any of them, but that did not preclude tenderness between us, or raunchiness. I was on a learning curve in all aspects of my life, professional and private, and sex was no exception. Some of the girls were so adorable that I fantasized about marrying them and having children. Again, as with Judith Silverman in college, it was what I ultimately wanted, I guess.

After about six months in Chicago, I had become very confident about my work, and I informed my agents that I wished to return to New York as soon as possible and become a star. David Steinberg felt the same way. Harry Kalcheim, a senior William Morris agent, would come out periodically to check on my progress, and David's, too, as we were both signed with Morris. Irvin Arthur of CMA would visit Fred. Fred was content not to hurry the matter, but David and I would petition old Mr. Kalcheim to start setting up things for New York. He would praise our work and say, "Just have a little patience. This is the perfect training ground for you."

"But Harry."

"Just be patient."

Around February 1966, there was talk of sending our company for a New York run. This was incredibly exciting news: the opportunity to showcase my stuff in front of the most important audience and critics I could imagine. When the plan was confirmed, it was decided that we would not do our current original show, but a series of classic sketches that had been performed by our classic predecessors. My comfort onstage, which had been nurtured in Steinberg's absence and continued with his return, even in my scenes with him, was now subjected to the terrible competitive test of who would do what and how much in the New York production. David, of course, would get the most, which I did not mind. It was disconcerting, however, to have the feeling that if I did not speak up and hustle, I could wind up with close to zilch for this, my New York debut. As we got closer and closer to the big event, David lobbied ever harder for additional scenes, like his sermons, as well as those wonderful parts that Alan Arkin had originated that David did so well.

Then one day, after I had poured ketchup over my french fries, I took a bite and experienced a pain in my gut as if someone had knifed me. The same thing happened with pizza, pepper, coffee, and almost anything that wasn't bland. I assumed I was getting an ulcer. My old fraternity brother Mike Geller was interning at Cook County Hospital, ministering to the down-and-out; his most interesting patient was a prostitute who had PAY AS YOU ENTER tattooed above her vagina. He prescribed Sparine, a stomach relaxant, to ease my condition, which it did. I was determined to relax and take good advantage of this fine opportunity instead of wasting my efforts on futile competition with David.

The show at the Square East, adjacent to the NYU campus, got

mixed reviews. Mostly, the critics complained that we were doing
previously presented material, and there is no doubt that they had a
point. In hindsight, Sheldon and Bernie should have had more confidence in some of the material *we* had created. Stanley Kauffmann
was the *Times* critic who reviewed us. Though I enjoyed his film crit-
icism in *The New Republic,* he was singularly underwhelmed by our
efforts. In a final blow, he mentioned in passing the names of the
actors, but he forgot to include mine.

　　We closed in four weeks, but we had been noticed by the business.
Judy Graubart and I did an animated Ruffles potato-chip commercial
in which she was the mother's voice and I was the father's voice. The
baby kept repeating "Ruffles have ridges" as we tried to understand
him. It became a classic, and even at union-scale pay rates, it earned
us each about twenty-five thousand dollars over three years.

　　But far more important—I had my first Broadway audition coming
up: for Mike Nichols.

Chapter Fourteen

Learning How

After returning from Chicago in 1966, I shared a huge West End Avenue apartment with two friends I had known since junior high school. It was an exuberant time. I was no longer financially dependent on my father, as I had a tiny nest egg and a modest salary from my first Broadway show, *Apple Tree*. I was truly on my own: free and twenty-four.

Each of us who shared the three-bedroom apartment had a room of our own. This was fortunate, not to say convenient, considering the various activities occurring at the pad, as we liked to call it. There was no more need for bizarre signals to warn one's roommate that he was approaching. No more embarrassing intrusions, like opening the door and seeing either hairy or smooth buttocks pumping happily away, depending on who was on top.

I performed eight shows a week at the Shubert Theater, albeit in the small chorus with a few speaking lines, and I would moonlight ambitiously after the curtain came down by going down Forty-fourth Street to the Improvisation Club to try out stand-up comedy material. Before leaving the theater, I would frequently smoke a few puffs of the dried leaves of the cannabis sativa plant. This would put me in a slightly more receptive mood, to inure me to the terrifying fact that in an hour's time I could quite possibly be onstage, in front of a crowd of people who were not laughing, thereby making a humiliating ass of myself. I would share the sativa with my friend James Saxon, who was the lead dancer and assistant choreographer of *Apple Tree*, as well as an original cast member of *West Side Story;* he was one of Jerome

Robbins's premier dancers. James was an incredible cut of a man, six feet tall, with what appeared to be a six-inch waist and pure muscle in all four quarters. He was married to a beautiful dancer. Women loved him, and the feeling was mutual. He was a martial-arts expert, which came in handy, as his choice of ballet dancer as a profession did not sit well with certain parties in the rough neighborhood of his youth. The wonderfully incongruous thing was, James had been a tough New York City street kid.

We would have a short smoke and spray the shit out of the windowless dressing room with Air Wick; then I would go off to make people laugh, and he would go off to cheat on his wife. Initially, I carried a twenty-five-pound Wollensak tape recorder to record the improvisations that tripped off the top of my head. In a short period of time, I acquired the latest lightweight tape recorder, which, though still reel to reel, used small reels. Soon technology came to the rescue, as audio cassettes came on the market, and I would record my work on a still more diminutive device without having to thread the tape into the machine. Years later, at an event I hosted with Dick Clark to commemorate the tenth anniversary of the Sony Walkman, I related this saga to Mr. Morita, the founder of Sony. He was fascinated by the fact that not only music lovers would use the device. Though he showed a sudden acute interest in comedians, he appeared to have little or no sense of humor.

I actually got the idea from watching an ambitious young woman comedian named Joan Rivers use a tape recorder at the Improv while her husband-manager, Edgar Rosenberg, watched with a studied eye and took notes. It was at the Improvisation that I learned the art of stand-up comedy. Starting in the mid-sixties, the Improv was a place where professional performers could get up and do a turn in an informal, leisurely atmosphere, though a few amateurs made their way to the stage as well. The audience was largely composed of off-duty actors and performers, well before the club's reputation gained hold and civilians began packing the place. It was the only venue of its kind, and would be copied hundreds of times over in the comedy clubs that dot the American landscape today.

This was different from the Hootenanny Nights held in the

Greenwich Village clubs like the Bitter End and Café Wha?, where people could get up and attempt imitations of the Kingston Trio or Ramblin' Jack Elliott. Those were once-a-week affairs when the headline act had the night off. For the most part, the performers there had less polish than the Forty-fourth Street crowd. The Improv had no booked act working nightly; instead, it had a steady stream of established and up-and-coming performers, and some not so up-and-coming, who would drop in and sometimes get up to perform. One might hear that Liza Minnelli was coming or that Jackie Vernon was going to try out some new jokes for his next appearance on *The Ed Sullivan Show*. It was here that I first saw Lily Tomlin, who made the occasional trek uptown from her semipermanent perch at the Duplex, a little club in the Village. Rob Reiner and Richard Dreyfuss (we called him Ricky) came in several times and were great laughers and very encouraging to me. They promised to be my guides when I came to Los Angeles.

This anticipation about who might be dropping in became the club's true charm. It certainly wasn't the architecture or the location. Forty-fourth Street and Ninth Avenue was hardly upscale then, and it was amusing to see the celebrities make their way through a gauntlet of drunks and panhandlers. The club had a tiny stage occupied mostly by a piano, next to which was a storefront window that allowed the more aggressive denizens of the street to make faces and expose themselves while a performer was on. The parcel of land on which the club stood was rumored to have been part of Aaron Burr's farm in the eighteenth century. If this is so, his remaining legacy must have been the men's room, and it was undoubtedly during his tenure that it had last been cleaned. It was a toilet that could make you hold it in forever and *never* sit down, bringing to mind my mother's admonitions to me as a child: "Don't *ever* touch a public toilet seat! Put paper on the seat. Squat. Hover. Use someone *else's* ass if you have to." In order not to touch anything in the tiny, filthy room, I would push open the door with my buttocks and come out with my washed hands held fingers up, like a surgeon after scrubbing. The phone booth was located near the toilet, and was approximately the same size, which caused confusion for newcomers. Many was the man who looked for the men's room in the phone booth, then saw the men's room and was sorry he hadn't peed in the phone booth.

The club served food quite late, and the chef, a moody Latino named Louie, distinguished himself by attacking the owner's wife with a knife after an apparent crack about his meat loaf. His temper was exceeded only by his mediocrity at the culinary arts, though the fare was hearty and appreciated at the midnight hour.

I first walked into the club in October 1966, after *Apple Tree* opened to successful reviews. David Steinberg had told me about the Improv, and I decided to get up and perform. Bud Friedman and his wife, Silver, owned the club. Bronx-born Bud loved the role of host and developed several affectations, such as wearing a monocle and ascot, that drew impertinent remarks from the comedians whose jokes he would borrow for his introductions. He was a Korean War veteran and had a vicious scar on his leg to prove it. Bud knew I was a professional appearing in a Broadway show, so he invited me to get up anytime.

Several cast members from *Apple Tree*, including the play's stars, Alan Alda, Barbara Harris, and Larry Blyden, came to give me support the first time I performed. Though I was nervous, the result was a resounding success, after which I was approached by a strange man in a black suit and red tie who was ceaselessly tugging at his collar in nervous discomfort. "You were brilliant, man," he said, "and I'm a tough cocksucker, but you have to come here every night for three years to get it right." I had never seen him before, but he seemed to be royalty at the Improv. Then he got onstage and absolutely tore the place apart. While delivering drinks, a waitress bent over in front of him. He looked at her ass and said, "That's what we need around here: new faces." His jokes were funny, and the attitude he used in delivering them was hilarious—a kind of everyman loser always tugging at his collar, even though, in a bow to comfort and a blow to tailors, the collar was two sizes too big.

His name, I learned, was Rodney Dangerfield, though where a guy like him got a name like that I couldn't imagine. He was a fixture there, and just starting to have success in a new incarnation. Some of his material was worthy of comparison to Art Buchwald and Russell

Baker, pithy if inadvertent social commentary. "I'll tell ya, our parks aren't safe, our schools aren't safe, our streets aren't safe: But *under our arms,* we have complete protection." His first show-business career, as Jack Roy, had been promising, but he quit at the urging of his wife, who wanted more security, and he soon became a successful entrepreneur in aluminum siding. His heart, though, was elsewhere, and he continued to write comedy and offer it to comedians like Jackie Mason and Joan Rivers until he bagged the siding business and became Rodney Dangerfield: a name, he subsequently told me, that he got from the Manhattan phone book.

It is worth pointing out that at the time, few comedians wrote their own material. Rodney had several *Ed Sullivan Shows* booked, and shortly, he was to appear on *The Merv Griffin Show.* I was to spend several years watching him, listening to him, and learning the craft as I followed him around to many of his gigs.

Certain techniques were instinctive, though complicated, like understanding the nuances and construction of a joke and how to test it. I learned how to play the whole room and grab the audience from the start. Other aspects, while seemingly simple, were incredibly important, like how to use and hold the microphone, and whether or not to remove it from the stand. Rodney taught me to find out the composition of the audience. How many Jews? Italians? Blacks? How old are they? How much did they pay to get in? When do *I* get paid? What to do if the laughs aren't coming? I couldn't have learned any of this in any university in the country, even at the Yale School of Drama.

I was with Rodney at a small hotel he was playing in Cape Cod. It was a gorgeous sunny day, though there were thirty-knot winds whipping up the bay. Rodney suggested we go sailing in one of the hotel catamarans. "What do you know about sailing?" I asked. "What's there to know?" he answered. He gave Vinnie the boat boy a twenty-dollar bill that almost blew away. We got into the boat and were off.

Rodney was standing up with the wind blowing his hair, an exhilarated look on his face, repeating over and over: "This is too fuckin' much. This is too fuckin' much." He occasionally went to tug at his collar, even though he was wearing only a bathing suit. It felt more like a speedboat than a sailboat, and in ten seconds we were nine hundred yards from shore. Then he said, "I think I'll take a swim. Know what I mean, man?" We were still moving pretty good when he dived over the side. I did not know how to manipulate the sails so as to easily come around to Rodney in the water, so I pushed the rudder all the way to one side and made a nice tight turn of six miles. I finally reached the white speck in the water, and a pale arm reached over the pontoon. Rodney had come within a minute of drowning. As I helped him up onto the boat, in his exhaustion and panic, he still sounded like Rodney Dangerfield—a drowning Rodney Dangerfield. "That was too fuckin' much," he said as he coughed up half of Cape Cod Bay.

I went with him to Miami, where he played the Diplomat Hotel and had a kind of reunion with his father, with whom he had been estranged for many years. Phil Roy was in his early seventies and had throat cancer. He had not been around for his son's childhood, and only recently had they had a rapprochement. As we sat on the beach, his father, obviously proud, kept repeating in his fading voice that Rodney should keep hitting his "no respect" theme. "Jack, it's a good hook. Keep it up." The old man died shortly thereafter. Rodney kept hammering the theme at the Improv.

David Frye was a nationally known impressionist who also regularly worked out material at the Improv. Not only did he do excellent imitations of voices, he actually seemed to *become*, body and soul, the person he was imitating. He worked in the traditional way: naming the subject, turning his back on the audience, pulling up his collar, and turning back again as Lyndon Baines Johnson, Nelson Rockefeller, Richard Nixon, or Burt Lancaster. He could do a brilliant Bobby Kennedy. His body and face would change in an uncanny way.

I had met him in 1964 at the Café Wha? on Bleecker Street on a Hootenanny Night. I went down to the men's room before my set and noticed a man at a urinal with a mirror in front of it, doing an impression of James Cagney: "You, you dirty rat. I'm gonna get you like you got my brother." He repeated "dirty rat" a dozen times to get it right, all the while urinating, shaking, and closing his fly. I was not used to seeing such behavior at a urinal, so I considered retreating upstairs. I did have to go, though, and I was to perform shortly and was nervous enough without compounding my terror onstage with the urgency to urinate. I ambled nonchalantly to the farthest urinal from Cagney, who paid not the slightest attention to me.

Now here he was, three years later at the Improv, flanked by his writers, a real up-and-comer who was appearing on national television. He was also, for all his brilliance, a highly eccentric, hard-drinking, ill-tempered man who could enjoy and not enjoy his hard-earned success in a manic-depressive way. He was myopically focused on his career, which was his life. The night after Bobby Kennedy was killed, I saw a drunk David Frye crying in a secluded booth at the rear of the club. I went over to him, and he beckoned me to sit down next to him. "I'll be honest with you," he slurred. "Sure, I'm sorry that he's dead. But Jesus . . . Jesus . . . I can't do one of my best voices now."

He would often get into arguments at the Improv, and being five foot four, he usually withdrew from the dispute before punches were thrown, but he could rile people. In those years, Dangerfield was an excellent improviser, the new, more theatrical term for what Rodney called ad-libbing. He was as fast on his feet as anyone. One night Frye began to heckle Dangerfield from the back of the audience, and Rodney replied with some barbs that David took exception to, including: "David Frye, the great mimic. A mimic is one step above a juggler." A furious Frye had to be restrained by friends (it was easy), and he put forth a slew of profane but hardly clever vitriol. He got louder and louder until he was screaming. Rodney, microphone and cigarette in hand, shook his index finger at Frye as if addressing an eight-year-old child and said, "Don't you raise your voices to me!"

About a year or so after I first went to the club, I met Bette Midler, who had replaced one of the daughters in Fiddler on the Roof, then in a long run. She would come after the show, dressed in eccentric clothing that looked like it had been borrowed from Fiddler's wardrobe department. Bette was an extremely rare breed: a Jewish girl from Honolulu who had a totally New York sensibility. She would try out musical material every night, showing changes and experimentation from the night before. She was relentless in her attention to duty, in finding out what worked and what didn't. She tried ten different versions of "She'll Be Coming 'Round the Mountain," from a jazz interpretation to a ballad, before she dropped the idea. Accompanying her was Ray Johnson, the ever talented, ever patient long-time piano player at the Improv, who later became my accompanist and with whom I worked and traveled for several years. At first, with the bad lighting and sound system and Bette's unspectacular looks, the audience would sometimes be talking and inattentive, and she had to fight to gain their focus. But she had the energy of Judy Garland and the balls of Bette Davis and plowed on her merry way. It was amazing to see how talent wins the day, for in thirty seconds they would rapidly become enthralled by her.

By contrast, Caesar Peters was an impressive-looking black man, deep-voiced, handsome, and six foot six. When he ascended the stage, the audience would hush and pay rapt attention to his booming basso and imposing appearance. But Caesar was a man of modest talent and could not deliver the goods, and in a matter of forty-five seconds, the crowd was in rapt conversation, ignoring the big fellow.

Bud and Silver Friedman knew a good thing when they saw it and would supply free food and drink to Bette, as well as some guidance: This kid was a long way from home. They became her first managers. Bud got her a booking to perform for the Friars Club. The audience snickered at her Bohemian appearance, but once again Bette won them over with her talent and originality. I would frequently drive her home to her apartment in the West Seventies, near Amsterdam Avenue. She was an ever optimistic girl and determined to succeed despite an industry run by people who were seldom able to think out of the box, who slavishly imitated what had worked before. The prerequisites for a "girl singer," as the job title was known, included extreme good looks, considered as important as talent and ability. So Bette Midler, like Barbra Streisand before her, created her own standard for beauty and sex appeal and went on to kiss many a leading man in the movies.

I initially met Richard Pryor at the club in 1967. Though he was not yet well known, there was an exciting buzz about him. Richard was an exceptional talent, with the gift of virtuosic mimicry, excellent timing, and funny body language. He was trying out new ideas, which gave a spontaneous feeling to his set, including the parts that weren't improvised. The material was fluffy, apolitical, inoffensive, and very very funny. I was immediately a fan. He had made several successful appearances on summer shows and *The Merv Griffin Show* as a hilarious yet adorably puckish collegiate type given to wearing white sweaters. On several occasions, we got up and did improvisations together, along with Lily Tomlin. He was articulate and charming in our talks; and as I had not yet appeared on television and he had, he generously answered my questions. Richard pointed out that we created our material in a similar way, and he was right, though he improvised brilliantly without a Second City pedigree or any training. He liked me, and he liked my stuff, which pleased me tremendously, as the feeling was mutual. There was an air of innocence about him that was appealing; perhaps his midwestern Peoria, Illinois, upbringing, I thought. One night I asked him what college he had gone to, and he broke out laughing as if I had told a primo joke. "Man, that's funny," he said between giggles, with his hands flailing—he laughed with his hands, too.

"What's so funny?"

"I didn't go to college, man. I spent my childhood with the pimps and whores and shit like that."

I was shocked. He didn't seem like a person raised in such circumstances. I made fun of the fact that we came from such dissimilar backgrounds: me the middle-class educated Jewish boy, and he the survivor of a past I could hardly imagine—both comedians. It was revealed that as kids, we both had used comedy to avoid getting beaten up and had been class clowns.

Pryor and I hung out for several days, until he returned to California, but not before an incident occurred out on Forty-fourth Street, right in front of the club. Richard got into an ugly argument with his woman and began to slap her hard across the face, which was very disturbing. She had a bloody nose. It was a violent side of him I had not seen before, and it made me very uncomfortable. I sort of joked about it the next day, saying I was just a middle-class guy and he was obviously dangerous and did he do it often, because that sort of antic made me nervous. He said he understood perfectly how I felt; that he was drunk, that he and his girlfriend occasionally had their differences, that they had made up. He was his appealing self again, and it was a wonder to me that a man so likable could turn so suddenly into someone else. No doubt drugs and alcohol were a catalyst, but one had to contemplate his experiences as a child.

It was 1968, which was an important and difficult year that included the assassinations of Robert Kennedy and Martin Luther King, Jr., and several riots in American cities. It was a significant time for Richard, the straw that broke the camel's back. In the following years, his incarnation as a cute, nonthreatening collegian was cast aside, and a hard-edged, profane, more authentic Richard Pryor emerged. I never saw Lenny Bruce or Jonathan Winters, my prime inspirations, in person. But I saw Richard at Avery Fisher Hall, and he was the best comedian I ever saw live.

Besides performers at the Improv like Pryor, Bette Midler, Lily Tomlin, Robin Williams, Danny Aiello, and others who achieved big careers, there were those who tried and fell by the wayside in a kind of show-business Darwinism. Laura the waitress comes to mind. She was a pleasant, intelligent person and overqualified for her job, which she of course saw as temporary. A zaftig, hourglassed woman with big breasts, she was determined to pursue a singing career. Her specialty number was the Aldonza the Whore song from *Man of La Mancha*. When she was told she was up next, she would, like Clark Kent, remove her waitress outfit and change into a provocative costume featuring garter belts, seamed stockings, and a high-tech bra that pushed her bust upward at a thirty-degree angle. When she took the stage, she would transform herself into Aldonza the Whore, and at her prearranged cue, the meager spotlight would dim. All too often, the meager sound system would dim as well, and Bud Friedman, the self-proclaimed "charming, bearded host," would rush to the stage and try a series of low-tech microphone checks. He used a lot of blowing into the microphone as well as an annoying assortment of "Is this on?" "Check one two," hitting the mike, and a feedback squeal that could cause permanent deafness.

Laura the waitress would do her dramatic Aldonza the Whore

song with all the passion and anger she could muster, and the first row
of tables particularly, would get the in-your-face effect. Her presentation included thrusting her head back, her chest out, and her hands
on her hips in the manner of the naughty, haughty Aldonza. She had a
loud voice, and toward the end of the song, she would put her foot up
on the front table aggressively, causing the patrons in front to arch
back as if they were watching a 3D movie and somebody threw a
spear at the camera. Unfortunately, people in the audience were
often eating. Then would come a veritable musical assault that was
totally inappropriate for customers who were chomping into a steak
or a pile of ribs. I can only paraphrase the graphic lyric that she
screamed right into the faces of the front row, but it was something
like: "Born on a DUNG HEAP! Look at this kitchen maid REEKING
WITH SWEAT! I am Aldonza the whore!" This was abetted by her
ample underarm hair, which was far from an appetite stimulant.
Invariably, the victimized tables could be heard en masse: "Check,
please! Check, please! *Now,* please!" The owner didn't mind, as on a
busy night he could turn those tables over easily. One could imagine
Laura doing eight shows on a Saturday night and making Bud Friedman a fortune with her pounding references to dung heaps reeking
with sweat. At the end of her number, she would quickly change out
of her costume, back into her waitress apron, and give her customers
their checks. Food orders always diminished after Aldonza's performance. "Aldonza the Whore" was the chef's favorite song.

Danny Aiello was also a fixture at the club, though we initially
knew him as the maitre'd/bouncer. He was a gregarious man, devoted
to his family, who had seen hard times: a survivor, gently spoken and
polite to a fault. This humble demeanor was no doubt compensation
for the notion that Danny Aiello was one tough guy. He would often
join me onstage, along with the comedian Bobby Alto and a singer
named Bud Mantilla, to be the background group for my doo-wop
improvisations. I would create lyrics and a melody, and they would
create doo-wops and shooby-doobys as we went along. Danny's wonderful acting talent was still a secret to most of us then, but he was the
best bouncer I've ever seen. He could eject the toughest of them quietly and efficiently, with minimum force and tumult, so as not to dis-

turb the karma of the room. On very rare occasions, he used a short right hand to the belly that one could hardly detect.

Life at the Improv quickly became the locus of my social situation as well as my professional one. I have always been grateful that I lived during the sexual revolution, which, as revolutions go, was much more fun than the French or Bolshevik revolutions. Much to my joy, I found that a good many of the women I met were willing and ardent revolutionaries. There was no such thing as AIDS, and syphilis was practically unheard of, though one occasionally heard that this guy or that one got the clap. I got the crabs once, but that was more zoological than pathological. The chief concern had always been getting a girl pregnant. Now birth-control pills and diaphragms had become as ubiquitous in young women's purses as lipstick and house keys, and many young men consigned their primitive condoms to the ash heap of history. It seemed like everyone had sex with everyone: strangers, first dates, people passing in the night who knew each other for a few days or a few minutes. Frequently, bodily fluids were exchanged before names.

One got the feeling that long-term platonic relationships were an impossibility, as the lure of sex was inexorable. Friends who routinely discussed politics or the mundane would break down eventually, out of curiosity, the allure of the new, strange, and different being what it was. Undoubtedly, there was a thrill about going from the distance of casual friendship, to wondering what the sex would be like with this person, to the bedroom and shared intimacy. Sometimes such encounters ended the friendship or strained it, and other times people returned to the old relationship, their curiosity satiated. Some continued in the best of both worlds—friends and sexual partners— as it was generally given that one did not have to be in love with someone to fuck them.

Sex was a newfound freedom for many, especially women, and was looked on as a rightful and healthful function that one had best perform with some regularity. If you had to wait to fall in love before you had sex, you'd rarely have it, or you'd have to fall in love three or four times a month. Purely sexual relationships sprang up, and many of the guys and girls had regulars with whom the understanding was that they had sex and little else, by mutual agreement. They were able to turn the passion on and off like a light switch: roaring stud and passionate siren with bodies locked together one moment, and pragmatic adults the next.

There was a nice girl who occasionally got up to perform at the Improv if no other act was available. I will call her Baby, because I cannot remember her name, which is probably just as well. She sang and made an attempt at comic patter, with a mediocre voice compounded by no sense of pitch or rhythm. The jokes were stolen and stale and poorly told—I had heard one of them in the sixth grade. The audience was surprisingly tolerant of her good-natured ineptness, for she clearly did not have it. What she did have was a pretty face, darkish Mediterranean looks, brilliant eyes, and a body that everybody agreed, in the parlance of the day, "did not quit." Male customers, particularly, seemed to give her the benefit of the doubt, even in the midst of painful off-key high notes that cut through the brain, making everyone grimace and rise three inches from their chairs. Even though she finished eight bars ahead of the pianist, bringing to mind the definite need for a metronome purchase, she seemed oblivious to the fact that she had no talent. On the contrary, she was quite ambitious about her future career.

I was already established at the club, so she sought my advice on matters relating to her act, and there was a fair amount of flirting. Over a drink at the bar or a cup of coffee, she would ask a lot of questions and absorb the answers like a sponge. "Are my tunes right for me? Should I wear something more dressy? Should I wear my hair up? How do I get an agent? How do I get new jokes?" I could not tell her that none of these answers would help, that her best bet for a career in show business would be to work silent and naked. I would not hurt her for the world. Apart from being a showbiz interloper, she was an incredibly hot woman, and I desperately wanted to have sex with her. She, however, was a more cautious straitlaced type who insisted on putting off sex until our second date.

This turned out to be well worth the twenty-four-hour wait. All the passion, clarity, focus, and talent that she lacked onstage, she demonstrated three times over as a lover. She was knowledgeable, adventurous, and had the most wonderful smell about her; a gorgeous sun-tanned body with white stripes left by the straps on her bikini; full lips, beautiful teeth and skin, and dark curly hair. She was a natural and a devotee of *The Kama Sutra* who liked to say the things that men like to hear.

We went at it for quite a while, like two contortionists. Then, as her orgasm began to build, she let out with an extraordinary verbal barrage. She began repeating the same phrase over and over again: at first quietly, then increasing in volume until, at her climax, she was screaming it at the top of her lungs: "I want your baby . . . I want your baby . . . I want your baby . . . I want your baby! I want your baby!! I WANT YOUR BABY! I WANT YOUR BABY!! I WANT YOUR BAYYYYYYYYBEEEEEEEEEEEEEEEE!!!!"

There were two seconds of silence, which she broke abruptly: "Robert, do you think I should do an up-tempo tune for my opening number? The ballad doesn't seem to work at the beginning, maybe it needs a little more pep. What do you think? How about a vocal coach? Should I work with a hand puppet? How about a duet with me and the puppet?" Seconds before, she wanted my baby, now she wanted a hand puppet. We lay in bed as she continued to pepper me with questions and I continued to give evasive answers. It was not fifteen minutes (ah, youth) before I began to kiss her neck, which distracted her: "Do you think I should wear something more formal—oooh, stop that. Oooh, don't stop that. Yeah . . . oh yes!" We immediately got hot again and commenced to enjoy a second helping of the carnal, coital experience. And yes, she gave out with the same shouting at the appropriate time. "I want your baby! I want your baby!! I want your baby!!! I WANT YOUR BABY! I WANT YOUR BABY!! I WANT YOUR BABY!!! I WANT YOUR BAAAAAAAAAYBEEEEEEEEEEEEEEEE!!!!!! Do you think I should audition for William Morris? How about Broadway shows? I was thinking of having a nose job, do you think I should? What about music charts and arrangements?"

Not surprisingly, she faded from view at the Improvisation, though in the ensuing period, I met a couple of guys who had dated her before I did. She wanted their babies, too.

❉   ❉   ❉

I had moved to my own little brownstone apartment on 103rd Street, near Riverside Drive. It was the perfect bachelor pad, with a fireplace and bay windows framed by beautiful wood shutters. The three-story house had been the boyhood home of Humphrey Bogart before it was divided up into small apartments.

I was progressing steadily as a comedian and actor but felt the need to escape as much as possible from the pressure and competition of the pervasive phenomenon known as show business. One of my favorite avocations was feeding the squirrels in Riverside Park. This park was an Upper West Sider's idea of country, where one could find a modicum of peace and relative quiet. There was even a stone wall separating the park from the street, which stood as a portent that here the wilderness begins, albeit followed by the Hudson River and New Jersey. Flora and fauna abound in Riverside Park, though that counts poison ivy and rats as well. I remembered seeing bilingual signs warning of rat poison: PELIGROSO! PELIGROSO! I could see the "ratones" in question busily going about their business at the base of the wall, in perfect harmony with the pigeons and squirrels, who apparently did not discriminate.

I had, over a period of three weeks, coaxed a particular squirrel to approach me and accept peanuts from my fingers. This is no small attainment. Squirrels are wild animals: wary, nervous little rodents that, like rabbits and rats, assume that everything is their enemy. They do not, as a rule, come over to you like a golden retriever, to be petted and cuddled. Therefore, I felt tremendous satisfaction in the triumph over the trepidation of this notably cautious creature, a bit like I had conquered nature—without hurting anyone, of course.

On this particular day, I searched for my subject with a handful of peanuts. I could distinguish him from the others by a peculiar lump on his neck, so I called him Lumpy. Several other squirrels that I recognized clearly acknowledged me as "that big, two-legged thing with the peanuts." But none of them had the sense of adventure, or courage, or perhaps recklessness to come and take the nut directly from my hand; only Lumpy.

I heard a squirrel sound high up in a tree and looked toward it. Our eyes made contact at about the same time, and Lumpy skillfully scrambled down the large oak tree, chattering incessantly. At about six feet from me, he stopped and stood up on his hind legs like Trigger used to do with Roy Rogers on his back. I squatted down as I usually did, offering the peanut between my right thumb and index finger, along with a kissing noise. (Incidentally, the same sound that naughty construction workers made when any female passed by who was not their mother or sister.) As the squirrel came nearer, he seemed to do a ritualistic dance of hesitation, moving forward and back, then to the side and forward once again. It seemed that he was regressing and would not accept the nut unless I tossed it to him. Just when I was about to call it a day and throw the nuts to all the *ordinary* squirrels, Lumpy sashayed forward and nervously took the nut from my fingers. He retreated slightly to consume it, then came immediately back for a second helping. This time he sidled up more confidently but accidentally knocked the peanut out of my hand with his nose. Not realizing what he had done, he opened his mouth and clamped down on the tip of my index finger, mistaking it for the nut.

I felt the considerable pressure from his considerable jaws and was hesitant about pulling my finger out, for fear that a fair portion of it would remain in the creature's mouth. I couldn't say for sure, but I think the squirrel had similar thoughts. Several moments of panic ensued as the realization came to me that my finger was clenched in the razor-sharp teeth of a wild rodent. Suddenly, Lumpy disengaged, paused for a confused second, then dashed off over the wall. I looked at my finger and discovered a tiny puncture, with a minute droplet of blood confirming that the squirrel had indeed broken the skin. I looked over the wall and down at its base, where Lumpy had retreated, and saw a melange of busy animals, including some rats. A horrible thought possessed me. RABIES! Oh, shit no! Bitten by a squirrel that lives among hundreds of rats! Rabies for sure! Fifty needle injections in the stomach is the *good* news; an excruciating death, foaming at the mouth, the worst-case scenario. I remembered a graphic scene from the movie about Louis Pasteur in which an unfortunate rabies victim had a hideous convulsive demise.

Come to think of it, that ugly tumor on the squirrel's neck was a sure sign of rabies. My heart began to race. Hold it. This is ridiculous. I'm sure it's nothing. I'm going to a doctor.

I walked down to West End Avenue, where I had seen a physician's shingle. I rang the bell and was admitted to an office that must have been furnished fifty years earlier, complete with ancient medical equipment reminiscent of a low-budget *Buck Rogers* serial. The place was empty. The doctor was a stooped, elderly man with wire spectacles drooping down his nose and shabby suspenders holding up his pants. He had a German accent from a Marx Brothers routine. "Vot can I do for you, young man?" I looked down at the finger in question. There was no blood; the wound was almost imperceptible. I felt a bit ashamed. "Well," I said sheepishly, thinking for a split second I was Gary Cooper, "a squirrel bit me. Not on purpose, it was an accident." I fully expected him to chuckle or yawn, but he let out a torrent of excited oaths. "*Gott in Himmel! Mein Gott!* You must get to the hospital immediately! Immediately! Go go! The nearest is St. Luke's, Von Hundred and Thirteenth and Amsterdam! I only hope it is not too late! *Mein Gott!*"

I staggered out of his office to the street, my life reeling before me, and looked unsuccessfully for what seemed like hours for a cab. I had begun to run up to Broadway when it occurred to me that if the rabies had entered my bloodstream, I was only helping the filthy microbes spread by exerting myself. I'd best calm down. I began to walk in slow motion, like a dream sequence, to retard my circulatory system. I remembered this advice from a Roy Rogers movie in which a man was bitten by a rattlesnake and Roy advised him to stay calm so the poison wouldn't spread as quickly. As I recall, Roy sucked at the wound as well: the sign of a very, very good friend. I immediately dismissed any notion of sucking at my own wound, as the taste of rodent saliva seemed a poor trade-off for the good it might do.

I finally hailed a cab, ever so slowly and deliberately: "Taaaaaaaaaaaxxxxxxxxxiiiiiiiii!" I began to feel symptoms in the form of aches and numbness, and I was certain that my saliva was foamy. I arrived at the emergency room just in time to find a waiting room full of patients, about sixty strong. None were complaining about the six-hour wait for medical attention, even though many of them appeared critical. An assortment of gunshot and knife wounds, cardiac arrests and strokes, and a man with an ax in his neck all waited patiently for their turn. Enter me with an injury that appeared so minor that I believed it had actually healed in the cab. But those rabies! Should I rush to the front of the line? Doctors and nurses could be seen scurrying to and fro from behind curtains and IV bottles. There was much shouting and chaos that gave the place the aura of a MASH unit.

A triage was taking place in which those most severely injured or ill would be treated first. I panned the scene of the hideously afflicted and injured, the screaming children, the blood and the pain; then I looked down at my finger and could not find the wound. Worse, I could no longer even remember which hand the finger was on.

"Excuse me, Doctor, I was bitten by—" I tried to explain, but the doctor was rushing about, obviously preoccupied with the five-inch knife wound in the spleen of the flailing patient on the gurney. "Uh, Nurse my doctor told me that I must seek—" I tried again, but the nurse shouted something about losing number five. I approached an exhausted intern. "Excuse me, Doctor, but I was bitten by a squir—" "Can't you see I'm busy? Later!" he snapped. I was determined not to die a chump who was too embarrassed to go to the head of the line because he didn't want to seem pushy. "Doctor, I have an emergency here," I shouted.

"No time now," he replied, squirting a hypodermic of adrenaline into a dead man.

I was mad now. "Goddammit, I was bitten by a squirrel! You know how serious that is? I could be dying right this minute. I was bitten on the finger by a squirrel!" I screamed.

The doctor looked up at me. "You were bitten on the finger by a what?"

"A squirrel. Lumpy. He didn't do it on purpose, it was an accident."

"You were bitten by a squirrel! Hey, everybody, he was bitten by a squirrel! Let's stop everything else and kiss his squirrel bite and make it all better."

All at once every doctor and nurse began to chime in. "Oh my God, a squirrel bite," said a nurse as she pulled a sheet over her late patient's face. "Another casualty of that great scourge, squirrel bite," said the intern with the syringe. "Are you kidding, man?" said another overworked healer with a bloody apron. They all broke into a laugh that went on and on and increased in intensity. It was as if all the tension and horror of dealing with these formidable medical emergencies had exploded into deranged and inappropriate behavior. These people were falling down in hysterical fits, and it was extremely contagious. As a comedian, I would have been proud to get such laughs, were it not for the context and the venue. Unfortunately, this was not the Improvisation.

One of the physicians composed himself enough to approach me. "Which finger?" he asked.

"I'm not sure," I replied, "but this doctor on West End Avenue seemed quite concerned that I might have rabies, and I did see blood."

"Wait a minute. You're not sure? Holy shit," he said. I could hear the moaning of the unfortunate wounded in the waiting room, and a fight was breaking out among the impatient patients over who was next. He took my hand, searching unsuccessfully for the injury. "Quite a wound. Have you made out your last will and testament? I'll give you a tetanus shot," he said, chortling.

"Never mind a goddamn tetanus shot. What about the rabies? I'm telling you, he definitely punctured the skin, and he has close contact with rats, I saw them. This is my life we're dealing with. How can you be so sure I won't get rabies?"

"Rabies? There hasn't been a reported case in New York City since 1938. The only way to get rabies here is to French-kiss a rabid bat. Now get the hell out of here."

A nurse gave me a tetanus injection, after which I walked out into a gauntlet of disgruntled patients waiting for attention. "Who the fuck are *you*?"

"I been waitin' for three hours, asshole!"

"Wait your turn like everybody else, man."

"I'll kick your ass, you cuttin' into line like dat." I thought I would be beaten to a pulp, and took little comfort in the fact the beating was to be administered conveniently in the emergency room.

I made it to the street unscathed, but this whole incident ended my squirrel hobby and diminished my enthusiasm for the species

considerably. I had little truck with squirrels for some time after my
encounter. A few years later, I was engaged to do a show at Nicholls
State University in Thibodaux, Louisiana, just southwest of New
Orleans, near the mouth of the Mississippi River. We all know Den-
ver is the mile-high city; Thibodaux, Louisiana, has the presence of
mind, however, to be a mile *below* sea level. Or so it seemed. If someone in Minneapolis took a shower, these people had to abandon their
homes immediately and seek higher ground. They could be seen regularly on the network news, bravely looking to the future: "Guess
we'll jes hafta rebeeld ageen." Guess so. Or live on a pontoon.

These folks, who were regularly laughed at by flood-insurance
companies, made up for their perilous existence with some of the
finest eating anywhere, and a relaxed tempo of life that was a 33 rpm
to my New York 78. The contrast began at once, when my plane
landed somewhat tardily in New Orleans. Knowing I would be late
for planned interviews, I began spewing out a torrent of worry-laden
apologies to my airport greeting party, like an Evelyn Wood speed
talker. "Gee, I'm sorry. We'd better get moving here. Can we switch
the five P.M. interview to six-thirty? Or the five-forty-five to seven?
What about the radio guy, can he do it at the theater? Or, if not, what
do you think? Can we get there by seven?" The unhurried reply
seemed to take an hour and a half in the saying: "It's awlraht, Robbad,
y'all jes relax neow. Y'all can git theah at sebn . . . oah sebn-thoity . . .
oah eight . . . oah nahn . . . oah not at awl. We'll woik it out, don't be
fussin' 'bout nuthin'. Tonaght we gonna cook y'all a Cajun feast after
yo show." It was not my desire to be fussin', particularly about nuthin',
so I surrendered to the locals and the locale and enjoyed the ride in
the state university van, with six speakers blasting heavyweight
zydeco.

The show turned out to be wonderful, as I responded to a spirited
audience cheered, no doubt, by the realization that their campus was,
for the moment, not underwater.

A note here. Early in my career, I automatically assumed that
southern audiences would be less acute, less hip; in a word, dumber.
This has rarely proved to be the case, though there are enough vapid
audience members everywhere to go around. I personally believe

that comedy audiences have become less cognizant of the world around them, less well read, and generally expect more vulgar and gratuitously cruel humor than the ones I started with in the late sixties. College students seem to have less veneration for erudition and the pursuit of knowledge. Perhaps I'm wrong, but didn't this trend begin when Allen Ludden's *G.E. College Bowl* went off the air?

After my performance, members of the decidedly unintellectual men's phys-ed department spirited me off to a campus dining room. I was introduced to our chef for the evening, who offered me a fried oyster with a cayenne-pepper smack like I'd never tasted; and shrimp in a dark, sweet, peppery sauce . . . out of this world. The freshness of the catch was one of the secrets; I was assured these shrimp had been backstroking in local waters that very afternoon.

The chef was a cordial Cajun with a ponytail wrapped in a colorful bandanna, whose immutable smile revealed a large gold tooth with writing on it that I tried unsuccessfully to read. It could easily be interpreted as impolite to attempt to read something written inside a person's mouth. He had a French name and that intriguing accent of Americans of this region, at once French and North American, which one can hear nuances of in the accents of Canada and northern New York, not to mention hockey players. Remarkably, all of these northeners lived some fifteen hundred miles to the north of Louisiana, and all of them are part of the historical happenstance of seventeenth- and eighteenth-century continental American history.

As the chef produced one incredible dish after another, like fried Cajun turkey made with sweet peppers and onions, and a gumbo that should be declared illegal, I was transported to hitherto unknown heights of gluttony. I, who had never tasted a shrimp that had not been frozen, who had wondered if tuna fish was actually reeled up from the ocean in a can, along with the mayonnaise and the celery, thought I had eaten the best meal of my life. Just then my host the football coach said, "Hey Robert, y'all ever have squirrel?" "What?" I replied, thinking he had said: Hey Robert, y'all ever have squirrel? "Y'all ever have squirrel?" It's got to be a euphemism, I thought, probably a delicious, rich chocolate dessert that they call squirrel, like the famous chocolate turtle. Certainly they cannot be talking about those industrious little crea-tures that inhabit Riverside Park. Who would eat a squirrel?

Whereupon Gold Tooth opened the freezer and removed several plastic bags with frozen bloody carcasses. These did not appear to be delicious chocolate desserts. "Let me think," I lied. "Wait a minute, no, I don't believe I ever have. But I'm stuffed, I couldn't eat another thing. What does it taste like?"

"Like chicken, Robbad. Jes lahk chicken." Of course I recognized that answer as the all-purpose description for any exotic food that someone tries to talk me into tasting. Frogs legs? Tastes like chicken. Rabbit? Tastes like chicken. Alligator meat? Rattlesnake? A Buick? Tastes like chicken. "Squirrel is delicious, Robbad. It depends, though, how y'all cook it. You gotta make de roux, and de roux gotta be good," said the chef. "Nobody cook squirrel like I cook squirrel."

I had little reason to doubt him, as I knew no one who had squirrel in their culinary repertoire. A roux, it seems, is the spicy flour and wa-ter base for the sauce, which is like the nitroglycerine of the flavor world. The secret to successful squirrel cooking, the chef revealed, is in a powerful sauce and a very long cooking time. These are required, no doubt, to squelch whatever little waft of rodentia might remain in the thing. For let's face it. A squirrel is a *rat* with good public relations.

Chapter Fifteen

L.A. and Me

The city of Los Angeles and I have had an erratic relationship. I've had bitter disappointment there, as well as a modicum of triumph over the years. I have never become a full-time resident, though my profession has demanded my presence there frequently, Los Angeles being the obvious locus of the entertainment industry. I have made hundreds of trips and have kept an apartment there.

There are many reasons why I have made this choice which is illogical to a show business career and keeps one out of the loop. First and foremost is my emotional lifetime attachment to New York and its environs in which I was born and raised. All four of my grandparents came to the city from Hungary in 1903, found work, and settled here. It seems perfectly natural to love one's own soil, though in mobile modern America, it appears that many find it perfectly natural or necessary to leave it as well.

In my case, the decision was abetted by a healthy dose of New York chauvinism, espoused by my New York–based managers at the time, Jack Rollins and Charlie Joffe, and their chief client, Woody Allen. It was as if there were something inherently nobler about staying in gritty New York, with its superior culture, than succumbing to the land of make-believe. These were all stereotypes carried over in part from the well-known virtuous-theater versus decadent-movie debate, and the woeful tales of the literary giants who were eaten up and made irrelevant by the Hollywood studios. Faulkner and Fitzgerald come to mind, as their work was sought fervently only to be changed by a committee of bean counters eager to pander to the

ROBERT KLEIN

audience and the bottom line. Aside from that, there is no doubt that I love the genuine excitement and variety of New York and the changing of the seasons, despite the extra challenge of the high-wire act, which is what it is like to try to earn a living in the major-league entertainment business while living outside of Los Angeles. I have always been wary of the West Coast and have preferred the familiar territory of the East.

In a series of phenomenal coincidences, I was working in Los Angeles during the two major earthquakes of the twentieth century, the riots, the devastating fires in Malibu and Altadena, and the torrential rains of 1976. The earthquakes left a lasting impression on my psyche, as there is no experience in my life to compare them to, except the dream I apparently created while the first one hit in 1971, when I was sleeping in a hillside house on stilts in Laurel Canyon. My dream was fifty subway trains hurtling through the Columbus Circle–Fifty-ninth Street station at the same time. The earthquake of 1994 found me cowering in my bed on the eleventh floor of the Four Seasons Hotel in Beverly Hills. I thought I had met my end during the seemingly endless, violent swaying of the building; yet the only discernible damage was a miniature bottle of vodka that fell out of the minibar. To the hotel's credit, I was not charged.

These events have undoubtedly left a negative residue in my mind about Los Angeles, and have made me a faux pariah among my colleagues at Warner Bros., where I worked for three years on an NBC show called *Sisters*. Many of them speculated humorously that I had brought these disasters from New York. I am sure many of my California colleagues, besotted by astrology, tarot cards, and the mystical predictions of Nostradamus, believed it, though they never withheld their friendship or collegial spirit. Having been present for these catastrophes, I can attest to the fact that they have been met in Los Angeles with bravery and a community vitality that I have come to admire.

My childhood impression of the place, from television and a Bronx perspective, was that it was paradise defined: sunny, optimistic, prosperous, and beautiful. The television image of sun-drenched people in shirtsleeves at the Rose Bowl, in January no less, made me envious of the proverbial West and the wide open spaces. This feeling, I think, was born of my romance with cowboy heroes in movies from the early days of after-school television, in which kids my age galloped through the sagebrush and mountains on spotted ponies with Ken Maynard and Hoot Gibson, and never wore winter coats. My galloping was done on a horse of pillows on my bed in the sixth-floor apartment on Decatur Avenue, where we largely played indoors during the winter. I was captivated by the sunny backyards of Ozzie and Harriet and George and Gracie, the land of movie stars and movie making and eternal summer. I knew nothing about Horace Greeley, but west was nonetheless my favorite point on the compass. I even preferred the West Side Highway to the East River Drive.

As it turned out, I didn't get to California until I was twenty-five, ten years before I moved from the west side to the east side of Manhattan. I had recently signed with Jack Rollins, the best manager in the business for a young comedian. Among the performers he had guided were Harry Belafonte, Mike Nichols and Elaine May, Woody Allen, Dick Cavett, Joan Rivers, and Tom Poston. Based on his prestige and his support of me as an exciting new talent, Jack had gotten me a booking, sight unseen, on *The Dean Martin Show*, which was a stalwart NBC entry in that 1967–68 season. This was the definition of managerial clout. The deal was for three appearances, starting at twenty-five hundred dollars, a thrilling quantum leap in my prospects, as I had not yet appeared on talk shows, much less prime time.

I had developed about an hour of comedy material at the Improvisation Club, about half of which was suitable for television. Rodney Dangerfield had told Jack about me some months before and had arranged an evening at the Improv for Rollins and his partner, Charlie Joffe, to see me in action. A few days before the audition, Rodney was driving his Impala convertible down Seventh Avenue with me sitting next to him. Driving with Rodney was always a hair-raising adventure, his competence behind the wheel being the opposite of his talent as a comedian. His left elbow out the window, he would work the accelerator rhythmically in an on-and-off sequence, thrusting the passenger's head back and forth like a bobble-head doll. His right hand occasionally on the wheel, he would talk, gesticulate, tug at his collar, and maintain eye contact with the passenger instead of the road. "Know what I mean, man?" he would say in the middle of some riff or other, as if to make sure one was listening. In his fast speech, this was contracted into "Know mean, man?" It was impossible not to listen to Rodney, he was so funny, fascinating, and insistent.

After a particularly vigorous gesture with his steering hand, the car swerved, narrowly missing a horse and buggy, the kind that have no business on Seventh Avenue. There was an impertinent exchange with the silk-hatted driver, whom he called a fucking idiot, and then "Danger" (which was my personal nickname for Rodney) spotted the Stage Delicatessen on the right. He spontaneously decided that Jack should meet me here and now, before he saw me perform. Rodney was often spontaneous. He screeched and lurched to a halt, practically sending me through the windshield in front of the famous establishment, which in 1967 was still a mecca for celebrities and a favorite late-night hangout for Jack Rollins and his friends and associates.

Rodney double-parked in front. Taught my whole life not to intrude or be pushy, and having little chutzpah in these matters, I was reluctant to disturb the important stranger while he ate. To my protestations of "Are you sure it's all right?" Rodney would say only, "Yeah, yeah, don't worry about it, know mean, man?"

I thought of pragmatic things, like the space between my teeth and my abundant eyebrows, which were connected above the bridge of my nose.

I straightened my tie and pushed into place my windswept hair.

Inside, there were bright lights and noise and that wonderful smell of fatty cooked meat and pickles. I surveyed the celebrities who were there, and the abundance of eight-by-ten glossies on the wall of those who weren't. Rodney beelined for the proper table, filled with performers and managers who lit up at the sight of him: a sure sign that he was getting hot in the business. It was a scene right out of *Broadway Danny Rose,* the movie that Woody Allen made years later, in which Jack Rollins played himself, a manager sitting with a table full of showbiz guys in a delicatessen.

Rodney greeted the group with a joke, of course. "I'll tell ya. You

don't know *who* to believe. Last week I told my psychiatrist I got sui-
cidal tendencies. He told me from now on I got to pay in advance."
After a big laugh, Rodney presented me to a gaunt, lanky man with
billowing bags under his eyes: "Here's that kid I told you about who's
the next dimension." While I stood awkwardly over Mr. Rollins, his
party, and their pastrami sandwiches, he looked up at me with a
kindly smile over his half-glasses. "Hello, lad," he said, arching his
upper body back. This arched back was a posture I was to know well.
Jack is a heavy cigar smoker and, being a considerate man as well, he
had developed a habit in conversation of keeping both his cigar and
his mouth at a maximum distance from the person he was addressing,
so as not to offend. If he stood and conversed with an in-your-face
talker, it precipitated a kind of ballet, with Jack arching farther and
farther back until he looked like he could pass under a limbo bar.

Standing over him that night, I was cognizant of this retreating
movement and sensed that I should give him plenty of space. "A good
face for motion pictures," he said. I felt foolish. "I look forward to seeing you at the Improv, lad." Two things were certain: I had not said
one word besides "hello" and "thank you," and no one had ever called
me "lad" before.

Rodney apparently felt obligated to deliver an exit line: "I got no
beginning, no finish, and I'm weak in the middle." He got a big laugh,
and we returned to his convertible just in time for him to talk a cop
out of a ticket for double parking. He fed the police officer some
excellent jokes in that no respect-everyman style, and it won the day.
"I just had to go inside for a minute, know mean, man?" Cops loved
Rodney.

The next day, much to my surprise, I was telephoned by five of my
William Morris agents, all of whom were excited about coming to see
me: an expression of enthusiasm I had not seen from them in the ten
months since my return from Chicago. The senior agent, Lee
Stevens, who would run the agency in future years, cautioned me
about signing with a manager. He gave no reasons, but he was big-
time, powerful, and intimidating, so I appreciated his interest and
promised not to commit to anything without first consulting him. He
then presented a wonderful plum: He was bringing down the pro-

ducer of *The Merv Griffin Show*, Bob Murphy, and his staff to see me. They would come, not coincidentally, on the same night as Rollins. Why William Morris would not want two top people like Rollins and Joffe to join my team was a mystery to me, since it was clear that I never contemplated dropping my agents. The agency business had changed. Agents mostly booked jobs for their 10 percent, but for the most part they no longer formed and guided careers. That task was now the province of the manager, who typically got a 15 percent commission. Maybe Morris didn't want to deal with a difficult third party. I never knew.

It was March 1967, and I was working on *Apple Tree,* the musical directed by Mike Nichols. I loved meeting Mike, whose work I so admired, especially since I had recently completed my Second City stint. He, of course, was one of the pioneers of that whole scene. For my audition, I had stood on the bare Broadway stage, looking out at the house: Jerry Bock and Sheldon Harnick, the composer and lyricist; Stuart Ostrow, the producer; Jerry Adler, the stage manager; and Mike Nichols. There was a piano accompanist onstage to whom I gave my music. Mike and I made some small talk about people we knew mutually from Second City, like Sheldon Patinkin, Paul Sills, and Bernie Sahlins. I sang "Almost Like Being in Love," from *Brigadoon.* The instant I stopped singing, I yelled, "Thank you! Leave your picture and résumé, we'll get back to you." It was brazen, but it made everyone laugh, and the singing got "very good" and "nice job."

Mike came down the aisle to the stage and gave me several pages of script. "Go across the street to the Edison Hotel coffee shop and look this over. Come back in twenty minutes, and you'll read for us, okay?"

Now I really got nervous, because I sensed that the part was mine to lose. I returned at the appointed time, taking deep breaths to hide my trembling. *Apple Tree* was composed of three one-act musicals. I read the part of Mr. Fallible from Jules Feiffer's *Passionella,* a play about a poor female chimney sweep who gets her wish and becomes a movie star. Barbara Harris was set for the part. Then I read a scene with a young production assistant where Mr. Fallible, Passionella's boss, rebukes her. After the first reading, Mike asked me to think of Jules Feiffer's drawings, to be more whimsical, less caustic. I tried again with a little cartoonish flourish, to his obvious pleasure: He had directed, and I had understood and responded. I left the theater with a ton of hope and got the part the next day.

A few weeks later, I found myself at a New York rehearsal hall, with gorgeous women in tights and gorgeous men in tights. I wore pants and fell madly in love with the adorable star of the show, Barbara Harris. My overwhelming memory of that first rehearsal is Jerry Bock at the piano with Sheldon Harnick, singing the songs for everyone, in what they call a "zitzprobe" in opera. With the composers performing it themselves, it was quite personal and touching. Sheldon had a wonderful singing style for a lyricist, if you know what I mean.

After four weeks, the company went to the Shubert Theater in Boston for our out-of-town tryout. While Mike Nichols and the stars stayed at the Ritz-Carlton, we lesser mortals resided at the Avery Hotel, surely one of the most depressing dumps in God's creation. There should have been a sign at the front desk, right under the American Express sign: SUICIDES WELCOME. From my dismal tenth-story view of the alley, I could swear I saw a target on the pavement below.

Despite the lowlife digs, it was a heady time, Broadway show and all, but the company was small, and my lovely female colleagues were all attached. I felt some loneliness in a strange city. The Avery was located around the corner from the "combat zone," the honky-tonk block or two of cheap bars and strip joints, where sailors and their tarts strolled amid the shore patrol, with their pistols and bright white spats right out of an MGM navy musical. My neighbor at the hotel worked as an exotic dancer in a joint around the corner. She invited me to see her work, and I invited her to see mine. Her name was Lisa DeLure, though I fancy that that was a stage name. She was about thirty, blond, a tiny bit weathered with some pockmarks hidden by makeup, and a deep tobacco voice. Though she was Caucasian, she had the faint accent of a black woman, the kind that certain white athletes acquire, having spent so much time around their black colleagues' culture and sound. She would often make conversation with me when we encountered each other around the hotel. She might come in at two in the morning, catch me reading the paper, and sit down to discuss current events. She was reasonably well informed, but her points were laced with expletives: "those fuckin' Chinese Reds" and "that dickhead Johnson." She was crude and slutty, and I wanted her desperately, but to my mind she thought of me like a sweet kid brother.

One night I contrived to be in the lobby when she returned, and I told her I couldn't sleep. She invited me up to her room to get a sleeping pill, and there was her roommate, Yolande, a gorgeous but unconcious five-foot-eleven black woman, stretched out on the bed. From the punctures in her arm, I had a fair guess as to what was causing her slumber.

Here we were sitting on the bed, conversing as if the woman were a throw rug. I found it impossible to make a move on Lisa, especially since any sex would have to take place on top of a living corpse. Finally, the awkward situation dawned on Lisa, precipitated, no doubt, by a loud Three Stooges snore from her friend, who at least proved she was alive. We agreed to meet in my room. "I'll see you in five minutes, honey. There's certain things a girl's gotta do," she said. I wasn't sure what she meant, but it sounded like a good omen. She came to my room wearing a silk floral pattern robe for which sunglasses should have been required. After fifteen minutes, I was still talking the situation to death, my usual modus operandi of stalling, especially with such an intimidating, experienced woman.

Then (unconsciously?) I took out my harmonica. I put it in my mouth slowly and sucked out a wailing, plaintive, blues cry in E flat. Lisa's body tensed. She looked at me and said, "Ooooooooo, baby. Do that again." I obliged, this time with an even longer, more agonizingly sensual note. "Oooooooo, baby, more." I sucked even harder on the little Hohner, and she became more excited: "More. Ooooo, baby, more. Play that thing, baby."

I was sucking on the harp like a mindless maniac now, and she was going nuts. Finally, I could feel potential artery damage in my lip, so I stopped, but by then she was on top of me, whispering expletives, ripping my clothes off, taking charge. This is why I shall always have a particular attachment to my harmonica. It has amused me, gotten women sexy, and I even made fifteen bucks one night playing "Amazing Grace" on the BMT subway.

Opening night in New York, Mike Nichols had the whole cast lie down in the lobby of the theater in the afternoon. "Don't be nervous. I want you all to relax," he said. "Just remember, everything depends on this." It was a joke, but about half didn't get it, which increased their opening-night terror exponentially until Mike explained his intent.

It was an excellent and exciting premiere with good jobs all around. As the family and friends of the cast gathered onstage after the performance, my father approached Mike Nichols and introduced himself. Evidently mistaking Mike for a summer-camp counselor, Ben put a question to him: "How's my son doing?"

"Your son is very talented, Mr. Klein."

"Well, that's good." I was afraid he'd give the great Mike Nichols a twenty-dollar tip.

My crush on Barbara Harris grew with the knowledge that I would never be her lover. I was her friend and occasional confidant. I brought her several times to the Bronx Botanical Garden, near my childhood neighborhood, and we talked about our lives. It was a very romantic setting. I showed her the steep hill that was Decatur Avenue, which she found fascinating, the antithesis of her childhood turf in flat Chicago.

She was being wooed by several young-buck movie stars, Warren Beatty chief among them. "He won't leave me alone," she told me. How could I blame him? But she did not want to be rushed or pushed into relationships. She would sigh, her face in her hands, and, even with her brilliant talent and critical acclaim, reveal a sad confusion about her place in the world.

Eventually, she was nominated for a Tony Award, and the ceremonies, including a scene from our show, were to be broadcast from our *Apple Tree* stage, the Shubert Theater, on our Sunday dark night. Barbara was exceedingly nervous backstage and tried to beg off, saying she could not go through with the performance. Larry Blyden, one of the leads, rebuked her sternly, as if she were a schoolgirl:

"You're going to go out there. Your audience expects it. There are millions of people who will be watching you and will expect you to give your best." She broke down crying, but twenty minutes later, she gave her usual brilliant performance as Eve to Alan Alda's Adam, from our first act, based on a piece by Mark Twain. As a capper to the evening, she won the Tony.

The next night, during the regular performance of the first act, those of us in the dressing room heard strange words from the stage instead of the familiar chatter over the speaker on the dressing room wall. We all looked at each other and ran downstairs. There was a bewildered Alan Alda, looking helplessly on, while Barbara addressed the audience incomprehensibly, in a kind of psychotic reverie, totally ignoring the proper lines. Our stage manager, Jerry Adler, gestured from the wings to Alan. Should he bring down the curtain? A cigar-chomping stagehand was ready with the curtain rope in hand, looking to Adler for the signal. Finally, the audience caught on to the fact that they weren't seeing the show as planned. We knew we were witnessing the emotional disintegration of a wonderful and talented woman who at that moment had not the slightest idea of what was real and what was fancy. The curtain came down. Understudy Carmen Álvarez finished the first and second act. A call uptown brought Phyllis Newman, who did the matinees, to perform the third act. Barbara was out two months while Phyllis did the part. Jerry Adler has since turned to acting, playing the Jewish mobster Hesh on The Sopranos. Blyden died on vacation in North Africa under mysterious circumstances in the seventies. He was alone and possibly waylaid and murdered by nomads.

As the show had gotten good notices when it opened in October, and seeing that I would have employment for a while, I gave myself the thrill of buying a car for the first time on my own: a new 1967 stick-shift Volvo sedan. Broadway at the entry level was a proud step, but my sights were set on diversifying, on creating stand-up comedy material. When I had tried stand-up a couple of years before, on Hootenany Nights, I had often been the lone comedian among throngs of folksingers tuning, lots of college boys wearing denim work shirts, singing the blues on guitars purchased by their parents. I had mixed success then, but the maturity and experience from my tenure at The Second City had given me some professional confidence, and the laughs came. From the many nights that went well at the Improv, I proceeded over the next few months to improvise material, fine-tune it, and create a small body of work. When I felt ready, I asked some William Morris agents to come down and see me, but despite vague promises, they were unresponsive. It was only the heads-up about Rollins and Joffe coming to see me that brought them in a swarm.

The appointed evening arrived. Rodney played the impresario on the big night, totally in charge, with an anticipatory glint in his blood-shot eyes. He had a glass of red wine in his hand, constantly refilled by the club owner, Bud Friedman, as he dashed around barking orders like a caterer, about where the guests should be seated and when my performance should begin.

Griffin's people and the William Morris contingent were there at the appointed time of ten-thirty, but Jack Rollins, as would often be the case, was late. After twenty minutes of cabaret singers and corny introductions from Bud in the show room, Lee Stevens came out to the bar and began gently pressuring me to go on, knowing full well why we were waiting.

As the clock ticked away, I began to get nervous about keeping such important people waiting, and I appealed to Rodney. He got me into a corner near the bar. "Listen, man," he said. "Don't worry about Lee Stevens. Fuck William Morris. It's Rollins who's got to see you, know mean, man? Don't go on until he comes, he'll be here soon." Lee Stevens expressed concern about missing the last train to Great Neck, and Dangerfield stroked him, and I promised him a ride to his door in that eventuality. At last the most anticipated guests arrived, and Rodney ordered that the singer onstage be given several rude sig-nals, by way of blinking the lights, to get off. The flustered tenor hur-ried through the last bars of "If I Were a Rich Man" and took his seat. I made a note to apologize to him later.

Rodney took the platform that served as a stage and, wine in hand, got the audience's attention with a couple of great jokes and an insult to the talkative front table. He asked a bald man where he got "those haircuts with the hole in the middle." There was genuine electricity in the room; everyone knew what was going down and what the evening could mean for me. Rodney gave a brief and modest introduction, too modest for my taste, though he referred to my comedy as "the next dimension." He clearly wanted my performance to do the talking.

From the first minute, I launched into a ferocious show in which everything worked and the laughs rocked hard off the brick walls. I did stuff about public-school food: "Yankee bean soup that India rejected," served by a woman with a hairnet. It was a health rule to keep hair out of the food. Of course, her arms were incredibly hairy, but there was no hairnet on them; *they* were in the potato salad. I did a new piece about the loneliness of being alone onstage, auditioning for a Broadway show. I played an overly cheerful, nervous loser. I talked in echoes, to accentuate the atmosphere of the huge, empty theater. I did all of the voices, of course, the actor and the people out front. "Hello-oh-oh-oh-oh! My name is Robert Klein-ein-ein-ein!" Unlike my own experience, I made the director curt and rude. "Can we get on with it, Mr. Klein?" "Okay-aay-aay-aay! I'm going to sing 'Almost Like Being in Love-ove-ove-ove!' From *Brigadoon-oon-oon-oon!*" "All right, just do it, okay?" When I got to "There's a smile on my face for the whole human race, it's almost like being in—" "THANK YOU!" came the cry from the producer, and I froze with my arms spread apart in the middle of the song, holding the pose for a long laugh.

It was my best set to date, and fortuitously, in front of the most important people I had ever performed for. I looked frequently during the show at my distinguished guests, and they were laughing the big laughs, the kind that make your stomach hurt after forty minutes. The Improv regulars altruistically yucked it up even to material they'd heard before, and Rodney was beaming. I had scored.

Immediately following, amid kudos and well-wishers, Stevens cornered me with Bob Murphy and his *Merv Griffin* entourage. They offered an immediate and exclusive deal for five appearances, to hearty congratulations and backslapping from the agents. I was euphoric, though Lee Stevens would indeed miss his train, and I would have to drive him home to Great Neck. Rollins waited patiently until that group cleared out and then sat with me and his partner to discuss some ideas. While Stevens waited for his lift, Rodney entertained him at the bar. First of all, they stated that they would like to "work with me," which was a wonderful euphemism for becoming my managers. Second, while they thought the *Merv Griffin Show* offer was splendid, Jack advised me to turn it down. In his opinion, *The Tonight Show Starring Johnny Carson* was bigger and more vital to establishing a television career; he thought my television debut should be on that show. I could do *Griffin* later. He told me to keep writing material, and in a few months, he would bring people from *The Tonight Show*, which was taped in New York at the time, to see me perform. *The Merv Griffin Show,* on which I'd seen the young, brilliant Richard Pryor, and hilarious spots of Woody Allen, seemed pretty important to me and, with their offer, a bird in hand. But the next day I agreed to Jack's suggestion, and my career as a stand-up began.

I was soon booked into several major clubs: Mr. Kelley's in Chicago, opening for the great Sarah Vaughan; the Hungry I in San Francisco; the Troubador in Los Angeles; and the most thrilling commitment of all, *The Dean Martin Show.* The Troubador was scheduled for right after the *Dean Martin* appearance, since I would already be in Los Angeles and the club would not have to pay my airfare.

Rodney worked with me diligently to prepare the five-minute spot required for my network television debut. He explained that the American television-viewing public was vastly different from the hipsters and show-business people who comprised the audience at the Improv, and that whatever material I did had to be comprehensible to them. He did not put it in quite those terms. "Not the intellectual stuff, know mean, man? Don't make 'em have to think too much. You use some of those big words, and they won't know what the fuck you're talking about, know mean, man?" He emphasized that I should take the tried-and-true punchlines, the "never misses," rather than do a piece with some possible weak spots. In other words, take no chances; present only the best of the best. "Don't worry about using up material, you'll back up your truck and write more," he said. Being able to "back up the truck" was Rodney's way of describing those few comedians who wrote their own stuff.

I put together three bits that I practiced and polished and had a great deal of confidence in. Even the reasonably square audiences I encountered at my early occasional gigs responded enthusiastically, just like the hipster insiders at the Improv. They loved it at the small, run-down hotel I played, at the Knights of Columbus and the Jewish Temple. The routines never missed.

I performed my premier bit about substitute teaching at the Improv the night before the early flight to California. It was a tune-up, a confidence builder, and the Improv crowd gave me everything they had. Everyone made a proud fuss and wished me well in Los Angeles, as if they were sending one of their own to the Olympics. One of my friends, an Improv waitress, even made me a wonderful offer for the night that was almost impossible to resist. But, like a true Olympian, I demurred, for it was the night before the race, my event, and even sex had to take a backseat to the project at hand.

I needed my sleep, but that night I could not sleep for the excitement, and I stayed up all night. Jack Rollins, ever the night owl, also had no sleep, though we caught some winks in the first-class, generously proportioned reclining seats of the DC-8. It was my first experience in that exalted section, with its miniature crystal salt and pepper shakers, linen tablecloths, and filet mignon. Between dozes, Jack expounded on my wonderful future in movies, television, and on Broadway while I gaped in amazement at the Grand Canyon from thirty-seven thousand feet.

We finally arrived at LAX, and a driver met us at the luggage area with a printed sign with my name on it, which made me feel very important. We proceeded north on the San Diego Freeway, which I had heard mentioned so often on television in a comedic vein, famous for its traffic jams. But there were no traffic jams. There was only a wide, modern highway with beautifully marked exits and an abundance of Cadillacs and Mercedeses. Even the commercial traffic looked good, the trucks were so shiny and new. We got off on Sunset Boulevard, heading east toward the Beverly Hills Hotel, with Jack dozing and me looking out of the open window at the land of El

Dorado. Here it was October, and gorgeous flowers were everywhere, the scents of the unfamiliar eucalyptus and my favorite honeysuckle wafting my way, still summer, in contrast to the autumn chill we had left behind in New York. The sun was shining, the people appeared to be handsome and happy, and the traffic lights seemed to be favorable, an illusion about Los Angeles that I would have for several years.

Pulling up to the Beverly Hills Hotel was right out of the movies. I'd seen the famous sign and the well-known facade surrounded by semitropical foliage many times. The bellhops stepped lively in removing the luggage from the luxurious Lincoln, with a hearty "Welcome to the Beverly Hills Hotel." I was escorted to a beautiful junior suite consisting of a bedroom and a small parlor, with a private patio bedecked with two chaise longues and flowers, trees, and shrubs everywhere. Very generous, these *Dean Martin* people.

There were three gift baskets of fruit, cheese, and wine waiting for me in the suite. The cards read: "Welcome to the Beverly Hills Hotel. If we can do anything to make your stay more pleasant, please let us know." It was signed by the manager. Another read: "Welcome to L.A. Good Luck on *The Dean Martin Show.*" It was signed "Your friends at the William Morris Agency." The third gift basket, a miscellany of nuts and apples, came with a card that said, "Enjoy your appearance on our show," and it was signed by the producers, whose scrawl I could not make out. All of these flattering gifts had one thing in common. Though they were sent through exclusive Beverly Hills shops, the fruit was inedible: The apples tasted like potatoes, the pears were like granite, and the oranges, in the *land* of oranges, were rotten. There were also sour grapes. Nevertheless, these were the most luxurious hotel digs I had ever had and I made a note to take the soap and the shampoo home with me when I left.

All this, plus a bonus of three extra hours in the day and a tempo that, while not rural, was clearly slower and more relaxed than where I had come from. Wonderful. Putting my watch three hours back made me especially proud, as it reminded me that I was getting someplace: by far the farthest I had ever been from home. We had been expected at the NBC studio later in the afternoon for a meeting, with the taping scheduled for the next day, but Jack received a call telling us to go there immediately. We went in a taxi over Coldwater Canyon into the San Fernando Valley and then east to Burbank. I was taken with the beauty of the ride through the mountains, and that such dramatic topography could be located in an area so heavily populated and metropolitan. We arrived at the giant NBC complex. The guard at the gate courteously directed us to the *Dean Martin* offices with "Have a nice day." It was, I believe, my first "have a nice day," the first of thousands I was to hear in Los Angeles.

Jack Rollins, along with his great success, was known as a true gentleman, soft-spoken and polite with that ever present cigar. We sat in the production office, and Jack filled me with wonderful talk about how I would be a "sensation" on the show and in America. Suddenly, the show's director and coproducer, Greg Garrison, burst through the door: "Hey, Jack, you cocksucker, how you doin', you old son of a bitch, you look terrible!"

Jack answered calmly but with a little embarrassment at the crude entrance. This was definitely not his style. "Hello, Greg, how are you?"

"Here, Jack, have a *good* cigar, you cocksucker. Is this your boy wonder?"

We were joined by the head writer of the show, Paul Keyes, who went on the following year to lend his talents as a speechwriter in the Nixon campaign. Two other people came into the office, one of whom was a secretary. Garrison explained that they would be taping two shows the next day, which left no time for dress rehearsals. This was attributed to Dean Martin's disdain for rehearsal in general, and this week in particular. Garrison said I should do the routine I had prepared right there and then in the office, in order for them to get an idea of what I would be doing.

Working in an empty room goes against all the instincts of the stand-up comedian, who needs an audience response, and four people is hardly adequate for the proper effect. Jack assured them that the material was proven, killer stuff, and that a comedian needs a crowd to work to, and they should just be aware of that. Garrison assured Jack that they could compensate in their minds for the lack of big laughs, and they knew funny stuff when they heard it; not to worry. Jack confidently gestured to me with his cigar to begin.

I did the bit just as I had done many times before, while Jack beamed and puffed and laughed. I did it confidently and well. When I finished, Paul Keyes inquired if that was the end, and I replied that it was. Then Garrison and Keyes hit their palms gently on the table four times, which, I took it, was their version of applause. "Do you have something else?" Keyes asked.

In truth, I had prepared two other bits, but the first one, about substitute teaching, was my strongest and most reliable. "I had planned to do that piece, it's always very strong when I do it," I said.

"Of course, we understand, we'd just like to hear what else you may have," said Keyes.

I proceeded to do another five-minute piece about my grade-school days, which got three hits on the desk. All the while Jack was smiling. Garrison said something like "Very funny" and asked Jack to come next door for a meeting "to discuss some details." A young William Morris assistant dropped by, and we had a conversation about my first impressions of Los Angeles, his hometown. He was very enthusiastic about my appearance, but I was preoccupied by the reaction, or nonreaction, to the turn I had just performed. I wanted to vouch for the material, but that would be unseemly, as if I were a supplicant and not the latest discovery of Jack Rollins. Anyway, I knew this was not an audition, as I had the job.

After about twenty minutes, Jack returned alone, with a pallor more pronounced than his usual New York yellow and a profoundly melancholy smile. He said nothing for a few moments; he just shook his head. "They killed you in there, Robert, especially that Keyes, they just killed you, lad. It's a shame."

"You mean I'm not doing the show?"

"They won't put you on the show, but of course they'll pay you the twenty-five hundred."

I felt a knot in my stomach, as if I'd been told of a death in the family. I thought first of my parents and all the friends who had looked forward to my appearance, and of the humiliation of having to tell them. I thought of Rodney. Mostly, I saw this as the end: my work on television ending before it had begun, and the expectation of a big career dimmed. In the cab back to the hotel, I pressed Jack for details of the meeting, though reluctantly, as the account would undoubtedly intensify the pain. He told me that once they got to talking, Keyes insisted that "the stuff isn't funny," and guaranteed that it would go over disastrously on the show. Garrison agreed and added that without a dress rehearsal to test the spot, he didn't want to take a chance. He had of course failed to mention that the show made extensive use of a laugh machine, which boosted a host of untried, often unfunny sketches and a few stand-up comedians to boot. In short, if they so desired, they could make the audience laugh at the Gettysburg Address. Real live people had been laughing at this material for months, dammit.

Back at the Beverly Hills Hotel, Jack kindly suggested a cup of coffee to talk things over, but I declined, preferring to be alone. I was at absolute low ebb, overwhelmed with grief; yes, grief is the word. From the career euphoria, which had been nonstop since signing with Rollins seven months earlier, I was, after all, to fail. I began second-guessing myself. Maybe my successful audiences were nonrepresentative, maybe I wasn't ready for network television, maybe the stuff wasn't as funny as I had thought. I had not been this depressed since my college girlfriend, Judy, had broken up with me.

Jack Rollins, ever thoughtful, called my room and invited me once again to talk. We sat in the Polo Lounge, and Jack said all the right things, reminding me about the many positives I had going for me. Most important, he urged me not to lose perspective. These guys were wrong, he said, despite their important jobs, and had missed the opportunity to be the first to present a wonderful new talent. I found it difficult to pity them their loss, but Jack's encouraging words were welcome and helpful.

I looked about at the suntanned big shots who would never know me, making deals that would never involve me. Then Jack told me a story about an experience similar to mine. Mike Nichols and Elaine May had been booked on *The Jack Paar Show* and were relatively unknown to television audiences. At the morning rehearsal, Mike and Elaine asked for suggestions of subject matter from the staff and proceeded to do a hilarious improvisation based on those suggestions. The producers told them to do that on the show. Nichols and May explained that they couldn't repeat the rehearsal scene and that they wished to improvise a new one for the taping, saying that they wouldn't even remember most of what they had done, and in trying to perform and remember at the same time, they would lose all the spontaneity and probably bomb. The producers insisted, and the performers, not yet the major stars they were to become, reluctantly acquiesced. At the taping, as Mike and Elaine had predicted, the attempt at the sketch went into the toilet: very few laughs. After the sketch, Jack Paar stared at the audience with a "don't blame me" look: "Hey pal, I didn't book them." Years later, during the filming of *Primary Colors*, in which I appeared, I spoke to Nichols about this, and he said that he and Elaine had felt the same as I did after my debacle.

I declined dinner and, after a pat on the back from the disappointed and exhausted manager, retired to a lonely few hours in my hotel room to contemplate my grim professional future, if there was to be one. I lay on the bed and replayed the awful event in my mind over and over. After a while, I reluctantly phoned my parents and fought back tears as my mother let loose a barrage of motherly support. (My father, in worried shock, was already trying to figure out how he would explain the situation to his cronies at work.) She tried so hard to comfort me. If only my mother could explain to the producers at NBC: "Mr. Garrison, my son's comedy routines always make the people laugh, and he would be a wonderful addition to *The Dean Martin Show*, which I watch every week, by the way." "Hey, Frieda, you cocksucker, how you doin'? Here, have a *good* cigar."

After my mother's nineteenth "keep your chin up" and "there's always tomorrow," we hung up. The conversation had not helped, sending me back to the worst feelings of childhood: helplessness, failure, and solace from one's mother in a situation in which she can do nothing to alleviate the problem. There was still that knot in my stomach and the repeating thought, common after tragedy, of how happy I'd been only three hours before.

My phone rang. It was a television-writer friend of mine who had no time to talk but had an interesting message. A wealthy married woman who knew his family in Boston was staying at the Beverly Hills Hotel after dropping her son off at Stanford University. He said nothing outright, but he hinted ("nudge nudge") that she was a bit wild and adventurous and maybe even promiscuous, and that she had a fondness for younger guys. He said that as we were staying at the same hotel, she would like to meet me for a drink, and he had given her a big buildup that I was brilliant and young and in Los Angeles to do *The Dean Martin Show* blah blah blah. Hearing the name of the show was like a dagger in the heart, but I chose not to mention the morning's debacle to him.

The human heart is resilient, and the wild, adventurous, promiscuous part piqued my interest and lifted my spirits. I was at an age when carnal appetite alone could perform such miracles. "She's married?"

"Yes, but I think her husband is in Boston. Let me know what happens." He hung up, and I began to think about whether or not to call. It bothered me that she was married on two levels: the first, moral. In college, I had been hit on by that thirty-something married graduate student, which had made me most uncomfortable. Second, I did not fancy being the guy caught in bed with someone's wife, who is forced to exit by the fire escape while putting his pants on. This wasn't Laurel and Hardy here, this was real life. He *thinks* her husband is in Boston. All of this implied danger, a concept I had scrupulously avoided most of my life. Ah, it's just a drink, she must know what she's doing, I assured myself.

Then the phone rang, and it was the woman in question. "Hello, Mr. Klein? This is Glenda Cater calling." She sounded cordial but conventional, and, well, old, not to mention entirely proper. She had an upper-class twang, like George Plimpton, and the "Mr. Klein" formality did not sound like potential sex to me. She suggested we meet in five minutes at the Polo Lounge for a drink, describing herself and her clothing in detail, mostly designer names, so that I would be spared the task of asking every woman in the room if she was Glenda. I did not confess to not knowing a Gucci from a Pucci if my life depended on it.

I checked myself in the mirror, brushed my teeth, spritzed on some deodorant, and proceeded to the Polo Lounge. Upon entering, I looked around carefully only to discover to my horror that at least twenty women in the place met the description she had given me: bracelets on blondes who had names sewn and etched into everything they wore. There was the aggregate scent of very expensive perfume, accentuated by cigarette smoke. Picking a candidate who could have a son of college age reduced the number by half. Suddenly, that bizarre staple of the Polo Lounge of the time, the little guy dressed like the old Phillip Morris midget, wearing a bellhop's hat with a chin strap, was paging someone for a telephone call. "Mrs. Cater, paging Mrs. Cater. Mrs. Cater, paging Mrs. Cater." A blond woman of about forty-five gestured to the little man, who plugged a telephone into her table. It was she.

I stood back and observed her on the telephone, slightly to the side, about thirty feet away from her. I liked her legs and the elegant look of her foot in the Chanel pumps with the black toes. She was pretty, and not yet heavily lined, though nearly twice my age. Twice my age . . . oooh. Hello Oedipus. God help me. Mrs. Cater was wearing an array of expensive jewelry and a suit right off of Rodeo Drive, with a prominent Gucci imprint on her handbag. As she spoke on the telephone, she used her hands in clipped and definitive movements, and the bracelets kept banging against her martini glass like a church bell. An anticipatory shiver went down my spine, abetted by the rather titillating fact that I was watching her unobserved. Her emphatic tapping on the table, while talking, convinced me that she was addressing an inferior. Apparently, from the snippets I could hear, she had several subjects on her mind, among which were drapes and a scratch on her BMW. She appeared to be someone who was used to giving orders and getting what she wanted, and if she wanted me, I was definitely available. Hell, I hadn't thought of *The Dean Martin Show* in over ten minutes.

Her call was going on for quite a while, and standing there, I was becoming a serious impediment to the waiters and their trays of cocktails. I thought people were noticing me. I stepped up to her table, nodded, and smiled hello; she smiled and gestured for me to be seated, and she yacked on about dinner reservations at her club, a painting bought at auction, the sprained ankle of her horse, and the helicopter that was to meet her at the airport. It was good to know that we had so much in common. My presence and her eye-contact smile seemed to make her ease up on the poor battered assistant she was addressing, and after one last command and another admonition, she hung up. The diminutive bellhop immediately pulled the plug, removed the phone, and proceeded to scream someone else's name around the room.

"How nice to meet you, Mr. Klein. Harold has told me so much about you."

"Nice to meet you, too, Mrs. Cater. And Harold has told me . . . I understand you know Harold's family."

"Oh yes, Mr. Klein, from summers on the Cape." She sounded like the duchess of Windsor. I decided on a bold stroke. "May I call you Glenda?"

"Of course you may, Richard."

"It's Robert."

"Robert, of course. I hope I wasn't rude on the phone and all. I just had to get these things done. I could use another cocktail, how about you?"

"Sounds good, a martini would be nice."

"Wonderful. We drink the same drink. They make divine ones here."

I called for the waiter while she went on about how wonderful it was that we were both ordering martinis, as if this made us part of some important club. I was silently thankful that I had not ordered a Scotch and soda. She was a talkative sort and launched into a lengthy discourse about her trip to California: some business, some shopping, seeing friends, and dropping off her son at college. She fervently hoped he wouldn't get involved with those damned hippies who were protesting the war in Vietnam. Berkeley was full of them, she said.

She'd had so many problems on this West Coast trip. According to her, the trouble associated with dropping one's child off at college was comparable to torture on the rack. She seemed utterly disinterested in knowing anything about me or the reasons for *my* trip to California, which suited me fine. I was not anxious to discuss my fabulous career. She happily filled the air with the accent of a Boston Brahmin, going on about her son. He was certainly *my* favorite subject of the moment, considering that I was attempting to have sex with his mother. William's grade-point average was in no way my idea of conversational foreplay. "He made the dean's list last semester." What was I going to say? "I'm so happy he's doing well, how about a blow job?"

Still, she seemed pleased with the way I looked, observing me, though not at all salaciously, as if I were a pretty dress at Bergdorf's. Yet, after a half hour of chatter about many subjects, she gave not a hint of anything that would suggest she would seduce a young man, and I began to question the veracity of Harold's story. Mrs. Cater appeared to be a rich, conventional, and, unfortunately, moral woman, and there was no way I would make a move and be humiliated.

Then it happened, in the middle of the most inane subject: I felt her foot nudge mine underneath the table. "Oh, excuse me," I said. But she continued to talk on as if nothing were happening, and once again I could feel the gentle pressure of her foot. This was no accident. I could feel her stockinged foot ambling up my pant leg as she rattled on incongruously, this time about Republican politics. She looked around a hundred and eighty degrees to see if anyone was watching, removed her toes from the cuff of my pants, and, with the agility of a ballerina, placed them with precision on the rather stiff penis between my legs. Bingo, Mrs. Cater! This contact made her stop in midsentence, and she suddenly turned to a waiter and said with a most regal air, "Check, please." Maybe this day, one of the worst I'd ever had, wouldn't be a total loss after all. "It's so noisy in here. I'll meet you in ten minutes at Suite 306," she said matter-of-factly. I could feel my heart racing. She leaned toward me, smiling. I thought she was going to kiss me, but she wagged her finger in a scolding fashion and said, "But no funny business"; and she was gone. What did she mean by "no funny business"? Had saucy Glenda been just a five-second flash who had reverted to prim Mrs. Cater? On the other hand, she had invited me to her hotel room, for God's sake, which seemed to indicate to me that this woman had more on her mind than introducing me to her bridge club. No funny business? What the hell would you call rubbing my penis with your foot in the middle of a crowded public room?

As I stalled to stretch the highly anticipatory ten minutes, and having little experience as a gigolo, I still wasn't sure I wasn't being teased. I chose to take the optimistic road and concluded that since she knew I was a comedian, "no funny business" undoubtedly meant that she did not wish to hear comedy during sex. This presented no problem whatever, as I was sure Mrs. Cater had a minuscule sense of humor, if any. I also thought that good, passionate, uninhibited sex and humor were mutually exclusive.

I made my way uncomfortably down the hall, checking myself in the mirror, feeling quite conspicuous. At the appointed time, I knocked on the door, and she greeted me formally (Mr. Klein again), with a slight, elegant bow and a gesture to enter: very Claudette Colbert. Back to square one.

It was a huge multiroom suite. She sat me down at a discreet distance and launched into yet another spate of mundane chatter—conservative Republican politics again—as she poured two giant ready-mixed martinis. I finished mine in three gulps. She decried the Communist thugs who had stormed the Pentagon the previous day at an anti–Vietnam War rally in which the novelist Norman Mailer had been arrested. I pointed out that the rally had been relatively peaceful until many of the demonstrators were bloodied by nightsticks and rifle butts, and they were not Communists but Americans who, in good conscience, were against our involvement.

She said they deserved it. "We're at war, young man," she said in a frosty tone as she poured us another round. This discussion seemed no more conducive to sex than the subject of her college progeny, but she had struck a nerve, and it was making me angry. "We have no business in Vietnam, it's a civil war," I said.

"Oh, sure, let's just let the goddamned Communists take over anywhere they choose. You and your President Johnson. He doesn't think we should win in Vietnam, either," she said bitterly, and swallowed a healthy swig of her drink. "You Communists are all alike. You enjoy the benefits of a free country and then you seek to undermine it."

"What the hell are you talking about? I am not a Communist, and I and every other American have the right to protest the policies of our government. It's the right-wing fascists like you who are un-American, for Chrissakes!"

She downed the rest of her martini and came toward me slowly, menacingly as I sat in my chair. "How dare you call me that," she hissed, staring me in the eyes. I figured the evening was definitely over. "Why don't you go to Russia, where you belong?" She was quite attractive in her ideological rage, and despite the context of our conversation, I felt myself getting aroused. She was just above me now. "Don't you call me a fascist, you little revolutionary bastard." Suddenly, she lifted her skirt, revealing no underwear, straddled my lap, took my head in her hands, and kissed me wildly with a tongue like a boa constrictor. "I hate you," she whispered.

"I hate you, too," I said with a mouthful of her lips and tongue.

She looked at me, and her face metamorphosed into a wicked smile. "Let's have a hate fuck," she said sotto voce as she rubbed herself against me.

"A hate fuck?" The thought appealed to me in a decadent way, and the sound of such profanity from the lips of the imperiously proper Mrs. Cater shot right through me like sensual lightning. I squeezed her breast hard, and she moaned passionately and bit my lip. Sex, after all, can be construed as an aggressive act, and I determined to fuck her for the cause of free speech and righteousness. She pulled me up and led me by the hand to her bedroom, then pushed me down on the giant bed. "Take off your clothes, you subversive Commie bastard," she said as she removed hers with the studied technique of a topless dancer. Naughty Mrs. Cater standing there naked. Full, drooping breasts, with hips a good deal wider than her tiny waist. "Next year Richard Nixon will be president, and all you stupid, unpatriotic idiots will be squelched like a bug," she declared as she removed a vibrator and a little yellow box from the top drawer beside the bed.

"Nixon is a reactionary douche bag who'll never win," I shot back, displaying an erection to please the gods. She lowered herself onto my body and began to run her hands across every part of me. "Haven't you ever heard of the domino effect? If we let the Communists take South Vietnam, then it's only a matter of time before they conquer the Philippines, South Korea, and all the other little countries," she said while licking my ear and manipulating me in a most pleasant way.

"That's just an excuse that the government uses to intervene everywhere they choose," I retorted breathlessly, while manipulating her in a most pleasant way.

So it was to be sex—mindless, wild, and clearly political—exactly what I needed to take my mind off the catastrophe at NBC. She wanted it from every conceivable position, and she screamed with such passion and ferocity that I feared the occupants of the adjacent room would call the police or an ambulance. I pressed her arms above her head as I pumped in and out of her. "Nixon is a loser and a slimy politician," I said right into her ear.

"He is not. He's just what this country needs," she groaned, and matched me stroke for stroke. Then, just before her climax, she grabbed an amyl nitrate capsule, normally used for heart attacks, from the little yellow box and broke it near our noses, which released fumes that caused a feeling of unreality, as if I were hovering above the bed, with a heart rate of about three hundred beats a minute. Maybe the paramedics were not such a bad idea after all. The sound she made at orgasm was a long, loud roar that evoked images of a *Tyrannosaurus rex* consuming a lesser animal, and I shushed her and attempted to cover her mouth to dull the noise. It is revealing that, though engrossed, I was cognizant enough to be terrified that the police might be on their way, with me having a lot of explaining to do: ever the vigilant boy. We had orgasms simultaneously.

When it was over, she allowed herself ten seconds to calm down, then covered herself immediately with a robe, lit a cigarette, and sprang up from the bed, reverting instantly to the society-dame mode. She told me that I was "a delight" and "very well informed," and she threw me my pants. She retired to another bedroom and came out a minute later fully dressed and brushing her hair. "It was so nice to meet you, Richard," she said as she guided me out. She gave me a maternal peck on the cheek. "Goodbye," she said as she closed the door.

There I stood in the hallway, my heart still racing, the smell of her perfume all over me, not quite believing what had transpired in the last sixty minutes. At least she didn't care if I did *The Dean Martin Show*.

Thus was concluded my first day in Los Angeles, which had begun and ended with me getting fucked.

Afterword

There are times in a life when a word or a gesture, a song or a scent, can instantaneously send you back to a moment in the past. It could be a brief, benign moment: the certain way you turned your head to see a birthday present, or the first time fresh rain dripped in your mouth. It can also be a profound moment, catastrophic or triumphant, that you will never forget, that pops up unexpectedly in memory from time to time. The past is a dream world of events that are remembered with varying degrees of perspective.

I find I remember minute details of some things, yet am hazy on the larger episode of which they are a part. I remember faces better than names, always have, so some of the names in these pages are not the names of the people they represent. I remember lawyers better than faces, so some of the names in these pages are not the names of the people they represent. For the most part, these reminiscences are presented affectionately, but as with anyone's youth, mine contained heroes and villains, and I have no desire to get a phone call from a disgruntled eighty-year-old villain who denies his villainy. I have spent a fair amount of time speaking to people who lived those days with me, who reminded me of events I had forgotten and the fine points of ones I remembered. I am surprised at how much remains in my memory. Yet there are reasons why I chose to write about these particular pieces of my life, even if I was not conscious of them. Each of them underlines the basic influences in my youth, among them:

humor, love, sex, music, ethicalness, and fear. It is surprising to me in reading these stories how unsure of myself I was, how afraid I was of risk and rejection, and how intensely everything was felt, large and small. This intensity is one of the mixed blessings of being young. Mellowing, it seems, is one of the meager compensatory blessings of being old.

The book concerns events that happened to me from the ages of nine to twenty-five. It is by no means a comprehensive autobiography, but rather an account of events that stand out in my memory, that have a chronology all their own. During the concentrated personal investigation of my past that the writing required, I relived the events in my mind, sometimes painfully but mostly joyfully, in amusement. I fell in love again, got angry again, laughed again, felt the pride of achievement and the sting of failure as if it were yesterday. From a distance, through the gauze of time, I can see how trivial some of my problems appear now. But to a young person, his place in his social universe is crucial to happiness and function, and patience is a notion that must be gradually learned. These difficulties were certainly not trivial when they occurred; in fact, they were the overriding realities of my young life.

I received a fine education at Alfred University and had a wonderful time, though my account of that four years contains some agony as well. There was the broadening exhilaration of living in a community of smart, ambitious young people, with their vivacity and laughter, in a rural setting so different from my home. Unfortunately, there was also the cruel actuality of institutional bigotry. Alfred today is an excellent school where those onerous elements of college life are long past and forgotten, but they took their damn time about it, and that's the way it was when I was there. I remember with particular fondness my introduction to acting, especially the contribution of C. D. Smith and Ronald Brown, who had an abiding love for the theater and started a spark in me that has never been extinguished.

There are several accounts in these pages of relationships with girls and women with whom I was in love and in lust. It is my intention not to titillate but to communicate the excitement that sex held for me and its importance in my life, which has evidently been considerable. Though I by no means set out to write a treatise on how sexual mores have evolved, it struck me how clearly this plays out in the book, and how radical the change was by the end of the sixties. I wonder at our naïveté and desperation, those of us who lived on the hazy line of mutable moral attitudes: one foot in the nineteenth century and the other in the twentieth.

My narratives of romantic love, for me that rarest of conditions, were the most emotional for me to remember. Looking from the present, despite some heartbreak, I am grateful for having undergone its rigors, as subsequently I have met many a person who has, unfortunately for them, never been in love. I am certain today that despite my youth, I was truly in love in those instances, so there is no need for revisionism here. I am also convinced that loving and being loved in return is as high an achievement as any that one can attain in life, and worth preserving, though making it last is the tricky part.

There are a number of comparisons in the book between situations in my life and scenes from movies: "I felt like I was in a Gene Kelly musical." Perhaps I use them as a reference because, to me as a child, movies were glamorous products of imagination and talent in which problems got solved and people were happy. There have been moments in my life when I thought, This is just like a movie, a case of life imitating art, which imitates life to begin with. Maybe such thinking makes a happy episode seem more momentous, or a tough spot more manageable. At times the judgment is made retrospectively. When I hurt my thumb in the mechanism of an M1 rifle and howled with pain, I didn't think of a funny scene from a Laurel and Hardy army movie then, but I do now.

As far as my parents are concerned, they did their best to provide security, and there was no doubt that they loved my sister, Rhoda, and me very much. Good people, idiosyncratic people. My father takes it on the chin here a bit. He was a powerful personality and a gifted comedian who meant well, but he had a tremendous amount of anger in him. He underestimated the effect on his wife and children of his temper, made all the more frustrating by his consistent myopia about others' approaches to life. Whatever our faults, the Kleins engaged one another, made one another laugh, were never boring. Reticent we were not: We went for the laughs; we fought for time at the dinner table. It is far from coincidence that such a family would produce an individual who makes a living by his imagination. I want to thank them and a host of others who played a part in my life. If *you* played a part in my life and went unmentioned, please forgive me, as the Academy has asked me to limit the number of people I may thank.

Photo Captions

Chapter 1, "Careful Parents"
My father's favorite photo—the suit was high quality.

Chapter 2, "Challenging Mrs. Graux"
Careful parents and children at the beach—I had to wait an hour after eating before going swimming.

Chapter 3, "The TeenTones"
The TeenTones—we were on Ted Mack's Original Amateur Hour*—we lost.*

Chapter 4, "Push Like You Mean It"
Rhoda and the author.

Chapter 5, "Joe College"
The author as ROTC cadet, 1959.

Chapter 6, "Boy Hero"
The lifeguard at the Alamac Hotel, searching for drowning victims and girls.

Chapter 7, "New Passions"
The author as a Japanese warrior slashing at a terrified graduate student.

Chapter 8, "Tales of a Busboy"
The author and a colleague posing between breakfast and lunch.

Chapter 9, "Ducks in a Row"
A serious senior, 1962.

Chapter 10, "Yale and Beyond"
Graduation, with Rhoda and my mother and father.

Chapter 11, "Summer Stock and Hard Knocks"
Scene from A Thurber Carnival *at Casino in the Park Playhouse.*

Chapter 12, "Foreign Affair"
Elizabeth Schmidt in uniform in front of the Berlin pavilion, 1964.

Chapter 13, "The Second City"
Joan Bassie, the author, Fred Willard, Sandra Caron, and an unseen David Steinberg in The Original Amateur Hour, *our funniest sketch.*

Chapter 14, "Learning How"
Onstage at the Improvisation.

Chapter 15, "L.A. and Me"
The author with Jack Roy (aka Rodney Dangerfield) and his son, Brian.